The *The* SILVER APPLES *of the* MOON

T0315665

To Ann
For the love, the space and the time

The SILVER APPLES of the MOON

*An engaging, bittersweet
story of infatuation,
obsession — and football!*

JOE CLANCY

First Published in Great Britain in 2017 by DB Publishing,
an imprint of JMD Media Ltd

ISBN 9781780915562

Printed and bound in the UK

CONTENTS

The **BUILD-UP**

1. *Who Are Ya?*   9

2. *Here I Go Again*   23

3. *The Men in Black*   27

4. *The Maverick and the Mob*   37

5. *Rich Man, Poor Man*   47

6. *Take Five*   59

7. *Words*   70

The **FIRST HALF**

8. *Torn Shorts, Nylon Stockings, Clean Sheets and Dirty Deeds*   83

9. *Two Men and a Van*   95

10. *Dons and Dossiers*   105

11. *Siege Mentality*   120

12. *Wingless Wonders?*   132

13. *The Birds and the Bees*   138

14. *Model Behaviour?*   148

15. *Frank Exchanges*   159

16. *Yellow Card*   167

17. *Saluting the Captain*   173

18. *Hotheads and Redheads*   183

19. *Going Our Own Way*   195

INTERVAL

20. *A Bit of Fluff*   205

The SECOND HALF

21. Early Bird. Special!	221
22. Digging Deep	229
23 Sun, Moon and Stars	233
24. Love, Bites and Scoring	238
25. Missed Opportunity?	244
26. All Wrapped Up	248
27. Injury Time	250

ADDED TIME

28. Whatever Happened to…	261
QPR Results: 1975–76	277
Credits	282
Acknowledgements	282
Bibliography	282

The
BUILD-UP

1. WHO ARE YA?

Saturday, 16 August 1975: 9.00 a.m.

I have this ritual.

I set out at around nine o'clock, just after breakfast. Down the gravel driveway and out the front gates, turning right onto Wellesley Gardens. I say hello to Marianne Pleass from number 21 as she leaves for work, pause outside Aunt Sally's place at the intersection with The Glade, and then cross over onto that part of Park Road known as Beane Row to say good morning to Eddie.

I usually bump into the two Butler brothers as I head down the hill towards the shops, where I'm greeted by Noah as I walk by Berrie & Threads; before passing by The Horseman and then over to The Cabin. There I meet Mick Hanrahan, pick up the Daily Mirror and have a quick chat with Bernie Trout.

The whole thing takes roughly twenty-five minutes.

I do allow myself certain derogations from this ritual. For example, I don't have to encounter all of these people in that particular order. And if I do happen to miss one of them on my walk down to The Cabin but I bump into them on the way back, then that counts as inclusion in the ritual.

This ritual, this walk to The Cabin to buy the Daily Mirror, every Saturday morning, has evolved over the last two football seasons whenever we have had a home game. I kept a note of the people I met en route to The Cabin and then also noted the result of the match that day. Through a process of elimination, I arrived at a set of people that seemed to bring the team 'luck' if I happened to have bumped them that morning.

It may sound a little childish and immature but routines, rituals and superstitions are important to those of us involved in football. Many players, certain managers and even some fans like to have a regular behaviour pattern on match days that they believe will bring them good luck.

One well-known team manager is reputed to have a 'lucky' blue suit that he wears to all his team's games and, even though the suit is almost threadbare, he cannot be dissuaded from wearing it, such is his belief in its power to deliver the right result. A teammate of mine will always put on the left sock first. Another likes to be the third player out when the team takes to the field.

Fans too have their superstitious rituals. One might wear a particular item of 'lucky' clothing; another will maybe give the front tyre of his car a gentle tap before leaving home on match day. All of this is done with the firm conviction that failure to adhere to the ritual may bring bad luck and the wrong result.

Most managers, fans and players are in complete control of their match day rituals and include only simple activities that they can influence directly themselves. This is not surprising, given that football is such an insecure business. Things are rarely left to chance.

I prefer to make my ritual a little more challenging by including some elements of risk. So, although I have this regular route that I take on Saturday match day mornings and I include the four people that I can be certain of encountering on a regular basis — Marianne Pleass, Noah, Mick and Bernie — I am depending on the other four to unwittingly play their part in the uninterrupted continuation of my Saturday routine.

This can be risky.

Although most of the people concerned have reasonably predictable patterns of behaviour, they can on occasions deviate from these habits, thereby throwing my ritual out of kilter.

Last season, for example, Eddie took an unexpected weekend break and wasn't there on the Saturday morning when I passed by his house. This immediately had me worried about the result that day (we lost) so I resolved to drop Eddie from the ritual. Eddie was also away for the home game the following Saturday so I decided to replace Eddie with Bernie Trout that day. We won. So, Bernie was in and Eddie was out. Three weeks later, Eddie was back. I could not avoid greeting him as I passed by and as we won that day I could not push my luck by excluding Eddie from the ritual thereafter. So I now have Eddie and Bernie.

The main risk involved in my particular ritual is the requirement that other people be there when I need them, rather than it just being based on me remembering to do something specific myself. As if there wasn't enough insecurity already in football without me adding to it!

Occasionally, I trek to The Cabin on weekdays too, but because the pattern of weekdays is so different to Saturdays, what with other obligatory commitments plus training sessions, those Saturdays when we are playing at home are essentially the days on which I can be reasonably positive that the consistency of my ritual can be maintained, and that I will bump into the same patchwork of personalities to ensure the right result later that day.

Today, getting the right result is of paramount importance. It's our first game of the season. The feeling among everybody at the club is that this could finally be our year. So it's vital that we get off to a winning start.

Marianne Pleass is always the first person I encounter on my trek to The Cabin. The epitome of punctuality and dependability, you can set your watch by Marianne. Her home is only a few doors away from mine. All of the houses on Wellesley Gardens are exactly the same. Large redbrick three-storeys over basement residences with wide granite steps leading up to the front door from a short, curved gravel drive. Eight-foot-high walls surround the houses with black wrought-iron security gates fronting onto the pavement. The entire group of houses — and indeed the Wellesley Gardens roadway itself — was newly built about five years ago on land that was originally part of 'Aunt' Sally's large estate.

Every Saturday, just after nine o'clock, Marianne leaves her home at number 21 and cycles to wherever it is that she works. I usually only see her for the time it takes for her to nod a cold hello to me and then cycle the hundred yards from her home to the intersection, where she then turns right and vanishes from sight until the following Saturday, when she repeats the same routine. Marianne is a shy, retiring, single woman in her early thirties with mousey hair and dark brown eyes that may once have been beautiful, but now appear hard and penetrating like those of a frightened cat. If she wasn't part of my ritual, Marianne is the sort of person I would hardly give a second thought to.

If it wasn't for her death wish.

It is obvious that Marianne Pleass wishes to die. How else can one explain her habit of cycling the wrong way down the one-way street against speeding oncoming traffic? Marianne's progress down Wellesley Gardens is always hailed by a cacophony of car horns that she appears to be totally oblivious to, or studiously ignores. I once asked her why she did this: 'It's quicker,' she hissed through wafer-thin lips before pedalling off.

Marianne has a sister, Marjorie, who I sometimes see sitting in the bay window on the first floor, waving Marianne off in the morning. Marjorie is plumper than Marianne but other than that, they could be identical twins. Marjorie's appearances are too irregular for me to include her in my ritual.

'Aunt' Sally is not actually my aunt. In fact, in all these years walking past her house, I have never actually laid eyes on 'Aunt' Sally. Nobody of my acquaintance has ever seen her. So Aunt Sally's residence would probably be unremarkable if it wasn't for this slight air of mystery about her — and her gardens. Between gaps in the high hedge behind the railings or in places where parts of the outer wall have crumbled, you can glimpse the abundance of flowers and foliage and enjoy the aroma that gently assails the senses. The humming and droning of bees can also be heard during lulls in the noise of passing traffic. Nobody seems to know why we call her 'Aunt' Sally. Not only is she unrelated to any of her neighbours, as far as is known, but no family member ever seems to visit her.

A small, wizened, garrulous man of oriental extraction tends her large garden on its corner site at a fork in the road. I call him 'Tojo'. Well, I don't actually call him Tojo to his face, or to anybody else's for that matter. It's just that I don't know his real name. I think of him as 'Tojo' because that's the name given to him by the Butler brothers.

Dressed in spotlessly clean and freshly-ironed dark blue overalls, he arrives in one of those Reliant Robin three-wheelers every Saturday without fail, takes his instructions, carries out his gardening, housekeeping and shopping duties and leaves as unobtrusively as he came. He's been doing this for a couple of seasons and has, in effect, become my 'substitute' for the elusive Aunt Sally. So he has become an integral, if slightly peripheral, part of my ritual. I don't attempt to engage him in conversation. For the present, just seeing him is enough to count him in for that Saturday.

The architecture, tone and style of the neighbourhood all change once you cross the road at Aunt Sally's and onto Beane Row. The first thing you notice is that there are fewer trees. And the trees that do grow there are scrawny and ugly. The footpath is tarred rather than paved, and there are no grass verges. The houses are smaller too. In all, there are nine two-up, two-down terraced houses with little bay windows on the ground floor and shared covered alleyways providing access to the back gardens. Some have the original checkerboard pattern of tiny terracotta and cream tiles on the short path from gate to front door; others have replaced these with small flagstones laid on gravel. A small number of the houses have low brick front walls with railings, but most simply have wooden picket fences. The gardens are generally well kept, although one or two have been allowed go to seed. The overall effect is a jumble of styles with little or no coherence.

Eddie's house on Beane Row is number 9. It's the corner site immediately opposite Aunt Sally's and because it's an end-of-terrace house it's the only one to have a large side garden. I reckon Eddie hails from one of the Scandinavian countries — or from somewhere behind the iron curtain — and his real name is something like Edvard. But everybody calls him Eddie. And those of us who regularly engage in conversation with him all refer to him as 'Echo Eddie'. The moniker 'Echo Eddie' was also invented by the Butler brothers (of whom more anon) and all because Eddie's way of greeting you is to repeat your own greeting and add his distinctive nervous laugh. So your 'Nice morning' is met with a 'Nice mornink, heh, heh' from Eddie. Your enquiry as to 'How are you today?' elicits a 'How are you today, heh, heh' which is delivered by Eddie as a statement rather than a question. He's a big, bulky bloke, with black curly hair, chubby face and ruddy complexion.

Eddie is always pottering around in the front or side garden of the house. Not necessarily gardening, just pottering. Usually with cars. He has at least two vehicles under repair at any one time. Then there's the gate widening and building of an additional driveway that he is permanently working on. Most days, hail, rain or shine, Eddie is out there wearing only vest and trousers with the braces swinging down around his knees, messing about with cars or concrete.

Eddie lives here with his partner Svetlana. Tall, blonde and with an athlete's figure (rumour has it she was an Olympic gymnast) Svetlana drives a signal red Triumph Herald convertible that, despite its age, Eddie is not allowed to tinker with. Sightings of Svetlana are rare and regarded by all as memorable events. Usually you will first hear the clack-clack of her stilettoes on the driveway as she strides to her motor, trailing a pungent aroma of expensive perfume and with a fur coat carelessly slung over her shoulder, before driving away at speed with only a bejewelled arm visible, waving 'Adjo' to Eddie from the open driver's window.

A few doors down from Eddie and Svetlana is where Jacko and Billy Butler reside. Although they can be great company, honesty and the Butler brothers could never be described as close acquaintances. Not to put too fine a point on it, both Jacko and Billy would be more familiar than most with the inside of the local police station. However, they have always managed to maintain a consistent coherence to their double act, even when being questioned in separate interview rooms. So, despite deriving much enjoyment from the latest expensive consumer durables, acquired in dubious circumstances, they have yet to experience the joy of being extensively detained at Her Majesty's pleasure. But notwithstanding (or perhaps because of) their colourful background and even more colourful language, I have always been drawn to and amused by their company.

Jacko, who's in his late twenties, is the sharper and more vocal of the two. He's also usually better dressed, tho' that isn't saying a lot. Not unlike Adam Faith as 'Budgie' in the TV series a couple of years ago, Jacko looks taller than he actually is, with a head of permanently tousled fair hair and near perfect teeth that he clenches while speaking through them, resulting in a kind of sibilant hiss that becomes even more accentuated when he laughs. He is also an optimist when it comes to the weather, usually wearing sunglasses regardless of the season. His other permanent trademark accessory is a cigarette.

Billy, a couple of years younger, has dark hair and sallow skin. He gives the impression that he really admires his older brother and would like to be just like Jacko. He even tries to dress like him. Unfortunately, Billy is a late adaptor. By the time he gets round to shopping in Shepherd's Bush market for his Jacko-lookalike threads, the best of them have already been sold. So Billy has to make do with end-of-line styles and colours that only serve to reinforce his inferior self-esteem. Billy is also a little shorter than Jacko, but compensates for this by wearing footwear purchased from The Elevator Shoe Company via one of those little ads you see in most weekends' newspapers. Every day seems to be a bad hair day for Billy. His hairstyle (an oxymoron, if ever there was one) is never quite the way he intended it that morning, so he is permanently pulling at some part of it or attempting to flatten it down. In contrast to his older brother, Billy's misshapen teeth need a little work. Like daily brushing, for a start.

Things improve a little again as you head downhill, along Park Road to the Green. The houses are mostly detached, with red-bricked ground floor frontages and mock Tudor stucco and half timbering on the façade of the upper stories. The cars are parked in driveways rather than on the street and the gardens are neat and well-tended.

In the centre of the Green there's a little pond that attracts swans from time to time; and, towards the north-east corner, a small war memorial stands proudly erect. On the south-west corner, there's a more modern sculpture, like a bone. It's bone-coloured too but with sharp edges. Personally, I don't like it and I don't know anybody who does. I have no idea what it's meant to represent but I do know that it was very controversial at the time it was installed. Facing the Green, a scattering of small shops vies for attention. There's a small cinema too, known simply as The Screen on the Green. Beyond the Green, through Station Road, is Cheppington High Street.

The little antique shop opposite the Green is run by Noah Berrie and has been there for as long as most residents can remember. The cramped premises, just inside the tiny old shopping arcade, has an air of faded gentility to it, in keeping with the business, but in reality most of the merchandise on display appears to be pretty low in quality, even lower in desirability and has been cluttering up the shop for quite some time. More recently, Noah's son Bradley branched out into the fashion business with a unisex boutique called 'Threads' next-door to the antique shop. Although polar opposites in terms of merchandise and clientele, the two separate businesses tend to be known locally by the single, combined name of 'Berrie & Threads'.

Noah Berrie, who is in his sixties, is a genial 'old-school' gent, with perfect manners and a ready smile. He wears those distinctive round spectacles like the ones worn by Ghandi, only smaller, usually perched on the end of his nose so that he peers out over them at you. He's bald on top with tufts of snow-white hair just over his ears and he rummages about the shop with a permanent stoop. His well-worn greeting, 'Good Mornington, are we buying or selling today?' is a pleasantly familiar part of the soundtrack to my ritual.

Bradley probably fits most people's definition of being 'ruggedly handsome' and, from what I hear, devotes a lot of his time attempting to conform to his self-styled status as being 'popular with the chicks'. He definitely matches my definition of a number one horse's ass. Maybe that's just envy on my part but it is difficult to warm to a bloke who tries so hard to be 'groovy' (his term) when he has the physical stature of a rugby player, the dress sense of a Conservative MP and a vocabulary gleaned from Top of the Pops.

The Horseman is our 'local'. It's a Watney's house. For some strange reason, it is referred to by everybody in its possessive form – The Horseman's. The generally accepted belief is that this is an abbreviation of its original name, The Horseman's Retreat (as in: a place where a horseman could stop and have a quiet pint; not a reference to him retreating in the face of defeat). Circumstances and a singular dedication to my football career ambitions mean that I frequent The Horseman's only on very rare occasions, and then simply to imbibe the innocent pleasure offered by soft drinks. It is also no longer possible to meet the Butler brothers in The Horseman's as their presence has been elegantly deemed as 'permanently unnecessary' by the landlord, the diminutive, silver-haired Bernie Trout. This resulted from a heated altercation between himself and the brothers after two kegs of beer went missing while the delivery truck was momentarily unattended late one evening.

Pardon the pun, but old 'Trouty' is a bit of an odd fish. Although small in stature and of fairly slight build, Trouty still has the air of a man not to be messed with – a very useful attribute in dealing with gassy patrons in the public bar of The Horseman's at closing time.

Bernie doesn't actually work behind the bar himself. During the day, he is invariably to be found sitting unobtrusively at a table in a far corner of the bar, sipping coffee, taking calls and meeting a succession of business acquaintances with strikingly diverse dress codes and tattoos. In the evenings, he retreats to a cramped office at the back of the premises to continue these meetings, making only the occasional foray into the lounge to exchange greetings with favoured clientele.

In the manner in which most males (and I include myself in this group) will probably never fully appreciate, Bernie Trout holds a singular fascination for women. Or at the very least, for some of the women who frequent The Horseman's. He is not strikingly handsome, yet there is a certain presence about him when he strides into the lounge bar; exuding an aura of confidence and authority that is impossible to ignore. He is always impeccably, if casually, dressed. And then there is the permanent tan that he tops up via regular visits to sunnier climes, particularly Spain. Bernie loves to travel and has a particular fascination with flying. These attributes and the obvious effect it has on certain female customers do not exactly endear old Trouty to the male patrons of his establishment. As a result, Bernie Trout's origins, his acquaintances – and the source of his undoubted wealth – are a topic of constant rancorous speculation, none of which could be described as being exactly complimentary.

Trouty tends to converse quietly in very measured tones, but whilst he has never been anything other than pleasant to me, always interested in how I am doing and very supportive *of the team; there is a permanent air of steely menace about the man which creates a distance between Bernie and the locals. I have never had any difficulty with him, however, and he inevitably seeks me out for a brief natter when I visit The Cabin as part of my Saturday ritual.*

The Cabin is a confectionery, tobacconist and newspaper shop run by an Irishman called Mick Hanrahan. In keeping with the general memory malaise that appears to afflict the local community, nobody can quite remember why it is called The Cabin. The generally accepted notion is that when Mick first set up home here, he opened the shop in what amounted to a rather large wooden garden shed. As the business grew over the years, the original cabin became too small in which to transact business in Mick's unique way, so he built an extension of sorts to his home to accommodate the growing clientele. At that stage, one assumes that 'The Cabin' had already entered the vernacular of the community and so the name transferred automatically to the more modern establishment which, whether by chance or by design, retained most of the rudimentary features of the original, especially those relating to heating (lack of) and swept floors (ditto).

Mick is an unwitting pioneer of what the marketing men refer to nowadays as 'limited brand choice'. With the exception of cigarettes and newspapers, Mick carries only one brand in any particular category. This means that if you need to purchase tea, Mick will always have what you want — so long as you are happy with PG Tips. A second feature of the Mick Hanrahan retailing revolution is that, despite the fact that it purports to be a self-service shop, most of the products, with the exception of newspapers, are housed behind the counter. As a result, the ambience in the customer area of The Cabin always has a slightly bare feel to it (come to think of it, maybe that's why they call it The Cabin). A second consequence of this particular approach to retailing is that phenomenon so beloved of us British, namely, the orderly queue.

Within the cramped confines of The Cabin, the orderly queue acquires collective qualities of patience and stoicism as it snakes its way towards Mick before its ultimate objective is revealed: the exchange of pleasantries with Mick and the inevitable introductions.

Mick's grandmother was a 'matchmaker' in some part of southern Ireland. According to local tradition, a man would approach the matchmaker and discuss with him or her which women he liked in the area. The matchmaker would then advise as to which women were likely to be good potential matches for marriage, based on the matchmaker's knowledge of both parties. The matchmaker would then facilitate the introduction of the couple after first discussing it with their families.

In maintaining a semblance of this tradition, Mick's ambitions are probably more to do with generating friendships than becoming the equivalent of an in-shop dating service. And the disparate ages, ethnic diversity and barely subdued impatience of most of the customers militates against any serious romantic interaction; a situation that is not helped by such unromantic behind-the-counter props as boxes of teabags and spongy sliced bread. But Mick is nothing if not quietly resilient, not only in affairs of the heart but, more importantly, in matters financial. The conventional wisdom is that Mick built up a portfolio of valuable properties all over West London that now yields sufficient rental income to maintain him and his family in the manner in which they have become accustomed, and that he continues to run The Cabin simply to provide the particular kind of social interaction that he craves.

Mick's tall, bent, skeletal frame, thinning red hair and pasty complexion are complemented by a dun-coloured shop-coat, smelling of fresh toast, that he wears at all times giving him a near-death appearance. The once raucous laugh that might otherwise have belied this judgment has long since subsided into an extended wheeze which, to those not familiar with his instinct for survival, simply confirms the imminence of Mick's likely departure from this mortal coil. But to those of us who know him well, Mick is the man with eyes full of dancing and a mouth full of smiles.

Mick has a son who very occasionally helps out in the shop. He's in his late twenties and is the complete antithesis of Mick. Small, thick-set and dour, with unkempt red hair and straggly ginger beard, he is, for reasons best known to themselves, referred to by many of the regular customers as 'Cattle'. Although born and bred in London, he is assertively Irish about everything he does. So, while Mick is never offended by Irish jokes (and has been known to tell a few good ones himself) 'Cattle' generally has a few cutting ripostes up his sleeve, usually directed at our British sense of propriety. Although most customers treat 'Cattle' with a degree of circumspection, he has never been anything other than polite to me. On those rare occasions when Mick himself is away, 'Cattle' will usually have some of his favourite music playing in the background. He calls it his 'wolf' tones but it sounds just like any other folk music to me. He's married and lives nearby with his four boisterous children, uncharitably referred to as 'the herd of Cattle' by some of the unkinder elements among Mick's clientele.

When I enter The Cabin this morning I have already successfully completed the initial stages of my match day ritual. I've met Marianne Pleass, Tojo, the Butlers and Noah. So only Eddie, Mick and Trouty remain. Something strikes me immediately as being different and it takes me a moment or two to work out what it is. Usually, the one person guaranteed to be already holding court in the queue is the redoubtable Bernard Trout. And with the need for one of Mick's introductions long past, Trouty and I inevitably eschew small talk, preferring instead to begin an initial scanning of our respective newspapers. But today, no Bernie. This throws me, because hooking up with Trouty in the queue has become a part of my Saturday home-game ritual. I decide to forfeit my place and dawdle for a few minutes at the side of the queue, in the hope that Trouty will turn up for our regular brief exchange of pleasantries. But still no Bernie.

When I rejoin the queue, I pick up on the main topic of conversation ahead of me, which is yesterday's verdict in the trial of a group of people known collectively as 'The Birmingham Six'. There's a stark headline on the front of today's Daily Mirror that simply proclaims:

THE GUILTY

in large letters, and above this headline there are pictures of each of the six blokes found guilty of the Birmingham pub bombings carried out by the IRA last November, which the Mirror describes as 'Britain's biggest-ever mass murder'. They were all sentenced to life *imprisonment. The only issue now to be decided is what minimum period they will have to serve in prison. Judging by the tone of the trenchant opinions being expressed by those in the queue, nobody wants to see these guys released. Ever. There are also photographs on the front page of some of the victims.*

A few of the newspapers warn of possible reprisals by the IRA, but the general consensus in the queue is that this is unlikely. Despite the car bomb in Belfast yesterday, which injured about thirty people, the feeling is that the IRA's ability to mount a major terror campaign in mainland Britain has been seriously compromised by yesterday's convictions of the 'Birmingham Six' and the arrest of the 'Guildford Four' in December of last year. I'm not convinced. I don't think we should be complacent about these things.

I am still skimming the report on this story on the inside pages when I become conscious of a presence in the queue behind me.

It's nothing she says, no particular movement she makes; no aroma of perfume that signals her presence; just the merest hint of apple blossom from her hair and the quiet rustling sound of the pages of a newspaper being perused. I'm tempted to turn round, but her proximity to me means that this will seem awkward and contrived. And anyway, what will I say?

I finally reach the counter to be greeted by Mick:

'Ah, Dawhee, me bucko.'

I have no idea why he calls me Dawhee. Mick tends to know every customer's name. But he also tends to have little nicknames for some of them. Why 'Dawhee' for me? I don't know. It just crept in over time and by the time I became curious about it, it had already become established.

I exchange the usual banter with Mick about how the team has done pre-season and our chances against Liverpool today. Mick reckons we are really up against it. He reminds me (as if I needed reminding) that the Liverpool line-up includes such household names as Emlyn Hughes, Kevin Keegan and John Toshack.

I make no mention of the story on the front page of the newspapers. I've never discussed Irish politics with Mick in any detail. Mick's usual response when anybody tries to raise it is to purse his thin lips, sigh and then hiss loudly through clenched teeth.

Today, Mick wants to know if there is any truth in the story that Gerry Francis is to captain England against Switzerland in Basle next month. He points out the two articles in my Daily Mirror, one by Nigel Clarke to the effect that Alan Ball's omission from the Arsenal team today will open the way for Gerry to captain England; the other, by Kevin Moseley, concludes that Francis has the right pedigree for the job. I tell him that I've heard the rumours but that Gerry hasn't spoken to me about it yet. Mick appears momentarily disappointed (he likes to have the inside track on these things so that he can give his customers an exclusive before the newspapers get it) so I give him a conspiratorial wink. I've no way of knowing how he interprets this, but it seems to do the trick in quelling his curiosity.

The truth is that Gerry Francis and I do not really hit it off. I admire Gerry a lot, I really do. I respect him too. And that respect is his due. After all, he is the team captain. But Gerry does not always welcome my point of view at training sessions. My 'interventions' as he likes to call them. I prefer to think of them as valuable contributions. So you will understand when I tell you that I am probably the last person that Gerry Francis is likely to confide in.

I pay Mick for the Mirror and ask him casually if Trouty has been in earlier, but Mick says he hasn't seen him all week. This is starting to bother me now. What if Trouty doesn't show?

I am still preoccupied with the absence of Trouty when Mick does his usual 'before-you-go' routine:

'Before you go, Dawhee, allow me to introduce you to Miss Dell.' Slight pause. 'Miss Lisa Dell.'

And then, as an afterthought: 'Miss Dell is a classical dancer.'

I turn round to face the young woman. She is a few inches taller than me, thin and angular in stature. Her skin looks naturally tanned and she has a distinctly Mediterranean appearance. With long, dark hair and a slightly hooked nose, she has an imperious, almost aristocratic demeanour about her.

'Pleased to meet you,' I say, extending my hand.

She shakes my hand firmly, looks me straight in the eyes and asks (without any trace of a foreign accent): 'And who are you?'

'This,' interjects a smiling Mick, rubbing his hands together nervously, 'is a young man destined for football greatness.'

Eight months later:

Saturday, 24 April 1976: 1.40 p.m.

Who are ya? Who are ya?
Who are ya? Who are ya?

Outside on the terraces, the early-arriving QPR supporters are reacting to today's opponents in the typical tribal fashion of all home fans. Out on the pitch, in bright sunlight, the Leeds United players are strolling about in their tracksuits, familiarising themselves with the conditions. I'm sitting in the home dressing room at Loftus Road. Most of the squad is here already. The familiar blue-and-white hooped shirts are on their numbered pegs, and the rest of the kit is all laid out, sock ties, gum, fruit and those new, garish blood-orange GOLA tracksuit tops with the hoods. The Gaffer, Dave Sexton, is not here yet. He's probably having a chat with the Chairman, Mr Gregory, or some of the other directors in the lounge upstairs.

It's early, so the atmosphere is still informal. There's tension but it's not a shared tension. Everybody involved is nursing his own private thoughts: setting individual goals; mentally visualising and playing out specific scenarios involving his immediate opponent on the Leeds team. *How can I stop him from playing to his strengths? What plan does he have to deal with me?* But I know what everybody is thinking deep down, the overriding concern that dwarfs all others: anything less than a Rangers victory over Leeds today will hand the title to Liverpool. No more, no less. A win for QPR today means Liverpool will then be under pressure to beat Wolves away from home in their last game on 4 May in order to wrest the title away from Rangers. The conversations initially are very much one-on-one; a few questions, a little encouragement, but nothing too heavy, all murmured and very low-key. At least outwardly. Inside, stomachs are churning, pulses are racing and, as the clock ticks on, the odour of nervous flatulence begins to permeate.

Among some of the non-playing staff there's a sense of something already achieved, a job well done: QPR have already qualified for Europe for the first time in the club's history with one game still remaining. But what do they know? It's the First Division title we're after. That's the Holy Grail. It's still possible for us to win it. But lose today and we've blown it.

There are a few favoured media people here, newspaper reporters, some technical bods from ITV's *The Big Match*, a few administrators, a scattering of hangers-on – even the lads who have 'privileged seats' along the touchline and act as unofficial ball-boys are allowed in at this early stage. The touchline at Loftus Road is so close to the pitch that official ball-boys are not really needed.

For some players, all this activity is useful in helping to provide a bit of distraction; to ease the rising tension. Others cannot wait for the moment when the non-combatants are ushered out, the doors firmly shut and the Gaffer reiterates key messages and gives his final instructions.

In the meantime, we just wait.

The emotion, the adrenaline rush, that footballers get from the atmosphere generated out on the terraces and inside the dressing room are feelings you can only experience if you are directly involved in the game. These emotions exceed anything that you will ever feel in life outside football.

The questioning from the terraces is becoming more insistent by the minute:

'*Who* are ya? *Who* are ya?'

I've always reckoned this to be a fairly mindless chant. For those readers who do not attend football matches regularly, let me explain. This chant is usually directed by the home crowd at the best-known player or players in the opposing team. It's designed to undermine them; to belittle anything that they have achieved. It's a particularly popular chant when one of the big 'marquee name' players does something that's embarrassing, like completely mis-kick the ball, or slip and fall over. It says 'you may be a big name on your own patch, mate, but round here you mean nothing. We don't acknowledge your reputation here.'

To start chanting this at the opposition before the match has even started, before a ball has been kicked or a tackle made, defeats its very purpose, in my view. It only gees up the opposition. Makes them strengthen their resolve to really stuff us.

To do it to this Leeds United team is totally counterproductive. First, because almost every single player in this Leeds side is a household name. Secondly, Leeds United have achieved more than most other sides can even dream of. And they are still in with an outside chance of finishing above us this season, lying two places behind us in fourth, six points behind but, crucially, with a game in hand.

Thirdly – and most importantly – the culture built up by Don Revie during his tenure as Leeds manager means that they are likely to bridle at the insult and, therefore, more likely to make you pay handsomely for your temerity. So today, of all days, is not the day to poke fun at Leeds.

Here are a few of the Leeds team strolling around the pitch out there that the baying crowd claims not to 'recognise':

Goalkeeper David Harvey: With 174 league appearances, Harvey has also played in two FA Cup Finals and won 15 caps for Scotland.

Paul Reaney: Over 500 appearances for Leeds and an England international.

Trevor Cherry: Another England international with over 400 league appearances.

Paul Madeley: Versatile England international who has played in a number of positions over his 400 league appearances.

Norman Hunter: Yet another England international with over 500 league appearances.

Billy Bremner: Combative, inspirational captain of Scotland in their magnificent recent World Cup odyssey, Bremner also captained Leeds to many of their successes in recent years and has played over 600 games for the club.

Eddie Gray: Scottish international with over 200 league appearances for Leeds.

Peter Lorimer: Scottish international and one of the big successes at the last World Cup. Almost 400 league appearances and over 140 goals for Leeds.

Allan 'Sniffer' Clarke: Leeds broke the British transfer fee record to sign him from Leicester. With over 400 league appearances and over 200 goals, Clarke is another England international.

Duncan McKenzie: Scorer of spectacular and crucial goals for Leeds since his transfer from Nottingham Forest.

The interesting team news is that Carl Harris is replacing Peter Lorimer at number 7. Harris scored on his league debut against Ipswich but most of his appearances for Leeds since then have been as substitute. He also won his first Welsh cap (against England) this season. Lorimer has been named as substitute.

A late change from the match programme is that 'Sniffer' Clarke is out injured today and is being replaced by Paul Reaney at number 8. Reaney is a full-back, so the team has a decidedly defensive look to it and may be happy to settle for a point.

Here's how Leeds, playing in their all-yellow away strip, will line out this afternoon:

1. DAVID HARVEY
2. TREVOR CHERRY   3. FRANKIE GRAY
4. BILLY BREMNER   5. PAUL MADELEY   6.NORMAN HUNTER
8. PAUL REANEY   10. DUNCAN McKENZIE
7. CARL HARRIS   9. JOE JORDON   11. EDDIE GRAY
SUBSTITUTE: PETER LORIMER

I reckon it's more likely that, when the team takes the field, Cherry will wear the number 8 shirt and Reaney will play at number 2 but, either way, the defensive quality of the Leeds side is unlikely to be diminished, as Reaney is also an England international.

But we're not short of international players ourselves at QPR. As one media observer succinctly put it this morning: 'Nine of the QPR first team out there today have already been capped for their country.'

Here's how the QPR team sheet reads:

1. PHIL PARKES
2. DAVE CLEMENT   3. IAN GIILLARD
4. JOHN HOLLINS   5. FRANK McLINTOCK   6. DAVID WEBB
8. GERRY FRANCIS   10. STAN BOWLES
7. DAVE THOMAS   9. DON MASSON   11. DON GIVENS
SUBSTITUTE: MICK LEACH

The QPR match programme is one of the few, if not the only, match programme that continues to set out the teams in the old 'W' formation with half-backs and inside-forwards. Teams don't really play that way any more. Not since the 1966 World Cup, anyway. And QPR certainly don't with Dave Sexton as Manager. Most match programmes today simply list the players sequentially in numerical order but at QPR some old traditions die hard.

Today's programme is 'a special souvenir edition'. Instead of the usual, familiar quirky motif of chequered squares on the cover, there's a series of flags – presumably to celebrate Rangers qualifying for Europe for the first time. Whether we play in the European Cup or the EUFA Cup only the next ten days will tell. The price of the programme has been increased from 15p to 20p, presumably to offset the cost of printing photos in colour on the inside pages too.

Another reason to celebrate today is the announcement that the QPR match programme has won the award for 'Best Programme in the League 1975/6'. According to the programme notes, the Charles Tew Trophy will be presented to the editor at the Clarendon Restaurant in Hammersmith next month. The Editor is Club Secretary Ron Phillips, a really nice bloke who well deserves this award.

I thumb through the programme distractedly, just scanning for interesting bits. But it doesn't reveal anything that I do not know already. Rangers' brilliant winning streak since the beginning of the year would normally have guaranteed that the First Division Championship trophy would come to the club for the first time in its history. That bad result last week at Norwich, however (we lost 2–3) means that we must beat Leeds United today (as if I needed reminding) and, even if we win, we must still wait until Liverpool and Manchester United play their final games in early May before we know the destination of this year's first division championship (sound familiar?).

For Liverpool, who are not playing today, this is 'a day of agonising inactivity' as one media commentator succinctly put it. And I can relate to that. At least we will know our fate after an hour and a half of agonising activity. If we win, then Liverpool must wait – and they will not exactly be looking forward either to their final game of the season: that visit to Wolves, who are themselves fighting a battle – against relegation from the First Division.

Going into today's match, the top of the First Division looks like this:

	P	W	D	L	F	A	Pts
Liverpool	41	22	14	5	63	30	58
QPR	41	23	11	7	65	33	57
Man Utd	39	22	10	7	65	39	54
Leeds Utd	40	21	9	10	64	42	51

So, if we lose today, then Liverpool will win the title. It's as stark and as simple as that.

2. HERE I GO AGAIN?

Saturday, 16 August 1975: 9.20 a.m.

We're both going out the door of The Cabin at the same time. I've got my Daily Mirror; she's carrying The Guardian. I'm doing the gentlemanly thing, gesturing and mumbling that she should go first, holding the door open for her. She doesn't say anything and doesn't look directly at me but smiles lightly in disinterested acknowledgement.

We both pause momentarily outside. Her Mediterranean complexion is much more striking in the bright sunlight, her large earrings and bangles (no rings I notice) catching the rays, giving her an almost exotic appearance.

'I haven't seen you in The Cabin before,' I declare, awkwardly.

She half turns, looks straight at me, smiles and then waits the longest five seconds I have ever experienced, before replying:

'Well, we only moved into the area a few months ago. And anyway, I usually get here a little earlier than I did today.'

I wonder momentarily about the 'we' but she has already moved on. I follow a step or two behind, not sure whether the conversation has concluded or not. She lopes across the road to the Green and passes the little war memorial, before stopping again at the traffic lights. I catch up with her at this point. She's wearing a uniform-green coloured sleeveless T-shirt and a long flowing skirt – white with little motifs on it – like one of those skirts you see in the window of Laura Ashley's. And brown sandals. She's also wearing a scarf over her shoulders – the same material as the skirt, I think – knotted loosely at the front. I wonder momentarily why she is wearing a scarf on such a warm day but then, what do I know about fashion?

Anyway, I'm desperately trying to think of something to say.

'Do you come to The Cabin every day?' is my highly original solution to restarting the conversation.

She stops and turns. That look again. Another agonising five seconds.

'No,' she shakes her head and I reckon for a moment that she is one of those people who speak only in monosyllables. But then she suddenly continues. 'I cannot shop there on weekdays as I have to leave early in the morning to attend classes.' Her accent is very English middle class and betrays no foreign influence whatsoever. For some reason, this emboldens me.

'Where do you have to go for these classes?'

'The West End,' she replies. 'Near Covent Garden.'

'That's a bit of a journey,' I declare, sympathetically.

She stops again. Bloody hell, this is like driving in rush hour traffic. This time she smiles. But it's the kind of smile a mother would bestow on a child that had just said something amusing.

'Not really. One gets used to it. I take an early train from Cheppington Holt and, five stops later, I'm on the Tube heading for Covent Garden.'

She walks on again and I kind of toddle along beside her, feeling a little childish.

'What about Sundays?' I pipe up, immediately conscious that I may be sounding a little pushy.

'No, I go to church on Sunday mornings. It's in the other direction so I use the shops near the church to pick up whatever we need.' Then she stops and looks straight at me. 'What about you?'

'Me?' My first thought is that she's asking me if I go to church on Sundays, but I needn't have worried.

'Yes. Do you walk this way every day?'

'No,' I reply, relieved, before rushing into a dry-throated explanation, 'mostly on Saturdays. And then only when we have a home game. Occasionally, I come on weekdays too, but with my other tedious commitments plus training sessions, you know how it is…'

My voice trails off. I don't really know what to say next. She is still staring at me as if waiting for me to finish. Obviously, she doesn't know 'how it is'. She doesn't even know what I am talking about. And I cannot find the words to finish even a simple sentence. She purses her lips slightly, gives a little 'Hmmm', and gazes across the road. Just then, the lights change.

She heads towards the cluster of small shops and I follow. It's a little early for Noah's son Bradley to open his 'Threads' fashion boutique but I can hear him inside testing the sound system as he sets up the mood music for the day. Noah Berrie is already there, setting out a selection of his wares, just outside the front window of the little antique shop at the front of the shopping arcade.

'Good morningston, my friend. Buying or selling today?' Noah calls after me. I stop, but Lisa Dell walks on as if our conversation has already ended as far as she is concerned. I mumble some pleasantry or other to Noah before making up the lost ground. The Horseman's is closed and quiet. This is in marked contrast to the Olde Fayre Green cafe, which is already open, and doing a brisk trade if the clatter of china is anything to go by. Lisa Dell pauses by the window to inspect the limited menu, tapping her open palm with the folded newspaper, before strolling on.

One unusual thing that I notice now is the way she has folded her newspaper. Like all tabloid readers I fold my Daily Mirror once, horizontally, across the centre. Broadsheet newspapers tend to come already folded in this way. Most people then add another fold — vertically — so that the final shape is compact. Not this lady. She adds a second horizontal fold so that the newspaper ends up long and narrow. She then holds it to all intents and purposes like a pointer or a baton.

The second thing I notice is that we are both heading in the same direction.

She has a slow, gentle, almost loping stride. I usually tend to walk at a brisk pace. She doesn't walk in a straight line either but meanders along the footpath, appearing to be fascinated both by the gardens, grass verges and gutters. It's as if she sees something in nature that I am missing. Slowing my pace to match hers makes me feel awkward and I cannot get any rhythm into it. I wonder, does she even realise that I am trying to walk beside her? At the moment we are like two trains that run parallel for a few seconds and will soon veer off in separate directions. I'd like to get the conversation restarted but cannot think of anything to say.

'Mick said you were some kind of dancer,' I venture, at last.

She turns slowly and stares at me as if surprised that I am still there. I cannot quite decide whether the look is one of pity or condescension, but I am suddenly conscious again of the difference in height between us. She is an inch or two taller than me.

'I'm studying dance,' she says emphatically, looking down at me; talking down to me.

'You mean like ballet.' I'm trying to keep the dialogue going, but I'm uncomfortable about getting into a conversation where my knowledge limitations will be shown up.

'Hmmm,' is all she says. I'm not sure if this means 'Yes', or if it's her way of thinking out loud: 'How am I going to keep a conversation going with this cretin?'

My mind has gone blank and I cannot think of anything to say that will restart the conversation. We walk in silence past the Butlers'. Unfortunately, they are not around to provide any much-needed diversion.

Then she suddenly asks, again without stopping and without looking directly at me: 'And what is your football team called?' The way she says 'football' makes it sound as though she regards the game of football as being on a par with 'pimping'. At this stage, the level of my self-esteem is positively subterranean so as we near the fork in the road, I decide that whichever route she is taking, I am definitely going the other way.

'Rangers,' I state, proudly, wounded pride pumping the strength back into my voice.

Getting no reaction, I elaborate: 'Queens Park Rangers.'

Still nothing.

'QPR,' I emphasise, helpfully. (Who is this woman and where has she been living?) 'Ah,' she says, a bit like the earlier 'Hmmm'.

Thankfully, we have reached Eddie's house at this stage and Eddie is out early as usual, messing with his motors.

'Morning Eddie,' I say, slowing down as I approach.

'Mornink, Eddie, heh, heh,' Eddie mumbles nervously, wiping both hands on his vest, his eyes darting swiftly from me to Lisa Dell.

I do a quick introduction. Lisa extends an impossibly long arm towards Eddie at a height where it appears she expects him to kneel and kiss her hand. Eddie doesn't shake her hand in the way that any self-respecting Englishman would do, but rather holds it in his right hand and then gently covers it with his left, muttering something in whatever language it is that he speaks. He does all this effortlessly without appearing in the least bit self-conscious. Lisa blushes. And then she utters something to him in a lingo akin to his own. There's lots of gesticulating and smiling going on: nauseating, continental stuff. Eventually, Lisa manages to drag herself away. I have a brief conversation of sorts with Eddie about our prospects against Liverpool today before we move on.

'What a charming man,' she smiles, as we continue towards the corner.

'Dirty dog, more like. You know, I've never heard Eddie utter as many words as that in all the times I've spoken to him.'

'*Maybe you should talk to him about things other than football.*'

Aha, I conclude, that's what caused the mood change earlier. She knows nothing about football. And has even less interest in finding out.

I notice she is drifting to take the left-hand turn at the fork, past The Glade and up Forest Hill Road towards Hazel Wood. Thankfully I'm heading on my usual route home – to the right, up Wellesley Gardens.

'*Nice meeting you,*' I say with as much enthusiasm as I can muster in the circumstances.

She seems a bit taken aback at the suddenness of this, but then realising that this is the point where I must veer off, she recovers her poise, extends her hand, looks me straight in the eye and says:

'*Well, the best of luck this afternoon.*'

I shake her hand awkwardly.

And with that she's gone.

It suddenly starts to drizzle so I cross the road swiftly and step into the relative sanctuary afforded by the high hedge at Aunt Sally's. I discretely watch Lisa Dell lope her way very slowly up Forest Hill Road. She stops to talk to some kid, then picks up something from the pavement and walks on until, eventually, she disappears over the brow of the hill hand-in-hand with one of the kids. I have the distinct feeling that she knew I was watching her but she never looked back. Then, with a few choice phrases learnt from the terraces at Loftus Road, I quickly deal with the lewd comments of the few layabouts sheltering under the hedge who are also staring after her, note the time and, with the sun now making its reappearance, I decide to move on.

A strange lady, that Lisa Dell. I felt awkward when I was with her but now that she's gone, I'm suddenly disappointed that I didn't get to talk to her a bit more. Funny that. But she seemed nice, if a bit toffee-nosed. Good looking too. Beautiful, in fact. But what would I talk to her about? She obviously knows nothing about football. And cares even less. Dancing? Bloody hell. No, we obviously have absolutely nothing in common. I'd reckon she's a bit older than me, too. Don't know why I think that. The way she talks; that air of confidence, maybe. And taller. And as for that gangly walk! Can she really be a dancer? A classical dancer; that's what Mick said. But then she said she was studying dance. That could mean anything. Still, she did take my mind off Trouty for a few minutes. But I don't think I'd like to go through all that effort of trying to make conversation with her again any time soon.

I glance anxiously back down Park Road in the hope of seeing Bernie Trout entering the side door of The Horseman's, intending to dash back to have a quick word with him so that the match day ritual might be maintained.

Nothing.

This leaves me with a distinctly uneasy feeling about today's game. It's the first match of the new season and already the ritual is broken. I worry how this will affect the outcome today.

Liverpool are the team that most people are backing to win the title this season. They will be looking to put down a marker today that signals their determination to win the First

Division by taking two points from their first game. Away from home, too. Winning away from home is not a problem for them. They did it here last season, beating us 0–1 at Loftus Road. They are physically strong and will be very difficult to break down. Scoring goals against Liverpool will not be easy. And QPR have never beaten Liverpool.

Ever.

Saturday, 16 August 1975: 4.40 p.m.
Queens Park Rangers...2   Liverpool...0

3. THE MEN IN BLACK

Eight months later:

Saturday, 24 April 1976: 2.40 p.m.
Black is the traditional colour worn by the match officials, and 'the man in black' is widely used as an informal term for a referee. The referee for today's game against Leeds United is Mr W. J. Gow of Swansea. The linesmen are Mr V. H. Wood (red flag) and Mr A. J. Parsons (yellow flag).

Getting the flag colours right can be as important to the fans as it is to the players. Typical terrace witticisms such as 'Hey, Woody you're as thick as a f*!*!+ing plank' are unlikely to work to maximum effect if mistakenly directed at the venerable Parsons.

I find it interesting the way referees and linesmen are always listed with their initials. Not just their first name initials, but their second names too. So, whilst the players are simply 'Billy' or 'Jack', referee Gow is Mr W. J. Gow. Presumably this is intended to convey authority through creating a little social distance between the chummy 'Daves' and 'Dons' and the more authoritative A. J. and V. H.

I'm told that in rugby, there was time when players were listed by their initials too, and of course rugby, with its strong elitist origins, emphasised the class divide still further by having more than two forenames, as well as having double-barrelled surnames. So you might end up with somebody listed in the match programme as A. J. F. Fortescue-Smythe, playing in the pack, while among his teammates he was probably better known by his public-school nickname of 'Squiffy' or 'Bunty.'

Anyway, I'm not sure it would work for the players and supporters at QPR. I can't imagine skipper Gerry Francis being happy to be listed as G. C. J. Francis (Gerald Charles James) or goalkeeper Phil Parkes as P. B. N. F. (Philip Benjamin Neil Frederic). The piss-taking in the dressing room would be merciless. No, for us, it's all schoolyard names like 'Bowlesey', 'Gilly' and 'Parkesy'.

And then, of course, there's 'son', that derogatory form of address so beloved of senior players but particularly of team managers because it suggests an easy familiarity but more importantly, it confers inferiority.

You'll have noticed how football managers and senior players refer to anybody that's a year younger than them as 'son' or 'The Boy'. In training sessions, it's 'lay it off now, son' and 'mark your man, son'. In media interviews it's, 'The boy Lee Royd done really well.'

The rules seem to go like this. Anybody who was at the club before you is entitled to call you 'son', regardless of his and your age. Anybody who is older than you (even by a month or two) is entitled to call you 'son'. The Manager is entitled to call you 'son' (and anything else he chooses, depending on his mood at the time) even if he is younger than you are. You, in turn, must always refer to him as 'The Gaffer'.

A small minority of television and radio commentators have an entirely different approach to players' names. In a puerile attempt to convey greater insider knowledge of a club or imply a deeper friendship with the player concerned, these commentators will frequently refer to him in terms in which he has never been publicly referred to before. So, Rodney Marsh is 'Rod Marsh' and Teddy Sheringham becomes 'Edward Sheringham'.

Me? It makes no difference to me what people decide to call me – as long as my name is on the team sheet. David, Dave, Davy – even Dozy Bastard! I've been called lots of names in my time.

Still am.

Saturday, 30 August 1975: 8.45 a.m.

It's a quiet morning. The traffic seems slower and more intermittent, for one thing. It's as if every second car is off the road today. Marianne Pleass has her bicycle propped up against one of the pillars at the end of her driveway and is busily pumping air into the rear tyre. I stop and offer to take over and finish the job but she mumbles something without raising her head that I take to be a 'no-thank-you-I-can-cope'. I hover, anyway, and attempt, unsuccessfully, to make conversation. Then I notice a theatre programme sticking out of the basket on the front of her bicycle. On closer inspection, I see it's for a show called A Little Night Music in the West End.

'Any good?' I enquire, holding up the programme.

'Yes. Excellent,' Marianne replies, frowning momentarily at my impudence in extracting the programme from her basket.

Marianne and I never have real conversations. We simply exchange sentences that have loose connections to each other but would never exactly qualify as flowing dialogue. We rarely even make anything more than fleeting eye contact.

'Adelphi Theatre...Jean Simmons...Joss Ackland,' I read aloud. Okay, so it wasn't a question, but I did expect something more than:

'Yesss.'

Having pushed enough air into the tyre to inflate a small dinghy, pinched its rock-hardness and exhaled almost as much air again in an exasperated sigh, Marianne is finally ready.

I make one final attempt:

'Are there are any numbers in the show that I might know?'

She straightens up, turns and half smiles. 'Send in the clowns?'

I take this to be a dig at me and at what she perceives to be an inane question. Then she readies her bicycle for today's suicide mission before pedalling away, bouncing onto the road from the edge of the pavement and off into the contraflow. Even the car horns that greet her hazardous arrival seem a little more subdued, a little less impatient, this morning. It's as if the world is on its best behaviour.

I cross at Aunt Sally's and wave to Tojo, who is driving his Reliant into the driveway. This makes a change from his usual practice of leaving it parked with one wheel up on the pavement. I immediately bump into the Butler boys whose demeanour appears decidedly at odds with the general relaxed atmosphere of the day. Jacko is wearing sunglasses and his long, double-breasted leather overcoat. He was a bit put out when I dubbed it as his 'Gestapo coat' the first day he wore it. It's unbuttoned as usual and his hands are thrust deep into the pockets. He's fidgety and the bottom half of the coat is flapping about, giving him the appearance of a bird that's about to embark on its maiden flight but lacks the self-belief to take the big leap.

Billy looks decidedly shifty, pulling at his hair while trying to appear nonchalant. Making eye contact is not a feature of Billy's method of social interaction. He's wearing a sort of latex or PVC-imitation version of Jacko's leather overcoat that he bought from a stall on Portobello Road. I've seen him wear this before. On cold evenings, the material almost freezes and becomes as hard as metal, locking Billy into what looks like one of those spacecraft re-entry capsules. Billy's 'metal jacket' is shorter than Jacko's leather version and reaches to just above his knees; perfect for knocking four pints of Watneys Red Barrel off a bar table. Which is exactly what he did one evening while trailing Jacko into The Horseman's. True to form, they didn't hang around to apologise or buy another round that night. And it doesn't look as if they intend stopping for a natter today, either.

'Aren't you going the wrong way?' I ask deliberately, seeing their discomfort.

'Nah,' mutters Billy, striding straight past me, while attempting to scratch his hair into place.

'Gotta see a man about a dog, mate,' Jacko mumbles. 'Right Billy?'

'Right on, Jacko,' confirms Billy, quickening his step. But Jacko obviously doesn't wish to appear rude. 'Look, mate,' he promises, 'we'll catch ya later, okay?'

And off they go. Or scarper, to be more precise. They disappear round the corner, along The Glade and up Forest Hill Road towards Hazel Wood in a matter of seconds. I half expect to hear a police siren but perhaps they are in a hurry on legitimate business this morning. I'm lucky I bumped into them when I did, then. Normally, they would stop for a natter but no matter, the ritual is intact. Marianne, Tojo, Jacko and Billy. Now for Echo Eddie:

'Nice morning, Eddie,' I say. 'Quiet.'

'Nice mornink, heh, heh.' And then he adds, 'Quite,' as if imitating the quintessential Englishman.

'Kipper play today, heh, heh?' He asks suddenly.

'Yeah,' I reply, 'QPR play today.' (I had solved that particular piece of translation one frosty Saturday morning last season.)

'We have policy today, heh, heh,' he declaims, and I'm not sure if it's an announcement or a question. But then I'm never sure of anything with Eddie.

'Policy?' I ask, wondering what can he mean?

'Yes, heh, heh. Policy today.' He extends his right arm in an exaggerated HALT gesture: 'Stop policy.'

Suddenly the penny drops and I twig what he is on about.

'Yeah,' I reply, trying not to insult him by laughing out loud. 'Our policy is to stop them playing.'

But Eddie is not entirely happy with my summary. He seems concerned that I have misunderstood his tactics and wants to expand the conversation.

'Policy,' he nods furiously. 'Stop,' he shakes his head negatively and pauses interminably while searching for the right word; 'Block.' He appears relieved to have gotten it out at last. So am I.

There are some days with Eddie when you know it's not the time to get into a deep conversation of more than two or three sentences. I'm thinking: 'Stop', 'Block' – same thing, really. So I thank him for the tip and move on.

He continues to explain as I walk away, calling after me, still agitated that I have not fully understood him. It's only when I round the bend on the last lap into the town that I finally get what he was trying to tell me.

There's a small police roadblock roughly a hundred yards before The Horseman's. Eddie was forewarning me. He probably said Polizei and not policy.

A couple of panda cars are parked at an angle on Park Road where it meets the Green and three policemen in uniform are stopping traffic and questioning the drivers. I immediately think of the fleeing Butler boys, and then just as quickly reprimand myself for the fact that I continue to harbour serious suspicions about them.

Then I think of Trouty. He still hasn't shown up. Could this roadblock be related to his disappearance? But then, as far as I know, he hasn't officially 'disappeared'. Nobody has reported him missing as far as I can tell. He's just not around. His absence seems to bother me more than it does anybody else. Maybe he's just flown off somewhere to top up his tan and I'm just being selfish about it because it has thrown my ritual out of sync. Wherever he's gone, hopefully he'll be back soon.

I slow as I reach the roadblock in the hope that the Old Bill will stop me for questioning. That way I will be able to question them and establish if it is Trouty who is at the centre of their investigation. But the copper just smiles as if he recognises me and waves me through. Damn.

I stop at Berrie's to say hello to Noah. 'Good mornington my friend; today, you are most welcome if you're buying. But if you are selling, then I must warn you that I will need to know the provenance of the merchandise.'

It takes me a moment or two to work out that this is Noah's little tstolen goods' joke in the light of the amount of police activity in the area this morning. I don't believe that Noah would ever knowingly handle stolen goods, but there was one occasion a few years ago when some merchandise he bought from the Butler brothers turned out to be of considerably greater value than either Noah or the brothers realised. An eagle-eyed collector brought it to the attention of the boys in blue and the resulting investigation caused Noah some considerable embarrassment. The Butler brothers claimed under questioning to have purchased the merchandise some time previously and that they were ignorant of its real value. No charges ever followed.

I ask Noah if he has any idea what the roadblock is all about, but he just shrugs and shakes his head. We discuss the possibility that it could be linked to recent IRA bombing activity. Noah isn't sure but he senses my apprehension:

'Hazak Ve'ematz,' he says as we part. 'Be strong and brave.'

Lisa Dell is at the front of the queue in The Cabin. I don't spot her at first. She looks different. She's wearing a long skirt, with a short-sleeved smock and a long silk scarf wrapped loosely at her neck. All plums, rusts and beige, she looks like she just stepped out of an advert for Biba.

But still no Bernie Trout.

Now I'm really worried. I need to think my way out of this. And the last thing I need right now is another struggle to make conversation with Lisa the lapdancer. So I stick my nose in the Mirror and pretend to be deeply engrossed as she pays Mick for the Guardian and leaves. I can smell the apple blossom from her hair as she passes me on her way out but I keep my nose in the newspaper.

The front page makes for depressing reading:

DEATH OF A HERO

is the headline over a photograph of a crumpled body lying under a blanket in front of the shattered front windows of a K Shoes shop. According to the report, a bomb in Kensington last night killed a member of Scotland Yard's bomb squad who was trying to defuse it. Is this the reason for the roadblock, I wonder? It's the third terrorist bomb this week. Thirty-three people were injured on Wednesday in a pub bombing in Caterham down in Surrey. And then another seven hurt in an explosion on Oxford Street on Thursday. All believed to be the work of the Irish Republican Army.

I don't ever discuss things like the IRA bombing campaign with Mick. I know Mick likes to give his opinion on it and I've heard him give it, but quite frankly, it all got far too complicated for me. What I did work out is that Mick is for the aims of the IRA (a United Ireland) but against its methods (violence) and I'm content to leave it at that. I tend to keep well away from political and religious conversations generally. Instead, Mick and I usually confine our chats to what we call 'the third picture'.

Mick has three pictures pinned side by side on the back wall of The Cabin. The first is of former US President John F. Kennedy, who probably had some Irish connections. In the centre is a picture of some pope or other, whose name and number I cannot remember. His right hand is raised in a kind of blessing but with two fingers raised in what you might reckon was a vulgar sign if it wasn't for the fact that he's a holy man. The third picture features Liam Brady, the young Arsenal midfielder. Mick is a major 'Chippy' Brady fan and tends to wax lyrical about Brady's 'cultured left foot'.

Now, I know that it's highly insensitive and selfish of me to be thinking of my own ritual at a time like this, but when I reach the counter I cannot resist the opportunity to immediately ask Mick if Bernie Trout has been in.

Mick, who usually knows everything, has seen and heard nothing of Trouty since our last conversation. He doesn't appear too concerned, either. Like it's normal behaviour for ol' Bernie to just vanish into thin air. Mick seems more intent on establishing if Gerry Francis will play today or if his hamstring injury will rule him out. And impressing upon me that I have 'just missed Miss Dell'. He appears surprised that I am taking my time paying him and peppering him with more questions regarding Trouty and not fleeing out the door in her wake.

I tell Mick that I spoke to Gerry last night on the phone and that I reckon Gerry will play, but that he will probably want to be replaced before the end of the game so as not to put too much strain on that hamstring. This is only true in the sense that this is what I reckon will happen today. As for speaking to Gerry on the phone last night, well, Gerry is unlikely to take a call from me after our brief but heated altercation at this week's training session.

Mick asks me how the 'ritual' is going today.

'Good, so far,' I tell him. 'I've got Marianne, Tojo, Jacko, Billy, Eddie, Noah and now you. The only one I'm missing is Bernie Trout.'

'And how were they all?'

'Oh, the usual. Eddie was a bit confused by the police roadblock, I reckon. Anyway, he was trying to make himself useful around the garden.'

'Useful? Useful, is it?' Mick is in one of his acerbic moods this morning. 'That man is about as useful as an ashtray on a motorbike.'

'Well, at least he tries.'

'And how was Marianne Pleass?' he asks, pronouncing it 'Please' and not 'Plass' the way Marianne does.

'A bit sour, this morning, I thought. She had a flat tyre. Not a lot to say for herself.'

'Huh, typical. She's either Miss Please or DisPlease. One day she has nothing to say for herself; the next day she has a mouth on her like a skipping rope.'

This revelation about the talkative side of Marianne surprises me, but I decide not to interject.

'As for your Mr Trout, I'm sure he'll turn up — and probably when you least expect him to. Mr Trout's the kind of gentleman who would go through a revolving door behind you and come out in front of you.'

But I'm not in the mood for Mick's humour. I tell him that somehow I have got to get the ritual back into sync; that we managed to get away with Trouty's no show for the Liverpool game but that I can't go through the whole season this way. I point out that although we got a couple of reasonably good mid-week results and a great away win, this only makes today's London derby against West Ham an even more crucial game for us.

Mick concurs, but makes some positive noises regarding our form to date, especially in the Liverpool game.

'Concentration, Dawhee me bucko: Rangers had it, Liverpool did not,' Mick pronounces emphatically. 'Even their manager admitted as much after the match. You heard what Bob Paisley said: "One or two of our lads didn't do their own jobs but ran round trying to do everyone else's — they were even trying to sell programmes!"' laughs Mick, doing a very passable imitation of the Liverpool manager's accent.

But I know he is just humouring me because he keeps standing on tiptoe and looking over my shoulder at the front door as if he is expecting someone. Eventually he smiles, looks at me and winks.

'Godspeed,' he says and hands me my change. 'Hurry along now.'

She is lingering outside as I exit The Cabin. She has a floppy-brimmed hat on and brown-tinted wire-framed sunglasses. I stop and pretend to scan those small advertising cards in the window looking for lost dogs and flat sharers, in the hope that she will move on. Damn. This is all I need today.

'Are you looking for something or someone?' she asks, nodding at the small ads board.

I'm tempted to say, 'Yeah, I've lost Bernie Trout and I'm thinking of putting a card on the board here offering a reward for any information about his whereabouts,' but all I do say is: 'Not really.'

'Did you win that match?' I'm surprised at the question, because it's two weeks since we bumped into one another. At least she remembers something of that encounter. Perhaps she has suddenly become interested in football.

'Yes. We beat Liverpool 2–0,' I say proudly, pausing briefly, newspaper still open, before walking on. 'I've just been chatting to Mick about it. Mick thinks Liverpool are a really good side but they lacked something against us that day, while we...'

'The best lack all conviction while the others are full of passionate intensity,' she announces rather melodramatically.

'Spot on,' I say. 'Where say. 'read that?'

'Yeats,' she smiles lightly, 'and I hope I've quoted him correctly.'

'I know most of the sports reporters and I've never heard of him. What paper does he write for? The Guardian, I suppose,' I say dismissively and start to drift away but she sets off with me, matching my stride as we head up Park Road.

'Did you perform well?' she asks suddenly, removing the hat and sunglasses.

I ignore the theatrical language. 'Yeah, I was happy enough with my own small contribution,' I reply a little sarcastically. 'But that was two weeks ago. Since then we drew 1–1 at home to Aston Villa in midweek, beat the champions, Derby County, 5–1 away from home and drew 2–2 with Wolves at home last Tuesday night.'

I can see her eyes begin to glaze over with boredom at this sudden data overload. She obviously has not developed an interest in football since we last met.

It seems that neither of us knows what to say next, so we walk on a bit in silence. I ask if she knows what the police roadblock is all about.

'It's probably related to the IRA bombs in London over the last few days,' she suggests.

'That poor man killed and all those people injured. I just don't understand the point of it all.'

'Bastards,' I say. 'And the Government does absolutely nothing about it. We need an election. A new Government. Or at least a new Prime Minister. That Harold Wilson is just useless.'

She frowns but says nothing. A Labour Party supporter, maybe. We walk on past the shops; turn at The Horseman's and up Park Road. When we pass the Butlers' place I don't mention my earlier suspicions that the roadblock might have been related to them. She doesn't know them so it would be difficult to explain the reasons for my initial misgivings. We continue to walk on, not speaking for a few minutes. I'm trying to think of something to restart the conversation but she beats me to it.

'What were you humming, just now?' she asks suddenly.

'Pardon?'

'You were humming something back there as we passed The Horseman. What was it?' She is staring directly at me now and it's the kind of look that demands a response when coupled with a question.

'Oh. I didn't realise I was. Humming. Probably "Here I go again". I've been humming it all morning. Why? D'you know it?'

'One of The Hollies' earlier hits. Three-part harmonies. Yes.' She smiles. I take the emphasis on 'earlier' as an indication that she reckons the tune I'm humming is out of date and perhaps that I am too.

'It's the track they used to play at Loftus Road when the team ran out on the pitch before each match,' I explain, immediately. 'It tends to come to mind in the days before every home game and then I can't stop humming it.' I'm embarrassed by how juvenile the whole thing sounds.

She smiles that slightly condescending smile again.

'Hardly appropriate though, was it?' she asks quizzically.

'Why not?' I retort.

'Well, the lyrics, for a start. Don't you think that there's a certain tedium about them?'

'Tedium?'

'Well, you know, stuff like (she starts singing lightly here but in a deliberate drone and gently waves the newspaper in her hand as if conducting to the beat):

Here I go again
Here I go again.

'Same old; same old, here I go again - hardly likely to raise team morale was it?' she suggests

'I never thought of it like that,' I admit, starting to feel the anger rising inside me. 'Anyway, they used to play it for quite a few years when the team ran out. Then they changed it to something else. "The Pied Piper", I think it's called.'

'Good Lord,' she exclaims. 'Another depressing theme. How do they choose these songs?'

'Dunno,' I say, morosely, 'maybe it's the Chairman's favourite tune?'

'And what has your team won in all that time?'

I just shrug and say nothing, and hope that this is an adequate response.

'Well?' she insists.

'Well, not a lot, as it happens,' I reply, stung by the shame of it all.

'See,' she states baldly, 'QED.'

'Pardon?'

'QED,' she repeats, smiling. 'And, as every schoolboy knows, it stands for Quod Erat Demonstrandum. It's Latin.'

'Really,' I sniff sarcastically, hoping that will bring an end to the misery I feel I'm being put through.

'Yes,' she continues, 'roughly translated, it means "Which proves my case".' She seems so smugly self-satisfied with her cleverness.

'QPR: QED,' she repeats with a soft giggle, as if it's a football chant on the terrace. 'It has a certain ring to it, don't you think?'

I assume that the question is rhetorical, so I don't give her the answer I would like to give and we drift along in a kind of sullen silence. Thankfully, we are almost at the fork in the road.

'Who is QPR playing today?'

Her question stops me in my tracks. She is walking a few feet behind me but close enough for the question to be part of polite conversation rather than her calling out to me. I take a deep breath.

'West Ham United,' I state curtly.

She smiles. Then she extends her hand again, looks me straight in the eye and says: 'Well, I hope it all goes well for you this afternoon.'

'Thanks.' I shake her hand and we part. This time I don't watch her walk up The Glade towards Hazel Wood. I think: this woman is having fun at my expense, toying with my emotions. At any time this would be unfair. On match days it is unforgivable. Who does she think she is, anyway? Pretending to be interested then using me as the butt of her little joke. What was that she said about QE2, QPR? It has a ring to it? What's that supposed to mean? And it's not exactly memorable either, is it? Unlike that bleedin' Hollies tune that I can't get out of my head:

Makin' the same mistakes
Headin' for more heartaches
What can I do when there's nothing I can do
I looked in your eyes and I knew that I was through
Here I go again
Watch me now 'cos here I go again...

Best to just put her and her stupid questions out of my mind. I wonder again about Trouty as I quickly hurry up Wellesley Gardens. This is the second match day Saturday that he will be missing. *Maybe I should consider excluding him from the ritual altogether. It's early in the season so there is time to adjust my routine.*

I worry all the way home about the result today. West Ham are currently top of the table. Okay, so they rarely win any trophies, but they play attractive, flowing football and are generally considered to be the aristocrats of the game. We lost 0–2 to them at Loftus Road last season. This season, they've got Frank Lampard and Trevor Brooking in top form. We're missing both of our regular central defenders today. Thankfully, we've got the experience of Ron Abbott to call on, but Tony Tagg only made his first team debut a week ago so the pressure will be on him. I know we're only four games into the season, but losing to West Ham?

Now that would really hurt.

I've been hurt so much before
I told myself, yes I did
No more, no more won't get hurt any more
Here I go again
Watch me now 'cos here I go again…

Saturday, 30 August 1975: 4.40 p.m.
Queens Park Rangers…1 West Ham United…1

4. THE MAVERICK AND THE MOB

Saturday, 24 April 1976: 2.15 p.m.

There's no sign of Stan.

All the team is here in the dressing room but there's no sign of Stan Bowles.

'Stan the Man' is one of our star players – if not *the* star of the team. If there's one person who can unlock the Leeds defence today, it's Stan. Most likely Leeds will assign Billy Bremner or Norman Hunter to the role of man-marking Stan this afternoon, so his shins are likely to resemble the bruised blue and white of QPR by the time the final whistle blows.

Stan was born in Collyhurst, just outside Manchester, and began his career at Manchester City, but his quick temper and constant run-ins with the management and coaching staff resulted in him being released after a series of off-the-field incidents. I suspect it was the company he kept, not Stan himself, that got him into trouble.

He subsequently played for Bury, Crewe and Carlisle – and left each of these clubs amid some controversy before he joined QPR for £112,000 in September 1972.

It can't have been easy for Stan initially at QPR. In the first instance, he replaced another QPR folk hero, Rodney Marsh, who had been transferred to Stan's first club, Manchester City, just six months before Stan joined us. Still, Stan had no problem donning Rodney's number 10 shirt or being compared to him, outrageously claiming never to have even heard of Rodney on the day he joined QPR nearly four years ago!

Also, given Stan's history, some commentators were convinced that this was a risky investment on the part of QPR at the time. But to date, Stan has proved them all wrong. In addition to his sterling performances for QPR, Stan has also been capped by England. And he has established a strong rapport with the fans. After home matches Stan has been reportedly sighted walking the fifty yards or so to the Springbok to join the locals for a few drinks.

He's a bit of a character both on and off the pitch, is Stan. Horses, dogs – anything you can bet on – are his main interests outside of football, and occasionally he even manages to merge his professional and leisure interests. In a break in play, he will sometimes ask supporters on the terraces if they know the result of a particular horse race taking place that afternoon. On away trips, none of the team wants to share a room with him because when most of the players are getting some sleep ahead of the match the following day, Stan will still be on the phone from the bedroom at one or two in the morning – probably calling his bookie!

Stan is a quick thinker – and not just on the field. One story I heard in the dressing room recently concerns Stan and another QPR squad member, Don Shanks, who decided to go for a meal in a well-known restaurant after a night out at White City greyhound track. Shanks assumed that Stan was paying for the meal but it transpired that Stan had no money. Stan reportedly complained to the restaurant manager about the dishonesty of its clientele and its lack of proper security, claiming that his wallet had been stolen during the meal. In order to preserve the reputation of the restaurant, the manager allowed them dinner-for-two on the house. And gave them a few quid not to talk to the media about it!

Stan's preferred position is to play out wide on the right. That way, he can cut inside and pass or shoot with that deadly left peg of his. He is also a great 'shuffler' and can beat opponents at will. This inevitably results in him having to survive some pretty harsh tackling during the course of the match. Some commentators – and fans of rival teams – believe that Stan has a tendency to 'dive', particularly in the penalty area. Certain referees appear to have been influenced by this view and, as a consequence, tend to give tacklers the benefit of the doubt by not awarding penalties in legitimate cases. To be fair to Stan, although he is kicked a lot, he rarely loses his temper.

The Gaffer, Dave Sexton, has suggested to Stan that he avoids further injury to his ankles by passing the ball that little bit earlier. That was a brave move by the Gaffer. You cannot really coach Stan in this way. He is an intuitive footballer; does what he feels he has to do. Some players want to score. Stan wants to win. And he will do whatever it takes to make that happen – regardless of the cost to life and limb. Stan believes he can change the flow of any game – if only somebody will give him the ball early. He is intolerant of sloppy passing and will inevitably remonstrate loudly with the culprit. Even Dave Sexton does not have immunity from Stan's ire. After being substituted in an FA Cup tie away to West Ham last season, he flashed a 'gesture' to the Gaffer and vowed he would never speak to him again. Within a few days he was back in the squad.

Today, against Leeds, we really need Stan. And we need him to be at his best. So why isn't he here?

Saturday, 13 September 1975: 8.45 a.m.

Marianne Pleass seems to be waiting for me. This is unusual. She's already outside her front gate on the pavement steadying her bicycle and busily tidying the contents of the basket. However, she appears to be in no hurry to mount up and sail off against the oncoming traffic. But just as I approach her, she mutters her usual stilted 'morning' and almost immediately begins to move off. 'I hear you've made the front page of the Mirror today,' is her parting shot, as the double honk from a dark blue Ford Cortina trumpets her arrival in the wrong lane.

'How so?' I shout after her, but she obviously cannot hear me over the continuous sound being emitted by an oncoming bright green Mini, whose driver manages the near-miraculous feat of extending his arm and upwardly pointed finger out the window while keeping one finger of the other hand pressed down firmly on the horn.

What did she mean, I wonder? On the front page? Did she literally mean me? Unlikely. One of the family, perhaps? Possibly – but not in the Mirror. The team, maybe. Or one of the team? I hope it's not Stan again. Why couldn't Marianne have been more specific?

Well, at least I can tick off the first person on my ritual list, but I continue to feel unsettled, wondering what she could possibly have meant. There's only one way to find out so I quicken my step, with just a nod in the direction of Aunt Sally's oriental factotum (person number two) before I cross on to Beane Row. I say a quick good morning to Eddie (person number three – this is going remarkably well this morning) but I'm in too much of a hurry to be drawn into a conversation with him. No sign of the Butler boys at the gate. This is not really a problem as, in conforming to my ritual, bumping into any one of the boys will do. I can always simply knock at their door on the way back. The boys know all about the ritual and they usually make a point of meeting up with me somehow on these important Saturdays. Anyway, I needn't have worried this morning as both brothers eventually appear at the front door and wave extravagantly, still wiping the sleep from their eyes. I wave back, and then step up the pace downhill into the town.

'Good mornington, my friend. Are we buying or selling today?' calls Noah Berrie. He is in his usual jovial form standing outside the little antique shop, both hands clasped behind his back, chatting to his son Bradley.

'Maybe we should lock up the shops and put up the shutters today,' Bradley suggests loudly, obviously intending that I should overhear. Then he laughs that phoney horsey laugh of his. I hate that feeling where there's a joke on that I'm not getting. Worse still, when I suspect that the joke may be on me.

I rush across to The Cabin, and without even looking to see if Trouty is there I grab a Mirror.

SOCCER'S RING OF FEAR

reads the headline. I join the queue and quickly read on. It says that a large area of London faces chaos today at the hands of soccer thugs who follow Manchester United. The centre of the ring of fear is the Queens Park Rangers ground at Shepherd's Bush, where United are to play. Bus and train crews are to treat the district as a no-go area.

So, the Manchester mob is heading for Loftus Road. The locals will have good reason to fear the self-styled 'Red Army'. When Manchester United were relegated to the Second Division two seasons ago, this 'Red Army' of football hooligans caused chaos at grounds up and down the country. But football hooliganism is not unique to Man U supporters. Most teams have a hooligan element that follows them round the country, much to the chagrin of the clubs themselves. With Arsenal it's 'The Gooners'; the 'Inter-City firm' travels to battle on behalf of West Ham United, Chelsea has its 'Head-hunters' while the 'Yid Army' rumbles on behalf of Spurs. I think back to that infamous relegation battle when Spurs and Chelsea fans clashed on the pitch before Spurs relegated Chelsea last season. It made national headlines when it was shown on television.

These 'firms' were formed for the specific purpose of intimidating and physically attacking rival supporters. Some people believe that the attacks have nothing to do with football rivalry; that it's a wider societal issue for Britain that was created by the emergence of a subculture some years back. This subculture, epitomised by skinheads and supporters of the National Front, now uses football matches as an outlet for their pent-up 'aggro', racism and general disaffection. But from what I've heard, it's not just confined to this country; it's a worldwide phenomenon. Yet, for some reason, it's been dubbed the 'English disease'.

The authorities are still grappling with the problem of finding a cure for this 'disease'. The segregation of rival supporters inside football grounds has definitely helped, even if it graphically illustrates the problem when you see it on the telly. But it has come at a huge cost, with fewer young families attending matches and an increase in security and police presence at all football grounds.

As if we didn't already have enough problems policing the country right now.

There was another IRA bomb a week ago at the London Hilton hotel that left two people dead and sixty-three injured. Diverting valuable manpower to policing football matches instead of focusing on catching terrorists makes absolutely no sense. This Government has got its priorities all wrong.

But it's not the threat from IRA terrorists that is worrying me this morning. Most of the bombings have been targeted at well-known locations in central London. Nor does the story about the Manchester mob cause me undue concern – a lot of it could be media hype. No, what is really bothering me – and I realise that this may sound insensitive in the light of all that bomb carnage during the week – is Bernie Trout's continued absence.

I scan the queue but he's not here. Bloody hell. This is the third consecutive week that he's missed. I asked around during the week – I even popped into The Horseman's – but nobody has seen him. Even Sid, the guy who manages the place for Trouty, hasn't heard from him, but doesn't seem too perturbed about it either. But then Sid has no interest in football, and he definitely doesn't know anything about football rituals.

Mick is no help either, when I arrive at the top of the queue. He only wants to talk about the threat from the Man U fans – probably to avoid having to discuss the bombings.

'Bastards,' I say. 'Stupid, idiotic bastards. Why do they do it, Mick?'

'Well, Dawhee me bucko, I don't suppose there is much point in being an eejit unless you can show it. And speaking of eejits, did you meet the Butler boys on your way here this morning?'

'Just a brief glimpse of them when I passed the house. They had just woken up by the looks of them.'

'I'm not surprised, me bucko, I'm not surprised at all. I think I may have heard them on their way home late last night. I think everybody in the neighbourhood probably heard them.'

'Well I'm sure I'll bump into them on the way back.'

Mick asks me how the ritual is going this morning.

'Well, so far I've got you, Eddie, Noah and Marianne...'

'And how were they all?' Mick is obviously keen to keep the conversation going. Any conversation — so long as it's not about the bombings.

'Good, I think. I was hurrying so I didn't stop for long chats. Marianne was a bit curt, to be honest.'

'Hardly surprising, me bucko. Even her eyes are at cross purposes, some days.'

'Come on, Mick, some people might reckon that's not very Christian of you,' I say, wagging my finger at the picture of the Pope pinned on the wall behind him.

Mick ruefully throws his eyes towards heaven: 'And what do you think, me bucko?'

'Sometimes I reckon the world has too much religion — and politics.' I nod towards the picture of President Kennedy.

Mick smiles: 'But not enough football, eh, Dawhee, me bucko?'

I notice Lisa Dell chatting to Brad across the street when I leave The Cabin. Bradley keeps checking his watch and tapping it. I don't fancy getting into a conversation with either of them this morning — and certainly not both of them together, so, to avoid them, I stay on my side of the street and start heading up Park Road. Come to think of it, they might be well suited: two people with superiority complexes. I cross over at The Horseman's as I want to catch the Butlers on my way home.

Lisa sees me crossing and immediately ends her conversation with Brad. That's not entirely true. First, I hear Noah calling Brad's name from inside the arcade. Then Brad says goodbye to Lisa and goes in search of Noah. Lisa then walks on up Park Road just as I am crossing to her side. So our meeting is entirely fortuitous.

We exchange polite but fairly formal 'good mornings'. She's wearing a green camouflage jacket and maroon trousers with one of those red and white arab scarves — a keffiyeh, I think it's called — draped casually around her neck and shoulders. If it wasn't for the fact that all of this expensive-looking clobber looks as if it came off the rails of Swan & Edgar in Regent Street, you could easily mistake her for a paramilitary.

'So whom are you playing today?' she asks eventually, fingering the tassels of the keffiyeh.

'Manchester United,' I reply

'Ah,' she nods knowingly, tapping her copy of The Guardian. 'I just saw something in the newspaper about that. It was on the radio this morning, too. The police are expecting some crowd trouble, I believe?'

'Yeah, there's a small group of Man U so-called "fans" who tend to cause trouble wherever they go.'

'And the police have decided to stop them coming to the ground by public transport? I hear that they're closing the Central and the Metropolitan Line Underground stations close to the ground. Can they do that?'

'It seems they can,' I sigh, 'even though the fans likely to be most inconvenienced are the QPR supporters.'

'And the bus drivers have blacked the area too, according to the radio.' For a moment I'm tempted again to believe that she is developing an interest in football, but I know that this story has spread from the sports pages to the news pages, which is obviously where she picked up on it.

'Yeah, Mick told me about that. Football hooliganism has become a really big problem. They've already cancelled some of British Rail's so-called "soccer specials" following a number of very nasty incidents. Now there's talk of some kind of Government working party being set up. And they're seriously considering issuing ID cards to fans to cut out the hooligan element going to matches. Can you believe that?'

'I think that might be going a little far,' she counters, 'but keeping them off public transport might work.'

'Yes, but according to today's Mirror, the hooligan elements among the Man U fans have made their own plans to overcome the police blockade on public transport. They're hiring private coaches that will drop them a few miles from the ground.'

'Really? And they intend walking the rest of the way?'

'Yeah. So shopkeepers will be putting up the shutters and pubs will be closing until later in the evening.'

'Is Mick putting up the shutters? Is The Horseman remaining closed?'

'Don't be ridiculous,' I laugh, 'we're miles away from Shepherd's Bush. Anyway, I can't see Mick putting up the shutters for any mob of hooligans. And Trouty doesn't appear to be around to close The Horseman's even if he wanted to.'

'Shepherd's Bush. Is that where QPR plays?'

'Yeah. The ground is called Rangers Stadium, but everybody calls it Loftus Road. It's near White City.'

'Beside the BBC offices?' she perks up.

'Yeah. Quite close, actually. But the BBC hasn't exactly covered itself in glory this week either. It seems they wanted to install cameras at the ground but only to film the Man U supporters, not the match itself. QPR refused, so the Beeb is reported to be setting up cameras outside the ground instead, in case there is any violence'

'But isn't that likely to just encourage the violence? When the mob sees the cameras?' she asks.

'Probably,' I concede, 'but that's the way things are these days in football.'

'Do you ever run into problems with supporters of the other teams?'

'Well, there's a lot of hooligan trouble at the football grounds, but the worst thing is going out in the evening and getting hassled by mobs of supporters from other teams, mostly drunken ones.'

'I trust your team doesn't have any hooligan mobs as supporters?'

'Every team has them, including QPR. There's the C Mob and The Ellerslie Enders. They're well organised gangs.'

'And all over a football match.' She shakes her head in disbelief.

'I know. You'd need dogs to control them. Speaking of which, here's a couple of hooligans. And a dog. What's up, boys?'

'Watcha,' the Butler boys puff in unison, while they grapple with a mangy-looking spotted greyhound.

I begin to introduce Lisa to the brothers but it seems she's met them before and has bumped into them quite often, in fact, since they introduced themselves to her as she passed their garden gate one morning. All three of them have bit of a laugh about this and I feel totally excluded.

'Who's this then?' I ask, attempting to steer the conversation back to the present day.

'It's our new dog,' announces Billy, running his thick fingers through his greasy quiff. 'We're gonna run it at White City once we get it fit and ready.'

'Who's training it for you?'

'We's trainin' it ourselves,' Jacko inhales deeply and leans back against the gatepost as if daring me to take issue with him.

'Yourselves!' I say, taking the bait. 'What do you guys know about training dogs? Just because you spend every spare hour at the dog track, doesn't mean you know anything about training a dog.'

'It's not complicated, me old china,' laughs Jacko, deliberately blowing smoke in my direction. 'Ya just need to exercise it regular-like.' Then, giving me a conspiratorial wink, he adds, 'Then all ya need to know is how much to feed it.'

I have no idea what this last comment means but Billy seems to find it funny, so I suspect it's something dodgy.

'Where are you training it?' I ask.

'Over on the Common. Lots of room there,' replies Jacko.

'And it's just a short walk from 'ere,' pipes up Billy.

'You're keeping the dog at home? Where? In that postage-stamp size back garden of yours?'

Before either of them can respond, Lisa, who has been standing back looking slightly bewildered, suddenly interjects. 'What's the dog called?'

The brothers exchange glances before answering as if silently agreeing on what their answer should be. Now I know there is something not quite right about all of this. But I shouldn't be surprised.

'Roxboro Roy.'

'Roxboro Roy?'

'Thassit. Roxboro Roy. Aintya, boy?' Jacko distractedly rubs the dog robustly. 'But we woz thinkin' of renaming 'im "Stan-the-Man", wasn't we Billy? We thought you'd appreciate that, wot wiv your Stan bein' into the dogs an' all. Right, Billy?'

'Right on, Jacko,' says Billy, who is still grappling with the hound and has his hands full. Or rather he has his hands wet.

'Aw f***,' cries Billy, suddenly. 'He's only gone and done a Jimmy Riddle all over me.' At this point the hound breaks free and bounds up the hill with Jacko in hot pursuit and Billy frantically searching for a piece of absorbent material. I can see him eyeing up Lisa's Guardian, so I quickly shove the Mirror at him.

He grabs it but the SOCCER'S RING OF FEAR headline momentarily catches his attention. 'There,' he quips, scrunching up the front page and dabbing each palm, 'I've dried my piss-wet hands on those Man U fans.' Then he stuffs the remainder of the newspaper into his overcoat pocket and takes off after Jacko and Roxboro Roy, who have by now vanished from sight.

I look quizzically at Lisa, as if to ask 'shall we go after them?' She nods and we walk swiftly in the direction of the pursuing pair.

Suddenly, from a few doors away, there's a scream followed by a whimper and then by an excited, heavily accented voice, proclaiming, 'I have dog, heh, heh. I have dog.'

We arrive to see Svetlana pinned against the side wall of her house by nothing other than abject terror and Eddie, having wrestled Roxboro Roy to the ground, now has the hound ensnared in a complicated kind of headlock. The dog isn't barking exactly but is issuing high-pitched sounds not unlike those made by a cheap house fire alarm when the battery is running out.

'I have dog, heh, heh. I have dog.'

The Butler boys immediately rush to liberate Roxboro Roy from under Eddie's heavy embrace. The dog is lying supine and appears to be seriously considering whether his long-term future might be better served by remaining interlocked with Eddie, but Svetlana crushes any such possibility by suddenly uttering a wailing sound in the direction of the dog, in what may be Swedish but is definitely hostile in tone. The hound staggers to its feet and makes an uneasy return to the brotherhood of Butler.

I decide to extract myself discreetly from the fracas and continue my journey towards the fork in the road. Lisa begins to follow. At this stage, the Butler boys are heading home with the cowering hound. Svetlana, I would imagine, is heading for the Valium. Halfway up the road Lisa stops, grabs my arm, glances back and explains: 'I believe Eddie is asking whom you are playing today.'

Eddie is indeed shouting something in my direction.

'Man U,' I shout back, hoping we're not out of earshot. 'Man U.'

Eddie straightens up, beams widely and flexes his muscles, obviously proud of his achievement in restraining the dog.

'I am man, heh, heh. Yes, I am man.'

'What an unusual start to the day,' exclaims Lisa, once we are well out of earshot. 'And what was all that "China" and "Jimmy Riddle" stuff, that the boys were going on with?'

'Cockney rhyming slang. "China" is from "China plate", meaning "Mate". A "Jimmy Riddle" is a — you know — a "piddle". The boys like to give the impression they're well in with some of the villains from London's East End — that they're originally from the East End themselves. But it's all just show. Those fake exaggerated, stage-cockney accents. It's all an act; totally over the top.'

'It does seem like a very complicated way to communicate, regardless of whatever prompted them to adopt it in the first place. To be perfectly frank, whenever I meet the boys I usually come away not quite certain of what they have been talking about. What's does "Must have a butcher's" mean?

'It means: "Must have a look". "Butcher's hook" rhymes with "Look".'

'What weird logic. What about "Apples and pears"?'

'Stairs.'

'Good Lord. And "Tin of fruit"?'

'Suit.'

'What's a "Ruby"?'

'Ruby Murray — a curry.'

'What about "Bristols"?'

'Haven't heard that one,' I blurt out quickly, then swallowing hard, 'but I'll ask around. Anyway, don't you have local slang where you come from?'

'I've never lived anywhere for long enough to pick up the local dialect,' she says wistfully and we walk on slowly, an awkward silence enveloping us. Thankfully, we soon reach the fork in the road.

'Are they good?' she asks, out of the blue.

'The Butler boys? They're good fun,' I answer, surprised at the innocence of the question. 'But I don't know that I would describe them as being "good". I suspect there's another side to them that maybe you're better off not knowing about.'

'I meant your opponents today, silly. This "Man U". Are they good?'

'Ah. Well,' I laugh, 'they're only one of the greatest clubs in the world. They've won League titles, FA Cups — even the European Cup.'

'Then, how come I've never heard of them?'

'Maybe that's because you don't follow football. But, more likely, it's because they went through a tough time in the last couple of years and they were relegated to Division Two,' I explain. 'Then last season they won the Second Division. So they were promoted and now they're sitting on top of the First Division, three points ahead of us in fourth place.'

'Sounds impressive,' she half whistles, but I know she hasn't really been taking in any of this.

'Yeah,' I say. 'Their manager is Tommy Docherty. He managed QPR...'

'Really?' she says, but without any real enthusiasm.

'...for about 28 days,' I laugh.

But she doesn't see the humour in this. She just stares at me blankly.

'And in that time, he claims to have given Gerry Francis his big break and he says that he has never stopped believing that Dave Clement is the best right-back in England.'

'Ooh, that's nice,' she says, as if this should mean a lot to me. She has brightened up all of a sudden, then: 'So, what are your chances today?' she asks, as if the previous bit of conversation never happened.

'Well, Harry Miller is tipping QPR to win,' I say, tapping my folded Daily Mirror. 'But United have got some top players in their team — Stepney in goal, McIlroy, Macari, Coppell...' I can see that none of this is of any interest to her, so I quickly finish: 'Both teams are playing well so I reckon it'll be a closely fought battle. But I'm hopeful.'

'Battle?' she raises her eyebrows. 'All the more reason to take care, then.'

I tell her I'm not worried, that I can take care of myself, and we part company. I cross the road to Aunt Sally's, where Tojo is loading some large cardboard boxes into his motor. I help him with a particularly heavy-looking box and for some reason I look back across the street. She is still standing there. She gives a little wave. It's not immediately clear if this is to me or to Tojo. I wave back. It feels like the most awkward, unnatural physical exercise I have ever undertaken.

'Take care,' she calls out, smiling.

I give a carefree shrug, turn away, and this time I don't look back. But, deep inside, I am concerned. Not so much about fighting on the terraces, rather how things will go on the pitch. I'm worried about the result today. No Bernie Trout, again. This is the third week in succession he's failed to show.

What will it mean?

Saturday, 13 September 1975: 4.40 p.m.
Queens Park Rangers…1 Manchester United…0

5. RICH MAN, POOR MAN

Saturday, 24 April 1976: 2.35 p.m.

Stan arrives in the dressing room eventually, with Chairman Jim Gregory in tow. At last. Thank Christ for that. He's probably been upstairs in the Directors' Lounge trying to bend the Chairman's ear concerning another advance on his wages. Jim has always indulged Stan and continues to do so. In truth, he probably sees a bit of himself in Stan.

In his late forties and bald on top, Jim has the air of a second-hand car dealer about him. This is not entirely surprising because that is what he is, essentially. There are two trademark items that Jim seems to wear permanently: a Crombie overcoat and a mischievous grin.

Today, however, Jim hasn't brought the Crombie overcoat with him into the dressing room (rituals are obviously not important to him!) and is dressed in a natty brown suit, cream shirt and brown tie. He appears a little nervous and constantly fidgets with his tie and strokes his chin or rubs his nose.

James Arthur 'Jimmy Boy' Gregory was reared in the Shepherd's Bush area of London and has supported QPR since he was a kid. A self-made man; the tales of his entrepreneurial skills are legion. One story has it that he took over running his father's fish stall at the age of 14 when his dad joined the army. Then, when his old man came back after the war, Jim set up in business for himself.

Another has it that whilst working for his mum and dad at their fruit and veg stall, Jim went out and brought three second-hand vans, sold all three in a day and repeated this on a regular basis until he had built up his initial capital.

He eventually set himself up in the second-hand car market as 'Gregory's Motordome,' and this, over time, became the basis of his personal fortune. He joined the QPR board in 1964 and was appointed Chairman one year later. Back then, QPR were a moderate, Third Division side operating from a shabby stadium at Loftus Road with a small but loyal following. Jim's commitment, hard work and, more importantly, the money he invested in the club eventually began to pay dividends, the three most notable achievements being the signing of Rodney Marsh in 1966, coming from 0–2 down to beat West Brom 3–2 to win the League Cup at Wembley in 1967 (thereby making history as the first third division team to do so), and winning promotion from the Third Division to the First Division in successive seasons.

Jim Gregory has overseen the modernisation of the Loftus Road stadium, adding new floodlights and building two new stands: one on South Africa Road, the other on the Ellerslie Road side of the ground. He was – and still is – also centrally involved in the buying and selling of players.

It is generally accepted that one of Jim Gregory's bravest decisions was to sell

QPR icon Rodney Marsh in March 1972. Rodney was immensely popular as an entertainer and match winner and seemed irreplaceable. But by selling Marsh to Manchester City for £200,000, Gregory created a war chest that enabled him to sign many of our current squad of players. Braver still was his decision to pay £112,000 for 'wayward' Stan Bowles in September 1972.

Jim Gregory has worked hard to keep Stan happy. Rumour has it that Stan usually needs his wages at least a week before he has actually earned them, in order to clear some debt or other. This means he is constantly requesting meetings with the Chairman to secure an advance. Over time, Jim seems to have achieved that delicate balance between firmness (saying no) and a bit of indulgence (giving in) and Stan respects him for that – as well as the fact that the advance sometimes becomes a loan that Jim does not collect on.

Today, Jim assures us, the expectation is that QPR will collect the two points needed at the expense of Leeds.

So, no pressure, then.

He wishes everybody good luck and shakes hands with each member of the team. Then, before leaving the dressing room to let the Gaffer give the final pep talk, he delivers this reminder to the whole squad: 'Look lads, it's going to be a full house here today. There are 80p tickets changing hands on the streets outside for £1.50. Now go out there and give those fans on the terraces full value for their money.'

Saturday, 27 September 1975: 8.40 a.m.

The chain has come off the bicycle this morning and Marianne Pleass is down on one knee trying to slip the chain onto the front sprockets. I offer to help but she shakes her head without looking up, and mutters something in a kind of guttural tone that betrays an angry impatience. I glance up at Marjorie who is standing in the bay window and I make one of those 'I don't understand' gestures with my hands (the kind I make to a referee who has inexplicably given a decision against me), but Marjorie just keeps staring out vacantly. Eventually, I return my attention to Marianne and tell her that I know how to fix the chain back in position in approximately ten seconds flat. She sniffs, stands up and turns to gaze up at the bay window with a resentful expression. I lay part of the chain on the front sprockets, lift the back wheel and rotate the pedals. The chain clicks back into position immediately. I steady the bicycle on its stand and step back. Marianne says nothing at first. Then, she reaches into a brown paper bag in the front basket of the bicycle and I hear a sharp snapping sound.

'Would you like some chocolate?' she asks.

I take the two pieces she offers and thank her. Then I notice that there's a dog-eared paperback book in the basket. It's got a kind of purpley-blue cover and what looks like a very long title. But what catches my eye is the large picture of a spanner. Well, it's a spanner at one end but the other end is shaped like a flower.

'Any good?' I ask, nodding towards the basket; then without waiting for an answer: 'What's it about?'

'It's called Zen and the Art of Motorcycle Maintenance. It's by Robert M. Pirsig,' she replies slowly, through a mouthful of gooey chocolate, all the while staring at the pavement.

The title throws me a bit. I cannot quite get my head around what the book might be about. I just don't see the connection between Zen and motorcycles. (Probably because I don't know what Zen is!) I pick it up and read aloud the text on the cover: 'This book will change the way you think and feel about your life. The most explosive book you will ever read.' I look over at Marianne with raised eyebrows.

'It's a philosophical novel,' she says, finally, 'an inquiry into values. It explores the metaphysics of quality.' She sounds as if she has learnt this off by heart. And it doesn't tell me anything.

Marianne breaks the remainder of the bar of chocolate in two, hands one half to me and waits on my response.

'Maybe you should buy a book about bicycle maintenance instead,' is all I can think of to say. And it falls as flat as, well, as flat as a flat motorcycle tyre...

Marianne doesn't react. The silence is broken only by the sound of both of us biting through the pieces of chocolate. I turn to squint up at the bay window again but Marjorie is gone. When I turn back to Marianne, she is already pedaling away to a fanfare of car horns.

I walk to the corner and throw the scrunched-up piece of chocolate wrapper in the litter bin. Tojo is sweeping up the first of the fallen leaves near the gate to Aunt Sally's. He's not having a lot of success with this, as the wind is whipping around the corner and blowing the little piles away. Tojo maintains his calm composure throughout and I consider momentarily asking him if he knows anything about Zen, but I think better of it; simply exchange waves with him and move on.

Across the road I see Jacko Butler leaning on the little iron gate outside his house. The sunglasses are on but, unusually for this time of the morning, he doesn't have a cigarette between his nicotine-stained fingers. I already know what's coming.

'How are you today, Jacko?' I ask

'Same as yesterday,' he replies somewhat despondently. 'Fackin' skint.'

'Sorry to hear that,' I sympathise. 'What's up? Bad night at the dogs?'

'Everyfink, mate. Lost me shirt at White City, then lost every stitch I 'ad trying to win it at back at cards 'round at Snozzer's place. So, you're lookin' at a fackin' financial nudist, so to speak.'

It's a little early in the morning for me to dwell on this particular visual analogy. Neither do I want to get into a discussion on the progress or otherwise of Roxboro Roy. So I change the subject to something of far greater concern to me.

'I don't suppose you've seen Bernie Trout in your travels this morning?'

'I ain't been doin' too much fackin' travellin' this mornin', to tell ya the trufe, mate. Unlike ole Trouty, who is always travellin' off somewhere. But now that you mention it, I ain't seen hide nor hair of ol' Trouty for at least a week or so. Not that I'm exactly seekin' 'im out, you understand. There's a bit of 'istory between ol' Trouty and me, as you is probably aware.' He smiles ruefully as if remembering some painful incident. 'Has he asked you to get 'im tickets for that Spurs match in November? Ya do know 'e's a secret Spurs fan, dontcha?'

'There's no secret regarding that, Jacko,' I correct him, 'Bernie has never tried to hide his allegience to Spurs as far as I'm concerned. He's always been up front about it. And no, he hasn't asked me to get him tickets for the Spurs match, but if he does, I'd be happy to get them for him. I owe him a favour.'

Jacko seizes his opportunity: 'Listen, mate. Can ya do me a fackin' favour and pick up a packet of smokes for me when yer in the The Cabin? Sovereign Extra Mild. I'll fix up wiv ya on yer way back.' Then, as I turn to move away: 'Oh, and a packet of Rennies for the bruv, too.'

I nod my consent.

'Peppermint,' comes a shout from an upstairs window. I look up to see Billy, elbows on the windowsill, rubbing the sleep from his eyes, his hair sticking out all over the place like a hedgehog. Not a pretty sight at this time of the morning.

'Right on, Billy,' I shout back, which seems to momentarily confuse him and leave him stuck for words. I hurry on down the hill into the town and decide to look in on Noah Berrie first.

Bradley is having difficulty with the mood music in Threads this morning. The speakers are giving him grief. The sound is going on and off intermittently. To make matters worse, the volume is going up and down without warning. Early morning shoppers raise their hands to their ears and their eyes to the skies as they pass. I take a quick peek in through the front window. Bradley is down on his knees at the back of the shop, fiddling with knobs and wires. Eventually he gets it sorted and stands up. I tap the window to get his attention, give the poor bastard a cheery thumbs-up, then skulk away.

'Good mornington. Well, are we buying or selling today, young man?' Noah's usual placid visage bears the pained expression of a man whose ears have been drip-fed with muddled morsels of mood music all morning.

'Neither, unfortunately – but your neighbour has a sound system he'll want rid of fairly soon.'

'Oh, that,' Noah tosses his head back in frustration. 'I did warn him about it but that's the younger generation for you. Never listen.'

'I shouldn't reckon anybody will want to listen to that racket for too long. Aren't you worried it will scare all your customers away? That sound would deafen anybody.'

'All my customers? Aha – a man with a sense of humour,' Noah wags his forefinger at me and laughs. 'Customers, indeed. With some of the merchandise I have in stock these days, it's blind customers I need, not deaf ones.'

'Well, you might need blind and deaf ones to shift some of these ancient LPs you have on the shelves.'

'Not so fast with the criticism, young man. I had a customer waiting for me to open at 9 o'clock this morning so that she could buy a few of those, what you call ancient, LPs.'

'What? This stuff?' I slide back the top dusty layer of the stack of albums. 'The soundtrack from Ben-Hur? Helen Shapiro? Lonnie Donegan? I can't imagine anyone wanting this stuff? Don't you have anything more modern? What about The Who or the Rolling Stones? Even the older stuff by rock bands is still much in demand. Some of them have become collector's items.'

'It wasn't that particular genre she was looking for,' Noah protests, slightly offended by my criticism of his stock. 'Actually, she wanted a particular LP of modern dance music. And, of course, I had it,' he adds a little smugly.

'Dance music?'

'Modern dance music.'

'Right. Well, can't hang around here all day. Gotta nip into The Cabin, get the paper — see what they are saying about our chances today.'

'I would try the café first.'

'Sorry?'

'She said she was going to the café. For a coffee. Late night last night, it seems.'

'Who?'

Noah smiles; raises his hand and just dismisses me with a wave. 'Kol tuv, my friend.'

I bump into Mick's son Cattle as I exit the arcade. He's with this other bloke that he introduces as 'O'Leary'. Tall geezer. Irish. No first name. And no small talk either. Unusual for an Irishman. Doesn't seem to want to hang around. Not surprising, really, I suppose, in the present circumstances. Cattle explains that O'Leary has got him some tickets for The Chieftains at the Royal Albert Hall on Monday week. This means absolutely nothing to me, so, after a bit of foot-shuffling and a few awkward pauses, they head off in the direction of the café. I stroll across to The Cabin.

There's nothing much in today's paper. Carole Augustine, the beautiful model in the Manikin cigars ads on the telly, has died tragically in Portugal. An overdose, according to the Mirror. But, in the sports section, there's an interesting article by Harry Miller highlighting the drop in attendances at football games this season. Of course, Rangers has never had a large following and the ground capacity is quite small, but even the bigger clubs seem to be suffering now.

I resolve to make my visit to The Cabin a quick one, as I'm dying for a cuppa myself. But Mick is having none of it. He asks me about the ritual. (I reckon that it's becoming as important to him as it is to me.) I tell him I haven't talked to Eddie yet this morning, but that I will pick him up on the way back. But that I've met Marianne, Tojo, Noah, Jacko and Billy — the usual suspects.

'Jacko and Billy. The usual suspects. How very apt, Dawhee, me bucko. How very, very apt. And what are they being accused of today, I wonder.'

I decide not to attempt an answer. I don't want to get Mick started on the brothers if I can avoid it. By way of diversion, I point to a newspaper clipping tacked onto the wall behind the counter that wasn't there before. Clipping is probably the wrong word to describe it, as it's large enough to obliterate the pictures of President Kennedy and the man I have since learned is Pope Paul VI. The 'third picture', however, is uncovered. The tousled-haired 'Chippy' Brady still stares out skywards at an angle as if waiting for the ball to drop at his feet, which (Mick assures everybody) 'Chippy' will instantly control with one touch.

The headline on the newspaper piece reads:

SLASHERS FINALLY MAKE THE CUT

It's an intriguing headline, especially as it's obviously from the sports section of a newspaper.

'What's so important about that story that it takes over from a former US President and a pope?'

Mick explains that the cutting is from a newspaper from his home town of Longford in Eire. The 'Slashers' are a Gaelic football team called Longford Slashers, and they have just won some major cup competition.

'Unusual name, "Slashers",' I smirk. 'Sounds like a bunch of blokes chasing each other around a football pitch carrying meat hooks and cleavers.' This elicits a few guffaws from the queue behind me.

'Does it now, me bucko?' I think I detect a steeliness in Mick's tone, and at first I reckon I've offended him by my condescending attitude.

'Well, I can't think of any English football club that would adopt a name like "Slashers", can you?' I say, by way of mitigation.

'No? What about Millwall?' He smiles. 'Yes, Dawhee me bucko; Millwall Slashers. With a name like that they would surely put the fear of God into anybody they play.'

'I think they do that already, don't they?' pipes up a voice from the queue and the general bonhomie of earlier is restored.

'Now, Dawhee me bucko,' Mick rubs his hands, 'what else can I do for you today? The Mirror, is it'?

'Yeah. The Mirror. Thanks, Mick. Oh, give me twenty Sovereign Extra Mild while you're at it, mate,' I add, pointing to the cigarette display behind the counter. 'And a packet of peppermint Rennies.'

Mick sniffs and his pale features darken. 'I take it they're not for you, me bucko?' Mick has always taken it upon himself to watch out for my health.

'No. They're for the brothers,' I say helpfully.

Mick doesn't move. He just stands there like a Customs Officer requiring further explanation.

'The Butlers. Jacko and Billy,' I oblige.

'Jacko and Billy,' Mick hisses resignedly. 'The Butlers. Now there's a gene pool that could do with a good dose of chlorine.' I know he doesn't like the Butlers. I've seen the way he deals with them whenever they come into The Cabin to buy some smokes — or 'snout' as they sometimes call it. No greeting, no banter, and definitely no introductions.

Mick forages among the shelves along the back wall, then lays the stuff on the counter: 'One Mirror,' slight pause, then slowly, 'and twenty Benson & Hedges Sovereign Extra Mild,' each word of the latter stressed and spoken as if the packet of smokes somehow sums up everything he needed to know about the Butlers as far as Mick is concerned. 'That'll be 36p — or seven shillings and thruppence in real money.'

It's been five years since decimalisation, but Mick has still not fully accepted the changeover.

'What about the peppermint Rennies?' I ask.

Mick hunches forward. 'Sorry,' he discloses in a half whisper, 'peppermint Rennies are out of stock.'

'I reckon spearmint might do the trick, at a push,' I suggest helpfully.

'Sorry, me bucko, but you're out of luck. Didn't I just sell me last pack of spearmint Rennies only five minutes ago.' Then, straightening up, folding his arms and gathering his breath he adds: 'Now, if the Butler boys are a little short of readies today, it's probably because they spent all their dough at White City last night betting on Rob Roy, or whatever they call him. Followed, no doubt, by a stint in some late-night curry house and rounded off by a few hours spent in a place of ill repute. So maybe a little unrelieved heartburn might teach them a lesson.'

I give him a moment or two to catch his breath after this diatribe before handing over a tenner. Mick gives me my change. 'Shrapnel,' he usually calls it. But not today. There's a heightened sensitivity around everything since the recent bombings: accents, language, parcels on trains — you don't make wisecracks about these things any more.

'Make sure you get paid, now...'

I know I won't get paid. The Butler boys are always happy to share their jokes and their time — but that's where their sense of generosity ends. I don't really mind.

'...and say hello to Miss Dell for me.'

I pause in my tracks, then turn around to face him.

Mick winks: 'She was asking about you earlier. Said she was going to the coffee shop.' He raises his hand: 'Godspeed.'

'Yeah.' This is beginning to feel like a conspiracy. But I had promised myself that cuppa anyway.

I don't spot her at first. She is sitting in the corner with her back to the door, engrossed in the newspaper. She is dressed entirely in black — T-shirt, jeans, boots and leather jacket with a red and white polka dot scarf knotted loosely at the neck. She's like a tall Suzi Quattro. But with too much make-up. I didn't think she wore make-up. I don't really like it. It makes her look older rather than younger. There's a fresh mug of hot coffee on the table beside an empty one so I wonder momentarily if she has been waiting for someone (me?) — or if she met someone earlier who has just left. I just stand there for a moment or two. Eventually, she looks up. She doesn't appear too surprised to see me.

'Ah, all in denim,' she smiles, looking me up and down. 'The uniform of the non-conformist.' I decide to ignore this little dig.

'What's so interesting in your newspaper this morning?'

'I'm just reading a review of The Rocky Horror Show. Why don't you join me?' She turns in her chair and Gregory, the owner, immediately rushes over to take the order. 'Are you coffee or tea?'

'Tea,' I reply timidly, suddenly realising that my throat is parched and I really do need one. Gregory, not normally so watchful or alert, is back with the tea in what seems like a matter of seconds compared to the time it takes him or Veronica to serve me when I am here on my own.

Veronica, a single mum in her early twenties, is the person who usually serves me. Gregory has a number of waitresses working there on a rota basis but it always seems to be Veronica who takes my order.

I squeeze into the chair in the corner opposite Lisa, and she clears space by pushing away the paper package on the table beside her. I can see that there's a couple of LPs inside the bag, but as it's not a record shop bag I decide that I know what's inside and resolve not to risk getting into a conversation that could end up being about modern dance music.

'The Rocky Horror Show,' I muse. Then I attempt to restart the conversation by lying: 'I think I heard something about it. What kind of a review does it get? Any good?'

'It was brilliant,' she says, holding my gaze.

'Oh, you've seen it, then,' I ask, taking a large swig of tea from the mug.

The burning liquid scalds my throat.

'Yes, about a week ago. It was awfully funny. Absolutely hilarious, in fact.'

'Hilarious?' I croak, swallowing hard. 'Isn't it supposed to be scary?'

'Not at all. It's a skit. A satire.' Then her expression suddenly changes to one of concern: 'Are you okay? You're not, are you? Hang on.' She half turns, raises her finger, demands water and within seconds Gregory appears with a small glass of the stuff, which I swallow in one swift gulp.

'Hot stuff,' I explain, pointing to the tea.

Lisa nods sympathetically. She waits until I am ready to speak again.

'Where was it showing?' I eventually manage to croak.

She raises her eyebrows quizzically.

'Where was it showing?' I point at the review on the open page in front of her.

'Oh. Chelsea. Kings Road. And it wasn't "showing"; it's not a movie — it's a live show.' The sympathy is gone and that slightly condescending air is back again.

'The Kings Road Theatre. Never heard of it,' is all I can think of saying.

'It was a cinema. Almost derelict and due to be demolished before it was transformed into a theatrical space. It holds less than 500 people so it's very intimate and a perfect location for the Rocky Horror Show. You should go see it. I believe you might enjoy it.'

'Nah, don't think so. I prefer going to the flicks.'

'Oh. And what good films have you seen recently?' She folds up her newspaper and rests her chin on her hands with her elbows on the table.

'I went to see a new one called Shampoo at the Odeon during the week.'

'With Warren Beatty and Julie Christie?'

'Yeah, that's the one. And Goldie Hawn. I like Goldie Hawn. A few of the guys recommended it. But I thought it was rubbish. Have you seen it yet?'

'No. And it's disappointing to hear that you didn't enjoy it. I heard it was an interesting film. All about a hairdresser but set against the background of Nixon, Watergate and presidential politics.'

'Sexual politics, more likely.'

'That too. It's meant to be a satire on the sexual and social habits of the sixties.'

'Dunno about the social habits, but there's plenty of sex in it and that poncey hairdresser was getting most of it.'

'I wouldn't call Warren Beatty poncey.'

'What would you call him then?'

'Well, sexy. I'd call him sexy.'

I say nothing. We settle the bill, leave the café and walk on in silence for a few minutes.

She keeps fiddling with the knot of her scarf and adjusting its position but eventually pats it into place.

'So, now that we seem to have exhausted the topics of films, theatre and the matter of Warren Beatty's sex appeal, or lack of, what's happening in the world of football?'

'Well, you'll never guess what I saw during the week.'

'Probably not, so do tell me.'

'I saw the draft of an article that will appear in the match programme today. It's all about the Man U game and it's strong stuff,' I say with undisguised excitement.

'How come you saw it before it was published?'

'The editor, Ron Phillips, knows of my interest in writing so he let me skim over it,' I explain, proudly.

'I didn't realise you had an interest in writing. So, what does it say that makes it "strong stuff" as you call it?'

'Well, the headline on the piece is THE MATCH THEY TRIED TO KILL and he's going to run it across two pages of today's match programme. It has a real go at the media. Basically, he's suggesting that the media exaggerated – or "embroidered and distorted", to use his exact description – the threat posed by the hooligans among the Man U fans; that it's only a small element – maybe a few hundred – of Man U's supporters that can be classed as troublemakers.'

'So he's claiming it's all the media's fault; that there was no real threat, no need to take all those security precautions?' (If she's feigning interest, she's making a good job of it.) 'But don't the clubs have obligations too? To the community as well a to their own supporters?'

'Of course they do. And he's not denying that. In fact, he intends listing in the article all the precautions that QPR took in advance of the match...' I stop, tuck the Mirror under my arm and begin to enumerate each point on the fingers of my left hand, '...liaising with the local police, briefing the stewards, arranging for the tie to be all-ticket so that supporters could be segregated—'

'So what actually did happen that day?' she interrupts animatedly, before walking on. (I reckon I really do have her attention, now.)

'The media obviously decided to ignore all that. You saw it yourself. The hysteria drummed up by the media in advance of the match regarding the possibility of violence was absolutely unbelievable. The fact that there was no trouble whatsoever the last time that Man U visited QPR was totally ignored by the—'

'But if that's the case,' she interjects again, 'why couldn't the football public make up its own mind about this. Could they not see it for what it was, scaremongering by the media in order to create a story?'

'Most football fans take their cues from the people in authority; the people who are expected to have the inside track on these issues. When London Transport announced that it would close the Underground stations close to the QPR ground, that gave out a signal that the people in authority – the people expected to know about these things – had hard evidence that convinced them that trouble was coming down the line.'

'But wasn't that a sensible move?' she asks, perhaps not unreasonably. 'One hears a lot of stories concerning trouble at Tube stations between fotball hooligans these days.'

'No, it wasn't a sensible move at all. On the contrary. It was generally known that because of the cancellation of the "football special" trains by British Rail, those Man U fans attending the match were all going to come by coach instead. So the only people inconvenienced by the decision to close the Tube stations were the QPR fans. Then the bus drivers decided to black the Shepherd's Bush area, which made things even worse for Rangers fans.'

'It looks to me as if your real gripe is with the transport authorities. Why criticise the media for alerting people to the possibility of danger? Isn't that one of their roles? Anything I read in The Guardian concerning it was very measured. Maybe it's just those red-tops of yours that are the problem?'

'Maybe you're right,' I concede. 'The Mirror certainly didn't help. One of its reports stated that huge numbers of genuine Man U fans had insured themselves against death or injury caused by their own rowdy supporters. Another had it that there would be a payout of £1,000 should any member of the Man U Supporters' Club be killed.'

'Good Lord. And you still buy that rag?' she asks, tapping my Mirror dismissively with her neatly folded Guardian.

'Well, the Daily Mail wasn't much better,' I retort, defensively. 'It put out a story that the police bill for the day would be enormous and that all of it would be borne by the taxpayer. The reality is that, as well as being one of the major rate payers in the borough, QPR also made a substantial contribution to the police cost on the day of the match.'

'Well, that's only fair isn't it? That QPR should pay for the police presence. After all, it's your QPR that stood to make substantial profits from the event.'

'Of course it's fair,' I snap. 'And QPR did make a substantial contribution to the cost of policing, but the point you are missing is that the security costs would have been much lower if the press hadn't generated all that hysteria.'

'Was it all the fault of the press? What about the television companies?'

'Well, the Beeb hardly covered itself in glory. The club had to ban their cameras from the ground when the BBC admitted that it only wanted to film the behaviour of the Man U fans and not the match itself. You know the way these things work; point a camera at a bunch of potential hooligans and they immediately feel they should start behaving like hooligans. The mere presence of the cameras can incite some of them to violence. Anyway, speaking of hooligans...'

'Gissthefags. Wot kept ya anyway?'

It's Jacko, rubbing his hands together and looking desperate. Billy is a little distance behind, dragging a comb through his damp hair. I take the smokes out of my pocket so that Jacko can see them but he makes no attempt to cough up the dough.

'Look, I'll settle up wiv ya later. Okay? I'm on my way to get some dosh right now.'

'White City? Snozzer's place? I'd have thought it was a bit early for that.'

'Nah, we're headin' for Joe Coral's.'

'The "Thrilla-in-Manilla". Next Wednesday,' interjects Billy.

Lisa looks confused.

'Betting on boxing,' Jacko explains. 'Putting our last few bob on Ali to beat Frazier.'

'One fight apiece and one to go. It'll be a Killa and a Thrilla and a Chilla, when I gets that gorilla in Manila.' Billy does a passable imitation of Muhammad Ali's boasting rhyme.

I hand over the smokes and we leave the brothers fumbling with the packaging.

Echo Eddie is in his garden unpacking some tools from a battered gun-metal grey cantilever toolbox.

'Morning, Eddie,' Lisa says.

Eddie blushes bright crimson.

'Mornink, mornink, heh, heh.' He starts to put some of the tools away, changes his mind and begins removing them again. 'You play tunes today,' says Eddie, except he pronounces it 'toones' the way they do in America.

'Not play,' Lisa laughs, 'just listen.'

Eddie looks confused. Lisa holds up the album.

'No,' Eddie shakes his head, then looks at me as if he expects me to translate for Lisa, 'you play tunes today.'

'No,' Lisa responds politely, 'I cannot play music. I don't play a musical instrument. I just listen.'

'No, no,' he insists gently to Lisa, then looks at me in frustration, 'you play tunes today.'

'Oh, Lord,' Lisa says, 'I do believe I've upset him.'

'I reckon 'e means "<u>The</u> Toons",' comes a voice from behind us. It's Jacko, relaxed and waving a lighted cigarette with Billy rolling up the rear, still trying to unscramble his hair.

'The Toons is the Geordies. From Newcastle,' mutters Billy. Then turning to me: 'QPR are playin' Newcastle today, arentcha?'

'I'm confused,' says Lisa to Billy. 'Geordies? Toons? Is that the nickname for the Newcastle football club?'

'It's not the nickname of the club,' says Billy confidently. 'It's wot the Geordies is called.'

'Why do they call themselves Toons?' asks Lisa. 'And how do you spell it?' Billy defers to Jacko on the spelling issue.

'T.O.O.N.S.' says Jacko. 'And they don't call theirselves Toons. Everybody else calls 'em Toons. It's 'cos of the way they speak, their accent, like,' he adds with no sense of irony whatsoever. 'See, when you say "I'm going into town", your actual Geordie will say "I'm going into toon". Tha's why we calls 'em "Toons".'

'Kipper play Toons today, heh, heh,' concludes Eddie.

Lisa catches my eye and silently mouths 'Kipper?' I shut my eyes momentarily in exasperation.

'Yeah, we play Toons,' I confirm. I'm slightly embarrassed that I didn't spot this one myself earlier and avoided all the unnecessary confusion. But call them Toons or call them Geordies, what I'm really concerned about today are the big names we are up against: Malcolm McDonald, John Tudor, Alan Gowling. These guys can score goals – home and away. They beat us 1–2 at Loftus Road last season. And no team has scored more goals than Newcastle United so far this season.

Saturday, 27 September 1975: 4.40 p.m.
Queens Park Rangers...1 Newcastle United...0

6. TAKE FIVE

Saturday, 24 April 1976: 2.45 p.m.

The Gaffer, Dave Sexton, has a final few words. Everybody gets his instructions. Every team member knows exactly what he has to do. The Gaffer looks relaxed but those of us who have studied him know that deep down, Dave Sexton is on edge too. He repeats the message that has been drummed into us all week by media commentators: you never underestimate Leeds United. Okay, so they are not the team that they were, but you write them off at your peril. You only have to look at how they fought their way back into contention after a hat-trick of losses back in February to know how resilient they can be. So we need a five-star performance from everybody this afternoon.

Leeds are already out on the pitch. We hear 'The Pied Piper' music starting up. That's our cue. And out we go to tumultuous cheers and applause. There's over 30,000 people out there – our biggest gate of the season.

The Gaffer is wearing a blue shirt, unbuttoned at the neck, with a dark tie with large diamonds on it. No 'lucky suit' for him. The Gaffer doesn't believe in all that ritual stuff. For him, it's strategy, tactics, preparation and attention to detail.

Less than ten minutes to kick-off.

After the initial pre-match warm-ups and kick-about, the nervous tension is building both on and off the pitch. Some of the players exchange high-fives. The players, club officials and fans alike seem to share a sense that at long last we are on the verge of a major, big-time achievement.

The Leeds players act as if they are aloof from all of the tension. They probably are, too. They've been here before. Totally professional – and focused. I decide to eyeball their number 5, Paul Madeley, who is the Leeds player standing closest to me. But he avoids making eye contact. He's not easily ruffled.

There's a blustery breeze blowing and the pitch is dry and firm, all of which will contrive to make ball control very difficult today. Leeds will be defending the school end in the first half, with our defence lining up in front of the QPR support on the Loftus Road terraces. Whatever advantage there might be in playing with that blustery wind behind you, QPR will have it in the first half. It's a cold afternoon but the strength of the sun belies the cool temperature. In the initial stages of the match at least, the sun will be directly in the eyes of the QPR defence when dealing with Leeds crosses coming over from the right wing. I try to point this out to goalkeeper Phil Parkes, but his face is a mask of concentration and nerves, and I doubt that he can hear me above the wall of sound emanating from the terraces behind the goal.

Five minutes to kick-off. The tension is unbearable.

Saturday, 11 October 1975: 8.50 a.m.

When I reach number 21 this morning, Marjorie is standing anxiously at the bay window with her right arm raised, holding a banana. Marianne comes round the side of the house and wheels the bicycle down the driveway, totally oblivious to this. I wait till she reaches me at the gates. I really cannot bring myself to greet her with: 'Hey, Marianne, your sister Marjorie is standing at the window waving a banana,' so instead I simply tilt my head in the direction of the window while raising my eyebrows. Marianne gets the message (maybe sign language could be our means of communication) and glowers at Marjorie before returning her attention to me.

'Oh,' she exclaims in frustration, 'Marje thinks I've forgotton my fruit.'

Marianne then delves into the basket on the front of the bicycle and produces an apple and an orange that she proceeds to wave back at Marjorie, one in each hand in a 'look, I've got them' kind of way.

Marjorie waves back in acknowledgement, still holding the banana. If either of them could dance, the whole thing might be a welcome distraction for passers-by. Instead, it just looks comical.

'Ah,' I say, 'the dance of the three fruits.' ('By two fruitcakes,' I'm tempted to add.)

'Five,' declares Marianne, suddenly and obviously totally oblivious to either my little joke or to how ridiculous they both look. 'Five. Part of my five-a-day fruit and veg,' she adds, pointing to the contents of the basket while mounting the bicycle.

'Good idea. Very healthy,' I shout after her as she cycles off. 'Live longer.' She waves without looking back.'But I doubt it,' I mutter under my breath, as she shapes up for a full frontal attack on a Land Rover Defender, eventually missing it by inches and almost colliding with a bright blue Renualt 5 in the process.

Tojo's wrinkled features are a blend of amusement and bemusement as I near the gate to Aunt Sally's.

'Kamikaze lady,' he says to no one in particular, 'she no go with flow.'

Then he addresses me: 'She very...' and here he makes a circular shape with his thumb and index finger and aims, as if firing an imaginary dart, '...individual lady.'

'Bullseye, mate,' I say to myself, 'she's definitely that all right'. To Tojo I simply say, 'Cheerio, mate,' and move off.

It is very obvious that there are more people walking on my side of the street this morning. I'm sure this must be because of the postbox on the other side. The security services have warned the public about the threat of letter bombs. You can keep an eye out for parcels or unattended luggage on a train, but how do you deal with letter bombs? Give'em a wide berth, that's all you can do.

The sun has gone in behind the clouds and the temperature has dropped, but Eddie is out in his vest, working up a sweat under the bonnet of Svetlana's red Triumph Herald.

'Who Kipper play today, heh, heh?' Eddie is being careful this morning. He always knows exactly who we are playing, but after the Geordie 'Toons' episode last time we met, he is obviously approaching the subject gingerly this morning.

'Everton,' I say.

'Ah. Everton, heh, heh, Everton. I have not been in Everton. Where Everton?'

'Liverpool,' I say.

'Liverpool? You play Liverpool? Again?' Eddie is baffled.

'No. Everton is in Liverpool.'

'Everton is in Liverpool today?' Eddie is incredulous.

'Everton is in Liverpool every day.'

'Every day?' Eddie is bewildered. I'm tempted to leave him in this condition, but eventually I take pity on him and explain that there are two football clubs in Liverpool. The fact that I hear the click-clack of Svetlana's stilettoes approaching may also have been an influencing factor in my decision to stay and explain. She is wearing blue cotton 'hot pants', a cream coloured T-shirt with an orange psychedelic tie-dye pattern, and a thick leather belt tied loosely around her waist. Not exactly the height of current fashion but very easy on the eye all the same.

'You-rrr giving my Eddie a gee-ography lesson,' she purrs and she puts a hand on his shoulder. Eddie wipes the engine oil off his hands with a rag and embraces her. Svetlana yelps and wriggles to avoid getting any viscous liquid on her T-shirt. There's a lot of grrrr-ing and purring until finally they manage to drag themselves apart.

'Carrr had problem starting today,' Svetlana explains, doing some interesting contortions while she checks for any oleaginous stains on her hot pants. 'And when it does start, no...' she looks around as if for inspiration, '...no, how you say...' Here she adopts a kind of both-hands-on-the-wheel posture while she jerks her groin back and forth.

'Poke?' I suggest.

'Yes, needs more poke.'

Eddie then says something to her in a language I don't understand, although it's fairly obvious from his demeanour as to what's on his mind. Svetlana giggles, Eddie laughs.

'Okay then, I make coffee. Five minutes,' Svetlana says, one hand on her hip, the other raised slightly with one finger in the air as if testing the way the wind is blowing. Then she gives me a knowing smile, swivels militarily and marches off in the direction of the kitchen. No invitation to coffee for me, I notice. I look at Eddie and wonder what she sees in him.

'No poke, no poke, heh, heh,' he mumbles as he troops after her towards the house.

'Dirty dog,' I call after him and start to move on. I immediately regret making this remark because he stops in his tracks and stares over at me, looking startled and a little guilty. I wave goodbye and walk on towards the town, but I have the distinct impression that Eddie is watching me all the way.

The sun emerges from the clouds again as I come within hailing distance of Berrie's Antiques.

'Good mornington. Today, I think you are buying,' Noah announces. Then, with one hand shielding the side of his mouth as if to prevent anybody eavesdropping, he whispers: 'I have something here that might interest you.'

'Oh, what's that?' I reply, not entirely convinced. He rarely has anything in stock that I would have the remotest interest in, but he's such a pleasant gent that I feel I cannot refuse the invitation.

'Come in, come in,' he takes me by the hand and leads me like a child into the inner recesses of the shop. 'I remembered what you said last time you were here. And when the opportunity came I snapped it up for you.' He clicks his fingers loudly as if to emphasise the point.

I remain sceptical, and it probably shows. Noah rummages around impatiently in a drawer and produces a faded Timothy Whites' paper bag.

'I think you might be in the market for this,' he says with mounting excitement, while still clutching the thin package to his chest. Now, I've been in this situation many times before with Noah, only for the contents of such packages to ultimately turn out to be entirely underwhelming. This time, however, he has really turned up trumps. Out of the bag he slowly draws an EP that I recognise immediately, from Keith Richard's distinctive check shirt on the cover, as one I have been on the lookout for.

'It's "Five by Five" by the Rolling Stones,' I exclaim. 'How did you come by that?'

'Mystery of the trade, my son; a mystery of the trade.' Noah stands there beaming for a moment, still not handing it over. I reckon he is savouring the moment; he has finally secured something for me that I have always wanted. We agree a price for it (ridiculously cheap as far as I am concerned, but Noah will accept nothing near the value that I put on it), and he eventually hands it to me. I examine it, turning it over to speed- read the liner notes by Andrew Loog Oldham. Classic! I ask Noah if he has any others and he gestures towards a couple of large cardboard boxes and says he bought a job lot from a small second-hand record store in Portobello Road that was closing down. The nearest box is already open and I rummage around. 'There seems to be at least two of everything in here.'

'Two of everything, just like Noah's Ark,' he replies quickly, as if he had rehearsed this quip beforehand.

I feel that I should hang around a while longer in the shop; that leaving too soon would somehow appear ungrateful after all the effort he obviously put into sourcing something for me. But we soon run out of things to talk about. I pretend to rummage around a bit further in the box, but there's nothing else in there that I am really interested in. I thank him profusely once again, we say our goodbyes and I head towards The Cabin, humming the infectious rhythm of 'Around and Around', the Chuck Berry number covered by the Stones on that EP.

I join the short queue in The Cabin. The joint isn't exactly rockin'. I stand behind this big fat bloke with a florid complexion, who's carrying a cane under his arm. I pick up the Mirror and flick through it. A headline that reads TICKLED BLUE catches my attention because of the colour-connection to QPR, but to my disappointment it's a piece about the first party conference of the new Conservative leader, Margaret Thatcher. 'Queen Maggie' they're calling her, and it seems she received a tumultuous welcome at the conference. She waved a blue feather duster at the crowd – Ken Dodd style – and they loved it. It all sounds a bit too

American razzmatazz for me. But she did make one very funny comment about the Labour party being like a pub where the light ale is running out. 'All that is left will be bitter, and all that's bitter will be left,' she said. Nice one, Maggie.

On an inside sports page, the Mirror has a few paragraphs on the doubt over Don Masson's fitness for today's game. Don suffered concussion during Tuesday's League Cup tie game against Charlton and spent a night in hospital. We will miss him if he doesn't make it.

Suddenly I feel the prod of what could be a feather duster in my groin. It's the bloke in front moving very slightly from side to side as he impatiently waits his turn, and his cane keeps jostling my private parts. Each time it happens, I move the cane away and the fat bloke attempts to turn round to see what I'm at, but his bulk prevents him from getting a clear view of me. Eventually, after a particularly painful prod, I move the cane more forcibly to one side, at the very moment when it comes to the fat bloke's turn to be served.

'I say——' he starts, but Mick immediately nips in with one of his famous introductions and defuses whatever situation might have arisen.

'This is Colonel Martin,' gushes Mick. 'Colonel Martin has just moved into number 5, a few doors away from you on the other side of the street.' Mick introduces me to the Colonel, who displays very little interest in me at first and absolutely no interest whatsoever once the word 'football' is mentioned. I'm surprised to hear he has moved into number 5. I know the house well, as it's on the corner with a commanding view up Forest Hill Road and down Park Road, and I hadn't noticed a For Sale sign outside. So I wonder if Mick has got it wrong. But I don't get the opportunity to ask the old Colonel about this, as he promptly pays for his Financial Times and shuffles off, breathing heavily and mumbling under his breath, his face as pink as the paper.

'You know, me bucko, it's hard to tell if the Colonel is fast asleep or just slow awake.'

'Not one for my ritual, then,' I observe. 'In case I ever need a replacement.'

'I'm afraid not, me bucko. How is the ritual going this morning, anyway?'

'Okay, so far. I've got Tojo, Noah, Echo Eddie – and Svet——'

'I'm sure that was a nice bonus,' Mick interjects. He says it nicely, without any sexual overtones.

'Yes, it was. And Marianne, of course...'

'And how was Miss Please this morning?' Now there's a hint of disdain in his voice.

'A bit fruity, actually, since you ask,' I say, mischievously.

'I can't imagine that. Sure, she has a face that would drive rats from a barn.'

'Come on, Mick, she's not that bad,' I protest, albeit feebly.

'I used to see that virago with my own eyes every day before she took her custom elsewhere. Sure, she wouldn't get a hug off a bear.'

'So what happened, Mick? Why did she stop calling in here?'

'You don't want to know, me bucko. You do not want to know.'

'I reckon I need to know,' I said, rather self-importantly.

'You know something, me bucko, that woman would start an argument in an empty room. Now, I'm not one for becoming involved in conversations about politics, as you very well know, but when all these IRA lunatics first started this bombing campaign she was in here every day spoutin' off about how all the Irish were murderers and should be sent back home. I tried pointing out to her as politely as I could that, to most of the Irish of my acquaintance, this is home. Sure I've been living here for forty years – and I actually served in the British Army in the Second World War. But the last straw was when she started on about how the Irish were only over here to take what they could get and give nothing back. I'm afraid I lost my temper at that point, and told her a few home truths.'

'Like what, Mick? What did you say to her?'

I ask this more out of politeness that interest, because in reality I'm becoming concerned that the queuers are becoming restless behind me.

'Well, me bucko, you may not know this but I was the youngest in a very large family and my eldest brother left home in 1916 to join the South Irish Horse. You've heard of the South Irish Horse?'

'I'm afraid not, Mick.'

'The South Irish Horse was a cavalry regiment of the British Army that fought in the First World War. My eldest brother George left home to join the South Irish Horse in 1916, the year I was born. He was killed in the Kaiserschlacht – the so-called "Kaiser's Battle" – in 1918. So I have no memory of him, just one old faded family photograph is all that I have. And do you know the awful thing, me bucko...?' Mick's voice starts to falter here. 'He had no memory at all of me.'

I obviously look totally flummoxed, so Mick elaborates:

'You see, he had already...left...home...before I was born that year. 1916.' Mick's voice finally cracks.

I like to consider myself as a fairly cool person, not easily given to emotion, but I have to admit that Mick's story really got to me. I have no idea what to say next but Mick is not expecting sympathy from me.

'So you can understand why I wasn't taking any guff from Miss Marianne Pleass regarding what the Irish have contributed to this country.'

'What did she say when you told her? What did Marianne say?'

'Sure, she wasn't really listening, Dawhee, me bucko. That woman is like an alligator – all mouth and no ears.' A wry smile crosses his lips and the twinkle is suddenly back in his eyes as he recovers his poise. 'So, tell me, me bucko, who are you missing this morning?'

'The Butlers,' I say speedily, 'and Bernie Trout – I take it he hasn't been in?'

'Divil a sign of him. Would you not seriously consider a replacement?' Then, standing on tiptoe to look over the top of my head, he announces:

'Ah. I see Miss Dell has joined us.'

'You're not seriously suggesting...'

'I'm not, but now that you mention it, why not? Miss Dell is here like clockwork every Saturday.'

'But she knows nothing about football!'

'Knows nothing about football? What about Marianne; she knows something about football? Tojo; does he even know what a football looks like? And as for that Eddie fella; does *he know anything? Jacko Butler is like a lighthouse in a peat bog — bright but useless! And Billy Butler? Sure, there's enough straw between his ears to bed an elephant.'*

'I dunno,' I mumble. 'I'd feel funny about asking her'

'Why do you have to ask her? Tojo, Marianne, Eddie and Noah — they don't even know they are part of your ritual. They are only part of it because you think they're dependable. Well, Miss Dell is dependable. And I bet if you asked her, she would be delighted to do it.'

'I'm not sure. Maybe Trouty will show up. He's dependable. Or was.'

'Well, why not try Miss Dell as a substitute? Just to see how it goes while Bernie Trout is, shall we say, indisposed?'

'I suppose I could do that,' I say, but I immediately begin to wonder from the tone of his voice if Mick knows more about Trouty's absence than he is letting on. I hand Mick the 5p for the Mirror and leave, nodding to Lisa as I pass. She is deep in conversation with Sid Scabbard, Trouty's main man in The Horseman's.

'Godspeed,' Mick calls after me.

I hang around outside The Cabin until Lisa emerges by engaging the old Colonel in an excruciatingly tedious conversation about the weather. I found him studying the small ads in the shop window using his monocle, as soon as I exited The Cabin. I introduce him to Lisa, who charms him into a burbling wreck, and I eventually point him in the direction of Berrie's with the promise that it's an Aladdin's cave of undiscovered bargains.

But no sooner are we rid of Colonel Martin than Cattle arrives with what's-his-face — O'Leary — in tow. Cattle does the introductions, and this time he takes a little longer over it, no doubt because Lisa is here. It seems that O'Leary is going to be staying at Cattle's place for a few weeks. He doesn't say a lot and he seems like an okay bloke, but it's obvious that he has taken a liking to Lisa and she appears a bit taken by him. I try to establish exactly how long O'Leary will be staying at Cattle's but they both seem a bit vague about this. The conversation eventually fizzles out and we say our goodbyes.

'Nice man,' Lisa says immediately.

'Yeah. I reckon Cattle's a pretty decent bloke, behind it all,' I say, knowing full well who she was referring to.

'I meant O'Leary.' She stops as if to emphasise the point. 'He's good looking, don't you think?'

'Is he? He looked a bit scruffy to me,' I retort, walking on. 'His clothes were all crumpled and he obviously hasn't shaved for days. In what way did you reckon he was good looking?'

'In a noble way,' she says emphatically, sweeping aside all critical observations regarding O'Leary's appearance.

'Noble?' I smirk.

'Yes,' she continues with a wry smile, 'he has a noble bearing. Did you notice how tall he is? He looks straight at you when he speaks. And he has a nice voice.'

'He looked straight at you alright. Your Mister O'Leering,' I add, rather satisfied with my little quip.

'Now I believe you're being childish,' she retorts, and this has the dual effect of instantly putting me in my place and ending that particular discussion as far as she is concerned. We lapse into silence for a few minutes while I think of something to ask her that does not relate to football.

'So, any other trips to the theatre recently?' This is the best I can think of, but I'm uncomfortable even uttering the words.

'Hmmmm. Yes, actually,' she replies enthusiastically, pretending not to notice my discomfort. 'I went to see Kwa Zulu in the Piccadilly last week.' Then, sensing my unease that this is not a conversation I can make any meaningful contribution to, she elucidates, 'African dance. Kwa Zulu is the name of a homeland,' she explains. 'In South Africa,' she adds helpfully.

'I guessed as much,' I say. 'Bloemfontein. Ellerslie...'

'So you know something about South Africa then?'

'Not really,' I say morosely. 'Bloemfontein Road, Ellerslie Road, and South Africa Road are the names of roads that run around the QPR stadium.'

'Ah, I should have guessed there would be a football connection,' she says, making no attempt to hide her disappointment. 'I thought for a moment that you might know the historical connection rather than the link to Lotus Park...'

'It's Loftus Road, not Lotus Park. And the roads are all named because of a connection to some war or other,' I interject.

'Yes. The Boer War.'

'Whatever,' I say. I really hate it when someone exposes my lack of knowledge, whether intentionally or otherwise.

'Do you know what Bloemfontein means?' she asks suddenly.

'No. Should I?'

'Maybe not, but I thought you might be interested. It's Dutch and it means "fountain of flowers". I think that's a really beautiful name for a street, don't you?'

I say nothing and I reckon now maybe I've upset her by my lack of interest. Lisa goes quiet too. This is obviously not the best opportunity to raise the topic of the ritual, I decide, but I do need to get the conversation back on a more positive track.

'Was it any good, the African dance show? Is it worth seeing?' is my pathetic attempt to get the conversation restarted. But it seems to work, because she suddenly gets all animated again.

'Well, you might enjoy it. But would you appreciate it? Its rhythms; its raw emotion? Hmmm. Yes, I believe you would!' she suggests playfully.

'Mick says that you're a classical dancer. What's this classical dance thing all about?' I ask, in an attempt to show interest by broadening the conversation.

'Mick got it wrong, bless him.' She smiles. 'It's not classical dance I'm studying now, it's contemporary dance, although I did study classical dance too.'

'What's the difference?'

'Well, contemporary dance is "free-dance"...'

'Like ballet?' I interject.

'No, it's nothing like ballet at all,' she states emphatically. 'Ballet is rigid, with very strict posture control. Look,' she starts to do a few movements here (yes, right in the middle of the footpath) to demonstrate the point. 'Contemporary dance, on the other hand, is based on the idea of natural movement.' A few more elaborate movements here, and I'm starting to feel embarrassed in case somebody spots me in her company.

'Okay, okay, I get the point,' I almost shout. 'But what does it all mean?'

She seems genuinely disappointed and deflated by my lack of interest.

'What does it all mean? What does it mean? You don't intellectualise contemporary dance. It just is what it is.'

'Yeah, but there are no famous contemporary dancers, are there?'

'Of course there are. It's just that you've never heard of them because you live inside that little football bubble. Contemporary dance has its stars and its heroes, just like football.'

'Who's your favourite play...your favourite, ah, dancer, then. Who's your hero?'

'I suppose it would have to be Pina Bausch, probably the most visionary and influential figure in European contemporary dance.'

'Who does he ...where does he...?' I stammer.

'Who does he play for?' she laughs sarcastically. 'Well, he doesn't play for anybody because Pina Bausch is a she.'

'Sounds more like a bloke's name. What kind of name is Pina anyway? Sounds Spanish. Or South American.'

'Pina is short for Phillippina. And she's German. But after her graduation she left Germany with a scholarship to study at the Juilliard School in New York.'

'So what's so great about her now, then?' I'm conscious that I sound as if I'm sulking.

'Well, now she's a dancer; a choreographer, a modern dance teacher and a ballet teacher. And her style is quite unique. It combines movement and sound and elaborate stage sets. She also developed something she calls Tanztheatre and...'

'What's Tens Theatre?' I interrupt, impatiently.

'Tanztheatre. It's a fusion of radical theatre, surreal art, sexual drama and body language. And it involves consulting with the performers during the composition of a piece. We try to work that way up in Covent Garden as part of our dance studies.'

'What's the sexual drama bit all about?'

'Aha. I knew you would ask that question. Why don't you come along to one of our open days and maybe you'll find out? Perhaps you could even join in? There is a marvellous intimacy in dancing with other people in a contemporary dance group. But the really great thing is that it's all based around creativity and self-expression. Everybody can enjoy it – and it doesn't matter what kind of bodies they have.'

'Bodies? Sexual drama? Intimacy? Sounds more like an orgy.'

'Well, it's true that Pina has been described as the "dangerous magician of modern dance". Why don't you come along anyway? Watch us "tread the boards", so to speak?'

'No thanks. I reckon I prefer to keep my feet firmly on soil.'

'Then you'd like Pina Bausch. Her most recent work is called "Rite of Spring" and in it the stage is completely covered with soil!'

'Blimey, like dancing on a football pitch. Definitely not. It all seems a bit too high-brow for me.'

'But it's not elitist. I promise you.' She sounds as if she really wants me to go along. 'It's totally accessible.' She thinks for a moment, then: 'You like Top of the Pops, don't you?'

''Course. What's that got to do with anything?'

'Pan's People. You like watching Pan's People dance, don't you? Go on, I bet you do.'

'Everybody likes Pan's People,' I assert, a little sheepishly, 'but that's...I dunno, "pop-dancing".'

'So? It's dancing. Popular dancing.' Then the mini demonstration starts again and I have to admit that while I'm embarrassed to be standing there in case anybody spots us, I like what I'm seeing. But she stops suddenly in mid-movement and, extending both arms, announces: 'Visual entertainment,' in a kind of 'ta-dah' way, laughs and holds the position as if waiting for applause. I glance around to see if anybody is watching before three-clapping weakly.

'So, you'll come?' She asks eagerly.

'Er, no. Sorry.'

She appears genuinely disappointed by my lack of interest but any feeling of awkwardness is immediately banished by a sudden burst of applause and shouts of 'Encore, encore' from the upstairs window of the Butlers'. The two boys have pulled back the lace curtains and are jockeying for position at the small bedroom window.

'Oh, f**k,' I mutter under my breath but Lisa waves back at them. Suddenly Roxboro Roy pushes his way in between the two brothers and paws at the window. Then an old man appears in the other bedroom window, unshaven and wearing a yellowing string vest.

'That must be Mister Butler,' she concludes, smiling and waving up at him too. He waves back and the whole scene becomes pretty pathetic with three grown men waving like kids from the bedroom windows, with stupid grins on their faces. 'Yeah. That's him alright,' I confirm, disinterestedly, 'the Creaking Door.'

'That a really cruel thing to say,' she scolds, glaring at me with disapproval, 'why do you call him that?'

'Don't blame me,' I protest in mock hurt, 'the two boys gave him that moniker. He's been sick on and off for so many years now that they expected him to pop his cloggs ages ago.'

'Pop his cloggs?' she looks confused.

'Die,' I say emphatically, 'and leave the house to them. But you know the old saying: "A creaking door hangs longest".'

'Oh, I don't believe that,' she scolds. 'The boys are not like that.'

Just then the window opens and Jacko leans out, places his elbows on the sill and rests his head on his thumbs. 'Great show, Lise,' he shouts. 'Right Billy?' Butler Minor cannot quite squeeze himself through the available space in the open window but manages to shove out his arm, wrapped in lace curtain, gives a passable 'thumbs up' and shouts, 'Right on, Jacko.'

Lisa bows and this proves to be the last straw for me. I wave dismissively and walk away without even glancing back. But Jacko isn't finished yet.

'You comin' round for a game of five card stud tonight?' he asks.

'Nah, don't reckon I can, tonight.' I keep walking straight on without looking back.

'All 'e can fink of is today's game,' I hear him shout to Lisa, then: 'Hope you chew those toffees today, then,' he calls after me.

'And spit 'em out,' shouts Billy.

'Don't be such a dozy c**.' I glance back in time to see Jacko rebuke Billy with a nudge of his elbow and I can still hear Billy's injured protests as the windows slam shut.

Lisa catches up with me and we fall into step.

'What was all that about chewing toffees?' she asks. 'And spitting them out? More cockney rhyming slang?'

'Everton,' I explain.

'Everton? Everton Mints?' She looks totally confused. 'I don't understand. What's the rhyming connection to toffee?'

'Everton. We're playing Everton today,' I explain. 'Their nickname is the Toffees.'

She pauses, but only for a second or two. 'Ah, I see now. "Chewing the Toffees and spitting them out" means beating Everton comprehensively.'

'In Butler-lingo, yes.'

'But why toffees?'

'Dunno. Never asked.'

'Okay. So this team of confectioners — Mints, Toffees, Caramels or whatever they are called — are they any good?'

'They finished fourth in the League last season and they're currently lying fifth,' I reply, getting into serious mode for the match ahead. 'They drew 2–2 with us in the corresponding fixture last season and if Bob Latchford strikes form today, it could be a hard game for us.'

'Hard as toffee?'

I smile weakly. 'You've been listening to too many poor puns from the Butlers. All that waving and shouting — behaving like three stooges.'

'Hmm. I think they're very…ah…sweet,' she quips.

I decide to ignore this deviation from the serious issue of today's match. We stroll on in silence to the corner. I'm worried in case Don Masson doesn't make it today. The Gaffer seems reluctant to risk him. We've got a great standby in John Hollins, but we will miss Don's passing ability and his organisational skills if he doesn't pass a late fitness test. Lisa must sense that I'm preoccupied because she suddenly asks about the game again:

'But you've been doing well, haven't you? So far? Particularly at Lotus Park.'

'Loftus Road. Not Lotus Park. Yeah, we've done well so far. Won four games at home.'

'Well, I'm confident that today you will make it five.' And she gives me a little pat on the upper arm.

And on that positive note we part company.

Saturday, 11 October 1975: 4.55 p.m.
Queens Park Rangers…5 Everton…0

7. WORDS

Saturday, 24 April 1976: 2.59 p.m.

Finally, it's time to go. There's a bit of 'thumbs up' between one or two players as everybody takes up their positions, but it's obvious that this is being done more out of nervousness than a reflection of genuine confidence.

I shout my own few words of encouragement to the rest of the lads.

Most footballers talk a lot on the pitch. They talk to their teammates, offering advice, instruction, words of encouragement and, when necessary, criticism. They talk, or more accurately, they shout at the referee and linesmen, querying decisions and claiming advantages that are not always theirs by right.

They talk to the opposition too, seeking to secure an advantage by insulting or verbally intimidating the opponent in order to undermine his concentration and cause him to commit errors. This is sometimes called 'sledging'. Conventional wisdom has it that 'sledging' usually involves an opponent questioning the virtue of your mother, wife or sister and intimating that he already has 'knowledge' of her, possibly as recently as last night. The idea that this might be effective is laughable. Even at schoolboy level. Although in my younger schoolboy football days, I did have opponents who tried this particular approach by besmirching the reputation of my sister. As an only child, this obviously had little detrimental effect on my morale.

The reality is that for 'sledging' to work best the cutting remark needs to be close to the bone. And it doesn't get much closer than your own reputation as a footballer. So if, for example, you enjoy a reputation as a skillful passer of the ball, having your opponent constantly in your ear, making adverse comments every time your pass goes just that little bit astray, you are likely to be tempted to refocus on proving to him *how* you can do it better next time rather than in making the right call as to *where* you put the ball that will best benefit your team. And that little switch of focus might result in you making an error that could cost your team the match.

Talking on the pitch is a necessary part of the game and it helps the player to become totally involved.

When it comes to talking to teammates, some players are better at it than others. These 'generals' are not always the captain of the team, but they exude a natural authority on the field. It helps, of course, if they're experienced players and what they are saying is constructive.

Others, regardless of age and experience, just cannot help talking all the time, offering advice and barking out orders even when they are too far from the action to be heard. I'm afraid that I'm one of those. I've always been like that. Off the pitch I am quite taciturn by nature, but when I'm anywhere near a football match – even as a spectator – I cannot keep my mouth shut.

I must confess that I also use colourful language on occasions. This has sometimes gotten me into trouble. Referees and linesmen don't usually like to be sworn at. Neither do certain teammates. And I confess that the club has spoken to me on more than one occasion regarding my verbal interaction with visiting supporters on the terraces at Loftus Road. In my defence, I would point out that, outside of footballing situations, using foul language is totally out of character for me.

Usually.

Saturday, 25 October 1975: 9.07 a.m.

I'm heading down Wellesley Gardens. Weather-wise, it doesn't look like it's going to be the greatest day in the world. It's mild but a little cloudy. Given the rain we've had during the week, the pitch is likely to be slippery and a bit greasy. Sheffield United are our opponents today. They've had a disappointing start to the season and are anchored to the bottom of the Division One league table. They've won only one match to date and lost all of their six matches away from home. Small wonder, then, that they recently sacked manager Ken Furphy, appointing Jimmy Sirrell in his place. In theory, we should win it easily today. But in situations like this there's always the danger of complacency on our part. Although Sheffield United have been chopping and changing the team a lot during their depressing run of defeats, strikers Woodward and Guthrie have posed a consistent threat to opposing teams, week to week. And Tony Currie always needs watching. We must approach this match the same as any other. Impose ourselves on the opposition; score as early as possible; build the lead and never allow them back into the game. We won the corresponding fixture 1–0 last season. The question is: can we do it again today?

This opposite side of the street continues to be deserted, the postbox being treated by everyone as if it has the bubonic plague. The rumour is that the Royal Mail has even stopped collecting from it – because nothing is posted there any longer due to the letter bomb scares. But then I notice Colonel Martin emerge from number 5, and stride – if it's possible to stride using a cane, perhaps 'walk determinedly' is a more apt description – to the postbox, pause and make a great show of popping a letter in through the slot. Then he emits a phlegmy 'harrumph' that can be heard across the street before performing a kind of one-legged swivel, army-style, tucking the cane under his arm à la Charlie Chaplin, marching back across the pavement, through the gates of number 5 and crunching on up the drive.

Up ahead, Marianne Pleass is standing beside her bicycle on this side of the road, just off the kerb. She is talking to somebody in a Rolls Royce Silver Shadow that has pulled in with its engine idling. She appears to be giving the driver directions and eventually points the way up the road in my direction. She is wearing a dark beret and light-coloured trench coat and looks, to all intents and purposes, like one of those women you see in war films that are part of the French Resistance. All that's missing is a Gauloises dangling from her lips, a string of onions hanging from the handlebars and a fresh baguette sticking out of the basket.

The Roller eventually glides off, slows as it passes me and then accelerates up Wellesley Gardens towards the corner with London Road. Marianne doesn't wait but sets off bravely into the path of a virtual Panzer division of BMWs, Mercedes Benz, Audis and Volkswagens that sound as if they are doing a horns-in-harmony version of 'Deutschland Uber Alles'.

I gaze up at Marjorie, who is standing in the bay window, looking a trifle agitated. She is holding a bottle of bleach in one hand and what could be a bottle of Smirnoff in the other. I decide not to hang around.

At the bus stop I bump into Svetlana. Her Triumph Herald wouldn't start again this morning so she is taking the bus, while Eddie works on repairing the car. She looks stunning in a dark red leather trouser suit. Up close, the lines around her eyes are more noticeable and she looks older than she appears from a distance. But the figure is definitely that of a younger woman. I have never been in Svetlana's company on my own before so I stand chatting to her for a few minutes, enjoying the envious leers from passers-by and the macho honking of car horns. I ask her if she has seen Trouty, as I know she works in the bar of The Horseman's some evenings, but she explains that she 'haffent seen Bernart' for some time. Blimey, there's even something about that accent that gives off a sexual charge. Then, to my disappointment, the bus arrives. She kisses me lightly on both cheeks, the way continentals do and which I wasn't expecting, jumps on the bus and takes her seat without even glancing back. I mooch off happily with both cheeks burning.

I arrive at the corner of Aunt Sally's as Tojo is in the process of unlocking the battered old wooden gate so that he can park his Reliant Robin inside. He waves slightly distractedly. He appears bothered. Or a bit more bothered than usual.

'Can I have a word?'

The bloke must have been standing close to the wall, and under the overhanging branches of one of those tree-size shrubs that proliferate around the outer edges of Aunt Sally's garden. At first, I'm not even sure he is addressing me. Then he walks purposefully towards me out of the shade; stops, turns slowly and stares back at Tojo, who is hovering at the gate and fiddling with his key in the lock. Whatever look this bloke gives him, Tojo gets the message and vanishes into the leafy sanctuary of Aunt Sally's garden — jack-fast.

He is extremely tall and angular and carries himself like an ex-army man. He's wearing a fine herringbone worsted suit that is definitely more Savile Row than Harry Fenton. Thin and wiry, he exudes a kind of tough-as-teak strength; not a guy to be messed with. He introduces himself to me but I'm too startled to take in any of it. He doesn't shake hands. He flashes a business card but doesn't hand it to me. I think I hear words that suggest something military (Major?) or legal (Attorney?) but I cannot be sure as it is all happening very quickly and I'm a little taken aback.

'I was hoping to have a quick…ah… word with you,' he declares in a well-modulated voice. His accent is classless.

'With me? What about?' (Why am I suddenly nervous?)

'About my…ah…client. Mr Trout. Mr Bernard Trout. I believe that you are…ah… acquainted with him?'

Okay, so he's definitely not a copper. Must be a solicitor or something like that. And he obviously has news of Bernie.

'Sure. Bernie. I know Bernie.'

He blinks rapidly and repeatedly over a forced smile as if my use of the word 'Bernie' offends him.

'You were...ah...enquiring in relation to Mr Bernard Trout recently?'

'Was I? Hmmm. Let me think...'

'The Sid?' *he suggests, gently jolting my memory.*

This is obviously a reference to Sid Scabbard, who acts as landlord for Bernie in The Horseman's. Everybody now calls him 'The Sid', a bit like in the movie El Cid. Bernie once told me it means 'lord' in Spanish, so it's probably Bernie's shorthand for 'landlord'.

'Oh, yeah. The Sid. Yeah, yeah, I was asking the Sid about Bernie, now that you mention it.'

At my second overly familiar reference to 'Bernie', he immediately winces and starts blinking rapidly again over that pasted-on smile.

'You were,' *he states, impassively – almost threateningly.*

While this exchange is going on, I notice the old rusty letterbox on Aunt Sally's gate slowly opening. A pair of Oriental eyes peer out. Tojo probably cannot hear our conversation from that distance, but his eyes suddenly begin darting from side-to-side like a pendulum on acid. It takes me a moment or two to realise that he is trying to draw my attention to something. And then I see him; the second guy, standing further back under the sycamore tree. This one is definitely not a member of the legal profession. Or a copper. This one has villain written all over his unshaven mug, studded leather jacket, faded jeans, white socks and suede desert boots. He is peeping around the curve in the wall as it bends towards The Glade; leaning on the wall with his outstretched left hand as if for support or reassurance; nervously fidgeting on a shirt button with his right.

'F*'%k,' *I exclaim, pointing in his general direction.* 'Who's this?'

Major/Attorney doesn't even turn around. 'That's...ah...Charlie. He's with me; my... ah...driver.' *He raises his right arm slightly, bent at the elbow, palm facing outward like you see people do in those courtroom dramas on telly when they are being sworn in. Charlie recedes sharpish into the shadows.*

'What's your...ah...interest in Mr Trout?'

'My interest? He's just a guy I bump into in the shop sometimes when I'm buying the newspaper.' *I'm beginning to feel hacked off by this whole interrogation thing.* 'We have a bit of a natter. I don't have any f**king, what you call, <u>interest</u> in ole' Bernie.'

His eyelids are now batting furiously like a butterfly in flight, probably because my description of his client demonstrates an even greater familiarity than he would approve of. The smile is beginning to fade too but I decide to continue using the only weapon I have at my disposal that seems to upset him. Without waiting to be asked another question, I go for the jugular:

'Trouty hasn't been there for the last few weeks, so I asked around if anybody knew how he was.'

The smile has now totally vanished; the lips pursed into a firm thin line; the eyelids have stopped flapping and are firmly shut. In the silence, I can hear Major/Attorney inhale through his nose very slowly and deliberately. It's as if he is trying to calm himself; to restrain the urge to beat me to death there and then for referring to his client in this way.

'Have you ever done any...ah...work for Mr Trout?'

'Work? What the f**k. Look I'm a—'

'Yes, we know all about you,' he interjects, 'but I would prefer if we could conduct this... ah...conversation without recourse to the language of the...ah...football terraces. Now, has Mr Trout ever asked you to, how shall I put it, perform any particular...ah...service for him?'

'Service? What the f**k are you on about? What the f**k are you suggesting?'

'I'm not suggesting anything. I was merely...ah...asking. I take it from your reaction that your answer is "No". Thank you for your time. If we need to talk to you again we know where to find you.' At this point he drops his right arm to his side and with a barely discernible flick of his palm, he beckons to his colleague to join him.

I barely hear the purr of the engine as a Rolls Royce Silver Shadow with tinted windows almost immediately glides to a stop beside him. I'm too shocked to notice the registration number. All I do know is that Charlie is sitting in the back staring at me through a partially wound down tinted window. From what I can see of the driver, he is immaculately dressed and stares straight ahead. Major/Attorney gets in; the door shuts almost noiselessly, a bit like the dull thud sound you hear in the movies of a pistol being fired with a silencer fitted – which, in the circumstance, is pretty spooky. I give a little jump. The Roller cruises smoothly away.

I turn round in bewilderment just in time to see the rusting flap on Aunt Sally's letterbox slam shut.

'Who woz that geezer, then?' It's Jacko Butler, shouting from the other side of the road. 'And wot's 'e doin' round our manor?'

'Nobody.' I cross to his side of the road and we both fall into step along Beane Row, down Park Road heading towards The Cabin. 'Just some guy asking for directions.'

'Askin'? Looked more like he woz givin' the fackin' directions. You okay, son?' Jacko seems genuinely concerned. 'Ya look a bit shook, if ya don't mind me sayin' so, mate.'

'Look, I'm fine, okay?'

Just then Billy emerges from the front gate of chez Butler, which presents an opportunity to change the subject. But Jacko won't let it go:

'I woz just sayin', Billy, that our ole' mate 'ere looks a bit under the weather this mornin'. Wotcha fink?'

'Probably missed his breakfass,' mumbles Billy, before digging into the pocket of his Sander & Kay army surplus combat jacket and pulling out two warm sausage rolls wrapped in thin, moist tissue paper, each seasoned with tiny pieces of wool from the lining of his pocket.

'Hrrr,' he grunts, pushing a soggy Butler banger in my direction.

'No thanks,' I decline, curtly, 'I actually had a proper breakfast earlier.'

'*Suityerself mate,*' *says Billy, obviously delighted at the prospect of having both bangers all to himself. His delight is short-lived, however, as Jacko grabs one and quickly scoffs the by now disintegrating sausage.*

'*Ya know somfink?*' *asks Jacko through a mouthful of flakey pastry.* '*Ya can't beat home cookin', right Billy?*'

'*Right on, Jacko,*' *belches Billy and I leave them to it.*

Eddie is at the side of the house attending to Svetlana's red Triumph Herald as I pass. All the car doors are open, the bonnet is up, the radio is playing David Essex and there are toolboxes and cables all over the place. I'm too pre-occupied by my encounter with Major/Attorney to relish the notion of engaging in idle banter with Eddie. But I must stick to the ritual. I stop and call Eddie but he doesn't hear me over the car radio.

I resolve to catch him on my return journey and continue on my way to The Cabin. When I glance back, the Butler brothers, not exactly renowned for their ability to hold a tune, suddenly decide to join in the chorus of '*Hold Me Close*', *each with an arm around the other's shoulder and performing a kind of knees-up on the pavement outside the front gate as they belt out the outro:*

Dum, dar ah dah dah. Dum, dar ah dah dah,

Dum, dar ah dah dah. Dah. Dah. Dah. Dah.

Somewhere in the neighbourhood a frightened dog starts to howl. The brothers stop suddenly and look around as if trying to locate the source of the sound.

I stop by at Berrie's in the near certainty that some sense of sanity will prevail after the topsy-turvy morning I've had so far. I decide to confide in Noah about my being stopped by this Major/Attorney bloke. I don't make a big deal of it, so I just give him the bare facts, but I want to get the reaction of a sensible man like Noah. I know the Butlers would always look out for me but they would probably have a different way of dealing with it. And it would more than likely include the threat of violence. That's not the way I deal with things.

Noah thinks that it's a serious development and that it should be reported to the police. I tell Noah emphatically that I don't want to involve the police.

'*I don't see why not. If you do, you may even get some clue as to Mr Bernard Trout's whereabouts.*'

'*From the police?*'

'*Yes.*'

'*What would they know?*'

Noah laughs: '*Well, they would know if he was wanted for something; they would know if he was on the run; they would know if he was in prison.*'

'*Why do you think Bernie's in prison?*'

'*I don't think he's in prison. I don't know if he's in prison. But I do know — from you, I might add — that he's been missing for some time and a lengthy prison stretch might — I repeat, might — explain his absence.*'

'Why would Bernie be in prison?'

'Oh,' Noah sighs in exasperation, as if to say, 'where will I start.' I wait but he doesn't elaborate. 'I can't imagine Bernie in prison. He'd never survive.'

'Prison is tough on most people. Young people, especially. Take those four IRA bombers, sentenced to life imprisonment during the week. Two young men and two young women. Such a waste of lives.'

'They bombed a pub in Guildford.'

'They did.'

'They killed innocent people.'

'That too.'

'Then they should be executed.'

'They would be if they had been charged with treason and found guilty.'

'Then life is what they deserve and life is what they should serve,' I say, pleased with my little rhyming slogan.

'It won't be an easy sentence for them to serve,' Noah says. 'They won't make many friends where they're going. The prisoners and the gaolers — both will be out to give them a hard time.'

'They deserve it. The bastards.'

'They deserve to lose their liberty,' says Noah. 'That's what they have been sentenced to: loss of liberty — for life. Nothing else.'

'Well, they should have thought of that before they went around bombing innocent people in pubs.'

'I won't defend what they did. Nobody can excuse that.'

'I reckon we can expect reprisals from the IRA now that the sentences have been handed down.'

'The IRA have threatened nothing yet as far as I'm aware, my friend,' Noah says. 'Strange that, don't you think? They usually do.'

On my way across to The Cabin, I see the tall frame of O'Leary sitting on the park bench, this time without 'Cattle'. He is talking to another bloke who looks just as scruffy as himself. This other bloke has long blond hair and is carrying a department store bag. It's got bold grey and whites stripes and the name Switzer on it. Maybe he's German. I reckon the bag must have something breakable in it because he is holding it almost at arm's length, as if he doesn't want it to hit his knee. They both appear to be down in the dumps, but when O'Leary sees me approaching he gives me a little wave and smiles, displaying a mouthful of gleaming white teeth. But he says nothing as I pass. The other bloke just turns away as if embarrassed. I only wish Lisa could be here to see the cut of these two 'noblemen'.

I meet Lisa in the queue. We make small talk about some of the trivia in the newspapers; singer Karen Carpenter has quit the Royal Variety Performance due to illness; Lisa is more interested in the story about more Britons taking up gymnastics, due to the success of popular Russian

Olympic gymnast Olga Korbett — she says there is a strong similarity between gymnastics and certain forms of dance. My attention is drawn to a report that a cargo of nuclear waste from Japan is heading for Britain. Lisa thinks this is just scaremongering and the story doesn't have 'legs', as she calls it. I wish Trouty would leg it in here. Still no sign of him.

The Cabin seems like a haven of tranquillity after the experiences of the morning so far. But it doesn't last for long. True to his nickname 'Goose' Berrie (copyright Jacko Butler — who else?), Bradley makes an appearance after a few minutes, pushing his way past the others in order to join Lisa. He is all excited about the Ike & Tina Turner concert he attended last night at the Odeon in Hammersmith and insists on giving the customers at the top of the queue a song-by-song account of it. We all make polite noises. Personally, I'm a fan of Ike & Tina — although I'm not sure Lisa is — but I really can't take Bradley's affected enthusiasm. I've known the guy for years. Ike & Tina Turner are definitely not his bag. This is all about him trying to appear 'groovy' as part of promoting Threads. Ignoring our polite disinterest in his views of the concert, he continues with his 'you-shoulda-been-there' routine, that culminates in him suddenly attempting a strangled demonstration of 'River Deep, Mountain High' while looking straight at Lisa.

A few customers stop in mid-conversation and crane their necks slightly to see what's going on at the top of the queue. More customers give each other knowing looks; others try to stifle a giggle. But Bradley realises that he now has a captive audience and continues, louder and a bit more animatedly.

The raunchy lyrics are obviously getting to Bradley and his performance becomes even more excitable. Perhaps sensing that one day there might be a role for music in launching him on a serious political career, he plays to the wider gallery, glancing briefly at me with a look that says 'Are you getting this, mate?' and then finally doing a few 'ba, ba, ba, bumps' in an attempt to bring his performance to a natural conclusion.

The stunned silence that greets the ending would leave any ordinary bloke squirming with embarrassment. Not Brad. With a neck like his, a career in politics is definitely a runner. He tells us that he's planning to play all Ike & Tina stuff in Threads for the whole week and it's going to be 'far out'. Then, suddenly, having purchased nothing, he checks his watch, taps it a few times, checks it again and informs us that he has to 'split'.

There's an awkward silence for a few seconds after he leaves.

'Young Bradley has Van Gogh's ear for music, I think,' says Mick.

'Oh, he wasn't that bad a singer, was he?' asks Lisa.

'Singer, is it?' asks Mick incredulously. 'Now let me tell you something, young lady: if that bucko was shot for being a singer he'd die innocent.'

I do my usual business with Mick. He reckons QPR will easily beat Sheffield United today. He asks me about England's chances against Czechoslovakia in Bratislava this Thursday. Gerry Francis is captain once more and I tell Mick I believe that Gerry might be just the leader England need to become world-beaters again, after leading them to that 2–1 victory against Switzerland at the beginning of September. I bite my lip while saying this, because relations between Gerry and I have not improved much during the season to date. But deep down I do believe he is exactly the captain that England needs.

'Let's hope so, Dawhee,' says Mick, 'but you know what they say: one swallow doesn't make a summer.'

I leave with Lisa and we cross over onto the Green. I scan the area; thankfully, O'Leary and his German friend have gone. But they left something behind. The tip of the distinctive department store bag with the grey and white stripes is protruding from the top of the rubbish bin. Maybe it finally hit his knee and smashed whatever was in it. I'm tempted to go over and rummage in the bag to find out what it was, but I don't want to get into a discussion with Lisa about it. However, I do ask her if she has ever heard of the name Switzer, spelling it for her as best I can from memory. She says it doesn't ring any bells with her but would guess that it's a Swiss name. I decide to drop the subject and we press on.

'Who does he play for?' she asks, suddenly, smiling.

'Switzerland,' I lie. 'Well done. Yes, he played for Switzerland against England a few weeks ago,' I add, pleased as punch with my quick thinking. 'How did you know that? Switzerland isn't exactly famous for football. Aren't they more into cuckoo clocks.'

'Yes, well, for a start, I heard you discussing it with Mr Hanrahan in The Cabin a few minutes ago. 2–1 to England, I think you said. Secondly, I think the Swiss have contributed more to the world than cuckoo clocks.'

'Name me one famous Swiss person, then,' I ask with a snigger.

'Well, apart from Switzer the fictitious footballer, the person who springs to mind for me is Timothy Albrecht, the poet.'

'Poet,' I say disbelievingly.

'Yes. A Beat poet. Most people think he was German but he was actually Swiss.'

'Never heard of him. What kind of stuff did he write?'

'Nothing I think that you would be interested in. He only published one book of poetry and I happen to like some of his work. It's out of print now. In fact, I've been trying to source the book for some time but without success.'

'Okay, I'll keep an eye out for it.'

Lisa gives me a sidelong, sceptical glance.

'Thank you,' she says, a bit too politely.

Eddie has switched the radio off. Maybe he's had enough pop music for one morning. Between Bradley and the Butlers, I've certainly had my fill of Opportunity Knocks-style warbling. He doesn't appear to have solved the mystery of the un-triumphant Herald, though. He stands there, staring at the motor, alternately scratching his head and his exposed armpit. As soon as he sees Lisa he reaches for an old T-shirt and quickly slips it on, as if this greasy, stained top will make him more presentable. It's obviously itching him around the neck or shoulder blades because he keeps giving these rapid, exaggerated shrugs.

'How's the repair work coming along?' I ask.

Eddie just shrugs. But he doesn't respond.

'How are you today, Eddie?' Lisa asks.

Eddie shrugs again. Eddie also smiles at the same time. The resultant combination of uncertainty and happiness makes him look even more absurd than usual. As if he's imitating Mike Yarwood impersonating Ted Heath.

There's an awkward pause.

'Knives,' *announces Eddie suddenly, with a shrug.*

'Pardon?' *Lisa is confused. So am I.*

'Knives,' *shrugs Eddie again.* 'He play knives.' *Eddie double shrugs.*

Lisa looks at me suspiciously. 'You play with knives?'

'I think he means Blades,' *I explain.* 'Sheffield United are called the Blades. You know, Sheffield; cutlery, blades.' *I'm tempted to add* 'QED' *but I resist.*

Lisa looks at me pityingly.

Eddie beams and gives a triple shrug. It's all very disconcerting: 'Blades, heh, heh, yes Blades. Sheffield United, heh, heh.'

'Sharp as knives,' *I say by way of conclusion..*

Eddie stops shrugging. He also stops beaming and gapes at me strangely. I decide to move on. This conversation is going nowhere. Lisa takes the hint and says a more extended goodbye to Eddie. He relaxes.

We stroll on at a snail's pace. Eddie has switched on the radio again and the voice of Kenny Everett drifts up the street in our wake.

'It's the end of summer time today,' *Lisa says wistfully.* 'The hour goes back tonight.'

'Great,' *I say, adding, with as much double entendre as I can manage:* 'That'll be an extra hour in bed for the both of us.' *I knew the moment I uttered those words, layered as they were with a particular emphasis and innuendo, that it was a mistake. A stupid, immature mistake. A cheap shot. In truth, I said it in that way deliberately in order to annoy her just a little.*

'I beg your pardon.' *She stops dead and fixes me with a disapproving stare.*

Any chirpiness I had drains from me in that instant. 'Just a figure of speech,' *I say unconvincingly.*

We walk on for what seems like an eternity without exchanging another word. When we get to Aunt Sally's, Lisa mutters a sniffy goodbye without making eye contact and walks away quickly. I stand on the corner for a few minutes staring after her as she walks up The Glade towards Forest Hill Road, but she doesn't look back.

Bollocks. What a shit start to the day. First that Major/Attorney bastard, then that scratchy conversation with Noah about the IRA before bumping into O'Leering with the white teeth (who is probably an IRA sympathiser) then GooseBerrie warbling to Lisa, followed by Eddie with his stupid jokes. And to top it all off, I go and make a stupid comment to Lisa that I knew would irritate her. What the f**k was I thinking? She'll probably avoid me from now on and refuse to speak to me if we do meet.

All I need now is for us to get turned over by Sheffield United this afternoon?

Saturday, 25 October 1975: 4.40 p.m.

Queens Park Rangers…1 Sheffield United…0

The
FIRST
HALF

8. TORN SHORTS, NYLON STOCKINGS, CLEAN SHEETS AND DIRTY DEEDS

Saturday, 24 April 1976: 3.00 p.m.

Both teams line up for the kick-off, Leeds in their familiar Admiral away strip of yellow with blue trim and QPR in the traditional blue and white hoops. Referee Gow blows the whistle; Johnny Hollins taps it to Gerry Francis and the match that will define our season is finally underway.

It's scrappy stuff in the opening minutes with the elements contriving to make ball control very difficult. The pattern of the match is a little too frantic, with both sides attacking but giving the ball away far too easily. It falls to Don Masson to try to steady things down a little by delivering an exquisite through ball for Don Givens to run onto. Don cannot quite control it but luckily it falls to Stan, who immediately sets his sights on the Leeds penalty area. As Stan shimmies into the box, I half expect him to try to entice the Leeds defenders to trip him up and give away a penalty. (Stan has won a couple of controversial penalties for us in recent weeks, none more important than the one against the Arsenal on Easter Monday. That one was crucial in keeping us in the championship race.) Instead, Stan goes for goal but loses control of the ball and it bobbles harmlessly wide. It's the first constructive move of the match, however, and helps settle the nerves of the home crowd, who roar loudly in appreciation.

Minutes later Billy Bremner blatantly fouls Stan and gestures to the referee that Stan has dived. But the ref is having none of it and the partisan crowd howls its approval. Maybe this is to be our day after all. But the free kick comes to nothing. The number of fouls is increasing, and this only serves to confirm to some sections of the crowd that the 'dirty Leeds' reputation is probably well deserved.

Soon, Don Givens receives another curling pass from Don Masson and glancing up, quickly spots Gerry Francis arriving through the middle. He threads an inch-perfect pass between two Leeds defenders that Gerry smacks on target. But Harvey makes a brilliant save.

The atmosphere ratchets up a few more notches. There's still only about five minutes gone. I haven't touched the ball yet.

Another Leeds attack. This time it's orchestrated by Frankie Gray. He pushes deep into our half and then tries to play a one-two with Duncan McKenzie. Frank McLintock nips in for a vital interception, and then hits a back pass to Ian Gillard.

Gilly clears it and the ball eventually reaches Stan Bowles. Norman Hunter immediately bustles into him. Hunter gets a foot in and the ball goes out for a throw-in, rattling the Brentford Nylons pitch-side advertising hoarding before bouncing back. The linesman, Mr Parsons, inexplicably signals a Leeds throw. This incenses the crowd: 'Look, he's a bleedin' Leeds fan,' quips one wag. 'He's even carrying a yellow flag.' Whatever happened in the entanglement between Norman Hunter and Stan, Hunter's shorts have come off worst. And off they come – in front of thirty thousand people! Norman kicks them away and gets a fresh pair. Leeds take the throw but it comes to nothing. Then it's our turn to go on the offensive but their goalkeeper, Harvey, makes another brilliant save. There's still nothing between the teams.

This is hardly surprising as both sides have impressive defensive records. We've played 19 games in which we have not conceded a single goal (11 at home, 8 away). Leeds United have had 17 such 'clean sheets' (10 home and 7 away). Keeping a 'clean sheet' can be vital at the end of the season if the final placings are decided on Goal Average. When teams finish on an equal number of points, then Goal Average comes into play.

Goal Average is calculated by dividing the number of goals a team scores in all matches the team has played by the number of goals the team concedes. So if QPR has scored 100 goals and conceded 50 in a season, our Goal Average will be 2.

Goal *Difference* replaced Goal Average in the 1970 World Cup finals, and there is talk that this change will also be introduced into all English Football League matches next season.

Goal Difference is calculated by subtracting the number of goals conceded from the number of goals scored. So if QPR has scored 100 goals and conceded 50 in a season, we will have a goal difference of 50 (100-50). What's the point of the proposed change? Well, if Leeds has scored 80 goals and conceded 40 it would have a Goal *Average* of 2 , the same as QPR, but its Goal *Difference* would be 40 (80-40), so an inferior goal difference to QPR. Presumably the intention is to reward the teams that score more goals.

Saturday, 8 November 1975: 8.45 a.m.

I have mixed feelings about today as I begin my Saturday ritual. On the football front, things are looking up a little. After a creditable 1–1 draw away to Coventry last Saturday, we are lying joint third in the league table with last year's winners Derby County, just one point behind the joint leaders Manchester United and West Ham. We've played 15 matches, won 7, drew 6 and lost only 2, scoring 23 goals and conceding just 10. We've scored in every match so far, bar two — and both of those matches were away from home.

On the other hand, today's opponents, our North London rivals Tottenham Hotspur, have made a disappointing start to the season and currently lie in fifteenth position. Having beaten Middlesboro' on the opening day of the season, Spurs then failed to win any of their next 11 matches and it is only by virtue of a few drawn matches that they are not closer to the bottom of the league table. In the process they've already conceded 22 goals. So even though they beat us 1–0 in the corresponding game at Loftus Road last season, I'm confident that with home advantage we can win this one easily enough. The aim has to be not only to score as many goals as possible, but to also to keep a clean sheet. We've done that in the last five home games and it could prove vital in terms of goal average at the end of the season. The important thing is to have all our ducks in a row. For me, that means adhering to the ritual.

It also means that everybody else has to play their part. And that's the bit that's been worrying me on and off. I'm wondering in particular if Lisa will show up today. The way we parted company last time, it wouldn't surprise me if she decided to avoid me from now on. On the other hand, was it such a big deal? A reasonable person would probably get over it quickly. And it's been two weeks. So I decide to say nothing about it when (if?) we do meet today. Ignore it. Nothing to apologise for. Still…

Marianne Pleass is sitting astride her bicycle at the gates of number 21 as I approach. She has one foot on the ground and the other on the right-hand pedal, but shows no inclination to move off.

'Marje is not well,' she bleats sombrely, looking at no one in particular but obviously directed to me, since there's nobody else within earshot. I'm tempted to comment that I could have told her that years ago but I realise that what she means is that Marjorie is worse than usual, whatever Marjorie's state of 'usualness' actually comprises of. I'm also tempted to ask Marianne why she is telling this to me, of all people.

'What's the problem?' I enquire, instead.

'It's her nerves,' she whispers, and my interest immediately dissipates. Because if there is one subject that I know absolutely nothing about, it's 'nerves', especially when it concerns women of a certain age. I realise that this betrays a certain youthful impatience and a lack of proper respect on my part, but I know I have nothing constructive to offer by way of insight, sympathy or reassurance. Pre-match nerves, I understand. Defending-a-corner-kick nerves, I am very familiar with. Taking-a-penalty nerves, I'm a bleedin' expert on. Waiting-for-James-Alexander-Gordon-to-read-out- the-results-of-other-matches-on-BBC-Radio nerves is a chronic condition that I live with week in, week out. But I believe that women's 'nerves' is a malady that can only be fully comprehended by other women.

'That's too bad,' is all I can summon up the wit to utter. I squint up at the bay window but the curtains are drawn. Marianne doesn't seem to know what to say next either and starts adjusting the contents of the basket, as if waiting for me to say more. I notice a book resting among the chocolate wrappers and the 'five-a-day' fruit and veg, so I seize the opportunity for a diversion.

'Another book? What are you reading these days?' I enquire lamely.

'The Feminine Mystique by Betty Friedan,' she replies limply, and I suspect instinctively that I've blundered into another conversational cul-de-sac. I swallow hard but soldier bravely on.

'Any good?' I ask, scratching my head.

'Mmmm. It's interesting,' she informs me, but without any palpable enthusiasm. I assume this means that either the book is no good, or she doesn't reckon I would understand it. Probably the latter, I decide.

'What's it about?' I ask.

Now, whether it's a book or a movie, I'm always nervous when asking people what it's about because some people reckon you want them to go through the whole bleedin' thing, cover to cover, from opening to closing credits, the whole shebang. So not only do I not want to have the feminine mystique explained to me right at this moment, but I can see a red-leather-clad figure standing at the bus stop further down the road, which is all the feminine mystique I reckon I need for today. But I'm too late.

'It's about the role of women in society,' she announces, 'particularly women who stay at home. How trapped they feel. How stifling it is for them. Their terror at being alone…'

I'm tempted to say 'Like Marjorie?' but Marianne is now in full flow:

'She tries to provide answers — solutions — to women who want to pursue a career outside the home or further their education. For women who ask "Is this all?"'

'So, it's all to do with equality, Women's Lib, that kind of thing,' I say, and realise at once that the term 'Women's Lib' instantly undid any kudos I had gained by using the term 'equality'.

'Ms Friedman believes that a woman is every bit as able as any man to do any type of work or pursue any career and that contrary views are a result of conditioning by a male-dominated media. That's what I believe too.'

It strikes me then that I have never exchanged so many words with Marianne until that moment, but also that this particular exchange is likely to end soon.

'So you want women to be the same as men?' I ask, in my puerile innocence.

'Not at all,' she says, mounting the bicycle and setting off, without as much as a glance in my direction, 'that would be a very unambitious target.'

The woman in the oncoming lime-coloured, left-hand drive Citroen 2CV gives Marianne a loud blast as she cycles straight towards her. Marianne immediately takes corrective action but is hit by a rapid stream of invective from the Citroen driver that owes its origin more to the locker room than to the powder room.

I pause when I reach the corner. No sign of Lisa ahead of me. Pedestrian traffic past the postbox on the opposite side of the street is still practically non-existent. The IRA bomb in Mayfair a week ago has left most people still very much on edge. Even Colonel Martin doesn't put in a stiff-upper-lip appearance this morning. Fortitude in the face of adversity appears to be a fading virtue. We seem to be accepting this as part of the way we live now. I cannot understand it. And the Government seems powerless to do anything about it.

Svetlana looks a bit disgruntled when I arrive at the bus stop. But she does seem slightly pleased to see me.

'You talk to Edvard.' It takes me a second or two to establish that this is not a question but a request. An order, even.

'Two weeks to fix carrr!' She is prodding my chest with her index finger. 'Cannot find problem; cannot fix carrr.'

Maybe this isn't my day after all.

'*I'll talk to him,*' I promise her. '*Maybe I help him find problem. Maybe even help him fix car.*' (*I'm one of those odd people who starts to speak like a foreigner when answering a question from a foreigner.*) '*Oh, vould you?*' *she places a hand lightly on my arm and I decide there and then to make it a priority to get myself one of those car repair DIY manuals. Today, if at all possible. And maybe a bicycle repair manual while I'm at it, for you-know-who.*

I ask her about Trouty again and this time I get the distinct impression she knows something. She starts speaking in Swedish, or some lingo that sounds Swedish, but I distinctly hear the name 'Bernart' mentioned a few times. And not in a complimentary fashion either, from what I can glean from her tone. But I don't understand any of it and I get the impression she doesn't want to explain it to me. I ask her if she has seen Lisa. She smiles broadly but says no.

The bus arrives just then and I get the continental-kiss routine, a big 'thank you' and the merest squeeze on the right arm (but I may be wrong regarding the last bit). Then, the sexy, blonde, Scandinavian woman who does like men hops on the bus. And this time she does look back.

I bump into Tojo at Aunt Sally's gate and ask him if he happens to have any car repair manuals in his Reliant Robin. It takes a few minutes to achieve this feat of communication, as Tojo has very little English. He eventually gets the message. But I don't get the manual. He has nothing, he declares. Not in the car; not in Aunt Sally's workshed; not even at home. Nothing. 'Kaimu.' I decide not to ask him if he's seen Lisa.

I cross at the intersection and notice that the Butler boys are already way ahead of me, rounding the corner and about to slip out of sight as they amble towards The Cabin for their 'smokes'. I break into a trot, pausing only to acknowledge Eddie as I pass, and I catch up with Jacko and Billy just as they reach the Horseman's and are about to cross over to the Green. I fall into step and get straight to the point, asking them about the car repair manual.

'When d'ya want it for?' asks Jacko.

'Today, ideally,' I say, a bit too eagerly.

'Sorry, mate, can't 'elp ya then. We do 'ave a mate – Benny – who's kind of in the book business. But we couldn't get hold of 'im today.'

'Is Benny's shop closed today, then?' I ask. I hear Billy give a kind of childish giggle behind my back.

'Not exactly,' muses Jacko, smirking. 'But listen, wot kinda motor is it, anyway?'

'Triumph Herald. Eddie is having difficulty with it and he asked me if I could help,' I lie.

'Can't say as I'm surprised ole Echo Eddie's 'avin difficulty wiv it,' says Jacko, 'but I'm amazed he's asked you for 'elp, seein' as you're not exactly motor mechanic material now, are ya?'

'That's why I suggested the manual,' I say irritably.

Jacko gives Billy a knowing look. Billy returns the knowing look but it's quite obvious he doesn't know why Jacko is giving him the knowing look, if you follow my meaning. Jacko turns to face me head-on and, hands on hips, he throws his head back and loudly enquires:

'So, how is poor sweaty Svetty getting around these days, wivout the motor, then?'

Cue the sound of the penny suddenly dropping for Billy, who grins lasciviously while tongue-twisting, 'Sweaty Svetty, sweaty Svetty.'

'Bus, probably,' I shrug.

'Bus, eh. Must watch out for 'er then,' grins Jacko 'Right Billy?'

'Right on, Jacko,' drools Billy, and we enter The Cabin together. There are not many customers around this morning and neither is Lisa. Mick spies us immediately and it's obvious that the brothers' custom is not exactly welcome.

'And what can I do for you this morning, gentlemen?' Mick's greeting is a little frosty, the word 'gentlemen' being laced with as much icy sarcasm as he can muster. I decide to let the brothers do their business first. I grab a Mirror and pretend to be engrossed in it. The front-page story is about Britain having to go cap-in-hand to the International Monetary Fund to borrow £975 million. Doesn't this Labour government have any pride?

Jacko swaggers up to the counter while Billy hangs back to retrieve one of those TIME-LIFE inserts for books about 'The Old West' that has fallen out of somebody's newspaper onto the floor.

'Ah,' says Mick with feigned pleasantness, but deliberately avoiding eye contact with Jacko, 'if it isn't the evil of two lessers.'

Jacko pretends he doesn't hear and places his order. There appears to be no shortage of readies today and the two are stocking up with plenty of cigarettes, matches and packs of Fisherman's Friend.

'Anything else I can get you, gen-tel-men?' asks Mick finally, and without waiting for an answer, suggests: 'Dog food, perhaps?'

'Dog's gone,' pipes up Billy. Jacko just stiffens and stares at Mick.

'Is he, now? Is he, in-deed.' The insincerity of Mick's concern is palpable. 'Escaped, did he?'

'Prob-ly,' says Billy, as he gathers up some of their purchases. Jacko continues to stare threateningly at Mick. 'Just ran off this morning.'

'And still running, I suppose,' mutters Mick under his breath as he places the last packet of cigarettes on the counter. This is followed by an awkward pause.

'I fink he woz nicked,' asserts Jacko loudly.

But Mick obviously wants to avoid being drawn into this line of speculation: 'So, no dog; no dog food,' he concludes. However, he can't resist one last jibe at the brothers: 'Nothing else? How are you gentlemen fixed for Rennies?'

Jacko continues to fix Mick with that threatening stare and you can feel the tension rise. 'Pay the man, Billy.'

'Right on, Jacko.' Billy peels the required notes off a thick wad.

Sensing he has probably overstepped the mark, Mick offers a conciliatory farewell as he hands Billy the change: 'I suppose you gentlemen are off to the game this afternoon?'

'Hope so,' says Billy pocketing the 'shrapnel'. 'All depends wot time we finish working.' And with that, they shuffle out.

I let them go, promising to catch up with them later. I'm a bit miffed with Mick. Baiting customers is not his style, and while the Butler brothers may not be to everybody's liking, they do have their good points. I try to tell him this as tactfully as I can. But Mick is not for persuading.

'It all depends what time we finish working, indeed,' parrots Mick. 'Working? Working? You know something, me bucko? Those boys are too lazy to get out of bed to draw the dole.'

'I reckon you're being a bit hard on them, Mick.' Then I ask Mick if Trouty has shown up, but he still hasn't seen him.

'I'm surprised,' he muses. 'Very unlike Mr Trout to miss a Spurs match. Him being such a big Spurs fan. Specially against QPR. Very surprised, I am. Just the Mirror, then?'

'Yeah, just the Mirror, mate. Has Lisa been and gone?' I ask as casually as I can while handing Mick a ten pence piece. 'I didn't see her on my way here.'

'Haven't seen Miss Dell at all today.' He pauses before handing me my change. 'Now, you haven't gone and mislaid two friends, have you, Dawhee?' he laughs. 'To paraphrase that great Irish writer, Oscar Wilde: "To lose one friend may be regarded as a misfortune; to lose two looks like carelessness."' He leans forward: 'I wouldn't worry,' he smiles, 'I'm sure Miss Dell will turn up. But Mr Trout? Now, he's a different kettle of fish entirely.'

I smile weakly, pick up my Mirror and pocket the change, remembering only at the last moment to ask him about the car repair manual.

'Unfortunately, I don't stock them, me bucko. But you might try Mr Berrie's establishment,' he adds helpfully. I thank Mick for the suggestion, fold up the Mirror and stuff it into my pocket.

Mick wishes me 'Godspeed'.

I dash across the street onto the Green. There's a small group of workmen putting the final touches to the decorations around the war memorial and getting the surrounding areas spruced up for tomorrow's Remembrance Sunday ceremony. I cross again to the shops and I peer into the window of Threads first, in case Lisa is in there. I know Lisa has visited the boutique before, tho' I'm not sure if she ever actually bought anything there. No sign of her, so I don't go inside. There's just Bradley, talking to a couple of pretty 'chicks', as he calls them. Bradley is kitted out in all the latest gear, and would probably look the part if it wasn't for that short-back-and-sides hairstyle. Bradley tries to be hip by day and a member of the Conservative Club after cocktails in the evening, pretentious prat that he is. I duck into Berrie's.

'Ah. The return of the prodigal. Good mornington, my friend. Are we buying or selling today?' Noah always has a cheery welcome. He wears his poppy proudly. There's nobody else in the shop.

'Since when have I ever sold anything to you, Mr Berrie?' I ask. Everybody calls him Noah, but as his son Bradley is not that much older than me, I always call him Mr Berrie.

'True, true,' he laughs, 'but you've never actually bought much from me either. So, what can I do for you today?'

'I'm looking for a car repair manual. Just thought I'd check with you on the off-chance that you might have an old one in stock.'

'Let's check out back,' he suggests, heading towards the tiny storeroom. 'Which car type are you looking for?'

'Triumph Herald,' I reply casually.

He stops for a moment, turns and peers over his spectacles at me. 'Triumph Herald? Hmmm, I've heard they can be dangerous,' he warns, and turns again to open the door of the storeroom. 'High maintenance, too.' He turns the key in the lock and turns back to me again, 'Especially the older models.' He opens the door and we enter the airless room. 'I understand that my son, Bradley, took a test drive in one once.'

'Oh, yeah?' is all I can think of saying. 'What did he reckon?'

'Well, I think that he probably enjoyed the thrill of the test drive while it lasted but, in the long term, he didn't believe it was right for him. Neither did I. Too much mileage already on the clock.'

I'm feeling a tad claustrophobic in the little room and my head is swimming a bit. Probably something to do with all those family histories embedded into those dusty old books and faded photographs. Noah sorts through the piles of old books and eventually unearths something.

'I believe this is it,' he exclaims triumphantly. The rising dust is clearly visible in the shaft of light from the skylight window as he extracts a cellophane-wrapped volume from a pile of books sitting precariously on the edge of a shelf. 'It's the Triumph Herald Repair Manual alright. The pages are a bit dogeared and are fairly creased.' He flicks through it. 'It's certainly been well thumbed.' He looks up and kind of smirks: 'Very appropriate in the circumstances, then.' He blows the dust off the covers and we head back into the shop. 'Now, all we need to do is agree on the price.'

We settle fairly quickly on a price that's probably a better deal for me than it is for Noah. He tells me he is going to today's match with some of his family and friends who are coming down from North London, and that Bradley is going to mind both shops — with a little help from two of his friends from the tennis club.

'We're all ardent Spurs fans through and through in this family,' he says proudly, 'ever since the great "double" team of Blanchflower and Mackay back in the sixties. But you've probably never heard of them.'

'I've certainly heard of them, but I'm more worried about the threat from today's Spurs team: Martin Chivers, Steve Perryman, Ralph Coates.'

Noah smiles.

'Bernie's a Spurs fan too,' I say, quickly. 'Bernie Trout. You know…'

'Yes, I know Bernard very well.' Noah smiles again. 'How is he? Haven't seen him for some time.'

'Well, that's the thing,' I say. 'Nobody has seen Bernie for a week or two. But nobody seems too concerned. It's all very strange.'

'Let me tell you three things apropos Mr Trout,' advises Noah, rather seriously, 'three facts to bear in mind. One: There are many people who think that everything about Mr Bernard Trout and his business is strange; and two: Mr Bernard Trout is more than capable of looking after himself.'

'What's the third?'

'Mr Trout's interests are widespread.'

Bradley walks in just then. Noah bids me 'kol tuv' and wanders back into the dusty storeroom. I don't particularly want to hang around chewing the fat with Bradley for longer than necessary, so I simply ask him if he has seen Lisa.

'You know Lisa?' He seems surprised, but he continues moving around the shop in a vain attempt to appear knowledgeable and important, picking up things and putting them back in exactly the same position.

'Yes, yes I do. Have you seen her today?' Bradley has this way of always putting me on the defensive.

'You know her well?' he asks, ignoring my question.

'Yes,' I say, 'very well.'

'Lisa is a dancer, you know,' he announces pompously.

'Yes, I know.'

'A classical dancer,' he adds, 'you knew that?'

'She studies classical and contemporary dance, yes, she told me.' I try to make the emphases as light as possible, but just heavy enough to get under his skin. Which it does. His face contorts a little. 1–0 to me.

But he recovers his poise: 'She's got class, has Lisa,' he remarks, haughtily. 'Everybody in the golf club thinks so.'

Ouch. 1–1. I decide to settle for an honourable draw. This hasn't exactly been my day so far and maybe I shouldn't push my luck.

'Look Brad, I'm in a bit of a hurry,' I say impatiently, knowing full well how he hates to be called 'Brad'. 'Have you seen Lisa today or not?'

'No,' he states, but as I turn to leave, he casually adds, 'not yet.'

'Thanks, Brad,' I say coldly.

'What do you think of her trifle?' he quietly asks, as I'm halfway out the door. I pause. I don't know how to respond because I didn't really catch what he said. He pronounced it as 'trefull'. I think. Trefull? Truffle? Trifle?

'I beg your pardon?'

'Her trefull. Lisa's trefull.' He is standing back in the doorway of the little storeroom and raises his voice just a little so that I can hear from the front of the shop. 'Fascinating, isn't it? So perfect.'

At this stage, I decide that honesty is the best policy. I lean against the architrave of the front door, stick my head inside and shout back: 'Sorry, Brad, I really haven't a clue what you're talking about.'

'You haven't seen it then? Her trefull? She hasn't shown it to you?' he almost half whispers, as if referring to some intimate secret.

'Obviously not,' I reply, resignedly, and start to walk away.

'Then you don't really know Lisa at all, do you?' he bellows after me.

What does he mean? Her trefull? With that lewd expression on his face as he said it. Like it was something dirty or sexual. My cheeks are burning. My ignorance has let me down again. That's 1–2 to Bradley. It's a result. And I feel sick.

Even the sound from the stack of old books crashing down, the plume of dust that belches out the door and the sight of Bradley staggering about, coughing uncontrollably, provides scant consolation.

I try the Green again and walk round the little war memorial where she told me she sometimes sits if the sun is shining. No sign of her. Maybe she's decided not to turn up today? Maybe the 'words' we had last time we met, after my childish quip regarding summertime, upset her more than I even realised at the time. There's a lot of preparation activity for Remembrance Sunday going on at the memorial, so I decide not to hang around and instead I embark on a short walk around the park. On my second circuit, I spy O'Leary, sitting on the same park bench as before. He appears to be doodling on a sketch pad but I don't have time to get into a conversation now regarding his interest or otherwise in art. I get straight to the point and ask him directly if he has seen Lisa. I'm aware straightaway that my tone sounds accusatory but he smiles, showing those gleaming white teeth of his again, says he hasn't seen her this morning and then asks if I would like him to help me find her. I say 'no', rather more abruptly than I should, thank him and move on swiftly. I'm already running late. As I quicken my pace up Park Road, I momentarily wonder if I've misjudged O'Leary. He didn't have to offer to look for Lisa. But he did. On the other hand, maybe it was only because it was Lisa that he offered in the first place. If it had been anybody else, maybe he wouldn't have been so helpful. Still, it was nice of him to offer. Lisa would probably reckon it was 'noble' of him. Blimey, if that's what the nobility looks like these days, I would hate to bump into a few peasants.

And then I do.

Because as I make my way back up Park Road towards Beane Row, I become aware of a noisy commotion up ahead. I can hear Eddie's voice raised in anger, and I arrive just in time to see Eddie brandishing a spade while squaring up to Billy Butler and shouting, 'He sold my garden; he sold my garden,' while Jacko, cigarette dangling from his lips, peeps out apprehensively from behind a battered builder's delivery truck.

'Somebody tell me what's going on?' I demand.

'He sold my garden,' Eddie repeats, then looks at me: 'two times he sold my garden.'

Billy seizes the opportunity presented by my arrival to grab the spade and both of them now wrestle with it. Jacko emerges slowly from behind the truck:

'Aw, leave it out, mate,' he shouts, blowing smoke in the direction of Eddie's face, 'it woz a pretty shitty garden already.'

'He sold my garden, he sold my garden.' Eddie is almost in tears.

'Will somebody please tell me what's going on?'

Billy, displaying physical strength I was not aware he possessed, has disarmed Eddie at this stage and hands the spade to Jacko. Thus emboldened, Jacko has the air of a man who will not think twice about using it.

'It's the fackin' dog,' explains Jacko finally, 'the fackin' dog escaped this mornin' and now 'e's back and 'e's only gone and shit all over Echo's garden. Echo says he seen 'im do it.' He hands the spade back to Billy, walks over and puts his face an inch or two from Eddie's before screaming: 'The dog soiled Echo Eddie's fackin' garden.'

Billy splutters into laughter, scoops up a few dog turds on the spade and slings them at Eddie. Shit-slinging is not a talent that Billy excels in, however, and while most of the turds drop on Eddie, Jacko suffers some severe collateral damage, too.

'You dozy c**t,' Jacko screams at Billy.

'You dizzy cat,' echoes Eddie.

Both men, now united in their sense of victimhood and pockmarked with pieces of faeces make as if to move on Billy, the common enemy.

I swiftly step in between them and their intended target.

'I thought the dog was missing,' I say to Jacko. 'Nicked, you said it was?'

'Well, he came back, didn't he,' Jacko explains dourly, staring at the pavement.

'Came back?'

'That's wot I said. Came back. Released from captivity, you might say,' Jacko says, grinding the pavement with the edge of the spade as if to sharpen it. 'He woz in the garden when we got back from the shop. But 'e ran off again, the stupid mutt.'

'Then where's the dog now?' is the only thing I can think of asking that might distract the two Butlers.

It works. Jacko calls off his planned assault on Billy, who, in the act of side-stepping Eddie's charge, slips and lands in more dog shit.

'He must've ran off again,' explains Jacko, wearily.

'Must've done...' burbles Billy, looking for a clean spot to place his hands so that he can push himself back up on his feet, '...before Echo Eddie here stuck a spade up his arse.'

They all guffaw at this, although Eddie's laugh is notably less hearty than the other two. Nobody proffers a helping hand to help Billy to his feet but he eventually makes it, breathing heavily and wiping both hands on his coat. Then, while the brothers catch their collective breaths, I slip Eddie the car repair manual, telling him that I noticed he was having trouble fixing the car over the last two weeks.

'My Svetlana,' he whines loudly, almost crying with joy or relief, 'she will be so plist, so plist. No more bus to gym.'

I sense the two brothers look at each other knowingly. 'I wonder who Jim is,' Jacko smirks out of the side of his mouth. Billy titters.

'No more bus to gym,' echoes Eddie again. Then he gives us all the thumbs up:

'Tone em,' he implores. 'Tone em.'

'I'm sure she'll tone 'em alright,' quips Jacko, digging Billy playfully in the ribs. 'Right Billy?'

'R-r-right o-n, Ja-hacko,' rasps Billy breathlessly.

'No,' shouts a clearly frustrated Eddie. 'Today. Tone 'em. Tone 'em Hot spurts.'

Jacko gets it first: 'He means Spurs! Tottenham Hotspur. Tone 'em Hot spurts.'

Billy emits a noise somewhere between a croak and a laugh that sounds remarkably like the clatter of a machine gun.

'Tone 'em hot spurts: now I've fackin' heard it all,' declares Jacko. He puts an arm around the still spluttering Billy and the two brothers head off in search of the mutt, waving their arms above their heads like a couple of Spurs fans and singing:

Tone 'em Hot spurts!
Tone 'em Hot spurts!
Tone 'em Hot spurts!

I take my leave of a confused Eddie and walk slowly uphill, unfolding the Mirror as I go. There's not a lot to interest me on the news pages. Telly Savalas, who plays Kojak in that American detective series on TV, is in town to appear in Monday's Royal Variety Show and he's pictured with a couple of meter maids. An English cardinal died yesterday. And there's a report that an enquiry is to be launched into a sex scandal at a school in Hemel Hempstead where, it is alleged, there were amorous relationships between pupils and teachers. It's mostly trivial stuff. But on the sports pages, Harry Miller has a nice piece. It's headlined THE REVIE RANGERS and it features the five Rangers players who've been selected by Manager Don Revie to join the England squad for the forthcoming game in Portugal: Gerry Francis, Stan Bowles, Phil Parkes, Ian Gillard and Dave Thomas.

Yeeah! Who loves ya baby?

There's a piece on the back page too – about Stan Bowles. 'I'll mend my ways,' he says. This is a reference to his constant gesticulating during games which, some commentators believe, will not go down too well with foreign fans. The feeling is that it may jeopardise Stan's chances of playing for England in away games, despite being recalled to the England squad by Don Revie yesterday. 'I know I must stop it so I'm going to make a real effort and work hard on it,' Stan says. Yeah, right. I'll believe it when I don't see it.

All in all, it's been a morning of mixed fortune. Although it started positively enough, there were some unpleasant aspects to it. On the plus side, I managed to exchange an additional civil word or two with Marianne Pleass – even if it was about Women's Lib – which was nice; I got a little closer to Svetlana which was, well, even nicer; I got the motor manual that might solve Svetlana's car problem from Noah; and I managed to stay out of the confrontation between Mick and the Butlers, thereby maintaining my friendship with both parties. On the minus side, there was that encounter with Brad and his lewd reference to Lisa's trefull which completely flummoxed me. I need to sort out what he meant by that. And of course, Lisa never showed up today. That's unusual. Then there was the altercation I didn't manage to prevent – the one between the Butlers and Eddie. But that one's always simmering. No, what really troubles me is the continued inexplicable absence of Trouty and the more explicable 'no-show' of Lisa.

The more I think about that, the more I worry seriously about the outcome of today's game.

Saturday, 8 November 1975: 4.40 p.m.

Queens Park Rangers...0 Tottenham Hotspur...0

9. TWO MEN AND A VAN

Saturday, 24 April 1976: Early in the first half

Stan is sitting on the low perimeter wall that runs round the pitch, waiting to take a corner kick. Play is being held up because the referee is having stern words with one of the Leeds defenders and Stan has taken the opportunity to have a chat with a section of the crowd. Stan does this all the time. And the crowd love it.

Suddenly, one wag shouts, 'Where's the white van, Stan?' from a safe distance at the back of the terrace. Or rather he *sings* it, in the style of 'Make a new plan, Stan' from Simon & Garfunkel's '50 Ways to Leave Your Lover'. Stan smiles momentarily, then fires back some mischievous comment out of the side of his mouth. I didn't quite catch it but it must have been funny because the crowd suddenly bursts into raucous laughter. They have barely had time to recover when Stan hits them with what must have been an equally cracking follow-up punchline. This time the sound of hearty laughter rises even higher and ripples round the whole ground like a Mexican wave and everybody, somehow, seems to be in on the joke, even though only a small number could have heard it. But that's the effect Stan has on the crowd at Loftus Road. And it helps release some of the tension in crowd – and in the team.

The crack about the van relates to an incident involving Stan shortly after he joined QPR from Carlisle United in 1972. Although the story was well chronicled in the media at the time, the version I heard, related in the dressing room one afternoon, was less constrained by legal considerations and, more than likely, was heavily embellished.

It appears that Stan and Don Shanks, a former England Youth international full-back playing for Luton Town at the time, were returning to central London from a day out at the dog track and decided to park their van in Holborn to go in search of a burger. Shanks then goes and parks the van partly on the pavement outside the Wimpy bar – directly opposite Snow Hill police station. Having popped around the corner to buy a newspaper, Stan returns to the van to find Don on the ground surrounded by a few burly members of London's finest, some of whom (according to one version of the story) were pointing guns at poor Don's head.

It transpired that the van had stolen number plates on it. Worse still, the van was suspected of being used in a recent armed robbery! Stan had borrowed the van from a mate called Carlisle Peter. The thing eventually ended up in the Old Bailey. The judge dismissed the case against Stan and Don after Carlisle Peter testified that they had nothing to do with the van or the changed number plates. But Carlisle Peter got three years in the nick for changing the plates. According to Stan, 'Carlisle Peter likes to go in every now and then for a lie down.' It was all very embarrassing for QPR at the time. Still, it didn't stop the club signing Don Shanks from Luton two years later. But he's finding it difficult to break into the first team and has only managed two first team appearances this season, at home to Manchester City when we won 1–0 and away to Newcastle United – another win, this time 2–1.

Saturday, 22 November 1975: 8.40 a.m.

It's a mild morning. The sun has peeped through and it's directly in my eyes as I approach the entrance to Marianne Pleass's home. I can see her in silhouette as she wheels the bicycle out through the pedestrian gate (the driveway gates being more or less permanently padlocked). There appears to be a large head protruding from the front basket of her bicycle. It looks like a man's head, and I immediately think of our last conversation and her not-so-subtle hints regarding what she thought of men. The head is so heavy that the basket can barely hold the weight. Marianne is having difficulty keeping the bicycle upright as she wheels it across the pavement towards the road and her regular dalliance with death. I immediately run towards her, grab the handlebars with one hand, the saddle with the other and steady the bike.

'Marianne! What are you doing? What's this?' I demand, but I can see already that I had jumped to a hasty conclusion.

'What does it look like?' she replies. 'It's from my sculpture class. I've been working on it at home and later today I'm taking it into class.'

'But it's much too heavy for that basket,' I exclaim, relieved that she didn't actually ask me to tell her what I had suspected it was.

'It will be fine once I'm on the bicycle and get some momentum behind me,' she tut- tuts impatiently.

'But you won't be able to manoeuvre the front wheel. You won't be able to turn a corner. You do have to turn corners on the journey, don't you?'

'Yes, but it will be fine. Now get out of my way. I'm late already.' And with that, she makes a little run, leaps on the saddle and…And I close my eyes because I cannot bear to watch. But strangely, there is an eerie silence. No honking horns, no irate drivers swearing, no screeching of brakes and thankfully no sound of a breaking windscreen that would signal the arrival of a few pounds of hardened clay onto the lap of an unsuspecting driver.

When I open my eyes again, all seems to be moving smoothly and for some inexplicable reason I wonder momentarily what state Marianne's 'five-a-day' fruit is in by now, lying in the basket under all that weight.

Today, Tojo is cleaning the rust off the wrought-iron railings that provide an intermittent fence around Aunt Sally's garden. The remainder of the extensive boundary is made up of a mixture of crumbling stone wall and, in some places, no wall or railing at all, just stands of tall trees and dense undergrowth masking deep drainage trenches just inside the perimeter.

Tojo rises from his crouching position as soon as he sees me, stands to attention, gives a hint of a ceremonial bow and, as usual, waits for me to speak first. This is his standard method of greeting. If I simply say 'good morning' to him he will smile and politely utter something in reply, wait for me to walk on and then resume his duties. If I happen to make a comment about the weather or whatever it is that he is doing, I will get the exactly same reaction. So I've stopped attempting to engage him in conversation. If I see him at all, then I can mentally tick that box on the ritual list and move on. I reckon it suits both of us that way. Why make it more complicated than it needs to be? So I bid him 'good morning' and stroll on.

No sign of Eddie or the Butler brothers yet. It doesn't worry me – I'm sure to catch them on the way back.

As I arrive at the Horseman's, a very preoccupied-looking Svetlana emerges from the laneway at the side of the building, carrying a large, brown paper package, loosely wrapped with string. She brightens up immediately she sees me, changes direction and strides determinedly towards me.

'Oh, zank you, zank you,' she whispers breathlessly, giving my arm a gentle squeeze. 'You 'elp Edvard fix carr.'

I could happily stand there listening to her pronounce 'carr' all day, but I'm conscious of some passers-by staring at us.

'I don't suppose you've seen Bernie Trout in your, eh, travels,' I try to ask as nonchalantly as I can, while nodding towards the Horseman's.

I'm sure its not my imagination that her grip on my arm tightens for a moment before she releases it and smothers the parcel closer to her chest.

'I never see Bernart,' she states indignantly.

I wince mentally, annoyed with myself for having put her in this position, but she recovers her poise almost immediately and flashes that killer smile.

'Zank you, again,' she gushes. She gives a little wave as if dismissing me. Then she turns and marches across the road to where she has parked her newly polished car. A moment later, it glides away with the merest of growls.

Noah is chatting to Brad at the entrance to the shopping arcade. I had noticed both of them staring across while I was chatting to Svetlana. Brad is wearing shades to protect his eyes from the few minutes of intermittent sunshine promised for today. He looks as if he's had his hair professionally tossed for the occasion, too. What a jerk. His 'trifle' comment about Lisa on the last occasion we met still rankles with me, and I decide to avoid him in case he decides to bring it up again and expose my ignorant lack of worldliness. But Noah beckons me over.

'Young Bradley here is bringing me up to date on the latest developments in American politics,' says Noah proudly.

'The future is conservative,' Brad almost drawls. He checks his watch, tosses his head back and pushes both hands into the back pockets of his Brutus jeans with his thumbs sticking out. All that's missing is a Stetson. I can see the reflection of some clouds mirrored in his

shades as he announces: 'A whole new alliance will be forged after the next elections, you mark my words; the Republicans in the States and the Conservatives in Britain.'

'Those elections are a few years away yet, I keep telling him,' smiles Noah, wrapping his arm paternally around his scion, 'and a lot could happen between now and then. But he has the confidence and enthusiasm of youth on his side, so who am I to dampen that?' he shrugs.

Brad puffs out his chest, double-checks his watch in his familiar I'm-a-busy-man pose, and shifts his feet further apart.

'Nice brogues,' I say, staring at his feet in an attempt to embarrass him into realising that his footwear doesn't exactly chime with the Brutus jeans.

It doesn't work.

'Aren't they? Yes, Jermyn Street,' the switch from drawl to Guildhall is seamless.

Okay, I know Brad is his son, but Noah must be able to see what a total prat he is.

'Gotta split,' Brad suddenly says, self-consciously, to Noah and, brushing past me without a word, he heads for Threads. Maybe the dig about the brogues worked after all.

The sun comes out again.

'Well, are you buying or selling today?'

'Buying,' I say, 'I could be buying. Have you got any good dictionaries for sale?'

'I would have thought that a dictionary would be an indispensable part of your 'kit'?' Noah smiles.

'I need a good dictionary,' I say. 'A large dictionary, if you've got one.'

I had actually looked up the word 'trefull' in an old Handy Oxford Dictionary I've got at home, but found nothing. I tried for other meanings for 'trifle' but all I got were the obvious ones.

'Why a large dictionary?' Noah asks, slightly bemused by all of this. 'Are you looking for some deeper meanings?'

'I suppose I'm looking more for associated meanings,' I reply, not wanting to get into a detailed explanation.

'Then, what you need is this,' Noah coughs, extracting a well-thumbed paperback from under a dusty pile. 'It's a thesaurus,' he announces. 'Take it my friend, and if you cannot find the word you want then bring it back. No charge. However, if you do find the word you want, I guarantee you will never want to return the book and will reward me well for it.'

This seems like a fair arrangement, so I thank Noah and scurry over to The Cabin, clutching the book close against my chest, title inwards.

There is loud merriment and derision in equal measure among customers in the queue this morning. The focus of all this is the recent announcement by ex-actor Ronald Reagan that he intends entering the race to be the Republican party's nominee for the US presidential election next year. Some of the more politically aware are quick to point out that Reagan has been elected Governor of California twice already, but others simply scoff at the notion that an ex-Hollywood actor could ever become a credible President of the USA. This view is strongly supported by Mick, who has concerns regarding Reagan's intellectual qualities:

'Sure, if his brains were dynamite he wouldn't have enough to blow his nose!'

'I'd watch him all the same,' smirks Mick's son Cattle, who is helping out in the shop this morning, 'I read somewhere that he's an arch-conservative war-monger.'

This summation of Reagan's political leaning is not necessarily seen as a negative by many of the customers, resulting in some muted murmurings and whispered comments from sections of the queue concerning Cattle's own particular left-wing tendencies.

When it's my turn to pay, I ask Cattle as nonchalantly as I can manage how his friend O'Leary is.

'He's gone. He was only staying a few weeks,' Cattle replies without making eye contact.

'He's an artist?' I ask rhetorically.

Cattle looks up at me intently.

'I saw him with a sketchpad sitting on a bench on the Green near the war memorial,' I offer by way of explanation. 'I assumed he was an artist. He looks a bit like an artist, too.'

'Ha! Yes. He's an artist all right.' Cattle laughs as if there is some underlying joke. 'Lofty the artist. That's a good one.'

The 'Lofty' reference is obviously to do with his height. But there is something here that I'm not getting. An in-joke perhaps. I decide to leave it. I feel better now that O'Leary is gone but I'm a tad uncomfortable at being excluded from Cattle's little joke. I decide to switch away from the O'Leary conversation by asking Mick about Trouty, but he reports that there have been 'no sightings of your slippery friend all week'. Lisa is coming in as I'm leaving and, resisting my instinctive urge to ignore her for not turning up last Saturday, I nod as I pass. Surprisingly, she gives me a warm smile in return. I decide to take no chances and wait for her outside.

I scan the newspaper while I wait: LET LOOSE TO SLAUGHTER screams the front page. It's the story of Patrick Mackay, who was jailed for life at the Old Bailey yesterday after pleading guilty to the manslaughter of three elderly people. The paper reports on the general outrage that he was at large to rob and kill despite a history of violence going back to his childhood. I can understand people's fury, but this morning I'm more concerned about what I am going to say to Lisa regarding her messing up my ritual – or how I'm even going to raise it with her.

Lisa looks a little puzzled when she finally appears.

'Wow. I wasn't expecting to walk into a heated political discussion at this hour of the morning. You could cut the tension with a knife in there this morning. What's going on? What did you say to cause that?'

'It wasn't me...' I blurt out, before realising that she is only teasing me. 'Actually, it was "Cattle",' I continue calmly, explaining how the right wing versus left wing discussion had begun.

'They have obviously moved on a bit since you left. It's now a full-blown discussion on the security situation.'

'Well, "Cattle" will enjoy that. You know, there's something that bothers me about him.'

'What's that?'

'Well, for a start, he never seems to condemn the terrorists and he's always very ready to put across their side of the story.'

'They do have a side to their story. Don't you believe it is important that we understand the reasons behind what they are...?'

'No, I don't,' I interject vehemently. 'I reckon that their methods — killing innocent people and all that — nullifies their right to any hearing, regardless of the merits of their case.'

Lisa appears a bit taken aback by this. 'I can understand where you are coming from, but I cannot agree with you. Everybody deserves to be heard if they believe they have a case to make.'

'There's something else, too.' I pause for effect. 'About "Cattle".'

'What's that?'

'I'm sure you read the report of the investigation into the bomb that went off in Mayfair, the one that was thrown in through the window of Scotts Restaurant?'

'Yes, I did. One person was killed, I think.'

'Yes, and about fifteen others were hurt. Well,' and I pause here again for emphasis, 'it was a carbon copy of the bomb that went off in the Tattatoria Fiori — that's just around the corner from Scotts — almost two weeks previously.'

'So?'

'So, in each case — and here's the thing — a ginger-haired man was seen running away from the scene.'

'So?' she laughs.

'So, the police say they are hunting for the Ginger Bomber. And "Cattle" has ginger hair.'

Lisa puts one hand on my shoulder to steady herself as she tries to contain the laughter: 'You cannot go around accusing people of being terrorists just because they have ginger hair.'

'It's not just his ginger hair,' I exclaim irritably. 'It's all that rebel music he plays. And his politics.'

'What do you know of his politics?' Lisa asks incredulously. She stops, hands on hips.

'I know he's left wing, for a start,' I state defiantly. 'And he didn't seem to have much sympathy for the dead and injured in Scotts. He said it was a place for "political toffs" like Rockefeller and Lord Mountbatten.'

'Okay. Not very nice, I grant you but hardly conclusive evidence that he's a terrorist bomber.'

We resume walking.

'So what do you suggest we do?' I ask sardonically.

'I'm not suggesting we do anything. Correction: I am suggesting that we — and by this I mean you — do absolutely nothing. Go home. Forget about it. Concentrate on the game today.'

I say nothing.

'Who are your opponents today, anyway?' she asks eventually.

'Oh. Ah, Burnley,' I reply disinterestedly.

'Are they any good?'

'Not really. Not this season, anyway. They're down near the bottom of the league. And their star player — Leighton James — has been dropped because he asked for a transfer. I hear that Derby are interested in him.'

'No problem, then?' She smiles.

'Shouldn't be. But then, you can never take anything for granted. Like last Saturday week. What happened to you? You didn't show up at The Cabin.'

Lisa appears taken aback again and suddenly adopts that defensive air that I'm beginning to recognise.

'Nothing '"happened to me" as you so inelegantly put it. And since when did I become some kind of permanent fixture in your calendar?'

'Sorry, I didn't mean it like that,' I lie. 'We dropped a point at home, that's all.'

'Well, that's a pity. But if you must know, I was taking my first tennis lesson that morning.'

I know nothing about tennis, so it's not a conversation I can pursue. All I can think of to ask is, 'Is Saturday going to be tennis lesson day, then?'

'There you go again,' she exclaims in exasperation. 'As it happens, it's not, but I don't see that it's any of your business.'

We walk on up Park Road towards Beane Row in silence, both probably hoping for a distraction that will enable us to change the subject.

A few hundred yards up ahead, there is a new white van outside the Butlers' house. The only remarkable thing about this is that the van is new. Because there's always a white van parked outside chez Butler. Usually it's the same white van, the one with the big scratch on the front wheel arch that reveals that the van was not always white. Sometimes it's the same white van with the scratch on the wheel arch but with different number plates. To describe this van as new is also a bit fanciful, as it is only new in the sense that it is new to the Butler boys. But at least it looks clean, is neatly parked and doesn't appear to be laden down in the rear by the weight of god-knows-what cargo. The two boys are carrying what looks like a heavy roll of carpet out to the van. I don't get the opportunity to congratulate them on their new acquisition as they have already scurried back into the house by the time we pass. They mustn't have seen us approaching, as normally they would have stopped to chat with me regarding today's game.

'Can I ask you something?' Lisa suddenly stops.

'Ask away,' I say, stop and turn to face her.

'Why do you call him "Cattle"? Mick's son. Why do you call him "Cattle"?'

'Everybody calls him "Cattle".'

'I know,' she says impatiently, 'I suppose that's my question. Why does everybody call him "Cattle"?'

'Dunno. He's always been called "Cattle" as long as I've known him.'

'But his name is pronounced "Cauhal"; the "t" is silent.'

'What?'

'His name is spelt C.A.T.H.A.L. but the "t" is silent so it's pronounced "Cauhal".'

'Bloody hell! I never knew that. And to think that all these years I thought...'

'You thought it was a nickname; a derogatory term; an insult.'

'Yes, I did. Everybody did. You only have to look at him. How scruffy he is. And his kids too. You've seen them...'

'Ah, yes. The kids. The so-called "herd of Cattle". Well, you'll have to find another collective noun for them from now on. The "herd" of Cauhal doesn't have quite the same ring to it, does it?'

I'm stunned into silence. Everybody does call him 'Cattle'. To his face too. He never seems to mind very much, but then that's obviously because he believed all along they were simply mispronouncing his real name out of genuine ignorance and that didn't bother him. Not much, anyway. To him there was no insult in it. The insult was the sly way it was used behind his back. Unbeknownst to him. The way it was twisted to become a dig at him. And then as a putdown way of referring to his kids.

'How do you know all this?' I ask.

'That everybody calls him "Cattle"? Well, as you say, they call him that to his face. I hear it any time he is helping out in the shop. But I've heard the muttered asides too; the sly jokes regarding his appearance and the references to his beautiful children. So, one day, I asked Mick what his son's name is and he spelled it out for me and told me the correct pronunciation.'

'Bloody hell!' I feel really stupid and annoyed with myself. 'What should I do now?'

'You can continue to call him "Cattle", if you like,' she says helpfully, 'I don't believe he minds very much. But please, please do not use it to insult him behind his back or use it in reference to his children,' she pleads. 'Alternatively, you can start pronouncing his name correctly when you next bump into him in The Cabin.'

'But he's in the shop so rarely,' I protest. 'By the time I bump into him again, I'll have forgotten the correct pronunciation. What is it? Cayhill?'

'Cauhal. You won't forget it. I know you won't.'

By the time we arrive at the Butlers', the two boys are out again fussing around the van, polishing the wing mirrors with their sleeves.

'Wotcha,' they cry in unison as we approach.

'Good morning, boys,' Lisa greets them warmly. I reckon she does this to piss me off. I mean, they're nice lads and I've known them for a long time, but they represent everything that I reckon Lisa detests in people. They are largely uneducated, foul mouthed most of the time, dress like a couple of cheap villains and have no visible means of support. Okay, so I find them funny some of the time but, judging by everything that I know about Lisa from our conversations to date, these are definitely not the kind of people whose company she would crave.

'Wotcha, cock,' Jacko says, grabbing me around the shoulders. I wince and stare at him as if to indicate that he shouldn't use such language in Lisa's company. But Lisa just lets out one of her short little murmured laughs.

I'm on the back foot again. So I try to recover and change the conversation.

'Nice van,' I observe. Then I allow one of those pauses I've learned from Lisa before adding, 'Yours, is it?'

I sense an immediate change in the atmosphere and a sudden shuffling of feet. Jacko says 'No' at the exact moment that Billy says 'Yes', but Jacko recovers quickly:

'Wot Billy means is that we're road testing it wiv a view to acquiring it.'

'So you're thinking of buying it, then?'

'Yes,' says Billy at the very same moment that Jacko says, 'No, we're thinking of acquiring it.'

'I don't understand,' I say, hoping to embarrass them a little further.

'No, ya don't, mate,' Jacko says and fixes me with one of his trademark stares.

There's a few seconds of awkward silence and I can see Lisa's eyes darting from Jacko to me and back again. 'How is your dog?' she asks finally. She is trying to sound upbeat but there's an unmistakable apprehension in her voice.

'Gone,' Jacko replies without ever taking his eyes off me.

'Oh no,' Lisa exclaims, sympathetically.

'S'true,' Billy adds.

This gives me the opportunity to look over at Billy (I know I'm never going to outstare Jacko): 'Not again?' I ask.

'E's really gone this time,' sighs Billy.

Jacko sniffs loudly and the tension abates a little.

'When?' I ask, relieved that we seem to be leaving the delicate issue of the van and its provenance behind.

'That day 'e shat in Echo's garden. We never caught up wiv 'im,' Jacko replies curtly and strides purposefully away, terminating the discussion. We all follow him, away from the van and towards Eddie's place.

Eddie is standing knee-deep in a freshly dug trench near the house. He is red-faced and sweating profusely. He doesn't see us at first.

'Hello,' Lisa calls out to him.

'Halo, halo,' replies Eddie. He steps up out of the trench, mops his brow with a grimy towel and comes to the gate. He seems surprised to see us. Perhaps he was not expecting all of us to be walking together.

'Nice day,' I add, politely.

'Nice day, nice day, heh, heh.'

'Wotcha, cock,' shouts Jacko cheerfully.

'Watch the clock, yes; watch the clock, heh, heh,' Eddie responds, beaming.

Jacko gives Billy a knowing glance: 'Hark at 'im Billy, watching the clock, indeed. He does look a bit tired, tho',' he whispers quietly out of the side of his mouth, then:

'Late last night, woz you, Eddie?' he asks at the top of his voice.

'Laid last night, was laid last night, yes, heh, heh,' Eddie responds innocently.

This causes convulsions of laughter from the two boys, followed by high fives, much knee-slapping and coughing. I cannot stop myself from laughing either but I try to hide it from Eddie by turning away as if to continue home. The others follow my lead.

'Boys, please,' whispers Lisa imploringly to the two brothers, before turning to glare at me. But the boys cannot restrain themselves from keeping the thing going as we walk up the short distance to the intersection with Forest Hill Road and Wellesley Gardens.

'Did ya know, Lis', that Eddie keeps a parrot?' Billy splutters to get the words out.

'No, I didn't know that, William,' Lisa replies, keeping a straight face.

'S'true,' affirms Jacko, joining in. 'You knew that, dint ya,' he asks, suddenly turning to me.

'No,' I reply curtly. I'm fast becoming hacked off by all this 'Lis' and 'William' stuff. 'I didn't know that.'

'Well, s'true as I'm standin' 'ere. A few weeks ago — nice sunny evenin' it woz too — me and Billy is comin' 'ome after that Rangers and Man U game. Few bevies and a Ruby, ya know the usual. And Eddie? He's in the garden wiv the front door open. So we shouts "Come on you RRRs" to 'im. An' Eddie shouts back, "Come on you Arse, Come on you Arse". And then, very faintly from the kitchen we hear the fackin' parrot squawking, "Come on you Arse, Come on you Arse," and 'e kept at it until we woz out of fackin' earshot: 'Come on you Arse, Come on you Arse,' all the way down the fackin' street. Right, Billy?'

'Right on, Jacko,' parrots Billy.

The knee-slapping, coughing and wheezing now reaches fever pitch as the boys are almost bent double by the sharpness of their wit. And I have to confess that I join in, although not quite with the same gusto.

'Boys, that's plainly not true. I've never heard Eddie make any mention of a parrot. And you shouldn't continue to poke fun at him,' Lisa admonishes them sternly, adding another glare in my direction. We arrive at the fork in the road and say our rather strained goodbyes to Lisa, before she veers left, heading along the Glade and up Forest Hill Road towards Hazel Wood.

I continue on my way with Jacko and Billy tagging along as if shepherding me as far away from the white van as possible. The truth is that I had heard about Eddie's alleged parrot some time ago — from the boys themselves. Nobody but the Butler boys has ever heard the parrot (assuming it actually exists at all) but listening out for it has introduced an element of additional intrigue to the casual early morning greeting.

'Why did she throw me that glare?' I ask eventually. 'All she gives you guys is a gentle bollocking.'

'Look, mate,' explains Jacko, sympathetically. 'It's 'cos she expects_more from you. She knows we're a couple of wide boys. Right, Billy?'

'Wide on, Jacko,' smirks Billy, chewing on some gum.

And with that, the brothers suddenly remember that they need to get back to the van.

The spring has returned to my step. She expects more from me. That's nice to hear. But what exactly does she expect? More of what? In what way? Suddenly, I realise that I have never actually given Lisa anything. But what would I give her? Chances are I'd pick the wrong thing and risk upsetting her again. Then suddenly it hits me. That book! The poetry book by...bollocks, what was he called.? German. No, Swiss. Switzer? No. Albert?

ALBRECHT!! That was it. Timothy Albrecht. Don't remember what it was called but she did say he only ever published one book, so that should be easy. Sorted!

I sprint the last few yards home. Right. Now I'm ready for Burnley this afternoon. Okay, we haven't had a great record against them in recent years. I think of the last three times we have played them – and lost on each occasion: 0–1 at Turf Moor back in October, 0–1 at Loftus Road last season and a 0–3 thrashing away from home earlier that season. But today? Today I'm feeling confident.

Saturday, 22 November 1975: 4.40 p.m.
Queens Park Rangers…1 Burnley…0

10. DONS AND DOSSIERS

Saturday, 24 April 1976: 10 minutes gone

Leeds are on the attack again: Harris to McKenzie to Eddie Gray. But Don Masson intercepts and breaks it up with a robust tackle on Gray, makes time and space for himself and lays the ball off beautifully to Don Givens. The tackle was fair but Leeds fans howl for a foul and Leeds Manager Jimmy Armfield is immediately up off the bench, arms wide in protest.

Don is being watched today by Scotland Manager Willie Ormond and there is talk that he may get a late call-up for Scotland's forthcoming home internationals. So the last thing Don needs is to be cautioned or sent off. Still, this has not diminished his commitment to the tackle or to winning the ball back.

Don was another shrewd signing by The Gaffer from lowly Notts County – even at 29 years of age, he was a bargain at £100,000. He's a strong-tackling but highly creative midfield player and a great passer of the ball. He's at his best when commanding the centre of the park, bossing the team around, protecting the ball, organising the plays and generally dictating the pace of the game.

The other Don – Givens – was signed from Luton Town three years ago for £40,000. He was an immediate success, scoring over twenty goals in his first season to help QPR win promotion to the First Division. Originally on the books of Manchester United, Don is an outstanding central striker although he is playing a little deeper in the team this season. He's been capped seventeen times by the Republic of Ireland, scoring nine goals – four in one game against Turkey last October.

Jimmy Armfield took over as Manager at Leeds United in October 1974 and led them to the European Cup Final in the 1974–75 season where they lost 2–0 to Bayern Munich. The major task he faces now is to rebuild the ageing but still formidable side that Don Revie put together.

It is difficult to think of Leeds without Don Revie – and his famous dossiers – immediately springing to mind. Revie was an enormous success when managing Leeds from humble beginnings in 1961, winning league titles, several cups and European trophies, until 1974 when he left to manage England.

There were many people in football – and in the media – who envied Leeds' success, never giving them full credit for what they had achieved and taking every opportunity to criticise and ridicule the values of the club as represented by Revie. This resulted in something of a shared feeling of victimisation among the Leeds players; a sense of 'Leeds against the world'. When allied to the values of family and togetherness he had cultivated at Leeds, this bunker attitude was probably exploited by Revie to engender a spirit of indomitability among the squad.

Revie, despite being riddled with ritual and superstition, was obsessed with detailed planning and left little to chance.

The genesis of the infamous dossiers was a report that Revie asked one of his assistants, Syd Owen, to prepare on a young player at another club that Revie was interested in signing.

The report that Owen handed to Revie the following week was a revelation. Revie had never before seen such a detailed analysis of a footballer. Owen outlined how good the prospective signing was with each foot, the shooting positions he preferred, the positions he tended to take up when he didn't have the ball, and so on. It occurred to Revie that this type of analysis would be invaluable if applied to the teams that Leeds met each week. And that was how it all started.

From then on, Leeds would have the opponents for the following Saturday watched and analysed. Anything that might be to Leeds' advantage would be noted. The general strengths and weaknesses of the opposition would be highlighted as well as player-specific issues – if the goalkeeper was indecisive in dealing with crosses or if one of the centre-backs was weak on his left side.

The report would be handed in on the Monday morning and Revie and the Leeds coaching staff would spend the rest of the week working on it with the players. They would hold practice games in which the Leeds reserve players played in the same style as the opposing team in question. The first team would be given the task of stymieing the 'opposition's' attacking tactics and of breaking down their defensive system. For example, if the 'opposition' were not well organised in defence, the Leeds first team would practise decoy runs designed to pull their defenders forward so that balls could be played over their heads.

Leeds' legendary dossiers eventually became both notorious and ridiculed. Some sections of the media and rival teams became obsessed by Revie's dossiers and believed there was some secret formula involved in Leeds' match preparations, but it's obvious now that there was nothing sinister in them. They were simply part of the detailed, decisive preparations of a very professional – and highly successful – manager.

Dossiers are unlikely to be much in evidence in the Leeds dressing room today. The current incumbent, the avuncular Jimmy Armfield, is reputedly less decisive; prompting one member of the current Leeds squad to reportedly comment after a meeting with Armfield: 'That's it. Jimmy's indecision is final.'

Saturday, 29 November 1975: 8.35 a.m.

It's a bright sunny morning, but my mood is anything but. I think it's the prospect of running into Brad or Lisa, or both, without having resolved this trefull/trifle thing. I tried the thesaurus that Noah gave me but it only made me more depressed. Nothing at all for 'trefull', but for 'trifle' it had things like:

   'physical object'

'sweet'

'piddle'

'wanton'

'to play or toy with something'

The book was supposed to put my mind at ease. Instead it has started me thinking in a certain way. And not a way that I wanted to be thinking about Lisa. Especially not Lisa and Brad. I need to get this thing sorted but I'm not sure how without losing my temper (with Brad) and perhaps giving the wrong impression (to Lisa).

'What's in the basket today?' I ask Marianne Pleass, a little tetchily. 'Anything unusual?'

Marianne dips her hand into the basket and rummages around under a multi-coloured scarf.

'Would you like something to eat?' she enquires, pleasantly.

'No thank you, I've just had breakfast.'

'It's a ToblerOne,' she announces, holding up the bar and then opening the wrapper. She pronounces it 'Tobler 1', so it takes me a second or two to work out that she is offering me a piece of chocolate.

(Blimey, here we go again.) 'Thank you, but no. Watching my weight. Keeping fit and all that.'

'Don't you like Tobler 1? It's got honey and almond nougat in it,' she reads from the wrapper.

'Does it?'

'Yes. It's Swiss, you know.' She breaks off a piece and pops it into her mouth.

Bloody hell, I think, more Swiss. First Switzer, then Albrecht and now Tobler, but 'Really?' is all I can think of saying by way of response.

'Hmmm,' she chomps, holding up the remainder of the bar, 'that's why it's triangular.'

I'm still trying to fathom this non sequitur when she adds, through a mouthful of chocolate: 'Its triangular shape was inspired by the Matterhorn. In the Swiss Alps.'

'Right.' I have visions of this conversation graduating onto cuckoo clocks, so I try to wrap it up: 'You see a lot of them on sale in airport Duty Free shops.'

'Marjorie doesn't like them,' she continues matter-of-factly. 'She complains that the pointy bit hurts the roof of her mouth.'

I turn and glance up, half expecting to see Marjorie standing at the bay window with two pieces of Toblerone sticking out of her mouth, like fangs, and some chocolate dribbling blood-like down her chin. But Marjorie is just sitting there with a triangle of toast in one hand while she shades her eyes with the other; which is odd, really, because the sun is shining in the opposite direction.

'There's a bear hiding in there — on the wrapper — if you can find it,' Marianne says drolly, handing me the familiar yellow wrapper.

I take the wrapper from her, giving it only a cursory glance because I notice that a very concerned-looking Marjorie has suddenly stood up, and is now gaping down at me from the *window, her mouth a melange of marmalade and toast crumbs. I hand the wrapper back to Marianne with a mumbled 'Sorry, cant't find the bear' and I'm relieved to see that Marjorie has sat down again. Marianne then takes great pride in pointing out to me how the bear forms part of the snow lying on the Matterhorn on the pack illustration.*

'You should share that secret with Marjorie,' I suggest, but Marianne simply 'harrumphs', shakes her head negatively, throws the empty wrapper in the basket of the bicycle and pedals off towards near-certain death. I decide that I really cannot face looking up at the bay window again and I move on quickly.

As I pass Aunt Sally's gate, I notice Tojo puffing on an untipped cigarette, arms half- folded, while sitting against the bonnet of his Renault Reliant. I haven't seen him do this before. He has the guilty demeanour of a schoolboy smoking out of sight of the headmaster, but he looks relaxed enough to suggest he knows he won't be caught. I give him a thumbs-up as I pass. He coughs raspily and waves smoke in my direction in reply as I cross to the other side.

Eddie is sporting a battered red baseball cap to keep the morning sun out of his eyes. He is whistling tunelessly, intent on whatever tidying up he is doing in the garden, but he stops when he sees me passing.

'Morning, Eddie. I thought that was birdsong I was hearing there for a minute.'

'Burt Zong? Who is Burt Zong?'

'Bird song,' I say, slowly emphasising each word. 'You know, thrushes, robins, sparrows.'

'Ah. Like canaries, heh, heh,' Eddie is delighted with his powers of deduction.

'Yeah, like canaries,' I confirm. 'Or parrots.' I toss this into the avian mix to see if I get a reaction.

Nothing. I knew those Butlers were spoofing me last Saturday. Unless, of course, parrots are called something else where Eddie comes from. I decide not to probe further. Instead, we briefly discuss today's game. Eddie says he reckons QPR will easily beat 'Stuck City'. I tell him that I reckon it could be a close game. We conclude our conversation without any further linguistic difficulties and I decide to move on. As I turn the corner and walk the last lap towards the shops, I hear what sounds like 'Land of Hope and Glory' whistling through the air. But I could have been mistaken.

'Good morning, Mr Berrie,' I cough, politely, as I enter the musty shop.

'Good mornington to you, young man.' Somehow, I don't mind being called 'young man' by Noah Berrie. 'How are things with you today? How are you getting on with the thesaurus. I see you are not returning it, so perhaps I have made a sale?'

I'm not going to argue with Noah, so I settle up with him even though the book did not solve my problem, but it suddenly occurs to me that a book could still be part of a solution to things.

'Any old books in stock these days, Mr Berrie?' I enquire, getting straight to the point. 'I know you used to keep a few.'

'Call me Noah,' he insists. 'Call me Noah. Old books are my business. Come out back,' he beckons, adjusting his spectacles and pushing those tufts of snow white hair back behind his ears. 'To be frank, I don't really have much demand for old books these days. But come on in anyway and we'll have a little search.'

He guides me through the shop into the back to a little anteroom and switches on the light. There are floor-to-ceiling shelves containing pictures, framed and loose photographs, lots of bric-a-brac and some books. The room smells of the past, which makes me momentarily dizzy for some reason.

'Are you looking for something in particular, or just shelf-shopping?' he asks, peering at me over the top of his spectacles.

'I'm interested in anything you have by Timothy Albrecht,' I reply, hoping I sound comfortable pronouncing the name. 'There was just the one book by him, I reckon; a hardback and a paperback version. It's out of print now.'

'Hmmm, that's interesting,' he comments without turning around. He is running his index finger along the book spines searching the authors' names. 'Because that's the second enquiry I've had this week apropos Timothy Albrecht.' Then he turns round to face me, and with a quizzical smile asks: 'Why is this Timothy Albrecht suddenly back in vogue, do you think?'

'I've...no...idea,' I stammer.

'What kind of stuff did he write?'

'Ahm, poetry, mostly. He's a Beat poet. Was. Was...a Beat poet.'

'Oh. Like Ginsberg?' Noah brightens up. Then, seeing the blank look on my face: 'Allen Ginsberg?'

'I suppose so,' I say, distractedly. Then, as casually as I can, I ask, 'Who else...was, you know...asking about it?'

'Can't really remember who it was.' He is stoking his little grey goatee beard with his thumb and index finger in mock concentration, while barely concealing a wry smile.

'Well, was it a female or male?' I ask.

'Female, I think,' then after a pause: 'No, male. Yes, definitely male.'

'Which?' I ask impatiently.

'Male. Definitely male,' he confirms. 'A young man.'

'Young man?'

'Yes. A young man. Studenty type.'

'Studenty type?'

'Yes. Studenty type. Or maybe a teacher.'

'Teacher?'

'Yes. A teacher. And why do you keep repeating everything I say?' he asks, not unkindly.

I ignore his question. 'Did you have one in stock? A Timothy Albrecht?'

'Unfortunately not,' he sighs. 'But he did ask me to keep one for him if it ever turned up. Look, I have it on my list of books to look out for.' He holds up a tiny pad, spiral bound at the top, dog-eared and covered in scribbled notes.

'And what did you say?'

'I told him the same thing I'm going to tell you,' he replies, smiling.

'Which is?'

'That I promised the woman who was in here some weeks ago first call on any Timothy Albrecht books that cross my path.'

'Woman?'

'Yes. That very attractive young woman I've seen you talking to from time to time.'

'What attractive young woman?' I ask inanely.

'The one that my young Bradley has had his eye on ever since she first walked into Threads. Did you know he has actually asked her to do some modelling for him, for a flyer he's doing for the boutique?'

'No, I didn't know that. Is she doing it? The modelling?'

'Why don't you ask her yourself, young man?' he asks, straightening up, hands on hips and grimacing slightly. 'Backache. Lumbago, probably.'

I nod sympathetically and turn to go.

'I saw her heading into The Cabin just before you happened by.'

'Makes no difference to me,' I mumble unconvincingly and shuffle off towards The Cabin.

'Kol tov,' he calls after me.

Cathal is working behind the counter this morning and there's a bit of tension in the air. The main topic of conversation among the queueing customers is the murder of Ross McWhirter, shot dead by the IRA last Thursday. McWhirter, a co-founder of the Guinness Book of Records, had offered reward money to encourage people to inform on the IRA, and the speculation is that this is the reason behind his murder. He was shot at close range in the head and chest outside his home in North London and died soon after being admitted to hospital. The Mirror has a front-page headline:

DEATH LIST OF THE DOORSTEP KILLERS

above a story that suggests McWhirter may be the first of many on a death list drawn up by the IRA as part of a vicious new assassination plan.

Bradley Berrie is just ahead of me in the queue and with him, to my disappointment, is Lisa. His 'trifle' comment about Lisa a couple of weeks ago — or rather, the fact that I didn't understand what the hell he was talking about — still bothers me whenever it comes to mind and seeing him here this morning, particularly with Lisa, makes me feel sick to the stomach. I don't really understand why. Maybe it's because, deep down, I suspect it wasn't a compliment; more a slur on her character. Or maybe it implied a degree of intimacy between the two of them that...that what exactly? That I would prefer didn't exist? That I didn't expect? But then, I'm not entitled to expect anything, am I? Then again, maybe, it's because it was Brad who said it and it would be okay if it was somebody else. But I know deep down that it would still bother me. But then again, why should it? The more I try to work it out, the more confused I feel. Then I start to feel queasy and I think about turning round and *walking out. But Lisa turns, catches my eye and smiles and I know I'm trapped. I manage a croaky, almost whispered hello, hoping not to draw Brad's attention. He sees me alright, but ignores me. Which actually makes me feel worse. Like a nobody. He's dressed in his trendy-boutique-owner clothes today and expounding loudly and at length to all and sundry concerning the security situation. He boasts that, through his contacts in the Conservative party, he is aware that the IRA has drawn up a 'death list' of prominent public figures who have spoken out against them. He has it on very good authority that we are about to experience 'new peaks of horror'. He believes we should 'reintroduce the death penalty for Irish terrorists' and he goes on about the fecklessness of the Irish in general.*

Although a Londoner by birth, Cathal regards himself as Irish, which is why most customers treat him with a degree of circumspection when it comes to the vexed issue of Irish politics. Bradley, who has never made any secret of his disdain for Cathal, is obviously taking the opportunity presented by the Ross McWhirter tragedy to embarrass him. So far, Cathal has resisted the temptation to respond or become involved, but he is not the sort of bloke to let any aspersion go unanswered, so as Bradley nears the counter, you can feel the tension begin to rise. I can see Lisa whispering to him. Hopefully she will distract him, and she appears to succeed somewhat. But just as they reach the counter, Cathal stoops low to rummage for something on a lower shelf and then appears to spend an inordinate amount of time searching for it. Bradley leans forward impatiently and addresses Cathal's posterior.

'I say, "Cattle". I'm here for my NME,' he states pompously.

Cathal rises slowly and deliberately, then he stands facing Bradley with both palms on the counter.

'Your wha?' Cathal is pretending that he doesn't know who Bradley is, but appears genuinely confused regarding the request.

'My NME,' booms Bradley.

'Sorry...' Cathal raises his hands to both temples and furiously scratches his long, straggly strands of ginger hair.

'My EN. EM. EE. "Cattle". Are you a little hard of hearing?'

'Pardon?' Cathal winks at Lisa. 'No, don't think so. But are you sure you're in the right place?'

'I'm damn certain I'm in the right place. I get one here every week.'

Cathal shrugs and raises his right hand. 'Hang on a minute.' Then, without warning, he bellows, 'Da!'

Most of the customers cover their ears. But no answer comes from below. Cathal tries again.

'Da!'

'Yes. What is it?' Mick's wheezy voice floats up from the basement.

'There's a guy here looking for an enema. Insists he gets one here every week.'

'No, no, the EN. EM. EE. You stupid man. I have it on order, weekly.'

'Sorry?'

'The New Musical Express — NME — it's a weekly music newspaper.'

'Aaah. The NME. Sorry.' Then: 'Daaaa!'

'Yes, yes, what is it now?'

'Where do you keep the Enem...the Enem...the Enemeeee?' Cathal suddenly breaks into convulsions of laughter. There are a few barely stifled giggles from some customers in the queue too but not, I notice, from Lisa.

Muffled instructions emanate from below amid the soft thuds of cardboard boxes being thrown around. Cathal seems to comprehend the instructions, sources the NME, composes himself and then apologises, but without any real sincerity.

'Sorry about that. Couldn't resist it. Here's your NME — I'm actually a Sounds man myself.'

Brad ignores him, but instead of paying and moving on, he immediately opens the paper at the listings page. Lisa looks over his shoulder and there's a bit of whispering and pointing.

'So what's it to be this weekend, then?' enquires Cathal sarcastically, nodding at the listings page: 'Rory Gallagher at the Marquee Club in Soho? Queen at the Rainbow? — you'd enjoy that, I reckon. Maybe a blast of the Bay City Rollers? Or Shirley Collins — she's playing tonight in the Royal Oak Folk Club, New Malden?'

'Actually, I'm giving tennis lessons today...' announces Brad, haughtily.

I immediately shoot a glance over at Lisa, but she doesn't return my gaze. I feel sick.

Mick has stumbled up the rickety stairs at this stage, and arrives at the counter covered in a light sprinkling of dust, just in time to hear Brad continue:

'...and I'm also planning to do a little fox-hunting this weekend,' he boasts.

'Ah. Are you?' says Mick, feigning interest. 'Fox-hunting, indeed; "the unspeakable in pursuit of the uneatable", isn't that what Wilde said?'

'Who?'

'Oscar Wilde, Bradley,' Lisa chips in. 'The writer and poet.' Then she gently chides him with what, in time, was to prove a prescient observation: 'Bradley, I would have surmised that you of all people would be very familiar with the work and life of Oscar Wilde.'

'Yes, of course, Lisa. Wilde. Oscar Wilde. I just didn't catch what "Cattle" said.'

'A bit hard of hearing this morning, are we?' asks Cathal icely. 'A bit Mutt and Jeff?'

But Bradley has had enough at this stage. He folds his music paper, smacks his knee with it and storms out. Lisa hurriedly follows him out but avoids eye contact with me as she leaves.

Mick has that amused expression on his face that I've seen whenever a couple of cheeky kids come into the shop arguing over what sweets to buy.

'What spooked the bold Bradley, I wonder?' he asks of nobody in particular. 'What did you say to him?' he demands, turning to Cathal.

'Nothing...much. I don't really remember.'

'Well, off with you, then, down that stairs. Finish the work and don't be upsetting the customers.'

Cathal smirks; then, in vain, he scans the queue for some indication that his achievement in embarrassing Bradley was appreciated. Sniffing and muttering under his breath he stomps loudly down the rickety, bare, wooden stairs to the basement.

'I reckon he must have the Irish Alzheimer's,' says Mick, addressing the queue, 'he forgets everything except the grudges.' It's obvious that Mick retains his fatherly love for Cathal but no longer has any influence over him.

'I think that's being a bit hard on him,' barks an old dear immediately in front of me, wearing horsey-set clothes, two odd socks and the odour of yesterday's garden.

'Well, you know what they say,' says Mick 'the Irish are a fair people – we never speak well of one another.'

The old harridan cackles loudly, gathers up her Daily Telegraph and Horse & Hound magazine – which she refers to as 'my Nag and Dog' – turns and elbows her way sharply past me. She turns briefly as if she recognises me and is on the point of saying something, mutters something to herself instead and waddles out.

I turn back to Mick. He has that painted smile on his face which usually means he is busy but too polite to hurry a conversation with a customer. I ask him about Trouty. Mick shrugs and smiles as if to say, 'What can I tell you? Nothing.'

'You don't seem too bothered by his continued absence,' I counter.

'Let me put it this way, Dawhee me bucko. I feel the same way about Mr Trout as the Burnley players probably feel about Leighton James: not sorry to see him go!'

We have a very brief conversation about the fact that Leighton James was finally transferred from Burnley to Derby yesterday, for a near record fee of £310,000, and an even shorter discussion about the game today. Mick appears distracted and seems to want to get back to the 'stocktaking' downstairs. I take the hint.

Lisa is waiting outside. There's no sign of Brad. I know that this is my big opportunity to try to bring up the 'trifle' thing, but I haven't really planned on how to do it. Without looking and sounding like a prat.

'I wasn't expecting to see you today,' she opens, cheerfully.

I keep walking. 'Obviously not,' I reply curtly, 'but why not?'

She falls into step. 'Well, it's only been a week since we last ran into each other.'

'And?' I don't really intend to sound so abrupt, but this thing is nagging at me so much I just can't subdue my natural instinct – which is to sulk.

'Well, isn't it every two weeks? You know, a 'home game' – or whatever you call it.' We've crossed over at the Green and we turn up Park Road.

'Yeah, usually. But not always. Sometimes it can be just a week between home games on Saturdays; sometimes up to three weeks.'

'That must be confusing.'

'Not really.'

Sensing that this conversation is going nowhere, she quickly changes tack.

'And how are you feeling today?' she asks brightly.

'I was confident enough yesterday,' I reply. 'But today, I dunno. Gerry Francis will be missing with that hip injury. John Beck is a good replacement but John hasn't played this season, although he's been on the bench twice. Don Givens is missing too, so Mick Leach will deputise for him. And we have young Phil Nutt on the bench to give us cover in defence, but he's not really been tested at this level...'

'I meant, how are you feeling generally? I thought you looked a bit down in the dumps.' She looks genuinely concerned. 'And are we only going to talk football again?' she asks, obviously unable to fully appreciate the difficulties we face today.

This is my opportunity. And I make a hash of it.

'Not necessarily,' I say. 'Is there something important that you want to talk about?' I respond matter-of-factly.

'Well, don't you want to ask me how my week went?' I know by her tone that she has something to tell me that has excited her, but is unlikely to be of much interest to me.

'Okay, how was your week?'

'Mostly pretty ordinary, since you ask...'

'I see. So what's...'

'But you'll never guess who I met on Thursday,' she exclaims teasingly.

'No. I don't reckon I will ever guess who you met on Thursday,' I say, sounding more sarcastic than I would like.

'Flick Colby,' she declares with a triumphant air.

I 'huh' through my nose: 'Let me guess: a dancer.'

'Dancer, choreographer...and founder of...Paaaa-n's People!' she announces, in that 'tar-ah' way, again. 'Now, do I detect a — pardon the pun — a flicker of interest in that football-only brain of yours?'

'Which one of Pan's People is she? Is she the one with the...'

'No, that's Dee-Dee Wilde,' she interrupts, giving me a pitying look. 'Flick doesn't actually dance in Pan's People these days.'

'How did you meet her?' I try to sound interested, if not enthusiastic.

'Oh, she popped round to see us at practice.'

'Did any of the others come with her?'

'No. Well, Dee Dee, Ruth and Babs are rumoured to be leaving Pan's People at the end of the year. Too old at 29, it seems. So don't you want to know why Flick Colby came to see us practise?'

'Checking out possible new recruits, I suppose,' I say off-handedly.

'Spot on, my footballing friend,' she wags her finger at me twice for added emphasis, 'and who do you think she took a particular interest in?'

I say nothing but I'm sure I know what's coming.

'Yes! Youuu-rs truly,' she announces, in that 'tar-ah' fashion again.

'But you wouldn't consider it, would you?' I ask incredulously.

'Why not? Wouldn't you like to see me strutting my stuff on Top of the Pops?'

'I'm just surprised that you would even consider it. It's hardly real dancing, is it? It's just a lot of suggestive wriggling and jumping around.'

'Let's ask the boys, shall we? Let's hear what they think.'

The Butlers are coming out the gate as we arrive. Good for my ritual, but perhaps not ideal given the subject matter.

'Pan's Pimples? Never 'eard of 'em,' says Jacko with a straight face after Lisa has repeated her story, complete with all the sound effects and her dramatic gestures. 'Wot 'bout you, Billy?'

But Billy is lost for words and stares open-mouthed at Lisa. He doesn't have to say anything; the expression on his mug says it all. It's obvious that he spends every Thursday evening perched in front of the telly ogling the scantily-clad Pan's People while they slowly gyrate to Art Garfunkel's 'I Only Have Eyes for You', or whatever, on Top of the Pops. The notion that soon he might soon actually know one of them personally has him in a near-catatonic state.

'Ah, never mind 'im,' Jacko advises. 'Billy's not feelin' 'imself today.' Jacko then makes a great play of rushing to steady Billy and putting one arm around him while fanning him with his copy of the Racing Post.

'Maybe we'd better move on,' I suggest.

'Do you think Billy will be alright?' Lisa whispers.

Before I can answer, Jacko asks me if I can hang back and if he can 'have a word'. I tell Lisa that I will catch up with her and she moves off, looking a little confused.

Jacko sits Billy down on the garden wall.

'What's up, Jacko,' I enquire.

'Remember that card game we 'ad 'round at our gaff a couple of weeks back?' Jacko asks, staring at the pavement.

'Yes. I lost heavily. How could I forget?'

'Monday 10th, wozn't it?'

'No, it was a Wednesday, Jacko. Why?'

'I'm sure it woz Monday, mate,' Billy suddenly pipes up from the dead.

'No, Billy, it was Wednesday.'

'Why so positive it wozn't the Monday?' asks Jacko. 'Did ya have a game on Monday 10th?'

'No. We had a game on Tuesday 11th. At home to Newcastle. Fourth round of the Football League Cup. You remember — you were both at the game. Lost 3–1. That's how I remember it. I was hoping my luck would turn on Wednesday round at your place. What's all this about, Jacko?'

'Well, it's like this. It seems that a couple of likely lads did a job on one of the 'ouses up in Hazel Wood on that Monday. They got away with a few bits and pieces but one of the neighbours got a glimpse of 'em as they scarpered and, by a strange coincidence, the descriptions they gave are very similar to yours truly and the bruv here. Total coincidence of course, 'cos we woz playing cards wiv you. But, temporarily, you understand, it's a bit awkward.'

'How's that, Jacko?'

'Well, it's just possible that the Old Bill will come round to check out our alibi and, much as I hate to drag you into it, I may have to give them your name. Sorry, mate.'

'No need to apologise, mate,' I say, acidly. 'That's no problem at all.'

'Good,' he concludes, rubbing his hands. 'That's sorted, then.'

'No problem for me, mate. I wasn't in your house that Monday.'

'Look,' Billy suddenly becomes animated. 'You know the way things are. The Old Bill's got a file — one of those 'dossers' — on Jacko an' me. Any bit of villainy in this here neighbourhood and they reckon it's us wot's behind it. Wot's the big deal? You <u>woz</u> playing cards in our gaff one evenin' that week. Wot's it matter to you if it woz Monday or Wednesday?'

'It will matter to my name and reputation if it ever comes out that I told a porkie to the police.'

'But that's why I need you to do it.' Jacko starts putting on his Mr Reasonable act, 'Your name, your...reputation...'

'Gimme a break, Jacko, that sounds like your solicitor talking. That "Smiley" Cheeseman bloke.'

'Smelly Cheeseman, more like,' Billy mutters, scratching his stubble.

'Okay, okay. But let's leave Nick Cheeseman out of this.' Mr Jacko Reasonable is fast becoming Mr Jacko Desperate. 'Look, I need a favour. We need a favour,' he looks threateningly at Billy then back at me. 'Just this once. 'Ave I ever asked you to do anyfink like this for me before? No. And I'll never ask again. And I'll 'appily return the favour.'

'I can't imagine ever asking you for a favour like this.'

'Look, it may never 'appen,' Jacko starts play it down. 'Likely as not, the Old Bill will nick the real villains in the next day or so and never need to trouble you at all 'bout the alibi. And, anyway, it's not as if I've never, how shall I put it, "covered" for you, is it?'

Sensing that he has touched a raw nerve and that I may be relenting a little, he tries to close the sale. 'Look, me ole' mate, 'ave I ever dropped you in it?'

I cannot resist the open goal: 'Well, there was that watch you sold me last season...'

Billy sniggers but Jacko ignores this reminder of the rusty Rolex. 'Promise to do this one fing for me mate and you can ask me anything.'

'Anything?'

'Me 'ole china, all you gotta do is ask.'

'Okay, Jacko,' I say, dead chuffed with myself for thinking so quickly on my feet. 'Do you have any friends in the book business?'

'The book business. You mean like...'

'No, I don't mean like those boxes of dodgy books I've seen in the back of the van. I mean proper books. I'm interested in a book that is not generally available any more.'

'Not generally available,' he repeats slowly. 'Oh, you mean banned?'

'No, I do not mean banned. I mean out of print. No longer available in reputable bookshops. Do you know anybody in the second-hand book business that might be able to source a book that is out of print and no longer available in bookshops?'

Jacko strokes his chin.

'It's a simple question, Jacko.'

'Wot's the book called?' he asks finally.

'Dunno,' I reply, shaking my head. Billy sniggers and clears his throat.

Jacko raises his eyebrows and affects a phoney laugh:

'Dunno? Gordon Bennett, mate, you aint 'arf making it difficult. I presume ya know who wrote it?' *More sniggering from Billy.*

'A poet called Timothy Albrecht.'

'Albrecht?' *Jacko glances at Billy. This time Billy just shuffles. This is unfamiliar territory for him.*

'Yes.'

'Timothy Albrecht?' *asks Jacko. Billy sniffs.*

'Yes.'

'A poet?'

'Yes. A Beat poet.' *I'm beginning to understand now how Noah Berrie felt earlier this morning.*

'Crikey. Wot's a Beat poet, then?'

'Haven't you ever heard of Ginsberg?'

I pause. Nothing.

'Allen Ginsberg?' *I ask with all the condescending confidence I can muster. It works too, because Jacko suddenly looks a bit sheepish. Billy inspects the pavement. So I push on quickly:* 'Look, I don't have time to go into all that now. All I'm asking is that you ask your friends, contacts — whatever you call them — if they can source a copy of this Timothy Albrecht book for me — new, second-hand, hardback, paperback, whatever.'

But Jacko senses my discomfort in relation to my lack of knowledge regarding the details. And he can't let the opportunity pass without adding to it.

'Albrecht. Jewish, is 'e?' *Jacko smiles across at Billy.* 'Or a Kraut, maybe.' *Billy sniggers again, which is the last straw as far as I'm concerned.*

'I don't f**king know!' *I scream, clenching my fists in fury. An upstairs window opens nearby. Billy starts to look concerned about my intentions towards him.* 'Can you or can you not get it?' *I continue loudly.* 'Do we have a deal or do we not?'

'Calm down, mate.' *Jacko puts a hand on each of my forearms as if to restrain me from beating the crap out of Billy.* 'Course we 'ave a deal. I'll put in one of my special orders to Benny-the-book. Maybe you'd like to meet him first? He operates from just off the Portobello Road. We can nip up there after the game today, if ya like.'

'Look, Jacko. I don't reckon I want to know what one of your special orders is. And I definitely don't want to meet anybody called Benny-the-bleedin'-book.'

'Right, mate. Suit yourself.' *Jacko doesn't take offence at this implied slur on him and one of his mates.* 'We've gotta deal then,' *he extends his hand and I shake it.* 'I'll have a word wiv Benny-the-book and you'll talk to the Old Bill — but only if they ask. Right, Billy?'

'Right on, Jacko,' *replies a slightly chastened Billy.*

And they head back into the house. It's only when I'm running to try to catch up with Lisa that I realise that I forgot to ask Jacko about the missing dog.

I resolve to put the whole conversation with the Butlers out of my mind. But I do wonder what the real story is. It wouldn't surprise me if the two boys were involved in that robbery. But I've got to give them the benefit of the doubt. So why do they need an alibi? It starts to bother me.

There's no sign of Lisa at the intersection. I look up The Glade and beyond to Forest Hill Road but there's no sign of her. Damn. I'm annoyed now that I missed the opportunity to raise that 'trifle' thing with her, but I know deep down I'm not really ready to. Or maybe I'm too scared to find out what it all means. She could at least have waited. It's not as if I was chatting to the Butlers for that long. Maybe she had to meet someone. Or had booked a tennis lesson. With Brad? That would really piss me off. As if I didn't have enough to concern me already, what with the disruption caused to the team by all those injuries. Stoke beat us 0–1 at Loftus Road last season so they could be equally difficult opponents today — especially if Alan Hudson and Jimmy Greenhoff hit form. But we're a better team. On balance, I reckon we'll win. We're on the up again.

I know we are.

Saturday, 29 November 1975: 4.40 p.m.
Queens Park Rangers…3 Stoke City…2

11. SIEGE MENTALITY

Saturday, 24 April 1976: A quarter of an hour gone

A goal has to come. It's only a matter of time. We've had more of the possession but we haven't broken them down. Yet. Against any other side we'd be a goal up by now. Maybe even two. But this Leeds team is resilient. They battle for each other, I'll give them that. Bremner, Hunter and Jordan in particular. And they play on the edge. Some of the tackling is borderline. Not dirty. Not illegal. But definitely on the edge. You have to admire their sense of togetherness, the way they fight for each other. They certainly live up to the 'United' part of their club name. And they have a siege mentality – in more ways than one.

This siege mentality appears to be shared by each and every member of the Leeds United squad. They have it off the field as well as on it. No criticism or slight is left unchallenged. It's as if they feel victimised; unfairly criticised by the opposition; by rival fans – even by the media – who envy their success and how they achieved it. It's like they're in a state of mind where they believe that they're constantly being attacked, persecuted almost; like some kind of threatened minority. It makes them very wary of 'non-Leeds United' people.

Football managers will sometimes deliberately create a siege mentality in the club and among their players by highlighting the hostility that exists towards them from outside the club. Whether the existence of this hostility is imagined, genuine or exaggerated is irrelevant. The fact is that managers will use it to create this siege mentality and a 'circling of the wagons' so that everybody – management, players and fans – are united in standing up for the club, on and off the pitch, come what may.

They say that Leeds' former manager, Don Revie, deliberately fomented this illusion of outside hostility towards the club in order to strengthen the sense of family and togetherness (blood is thicker than water) that he was cultivating at Leeds. I don't believe that. I think that the hostility was real. Partly, it was based on envy – other clubs were simply jealous at what Leeds had achieved. But it also stemmed from a frustration that Leeds were doing it differently, through a combination of pragmatism and ultra-professionalism. The skills were there too, of course – nobody argued with that. But these skills were allied to a kind of ruthlessness that did not always endear Leeds to the opposition or to the watching public. To be fair, Leeds would probably describe it as ruthless efficiency. Either way, you didn't – and you still don't – mess with Leeds United.

Saturday, 13 December 1975: 8.40 a.m.

I hear the dog before I see him. At first, I reckon it's just some neighbour's dog barking at the postman. But then I hear screams coming from Marianne Pleass's front garden. I run towards the entrance of number 21. Through the black wrought-iron gates I see a petrified Marianne using her bicycle as a shield against an emaciated-looking Roxboro Roy, who is blocking her path, pawing the ground and growling. Marianne is calling for Marjorie. It's a pretty futile gesture, as Marjorie is standing inside the house with her back to the window and with both hands covering her ears. I immediately dash up the driveway.

'Here, boy. Come here,' I try to cajole the scrawny hound towards me and away from Marianne. But he doesn't even turn his head. His focus seems to be entirely concentrated on Marianne and her bicycle. I pick up a small pebble from the driveway and chuck it gently at him in an effort to distract him.

No luck.

I move slowly in a wide arc round to Marianne's side and face the brute. Then I notice that there's a bone lying on the gravel, which the wheel of Marianne's bicycle is preventing the dog from getting its teeth into. I lift the bike and the hound moves closer towards us. Marianne screams. I hear banging on a window behind me. Marianne transfers her grip on the bicycle to a vice-like grip on my wrist. I slowly take one step backwards; Marianne takes three steps very rapidly, trips on one of the garden gnomes and falls, pulling me down on top of her into a holly bush. The dog grabs the bone, turns and makes off down the driveway and out the gate. The pounding on the window becomes incessant.

I disentangle myself awkwardly from Marianne and we both stand there blushing and brushing the dust off our clothes. We've both suffered light scratches, but Marianne has a deep cut on her right knee. Stooping with difficulty, she rifles through the spilled contents of the basket, and extracts, of all things, a pack of sticking plasters.

'You should go inside and clean that cut first,' I suggest, wondering at the same time what else she keeps in the basket of that bicycle.

She rebuffs my suggestion with a dismissive wave of her hand and starts to peel open the pack, but a low growl from the gate convinces her that she had better go inside.

'We're prisoners. In our own home,' she wails as she limps towards the steps leading up to the side door of the house. 'Imprisoned. By that...that...creature.'

For a split second, I consider passing some comment on her sister Marjorie's self-imposed imprisonment in the house due to 'her nerves', but my thoughts are interrupted at that moment by the hound letting out a contemptuous growl as if responding to Marianne's insult. The large front window pane, miraculously still intact, now reverberates to a slower rhythm as Marjorie, slumped exhausted against the chaise longue and blithely resigned to accepting whatever fate is about to befall her, beats out an irregular tattoo like a dying heartbeat with her fist.

I head towards the growler at the gate, determined (but unsure how) to capture the hound and return it to the Butler boys. But I needn't have worried; Tojo, having been disturbed by the commotion, has arrived during the stand-off and now appears to have the matter in hand. He has a short stick that he is pointing directly at the hound's head and barking (I can think of no other description of it) something in what I assume is Japanese. The hound cowers sufficiently for Tojo to place some garden twine around its collar and bring it under *control. A few onlookers give a half-hearted cheer and there's a bit of desultory applause as Tojo hands the makeshift leash over to me. He gives a little bow and we both walk in silence towards Aunt Sally's, where I thank him, tug on the twine and set off in the direction of the Butlers'.*

Eddie is hanging some festive lights outside the house. He looks dumbfounded when I walk by his place leading Roxboro Roy, still crunching on his dirty bone.

'Who...you...?'

But I'm in a hurry and in no mood for one of Echo Eddie's fractured conversations. I want to get this animal back to its owners as quickly as I can.

'Derby,' I say, anticipating his question about who we are playing today and walking swiftly on.

'You are goink to race him in the derby?'

'No, course not,' I reply, stopping briefly. 'We're playing Derby today.'

For once, Eddie is temporarily lost for words. But he recovers his voice as soon as I move off again:

'That dog, he sold my garden.'

As if recalling their last encounter, Roxboro Roy appears anxious to move on too; he strains on the makeshift leash and the twine cuts sharply into my hand. I stroll on, thinking about how we will deal with the challenge from Derby County today. Last season's League champions and sitting joint top of the table with QPR after twenty games each. The Derby line-up that manager Dave Mackay has assembled is like a who's who of stars: David Nish and Roy McFarland anchoring the defence; Bruce Rioch, Colin Todd and Archie Gemmell controlling midfield; with Francis Lee and Charlie George banging them in up front. Thankfully Kevin Hector is injured and unlikely to play today.

A sudden tuging on the leash interrupts my reverie.

Billy is massaging the sleep out of his eyes as I approach. He is retrieving something wrapped in a small paper bag from the back of the van, and doesn't see us at first. He appears to be wearing pyjamas under a dirty overcoat and some kind of house shoes over his bare feet, that he drags along like slippers. Suddenly he starts rubbing furiously at his eyes and, recognising the lost hound, he crouches and starts slapping his knees and calling loudly. Despite his malnourished appearance, the beast has the strength to tear himself away from my loosened grip on the cord and bound into Billy's arms. I stand back and let them at it.

'You found 'im. You found 'im.' Billy makes to embrace me but I step further back. There's a kind of tang in the air that could be from either man or beast.

'Jacko, Jacko, get yerself out 'ere. Roxboro Roy is back,' Billy yells.

Man and dog then continue to smother each other in what has to be the most unhygienic display of affection I have ever seen. Then Billy produces one of his trademark lukewarm sausage rolls from his coat pocket and hand-feeds the grateful canine. He picks up the discarded bone, and for one awful moment I wonder if he is going to suck on it as part of 'Roy's Return'.

Finally, Billy tears himself away from the hound, straightens up, yawns and, handing me the scrunched-up paper bag, says:

'An' I got a little summink for you an' all.'

At first, I'm reluctant to accept it. It's got 'ABC Bakery' printed on the outside and I'm thinking it might be the remains of another snack that he has decided to share with me. But he pushes it at me. There's the slightest hint of yesterday's Cornish pasty from it. I take it and then I suddenly realise what it might contain.

'Is this what I think it is?' I ask, dipping my hand inside the bag and extracting a tiny hardcover volume.

Billy smiles, sheepishly.

'Timothy Albrecht! How did you get it? Where did you get it?'

Billy blushes, shuffles and stares at the pavement but offers nothing by way of explanation.

'Is it new?' I turn the book over and flip through the pages. It looks and feels new, but smells a little musty and some of the pages are lightly sprinkled with pastry.

'More "well preserved", if you get my meaning,' Billy explains. 'We 'ad to take the first page out, 'cos it had fings written on it.'

'What kinds of things were written on it?'

'Not written, exactly,' he dithers. 'More like drawings. Squiggles and that.'

'What kind of squiggles? Tell me. It could be important. I want to know' I insist.

Billy starts to blush that purple-red colour again, shifting from one foot to the other. 'Well, not the kind of squiggles you'd want a lady to see, if you know wot I mean. Body parts; sex fings. The bloke who owned that book woz some kind of sex maniac if you ask me, mate.'

Any further embarrassment is avoided by the slow arrival of the old dear I've seen in The Cabin on occasions. Today she is wearing odd shoes and is gasping a little as she navigates the slight incline. Billy maintains his position at the edge of the pavement as she passes us. In effect, she has to pass between me, Billy and the dog. It may appear slightly intimidating but Billy doesn't really intend anything by it, and is not really aware that he may be frightening the old dear. But in truth she doesn't appear too frightened by it, or even to be aware of it, for that matter. I give him the nod to create some space and the old dear struggles past us without any further impediment.

'Wot's ol' haggletooth bin sayin', then,' calls Jacko as he emerges into the daylight.

'Nothing much,' I shout back, noting Jacko's less than friendly disposition.

'Nuffink at all, ackshley,' Billy murmurs to nobody in particular. At this point the hound sprints towards Jacko, who gives him a friendly slap.

'Where 'ave you bin these past few weeks, then? Playin' away from 'ome have ya? Got a bit on the side somewhere?'

The hound barks and prances around him. Spotting that I have the book in my hands, Jacko struts down the pathway to join us.

'This is fantastic, Jacko. Thank you. Thank you both.'

'Read somefink from it for us,' demands Jacko, and I look up just in time to catch him winking at Billy. I attempt to ignore this request but they both insist, and I know by the *expressions on their faces that the purpose is to embarrass me. Billy grabs the book from me. He flicks through the pages, stopping randomly:*

"States of the U.N.",' he announces. 'Wot's that all about, d'you reckon?' He thrusts the book back at me.

'It says "States of Un",' I point out and, without further ado — or even taking a moment to have a precautionary glance over the text — I start to read aloud:

Unashamed
Unabashed
Uncensored,
Unforgettable
Unmissable

'Next verse…' (Christ, I realise, it's just a list of bleedin' words beginning with 'Un')…
Unseen,
Unsung
Untold
Unknown
Unrequited…
'…er…'

Unbridled…
The brothers contain themselves at the beginning, but they are pissing themselves laughing by the time I get halfway through. I stop.

'Unfinished,' yells Jacko.

'Unbeaten,' suggests Billy

'…at Loftus Road,' laughs Jacko.

'Unlucky…' shouts Billy.

'…in love,' adds Jacko.

'He's a Beat poet,' explains Billy, sarcastically.

'Deadbeat, more likely.'

The brothers explode into laughter again.

'Okay, okay, I didn't write this shit. And I don't understand it either,' I protest, slamming the book shut. Then I start to see the funny side of it and all three of us have a good giggle about it.

'Look, I never thought you'd manage to get it for me. So thanks again.' Then, remembering the terms of our agreement, I whisper, 'And whenever the cops come asking about that card game…'

'Aw, ya don't 'ave to worry 'bout that, mate,' Jacko says with a dismissive wave of his arm. 'It's all sorted. The witness changed 'is mind. It seems the old geezer woz a bit confused. Nice old geezer, that Mr Finchley. Right, Billy?'

'Right on, Jacko,' smirks Billy.

'You know him then?' I ask. 'This…Mr Finchley? You've met him?'

'Just the once,' asserts Jacko.

I begin to smell a rat.

'Changed his mind, did he?' I stare straight at Jacko.

'Changed 'is mind, mate,' Jacko holds my stare, never wavering for one second. 'And that's the end of it, an' all,' he adds emphatically. 'C'mon, Billy, let's get Roy the rover some grub.'

'Right on, Jacko,' yawns Billy, rubbing his eyes again.

'Just thought I'd let you know that I got the book.'

I decided to tell Noah as a matter of courtesy so that he could strike it off his list.

'Good mornington to you, too. And what book is that? If it's the one I've been looking for about Danny Blanchflower and the Spurs "double" team of 1961, I'll make you a rich man.'

'No, actually, it's the one that I've been looking for. Timothy Albrecht. Remember?' I take the book out of the bag and hand it to Noah.

'Ah, yes, I remember now,' he sniffs, slowly turning the pages. He begins to read some of it quietly to himself. Then he frowns and breathes heavily through his nose. Then he stops and peers at me over his reading glasses. I shrug. He sighs again, and examines the book a little more.

'It appears to be in good nick. Do you know its provenance?'

'Providence?

'Provenance; where it came from, its origin. Where did you get it?'

'Well, actually, the Butlers got it…gave it…to me.'

'And these are their notes and drawings pencilled in here, are they?' Noah makes a show of turning the book upside down as if trying to work out one of the drawings. 'Hmm. Yes, that would explain a lot. Can't say I'm surprised, though.'

He holds the book between his thumb and forefinger as if he is about to drop it into the dustbin but he hands it back to me. I take the book and flick through it again. Then, seeing my obvious discomfort, he mellows a little:

'The notes and drawings are all in pencil.'

'Yes,' I say non-committedly. I'm not sure how I'm supposed to react to this observation.

'So they can be rubbed out,' he explains sternly. 'Erased.' He waves his hand dismissively.

I nod and swallow hard. Noah is obviously annoyed about something. I don't like to see him this way.

'…before you give it to anybody!' he says through gritted teeth. Then he turns and walks to the back of the shop and I take this to mean that the conversation has ended. I place the book carefully in the paper bag, slip it into my pocket, stroll out and head for The Cabin. I don't like the idea of getting on the wrong side of Noah — and not just because he's an important part of the ritual. I really like the man. But maybe it hurt his pride that he wasn't able to get the book for me first. Or maybe he wanted to get it first so that Brad could give it to Lisa. They say that blood is thicker than water and it's probably true.

Anyway. There are other important things to be sorted today. I head for The Cabin.

There's a comment in the Mirror this morning from Derby Manager Dave Mackay. He's always felt Rangers are a gifted team, he says, but they are not among the sides he considers a real danger to Derby for the championship. You need a bit extra for that, he adds. A bit extra, indeed. Has he forgotten that we showed a lot extra when we thrashed Derby 5–1 on their own patch back in August? That's just the kind of comment that will get us really riled up for this one. But it will be difficult for us today without Stan Bowles. The Gaffer has left him out of the team because of Stan's personal problems. 'Stan rocked the boat,' he said, 'and the most important thing right now is to keep the boat on course. He isn't in this week because eleven players gave a magnificent performance at Manchester last week. But let me make it clear; Stan will be back. There is no greater admirer of his talents than me. He's a marvellous player and I want him here at Rangers.' So, the Stan Bowles story rumbles on.

But the really big story in all the papers this morning is the ending of the Balcombe Street siege yesterday, during which an elderly couple were held to ransom. The siege started about a week ago, when the police chased four IRA gunmen across London after shots had been fired through the window of Scotts Restaurant in Mayfair. The four men ended up in a flat in Balcombe Street, near Marylebone railway station, taking its two residents, John and Sheila Matthews, hostage. The men demanded a plane to fly both them and their hostages to Ireland. The police refused, resulting in the six-day siege. The gang are also suspected of having thrown a bomb through the window of the same restaurant a few weeks ago, killing one person and injuring others. And one of the men is rumoured to be wanted in connection with the shooting of Ross McWhirter a couple of weeks ago.

There is general consensus in The Cabin that the police tactics have been vindicated by the outcome, and a feeling that things will settle down now that the security forces have apprehended what they call an IRA 'ASU' (Active Service Unit). There's even a smattering of praise for Harold Wilson and the Labour government. Undeserved, in my opinion.

As I've said before, I don't like to discuss things like the IRA bombings with Mick. I know he supports the aim of a United Ireland but that he is against the IRA's violent methods. I'm content to leave it at that, but some of his customers seem to want Mick to declare his anti-IRA stance every time there is a bombing, shooting or security threat. The fat bloke in front of me with the monocle and cane — Colonel Martin — is at it this morning. Mick tries in vain to steer the conversation away from IRA gunmen and on to Christmas, but the eccentric old Colonel won't let it go. Having bought and paid for his Financial Times, he is standing there, cane under his arm, holding everybody up by having his say and putting Mick on the spot.

I pretend that the Colonel's cane is sticking in my ribs and I push it firmly away. Without moving his hips, the old Colonel turns his head left and then right in an attempt to see what is happening behind him. Eventually, he has to turn round. This distracts him sufficiently for Mick to wrap up the conversation and bid him farewell. The old Colonel mumbles something incomprehensible and ambles away reluctantly.

'Thank you and good morning,' winks Mick, at the back of the retreating Colonel.

'I haven't seen much of that old soldier since he bought number 5,' I say.

'Oh, he didn't buy it, Dawhee me bucko,' retorts Mick, 'he's just renting.'

'Why would a retired army colonel rent a large house like that at his age?'

'You know, me bucko, that's just the problem with young men like you. You think that everybody over the age of 40 is old and should be retired. Colonel Martin is ex-army all right, but he still works. He's got a desk job at MI5 — or is it MI6? Anyway, at some branch of Her Majesty's security service. But as for why he is renting and not buying, well, you will have to ask him about that yourself. Now,' he whispers, nodding at the sports pages of the open newspaper in front of him, 'I see that Stan Bowles is in the wars again.'

'That's putting it mildly, Mick,' I sigh.

Mick asks what the problem is this time. 'C'mon Dawhee, you can trust me with the inside track,' he promises.

I tell Mick that it's complicated, but I explain it as best I can. Stan Bowles has been having 'personal problems'. He lives with his wife and three kids in a flat and wants to buy a house. As usual, money is at the root of the problem — he doesn't have enough. Stan's predilection for gambling is a matter of public record but he's not a bad bloke and wants to do the right thing. He wants more dosh and the club is reluctant to give it to him.

Mick has been nodding sympathetically at all of this, but now he interjects:

'But what has Georgie Best to do with any of this?'

I tell Mick that there have been rumours that George Best wants to make a comeback and that Chelsea, Stoke — and QPR — are all interested in signing him.

'But he's way past it! Jaysus, Georgie Best is a "has been",' exclaims Mick. 'And he hasn't a single redeeming vice.'

'You may be right, Mick,' I say, 'but George Best can put an extra 10,000 paying customers on the gate every week.'

Mick shrugs. 'So?'

'So Stan's position — as I understand it — is that if QPR are prepared to shell out all that extra dosh for a "has been", as you call him, why can't they come up with the readies to pay more to a guy — Stan — who is turning it on for them week after week.'

'Seems like a fair position to me.'

'Yes, but the uncertainty caused by this whole rumpus has resulted in Stan losing a bit of form. As you know, he was dropped for the game away to Manchester City last week.' I tell Mick that being dropped really upset Stan, as he used to play with Man City and would have been looking forward to returning to Maine Road. Drawing that game 0–0 didn't help the relationship between Stan and the club, because Stan obviously believes that we would have won if he'd been playing. To make matters even worse, some QPR supporters cancelled their coach trip to Manchester last Saturday in protest against Stan being dropped. The club reckons that Stan's story has been getting too much media coverage, and this is distracting both Stan and the rest of the squad. And now Stan, who scored a hat-trick against them earlier in the season, hasn't been recalled for today's game against Derby. So he's upset.

'I can see how he would be,' Mick says, 'But, you know, me bucko, sometimes Stan is his own worst enemy, the way he talks to the media all the time. He's a great footballer that Stan Bowles, but he'd give a headache to an ambulance, so he would.' He slides his newspaper aside, finally releasing me from the Stan Bowles inquisition.

'Just the Mirror, then?' he asks.

'Yeah. Do you sell erasers by any chance? You know, the things used in school to rub out pencil marks.'

'I know what they are and what they're used for. Only I would have thought you were gone way past using one. But I do sell them. Well, which one would you like? A Big Ben shape? What about an Eiffel Tower? Or a Christmas tree shape — very seasonal?'

'Just a simple eraser will do the trick, thank you Mick,' I say, spilling a few coins on the counter. 'By the way, has Trouty been in?'

Mick shakes his head while he counts out the change.

'No, at least not on my watch. But Lisa's been and gone already this morning,' he says, suddenly perking up. 'Bought a few Christmas cards, too. Just popped round to the post office.'

I feign disinterest.

'I just cannot understand where Bernie Trout has got to,' I say. Dropping the eraser into my pocket, I fold my Mirror, pay what's due and wish good-day to Mick.

'Maybe when the spawning season is in full swing he'll make an appearance,' Mick laughs. 'All tanned, like a brown trout. Ready to lay a few eggs.'

I don't respond.

'Godspeed,' he calls after me, still laughing at his little joke.

I make my way across to the Olde Fayre Green café, order tea from Veronica and find a table by the window, so that I can see Lisa when she passes by. I pay for the tea and while I wait for it to cool, I slide the package out of my pocket and take out the book. It strikes me now as being surprisingly small and slim. The publisher's name doesn't ring any bells for me either. I spot where Billy or Jacko removed an offending page at the back. You wouldn't notice it unless you went looking for it, it's been that neatly done. I survey the task ahead of me and then try the eraser. I'm in luck! The writing was done with a soft pencil so it vanishes quickly and there are no indentations to arouse any curiosity. Soon the table is littered with the detritus of all the rubbing.

Mick's son Cathal comes in and makes for the table in the back corner. He doesn't look in my direction and seems a little agitated when he sits down, accidently knocking against the small jug on the table and spilling some milk. When Veronica attempts to mop it up with a napkin, he just waves her away dismissively. He doesn't order anything and keeps looking at his watch and then at the front door. He scans the room from time to time but doesn't appear to notice me. I decide to put away the book and peruse the Mirror instead. If I hold it up, I can gaze around the room over the top of it without anybody noticing.

When I look over in Cathal's direction a few minutes later, I discover he is staring directly at me. I lower the newspaper and nod but he doesn't acknowledge me. He just stares straight ahead. I wonder who he's waiting for. O'Leary? He hasn't been around for a couple of weeks.

Gone. That's what Cathal said when I asked him about O'Leary last time we met. Gone. But where to? No explanation. I begin to think back on some of the images from the television coverage last night of the ending of the siege in Paddington. One of the IRA gunmen was tall. Not unlike O'Leary, in fact. It was difficult to make out their faces on the screen, but the tall one could have been O'Leary. It would explain his sudden disappearance from the area. Maybe Cathal was providing cover for him. What did Brad call it? A 'safe house', that was it. Or maybe O'Leary was sleeping rough and just coming to Cathal's place for food. That would explain his scruffy appearance. He could be part of one of those 'Active Service Units' that Brad also referred to. Small units operating independently of each other. Maybe Cathal doesn't even know what O'Leary was up to. Cathal might have been used. He may be an unwilling accomplice in all of this. That's what probably has him so agitated this morning. Now that the IRA gunmen have been caught, Cathal has only just realised the trouble he's in.

The double knock on the window is like gunfire and it jolts me out of speculative mode. It's Lisa. She waves, obviously in hurry and not intending to come in for a cuppa. I hold up my hand in a 'hang on' motion, stuff the book back into my pocket and hurry out after her.

Without as much as a 'Good morning' I immediately start to tell her about my suspicions regarding O'Leary, but she's not impressed.

'But he's gone,' she says. 'You told me so yourself. You told me that Cathal had said so.'

'Gone, yes, but where to?'

'Home. He's gone back to Ireland for Christmas.'

'But you don't know that,' I say. 'You're just guessing.'

'I'm not guessing. Cathal told me.'

'You asked him? About O'Leary?'

'Yes. Just like you did.'

I don't really have an answer for that.

'Maybe Cathal was lying. Or maybe O'Leary was lying when he told Cathal he was going home. Maybe Mr "Lofty" artistic O'Leary was just planning to lie low until this operation was over so as not to involve Cathal.'

I can tell immediately that the 'Lofty' reference does not appeal to her.

'Must you use nicknames for everyone? It must come from that closed football environment that you operate in, where everything is reduced to childish, schoolboy humour.'

'What am I meant to call him?'

'O'Leary, like everybody else does.'

'No first name? Who goes around using just their surnames?'

'Picasso. Gaudi. Monet. There are just three examples. And don't you dare ask me what teams they play for.'

'I know the first guy's an artist…'

'Well done,' she says sarcastically. 'They are all artists.' I've never heard her use sarcasm before and it surprises me. I try to get the conversation back on an even keel.

'Who were the others again?' I ask. 'Camus…'

'No. Albert Camus was a writer.'

'I'll bet you don't know what team he played for.'

She stops and looks as if she is about to swing a punch at me.

'I'm serious,' I say. 'What team did he play for?'

She ignores the questions and sniffs a bit.

'Well, for your information,' I say, 'Camus played in goal for the University of Algeria team that won both the North African Champions Cup and the North African Cup twice each in the 1930s.'

'Not the same Albert Camus, surely,' she says, rather dismissively.

'The same bloke,' I say. 'He played until he contracted TB.'

'Good Lord, really?' she exclaims, obviously unconvinced. 'And what do you know of the great Camus's beliefs?' she asks in that slightly superior tone that she sometimes adopts.

'I know that when he was once asked about his time playing football, Camus said "What I know most surely about morality and the duty of man I owe to sport." Something along those lines, anyway.'

That stopped her, didn't it. Dead in her tracks.

'Well, you surprise me. I'm amazed to be honest.' She looks almost pleased, but for once, in all the time that I've known her, I can tell that she doesn't know what to say next. So she adopts my old trick of changing the subject.

'And where is all this James Bond terminology coming from, active service units, safe houses, operations, lying low? You're being very melodramatic, you realise that don't you? You're beginning to sound just like Brad. And speaking of Brad, the names of the IRA men who surrendered in Balcombe Street were listed in the report I just heard on the radio in Brad's shop, and for your information, none of them was called O'Leary.'

'Well of course not. O'Leary is probably not his real name.'

She throws her eyes skywards, stops and places her hands on her hips:

'Can we just drop this ridiculous conversation? Now? Or do you want me to walk back and ask Cathal straight out if he is aware that he has been harbouring a terrorist for weeks?'

'I reckon we would need more evidence first,' I say a little nervously, as I'm beginning to think Lisa will probably carry out her threat to speak to Cathal about it if I persist in pursuing this line of thought.

We both fall silent as we continue up Park Road. I reckon she is genuinely lost for words. Me? I'm pleased at how I got her on the Albert Camus thing. She walked right into it. Nutmegged.

'When is the next home game after today?' she asks eventually, when we reach the corner where Beane Row meets the Glade.

'Not until December 26th,' I say.

'Oh, I thought you had a game next week. Well, I have something for you, then,' she says quietly, dipping her hand into her hippie bag. 'Oh, it's just a little Christmas card. We probably won't see each other again before the New Year.'

I'm a little taken aback at this. Not just the little Christmas card (and it is tiny), but the vagueness regarding when we will meet up again. No mention of Boxing Day, when we play Norwich City. Just 'the New Year' and no specific date mentioned.

In certain situations, I sometimes get tongue-tied. There is so much I want to ask that I end up asking nothing. This is one of those situations. I say nothing. I just stand there fumbling with the Christmas card before pushing it into my back pocket.

'Thanks. I'll open it later.'

She seems disappointed.

'I have something for you too,' I say. 'But not with me,' I add lamely. Lisa puts a hand gently on my arm. But I know she doesn't believe me.

'Well, goodbye, then,' she says softly, with no traces of the earlier sarcasm and superiority.

I watch her walk along the Glade and on up Forest Hill Road. Across the street, Tojo is hauling a huge Christmas tree in through the gates of Aunt Sally's, humming loudly. I never asked Lisa what her plans are for Christmas. Is she going away? When will she be back?

As soon as she is out of sight, I rush across the street and, once round the corner, I pull out the Christmas card, rip off the envelope and read it. It's a fairly bland Christmas message. There's nothing particularly meaningful in the verse, but it's signed 'Lisa' with a nice flourish that finishes with what could be a tiny X. But then again, it might just be her handwriting style. No point in reading too much into it. It's the kind of card I would buy as back-up in case, at the last moment, I didn't have the nerve to give the card I really wanted to give.

I put the card back in my pocket and bin the envelope. I don't know why I'm disappointed. It's a nice card with a nice verse. It's just a bit...small. Insignificant.

I'm disappointed, too, that I totally forgot to ask her about that 'trifle' issue. Did I really forget? Or do I just not have the courage to raise it? Maybe I should try to forget all about it. Concentrate on more important things. Things I can influence.

I need to focus on this afternoon. Derby County, the current Division One champions. We beat them 5–1 at the Baseball Ground back in August and 4–1 here last season, so we have a good recent record against them. I'm confident we'll beat them – although we may not score as many goals as we did in tour previous two games against them.

I quicken my step, tapping my pocket to check that the card is still in there.

Saturday, 13 December 1975: 4.40 p.m.

Queens Park Rangers...1 Derby County...1

12. WINGLESS WONDERS?

Saturday, 24 April 1976: Twenty minutes gone in the first half
Suddenly, the home crowd senses that something is on.

John Hollins lays off a short pass to Don Masson. Don lets it run a little, then arcs a long sweeping pass into space for Gerry Francis, bursting through on the left. But before Gerry can reach it, Leeds winger Carl Harris, who has tracked back deep into his own half, makes a clean interception to avert the danger. Harris makes a long, raking cross-field clearance. The ball appears to be heading straight towards me and I tense myself to control it. But the Leeds number 7 has put a spin on it and it veers away from me and finds Eddie Gray. The left-winger controls it cleanly with one touch, his trademark jutting elbow signalling that he is about to embark on one of those mazy runs of his. He beats a couple of despairing tackles, goes tight to the end-line and crosses to the far post only for Joe Jordan to mistime his header fractionally. There's a collective sigh of relief all round at this narrow escape for us.

The two Leeds wingers could not be more different. At 27, Eddie Gray is already a Leeds veteran. A Scottish international with over 200 league appearances for the club, he's a winger in the traditional mode and very light on his feet. Don Revie once said of him that when he plays on snow, he leaves no footprints. At one stage last season, Gray worried that injury had put paid to his career, but eventually he made a full recovery. Capped eight times for Scotland, Eddie Gray was an integral part of that celebrated Leeds team which won so many trophies during the last decade. To date he has scored 35 goals for the club and also enjoys the distinction of never having been booked in his career. By contrast, Carl Harris is a complete novice. Harris made his first league appearance for Leeds only one year ago – almost exactly to the day – scoring on his debut against Ipswich. Since then he's had to be patient as most of his appearances have been off the substitutes bench. But that patience does appear to be paying off, as he won his first international cap – for Wales against England – earlier this season.

I still refer to players like Eddie Gray and Carl Harris as wingers, even though their roles have expanded far beyond what the traditional English leagues' wingers were expected to do.

By 1966, when England won the World Cup, Manager Alf Ramsey had developed a new style of play, following a period of experimentation while he was manager at Ipswich Town. Up to that time, using the old W-formation, wingers tended to be nimble, tricky ball players whose primary purpose was to beat the full-back, get to the by-line and cross for the big centre-forward to score. They were usually small in stature with a tendency to be crowd pleasers – even if it meant beating the same opponent twice before crossing the ball. They were not generally known for their defensive qualities, however, and dropping back to help a teammate in trouble never seemed to be a priority for them nor, to be fair, was it really expected of them.

Ramsey started to exclude wingers entirely from his teams and replacing them with attacking midfielders who could also track back into defensive roles. But the real advantage of the system was that it got the ball to the strikers swiftly by having them run onto through balls supplied by the midfield players.

This system had the additional advantage of unsettling opposing full-backs, who would normally expect to encounter a winger regularly haring down the flank towards them. Instead, the attacking midfielders were cutting through the centre of the opposition defence to score, as best exemplified by Martin Peters of West Ham and England, who Alf Ramsey described as being ten years ahead of his time.

The Ramsey system was employed in the lead-up to and during the 1966 World Cup and was credited in large part with the success of England, and led to his England team being referred to as 'The Wingless Wonders'.

Friday, 26 December 1975: 11.05 a.m.

It may be Christmas holiday time for most people, but for those of us involved in football, life goes on as usual. It's Friday, it's Boxing Day, but not only am I 'on duty' today — we're at home to Norwich City — but QPR has another game tomorrow, this time away to our other great London rivals, the Arsenal. Two matches on the trot means not much Christmas cheer for professional footballers. But one step at a time — today's game against Norwich is the one that I'm focusing on. They have two deadly in-form strikers in Ted McDougall and Phil Boyer, so they'll need watching.

There are no newspapers this morning and I know that The Cabin is closed for Boxing Day, but I go for a walk anyway. As it's a holiday and I leave the house later than usual, I don't expect to bump into any of the usual crew. But I bring that Timothy Albrecht book with me anyway. Just in case. I took the time over Christmas to erase any of the pencil scribbling that could be interpreted as rude or vulgar. As it's not a Saturday, I also permit myself the latitude of putting the ritual on hold till everything (and everybody) is back on schedule again in the New Year. No point in tempting fate. But I do bump into Marianne Pleass almost immediately, as she manoeuvres her bicycle out the gate. There is a large poinsettia plant in a seasonal pot, placed firmly in the front basket that, she tells me without making eye contact, she is taking it to a nearby relative. I ask her about the cut on her knee but before she can respond, a sharp rat-tat-tat of wood on glass announces the arrival of Marjorie at the first-floor bay window. She appears particularly giddy today as she waves excitedly at both of us, wearing a Santa Claus hat and holding a hand mirror and hairbrush. I wave a Christmas greeting in Marjorie's direction but she is staring worriedly into space beyond me, probably at the retreating form of Marianne who has, without warning, pedalled out onto the road into that special lane reserved for people with death-wish syndrome. I watch Marianne as she freewheels round the corner and out of sight. Mercifully, traffic is light this morning, but the repeated tinkling of a bicycle bell followed by a single blast of a car horn and a decidedly un-festive greeting from a hoarse male voice suggests that some things don't change.

It rained overnight so the streets are damp and dismal. The playing surface is likely to be muddy today and more rain is forecast so, all in all, it's the kind of day where it can be difficult to remain focused during the game. It's on days like this that results can unexpectedly go against you, so the superstitious side of me is looking out for any positive signs or signals that I can take comfort in. As Marjorie is the person least likely to be of assistance to me in this regard I decide to move on.

There's not many people out and about, except for a few kids who got bicycles for Christmas giving them a test run down Park Road. I walk quickly as far as the shops, all of which are closed, with the exception of Noah's place.

'Good morningon,' he hails me in his usual fashion. 'Just doing a bit of stocktaking.'

Through the dust, I can make out the old dear whom I've seen in The Cabin on a couple of occasions, dithering over a bundle of Japanese parasols in the back of Noah's shop. I catch Noah's eye and nod in the direction of the old dear:

'Buying or selling?' I ask.

'Can't seem to make up her mind,' mutters Noah, not unkindly, under his breath. 'She says she is looking for two parasols that will complement each other. Wants to make up a set, apparently.'

'From the way she dresses, I would have thought that complementation wasn't exactly her strong point.'

'That observation does you no justice, my friend,' Noah admonishes me gently. 'Remember, if everybody's taste was the same there would be very few wallpaper shops.'

I have neither the time nor the inclination to work out what Noah is on about, because in the distance I see someone who looks remarkably like Lisa coming down Park Road past the Butlers' place, with what appears to be a young girl skipping along beside her. I take my leave of Noah and quicken my pace back up the hill. It is Lisa. But who is that little kid with her? The young girl appears to be about 5 years old, is dressed in an angel costume, and seems to be having difficulty with her wings.

'Can I help?' I call out as I approach them.

Lisa looks surprised and a little embarrassed by my sudden appearance. 'Oh, hello,' she says, but without any real warmth.

'Fancy bumping into you today,' I say. 'Did you have a good Christmas?'

'Yes, indeed. Very nice.' She sounds irritated by something. Maybe the fact that I didn't give her a Christmas card. She appears eager to move on quickly, although the pace of her young companion holds her back.

'Where are you off to in such a hurry? I ask, and immediately reckon that perhaps I am being too familiar and have overstepped the mark.

Lisa stops and sighs resignedly: 'This is my cousin, Lynette,' she explains eventually. 'Lynette is an angel in the school play – aren't you, pet? She has a rehearsal tomorrow and is having some problems keeping her wings attached to this little harness.' She turns Lynette around to show me the problem with the harness.

'You never told me you had a cousin called Lynette,' I blurt out impulsively. Alarmed by my accusative tone, Lynette gives me a decidedly frosty glare and steps closer to Lisa. She is small for her age, blonde and fair skinned (so unlikely to be closely related to Lisa).

'We're hoping that The Cabin will be open and maybe have glue or pins – anything that will help sort out the wings problem.'

'Some hope. The Cabin is closed today.'

'Are you sure?' she asks despairingly.

'Positive,' I say, emphatically. 'There was a sign in the window all week saying it's closed Christmas Day and Stephen's Day, which I happen to know is what the Irish call Boxing Day.'

'Hell,' she fumes suddenly through gritted teeth. It's the first time I've ever heard her say anything that resembled a swear word. 'No shops open; no buses, no trains...' She stops suddenly and leans against the Butlers' garden wall. 'What a day.'

'Here, this might cheer you up.' I hand her the package.

'What is it?' she asks suspiciously.

'Take it. Open it,' I urge.

'But what is it?' she asks again.

'Just open it.' I wink at Lynette and this has the desired effect of making her feel part of this little ceremony. She giggles and smiles.

'I don't mean what's inside. I mean what's the occasion? Why are you giving this to me?'

'Why? It's a Christmas present. You remember – when you gave me the Christmas card – I said I had something for you. So, it's a day-late Christmas present, but a Christmas present all the same.'

She puts her hand to her mouth in shock. I know in that instant that she hasn't got a present for me; that it had never really crossed her mind. And I'm gutted. But Lisa's reaction is more than I expected.

'Oh, how kind of you,' she exclaims as she struggles to regain her composure. 'Can I open it here?'

But she's already started to remove the wrapping. Watching this action alone is worth all the effort I put into acquiring the book. She removes the wrapping paper very carefully – as if it would be disrespectful to simply tear it off. The book emerges from its loose wrapping with the back cover facing up. She stares at it then looks up at me slowly and holds my gaze for just a second before returning her attention to the gift. She turns it over and the 'oh' is short as she catches her breath. She opens the book lightly with her right hand, turning the pages over, recognising some of the lines that are obviously familiar to her. Finally, she exhales lightly.

'I don't know what to say. I'm lost for words.'

I resist the temptation to point out that this would be a first. Instead I just shrug and ask her if she likes it, while hoping that this moment, this moment when I've done something that has surprised and pleased her, will last just a little longer. But it gets even better.

'This is the best Christmas gift that anybody could have given me. You are so, so sweet.' And she touches my hand with her fingers. It only takes a second, approximately the time it takes to strike a chord on the keyboard of a piano, but the effect, like the sound, lingers and is sustained for what seems like an eternity to me. You read about moments like this in novels, you see them in films and on the telly, but until it happens to you, you really cannot explain what it feels like. Those moments in books, films and on the telly, however, don't usually have 5-year-old kids in them and this particular moment is interrupted by the sounds of wrapping paper being ripped.

'Oh' (longer this time and with a distinctively different emphasis). 'Lynette, you must not do that,' then, to me: 'I'm terribly sorry.'

'It's just wrapping paper,' I say, but Lisa retrieves the strips of paper, folds them neatly and places them carefully in her bag. I'm thinking that if all gift-giving was like this, it would be a pretty emotionally exhausting process. The spell has been broken, the moment has gone, but the Cupid's arrow has found its mark. Now we're suddenly back to sorting out the problem of little Cupid's wing. Would this be a good time to raise the 'trifle' issue? With a kid around? Maybe not.

'Fackin' 'ell, look who's 'ere.' Jacko Butler is suddenly upon us, smelling of cheap aftershave and stale Christmas cheer. 'Now there's three of ya. Is this 'Appy Families or wot?'

'Language, Jacko, there's a child present,' Lisa scolds. Jacko looks suitably chastened. She explains the problem with the wings.

'Can you suggest anything?' Lisa asks him, the clear implication being that I could not come up with a workable solution.

Jacko seizes the opportunity, and makes a big show of thinking intently on how he might provide a solution. Then suddenly:

'Broken its wing? Poor little thing! A spot of You-Hoo will soon put it right,' Jacko sing-songs the words of the ad for UHU glue. 'Just leave it to Uncle Jacko. I reckon I might 'ave just wot we need in the back of the van.'

Lisa seems overjoyed. 'Did you hear that, pet? Jacko is going to fix your wings.' Lynette beams and they all move happily up the few yards towards the van. I tag along a few paces behind.

Jacko opens the back doors of the van and crawls into what looks and smells like a large rubbish dump, mumbling, 'Now, let's 'ave a butcher's.' Eventually, he emerges with an almost empty tube of glue.

'This should do it,' he says triumphantly. At this juncture, Billy comes out the gate to join us, his cheeriness totally at odds with the greyness of the day. This is all getting a little too crowded for me.

'Look,' I say, unable to hide my slightly sullen tone, 'I need to get home. We've an important game this afternoon.'

'Gotta fly, 'ave you?' asks Jacko, nodding at Lynette's wings. This sets off a furious bout of contrived laughter from the two brothers. Lynette giggles. Even Lisa smiles weakly at this awful joke. I'm beginning to feel decidedly left out and down in the dumps. Not ideal preparation for today's game. I start to shuffle off slowly.

'Well, let's 'ope we stuff the Canaries today,' Jacko shouts after me.

'And the Arsenal tomorrow!' adds Billy.

'QPR has two matches in two days?' I think I hear Lisa exclaim — but I may have imagined it.

'Can I have a stuffed canary, too?' pipes up Lynette.

Cue another round of uncontrolled laughter from all concerned.

There isn't a sound from Echo Eddie's place as I pass by. The house looks dark and unoccupied, so they must have gone to friends for Christmas. A tiny robin hops from a withered shrub onto one of the planks of wood lying temporarily abandoned in the still unfinished garden.

But no sight or sound of a parrot.

Friday, 26 December 1975: 4.40 p.m.

Queens Park Rangers…2 Norwich City…0

13. THE BIRDS AND THE BEES

Saturday, 24 April 1976: Midway through the first half

Leeds are now attacking in waves. The build-up is patient but incessant. Bremner to Eddie Gray. Eddie Gray to his brother Frankie, overlapping on the left. The ball is swept across field to Carl Harris on the right wing. Harris floats in the cross and finds Joe Jordan's head. Jordan knocks it down to Trevor Cherry.

Bang! The power and velocity of Cherry's strike has goal written all over it.

But Phil Parkes makes a superb save from Cherry's fierce drive, and then flings himself at the feet of Duncan McKenzie when it seems like a certain goal.

The travelling Leeds fans are on their feet. They feel the game is beginning to swing their way:

Oh when the Whites, go marching in
Oh when the Whites, go marching in
I wanna be in that number
When the Whites, go marching in.

Most football teams have nicknames, some boast more than one. A few have rather interesting origins. Sunderland are known as 'The Black Cats' after the Black Cat gun battery which stood on the River Wear, whilst Sheffield United are 'The Blades', based on the city's association with the local steel and cutlery industries. Arsenal are 'The Gunners' in recognition of the club founders, who were workers at the Woolwich Arsenal military arms factory. And Chelsea's nickname, 'The Pensioners', originates from the Chelsea pensioners, based at the nearby Royal Hospital Chelsea.

The most common nickname used by Leeds fans is 'The Whites', a not entirely original nickname deriving from the simple fact that Leeds play in an all-white strip. Readers may be interested (and not a little confused) to learn that Leeds' original club colours were blue and white, and subsequently blue and yellow. So what happened? Well, when Don Revie became Manager of Leeds he changed the colour of the team strip (tho' not the colour of the club crest) to all-white in the style of the highly successful Spanish side Real Madrid.

A more interesting and original nickname for Leeds, tho' sadly now almost obsolete, is 'The Peacocks'. This stemmed from the original name of Leeds football stadium – 'The Old Peacock Ground' – at Elland Road. This, in turn, was named after a nearby pub, The Old Peacock. And Leeds have certainly ruffled a few feathers in their time.

Other football teams have 'bird' nicknames too. Norwich City, nicknamed 'The Canaries' due to the popularity of canary breeding in Norfolk, play in bright yellow shirts with green shorts and the canary is now part of the club's crest. Crystal Palace are known as 'The Eagles'; Brighton are 'The Seagulls'; Bradford City, 'The Bantams'; some wiseacre dubbed Sheffield Wednesday 'The Owls'; and 'Robins' are so popular that no less than four clubs, including Bristol City and Charlton, adopted this nickname.

Insects are popular as nicknames too. Barnet and Brentford have, rather predictably, self-styled themselves as 'The Bees', while waspish Watford answer to 'The Hornets'.

While some of the nicknames have interesting origins, most are based on fairly obvious associations with more mundane features such as the initial letter of the club name, the colours of the club or some aspect of the team kit.

Queens Park Rangers fans refer to the club as either 'QPR', 'The 'Rs' or 'The Hoops'. During the late 1960s, die-hard QPR fans (probably suffering from delusions of invincibility following a hard-fought 0–0 draw at home to Rotherham United on a wet and windy Wednesday evening in December) would sometimes refer to them as 'The Super Hoops'.

But that's typical football hyperbole for you.

Saturday, 3 January 1976: 8.45 a.m.

I'm worried in case today is going to be another one of those days when the ritual is under threat. Thursday, being 1 January, was a bank holiday and many people will have taken yesterday off too, made a weekend of it and probably taken a short break away. So there could be one or two 'no shows' this morning.

It's also our first involvement in this season's FA Cup. As a First Division club, we get a bye into Round 3 of the FA Cup, and today we're at home to Newcastle United. They are currently languishing in mid-table, a full ten points behind us so, with home advantage, the odds are in our favour today. Still, the FA Cup is famous for producing shock upsets so we must avoid complacency at all costs.

I bump into Marianne Pleass – literally – as she jogs out the front gate of number 21. She is all kitted out in brand-new running gear: vest, shorts and shoes. I step back and wish her a Happy New Year. She stops briefly, still jogging time and, noting my surprise, she explains that jogging is one of her New Year resolutions and that this is day three. She tells me that she and Marj got one of those thread-mills as a Christmas present to each other and goes on to tell me about their new fitness regime. Out of the corner of my eye I notice some activity at the front window that would suggest that Marj is giving the thread-mill a bit of a workout, but I cannot bring myself to look up. Marianne is impatient to go and jogs off at a steady pace. It's strange to see her without the bicycle. I watch her go to check that she is keeping to the pavement.

Tojo is sanding the railings beside the pillars at the gate entrance to Aunt Sally's place. The railings look as if they haven't had a lick of paint for years and are rusting and peeling badly. I wish him a Happy NewYear too. He waves back but without any great enthusiasm, which makes me wonder if the Japanese celebrate New Year at the same time as we do.

My spirits rise a little when I see Eddie in the garden. Not because it's Eddie, but because all the parts of the ritual seem to be kicking into place today, despite my earlier misgivings. Eddie has a coal bunker at the side wall of the garage and he's filling a large coal-scuttle to bring inside the house.

'Happy Noo Year, heh, heh,' *booms Eddie.*

'Many happy returns,' *I say.*

'Yes, we return, heh, heh, we return yesterday,' *grins Eddie.*

'Got Nit Are,' *comes a voice from the open upstairs window that can only be Svertlana's. At least that's what I reckon she said. She is obviously only just out of bed and is having her first cigarette of the day, leaning on the windowsill and blowing smoke skywards.*

'Many happy returns,' *I repeat, hoping that I have correctly guessed the sentiment being expressed.*

'My Edvard is bizzy this mornink. He hass lots of rezzelutions.' *Svetlana takes a long, deep draw on her slim cigarette.*

'I'll bet he has,' *are the only words that come to mind and I immediately regret uttering them.*

Svetlana smiles directly at me and exhales very, very slowly.

'No smoke wivout fire, right Billy.'

'Right on, Jacko.'

I turn to see the two brothers, slouching and smirking a few feet away. Jacko throws his eyes in the direction of Svetlana and then nods towards Eddie's coal bunker, presumably by way of explaining his 'smoke without fire' quip. Billy keeps his eyes firmly fixed on the upstairs window. Neither shows any inclination to be on their way. This is unusual as things have been strained between them and Eddie since the incident of the soiling dog. Both brothers look remarkably well scrubbed and are wearing their best bib and tucker – probably Christmas presents.

'We're off to the bookies,' *Jacko announces.*

'Having a little flutter on the FA Cup,' *Billy explains eagerly.*

'QPR must be worth a punt,' *I suggest.* 'You'll get good odds too, I reckon.'

'Nah. William Hill's offering 16–1 on the Rs. We woz thinking maybe Newcastle at 33–1. Good side; very underrated. Could be a good bet, eh Billy?'

'Who we playing today, anyway, Jacko?' *asks Billy, overplaying his role in feigning ignorance.*

'C'mon guys, you know we're playing Newcastle today. You can't bet against the team you support. Who are you really putting your money on?'

'Well, we might do the Rs as a long shot, but the smart money…'

'And that's us,' *interjects Billy.*

'…the smart dosh will be on the usual lot. Leeds and Man City are 10–1. Derby and Man U are on 11–1, Ipswich and Liverpool 12–1.' *The brothers are certainly bang up-to-date on the odds. It's the same with the gee-gees and the dogs. They always believe they have the inside track. They know a bloke who knows some geezer whose cousin is a stable-lad in some yard or other. Funny the way things don't always turn out the way they had planned, though. Something always happens to go wrong. I've long given up acting on the 'certain' tips they offer. I make my excuses and leave them to their calculations.*

I grab the Mirror off the stack as soon I enter The Cabin. The front page has a huge headline:

BLOODY NEW YEAR.

Britain has swept into 1976 on a wave of violence and sudden death, according to the story. In the first few hours of the new year it says at least thirteen people died violently; shootings, stabbings, strangulation – it's all there; a 5-month-old baby found dead in a house in Scotland and in Ulster, a woman who was injured in a bomb attack on New Year's Eve also died subsequently.

I turn to the back page. There's a short piece on today's match. Gordon Lee, the Newcastle manager, is honest enough to admit that we might give them a game of it this afternoon: 'They don't come harder than this,' he is quoted as saying. Typically, their outspoken striker, Malcolm McDonald, is more bullish. 'We have a little bit of pace up front,' he understates, 'and QPR's Frank McLintock and David Webb are not the quickest defenders around.' This pisses me off initially when I read it but then, I think, he may have a point. Anything can happen – and frequently does – in the FA Cup. And Newcastle United have been a real thorn in our side this season, knocking us out of the League Cup when they beat us 3–1 – at home – last November.

Mick is beaming when I arrive at the counter.

'Well, Dawhee me bucko, you were privileged to see a class footballer last Saturday,' he proclaims.

'Yeah, Phil Parkes played a blinder for us in goal. Even the Arsenal fans on the North Bank applauded his performance. He made at least three world-class saves. I reckon he's now a certainty to take over the England goalkeeper's spot from Ray Clemence.'

Mick slaps his knee and roars in delight at my response. 'It was young Master Brady I had in mind, as you well know, me bucko.'

'Brady played okay,' I say, deliberately underplaying the Arsenal midfielder's performance. 'But he couldn't stick one past Parkes.'

'No, but Kidd got one – under Parkes if not past him.' Mick roars with laughter again at his own witty reference at the one mistake Parkes made in the whole game. I decide to let it go.

The Cabin is quieter than usual this morning. No sign of Trouty. I don't even ask Mick if he's seen him. There's not much point. I'm already hatching a plan to replace Bernie. It's the one and only New Year resolution I've made. No sign of Lisa, either, which is worrying. I do ask Mick about Lisa but he hasn't seen her this morning. Then I tell him about bumping into Marianne Pleass out jogging earlier.

'Jogging is it? Another one of her fads, no doubt. I bet it won't last.'

'She seems quite committed to keeping herself fit,' I say, trying to gently egg him on.

'Sure, wouldn't the cycling do that?'

'Well, maybe she's trying to lose a bit of weight, then,' I suggest.

'Lose weight, is it? Sure she hasn't as much on her as would dust a fiddle.'

I decide not to pursue the topic. We have a brief chat about today's game, then I'm off. On the way back I call in to see Noah. I ask him about Lisa but he hasn't seen her either. Then Brad arrives. He makes a big deal of wishing me a Happy New Year, pumping my hand vigorously and clapping me on the back. Noah asks him about Lisa. Without even looking in my direction, Brad tells Noah that Lisa mentioned to him last night how she intended calling in to see Aunt Sally this morning. Aunt Sally? Nobody goes in to Aunt Sally's place except old Tojo. I want to know more, but no way am I asking Brad. I make a point of thanking Noah and hurry away.

I reach the fork in the road jack-fast. Tojo has either finished or abandoned his sanding of the railings. I don't really want to be seen hanging around on the corner, or to have to explain to Lisa if she arrives from another direction that I'm waiting for her, so I cross the road and bear left onto The Glade, which forms the other boundary to Aunt Sally's house. This is the route that Lisa takes when she's going home. It has particularly high walls and overhanging trees that I can linger under without being conspicuous.

I wait. No sign of her. As I cannot see over the wall I decide to give it ten minutes, in the hope that Lisa will emerge from the wooden door set into the wall beside me. Alternatively, if she comes out through the main gates I will still see her from this vantage point.

But what if she's not in there? Where else can I look? It's a reasonably sunny day but it's windy, I'm cold — and I'm not dressed for hanging around. Still no sign of Lisa. I decide to give it another five minutes.

I try to appear nonchalant to passers-by, casually perusing the Daily Mirror, but I cannot concentrate on it. Eventually, I hear something. The voices are faint at first but soon I can detect that there are three of them. Lisa is definitely in there, but doesn't appear to be in any great hurry to come out. I can hear Tojo, sounding very animated. And then this booming, authoritative voice which I take to be 'Aunt' Sally and which does not fit the mental image I have of her at all.

Eventually, the wooden door opens and Lisa walks out, turns right as if heading for home, and I step out to confront her.

'Where have you been?' It sounds stupid for two reasons: one, I have no right to ask the question; and two, I have just seen her walk out of Aunt Sally's gate, so I obviously know where she's been.

'Oh,' is all she says, rolling her eyes and clenching her fists. She is obviously irritated. 'What now? Are you following me?'

She stops suddenly as if deciding what to do, then turns round and walks back quickly towards the corner, crosses the road at the pedestrian crossing, then turns again and walks up The Glade on the other side of the road to me. Then she decides to sit down on the low wall directly opposite me. I wait for a break in the traffic and cross over to her.

'Look, I'm sorry,' I say.

She looks up and stares at me for a long time.

'Don't mind me,' she says, finally.

'What's up?' I ask.

'Nothing, really. I've just heard a very sad story, that's all.' She sighs and appears to be on the verge of tears.

'About what? About who?'

She nods across the road, pursing her lips.

'Aunt Sally?'

She nods again.

'How did you meet her? I don't know anybody else who has met her. I don't know anybody else who has even seen her.'

'I wrote to her. I put a short note into a Christmas card and posted it to her. I told her I would love to see her garden and enclosed my address. A few days later I had a reply inviting me to call in this morning for coffee.'

'That was quick. Must have been hand-delivered by Tojo.'

'Mmmm. She pauses, tight-lipped, for a few moments. 'His name is not Tojo, by the way, it's Daisuke.' She spells out the name slowly for me. 'You really should try to get these things right. It may be okay for footballers to have childish schoolboy nicknames for each other, but in the real world people expect more.' She states this in a calm, matter-of-fact way; it's a piece of friendly advice rather than an admonishment.

'Okay. Fair enough,' I say, 'Daisuke it is, then.'

'I believe it means a combination of "Great" and "Help" – but don't quote me on that,' she says, cheering up a little.

'Describes him very well, though, "Great Help" – don't you think?'

'Yes, I do. He's been with them a long time,' she says and her lips start to tremble again. 'He's been with Aunt Sally a very long time.'

She shows no sign of standing up so I sit on the wall beside her. I feel I should put my arm around her to offer some comfort. But for some reason I can't quite bring myself to do it. Eventually, she relaxes a little but says nothing for a while, then:

'Sally was married, you know...' she informs me, staring intently at the cracks on the pavement.

Hearing the name 'Sally' without the 'Aunt' prefix immediately undermines the established mental image I have always had of her as a dark, brooding recluse to something far jollier, tho' still a little vague.

'...to an Italian count,' she continues, making the presumption that I am interested in that kind of stuff. 'I cannot recall his full title but it sounded very grand indeed, although Sally assures me that it was one of those aristocratic Italian families that fell on hard times a few generations ago, so it's not as if he had money or land or a castle or anything...'

Her voice trails off. I feel there is more coming so I say nothing and let her resume in her own time.

'It's a very sad story, actually.'

'Why?'

'She was married to Cosimo for more than ten happy years, and then it all suddenly ended. Literally. She was always a bit of a stickler for detail in terms of how the garden was laid out, and it seems that one day Cosimo bought her this plant...'

'He bought her a plant?' I repeat, quite unable to believe that any sad story could hinge on the purchase of a plant.

'Yes. And Sally's immediate thought was that this particular plant wouldn't look right in her Victorian-style garden where everything fitted into a set pattern. She thought at first that she had managed to suppress her instinctive negative reaction, but it seems that Cosimo saw the disappointment in her eyes. The fact that how the plant looked meant more to her than his gesture in buying her a plant in the first place stunned him, and he concluded that this was a sign that their relationship was now based more on comfort than on love. She apologised, of course, when he mentioned it, but to him the damage was done. "One can apologise for one's actions but not for one's feelings," he told her. From that day on, it seems that the relationship was never quite the same again. She did everything she could to reassure him that it was simply a momentary thing, but Cosimo found it hard to believe and accept this.'

'And all because of a plant?'

'I don't think you quite understand,' she replies matter-of-factly.

'What happened then?'

'Well, he probably loved her too much to leave her so he just withdrew into himself.'

'What a prat. Why couldn't he just get over it and get on with it?'

'Well, that question shows that you have a lot to learn about love. He withdrew into himself. He didn't freeze her out or behave in a nasty way to her. He just didn't believe that she loved him – really loved him – any longer. At least not in the way that he wanted her to. She admired him? Yes. Needed him? Yes. Wanted him, even. But loved him?' Lisa shook her head sadly. 'Not any more, he thought.'

'So he didn't leave her?'

'Not in the way that you mean; not physically, no. But he did leave her emotionally. And in the end, he did leave her physically, too. He took his own life.'

'Bloody hell. All because of a poxy plant?'

She gave me another one of those you- don't-understand-these-things-and-you-probably-never-will looks. So I try another tack:

'Is that when she became a recluse?'

'She's not a recluse. It's just that you never see her.' Then she stops, turns, and with hands on hips launches into a tirade. 'Do you know what really irritates me about you? If something doesn't happen directly in that small, enclosed, schoolboy-humour world that you inhabit, you cannot accept that it happens at all. Or that it has any value. She did not become a recluse. She changed. She changed things. She changed herself.'

'There's no need to get all worked up over this new-found friend of yours. This old lady you've known for – how long? – an hour? Two hours? So she changed things. Like what, for example?'

'Okay, maybe I'm being too hard on you. I apologise for the tone – but not the content – of what I said just now. It's just that I think her story is so very sad. What did she change? Well, she tried – is trying – to change herself; from the impulsive, impatient person she used to be to someone more…measured, I think is the word she used. She also changed the garden.'

'The garden? She changed the bleedin' garden!'

'Yes, she changed the garden. Have you ever seen her garden?'

'Not really. Just glimpses through those gaps in the walls and hedges. I've often smelled it, though, when I've been walking past. It's quite nice.'

'Well, the garden used to be laid out just so. Typically Victorian patterns and planted out bedding; all neat and geometric; everything in its place and all colour co-ordinated. After Cosimo died she transformed the garden into the wild Robinsonian style—'

'What's that?' I interject, but she continues in full flow as if she didn't hear me.

'William Robinson was this brilliant nineteenth-century garden designer who believed in natural, wild gardens, as opposed to formal ones. Aunt Sally converted her garden to the Robinsonian style by bringing in trees, shrubs and herbaceous plants from all over the world. You really should see it. Even a Philistine like you could hardly fail to be impressed. She's got beautiful rhododendrons and azaleas that will be breathtaking when they are in full colour during May and June. She has an enormous range of Alpine plants in this magnificent rock garden and a bank of heather that I would love to see again in autumn. It has all the simplicity of an English country garden but on a grander scale. It has very dense planting with very little soil visible. It all looks so natural; so beautiful. And then there's the apiary…

'She keeps birds?' I interject, thinking I may have finally solved the mystery of ownership of the squawking parrot, which had been misattributed to Echo Eddie.

'Apiary,' Lisa corrects without changing tone. 'Sally keeps bees, gathers the honey and…'

'It all sounds very impressive,' I interrupt, 'but what has any of this to do with poor old Cosimo?'

'Don't you see,' she asks and, without waiting for a reply: 'This was her reaction to the fact that her previous obsession with order and formality had resulted in the breakdown of her relationship with Cosimo. It was a gesture on her part; part of her big public gesture. To reject the old way that had failed her.'

'Okay, so it was a big gesture, but hardly a public gesture. You can barely see the garden through the hedges.'

'You still don't get it, do you? Why would a woman take the trouble to deliberately go out wearing odd pieces of clothing and invite ridicule from every oik on the street if she was not committed to making a public statement about her rejection of order and formality?'

The penny finally dropped. 'That's Aunt Sally? The old bag lady with the odd shoes that don't match is Aunt Sally?'

'Oh, so you have met her, then?'

I don't know what to say next, but I need to say something.

'I always thought she was a bit, pardon the pun, odd – but in a loopy kind of way. Cripes, to think that was Aunt Sally all the time.'

Lisa says nothing but she looks less pensive.

'How come I never twigged it was her?' I ask myself out loud.

Lisa suddenly stands up. 'Maybe it's because she has never shown any interest in football,' she says, stoically.

I decide not to respond and wait a few seconds before seizing my opportunity.

'Speaking of which,' I pipe up, 'I'm glad I did bump into you today.'

'Why so?' she asks with resigned disinterest and sits down again.

'Well, last time our paths didn't cross on match day we were held to a scoreless draw. The same thing could have happened today, if I hadn't bumped into you.'

'Don't be ridiculous. You're taking this ritual thing of yours much too seriously. It's all just coincidence. And anyway, you didn't just bump into me – you were skulking under the trees.' Lisa stands up again, says she's just remembered she needs to get to the high street to pick up a few things, and starts to walk back to the corner. I walk back with her.

'Look, this is important to me. Whether you believe in it or not; whether or not you reckon it is all coincidence – it affects me. It affects my mental preparation, it affects my performance – it affects my life. Isn't that important?' I just stop myself from adding 'to you?' but I reckon she read that into it anyway.

She stops at the corner and studies me with feigned sympathy, but treats the question as rhetorical.

'Look,' I start again, 'we've been bumping into each other all season. We both go to The Cabin at roughly the same time on match days. And when we do bump into one another… well, eh…QPR have tended to get a good result. We haven't lost a league match at home all season. Our worst league result at home was a 0–0 draw against Spurs and…'

'…that was the one day we missed each other,' she interjected.

'Exactly,' I said, feeling better at her description 'missed each other'.

'So, what are you suggesting?' she asks immediately.

'All I'm asking is that, as both of us are heading to The Cabin anyway, that we arrange to meet up on the way there or on the way back.'

'Like a date,' she concludes.

'No, not like a date. It's not like that at all.'

'So you're not asking me out on a date. What would you call it, then?'

'I don't know. It's not that I don't look forward to our conversations – well, some of them anyway – but why do we have to call it anything at all?'

'We don't. I just want to be sure what you have in mind.'

'That's all,' I reply, conscious that it all sounds rather pathetic. 'And it's only until the end of the season, the end of April – four months away, or thereabouts. Is that too much to ask?'

She makes a point of pondering over this.

'Okay, I agree,' she smiles, to my surprise. Then, holding my gaze, she asks firmly, 'And what do I get out of this arrangement? Because, despite your undoubted intelligence, the only subject you ever talk about is football; I'm not being taken anywhere interesting; I don't even get the opportunity to go Dutch.'

'Dunno. What do you want out of the arrangement?'

She thinks for a moment, then smiles coyly: 'Well, you could explain the off-site rule to me.'

'Offside, it's called offside,' I retort impatiently.

'Well it said "off-site" in The Guardian. I read it only yesterday.'

'That must have been a spelling mistake. And anyway, since when have you started reading football reports?'

She just shrugs.

'So, okay, it's a deal, then. The offside bit,' I say. 'But not today,' I add hurriedly. 'I'm late already. Let's do it before the next home game against Birmingham on the 17th.'

'It's a deal,' she confirms, 'not a date.'

I nod in acknowledgement.

With that, I start to drift away and up Wellesley Gardens.

'Who are your opponents today?' she calls out after me.

'Newcastle,' I shout back, happier now that we've made some kind of contact, however brief. 'They're called the "Toons". Remember?'

'You mean the "Magpies",' she smiles, turns and heads back down Park Road.

I feel better now. About everything, including the game today. Okay, so Newcastle have been a bit of a bogey team for us in recent times. They beat us 1–3 – at home – in the fourth round of the Football League Cup in November. Then drew 0–0 with us at Loftus Road in the FA Cup and beat us 1–2 in the replay at St James Park…Then, suddenly, it strikes me. 'Magpies,' she said. 'Magpies.' How could she have known that Newcastle are also called the Magpies? Maybe Lisa knows more about football than she lets on. That would be good news. I resolve to ask her next time I see her. And I will definitely ask her about 'trifle' too. But the circumstances have to be just right.

In the meantime, Toons or Magpies, we have to beat Newcastle today. We owe them.

Saturday, 3 January 1976: 4.40 p.m.
Queens Park Rangers…0 Newcastle United…0

14. MODEL BEHAVIOUR?

Saturday, 24 April 1976: Twenty-five minutes into the first half

The home crowd is not happy at the number of fouls being committed by Leeds. The fouls are not nasty, just enough to interrupt the rhythm of our attacks. It's an easy issue to get worked up about. Leeds have a reputation, deserved or not, for this type of play. Not just fouling but general gamesmanship. They would probably call it 'professionalism'; extracting the maximum possible advantage from each and every situation. It's hard to argue with that approach – provided it is done strictly within the rules. But, to be fair, it's not all one-way. Gerry Francis gets a little nudge on Bremner that the referee spots, and Leeds would be within their rights to be totally pissed off at a couple of the tackles on Paul Reaney.

In the early years of the Revie era, Leeds earned a reputation for being a very defensive side. That reputation has stayed with them, even though it is generally acknowledged by those in the game that Leeds became one of the more attractive teams to watch. But they never forgot their roots – and how to look after themselves on the pitch should an opponent attempt to 'try it on' physically with them. Retribution would usually be meted out in equal measure.

This reputation was the anthisisis of how Brian Clough – who replaced Don Revie when he departed Leeds to take over as Manager of England almost two years ago – believed that football should be played. Clough was a dreamer, an idealist who wanted his teams to win by adhering to his belief in the beautiful game. He called a spade a spade – and he called it loudly, regularly and to the widest media audience he could find. His outspoken criticisms of Revie's Leeds formed a theme that he returned to again and again. This behaviour made him enemies within the game, although nobody could argue with his talent for getting the best out of what many observers would have classified as 'ordinary journeyman players'. Neither was he afraid to pay big bucks in transfer fees for players he believed would slot seamlessly into his team. And it was 'his' team. Wherever he went, Clough invariably blended the outstanding and the ordinary into a cohesive, highly effective unit that was exciting to watch, week in, week out.

Until he joined Leeds United.

Clough saw Don Revie's methods as representing all that he thought was wrong with the way the beautiful game had been heading. Even before he took over from Revie at Leeds, Clough had been sniping at what he saw as Revie's 'win-at-all-costs' approach. While acknowledging Leeds successes, he bemoaned the tactics used to achieve them. So it surprised the world of English football when 'Cloughie' – or 'Old Big Head' as he was dubbed by some – replaced Don Revie as Leeds' Manager. Not just because of how critical he had been of the Leeds players, branding them as 'cheats' and highlighting what he saw as their poor disciplinery record. But because Revie himself had already indicated, perhaps obliquely, that his preferred choice as new Manager was the Leeds midfielder Johnny Giles, a suggestion that probably had wide support among the Leeds playing squad, supporters and some of the Board of Directors.

But the job went to Clough, possibly on the basis that he might be better equipped to achieve the one thing that Revie had failed to do. Win the European Cup.

Reports differ on what happened during the first few days of Clough's reign at Leeds. He was criticised for not getting the Leeds 'family' (players, coaches, administration staff, tea ladies, et cetera) together to outline his vision for the club. Instead, he is reputed to have had conversations with players singly and in small groups, during which he told them that they could throw all their medals in the bin, as they had won them unfairly. This would be a typical Clough tactic: say something outrageous to silence people, and then take control of the conversation and dominate it. Not the kind of behaviour to endear him to a bunch of highly talented, successful and much-admired players.

In fairness to Clough, he contended that the players saw themselves as Revie's players, some of them still used the term 'The Boss' to describe Revie even though he had already left the club. There are also suggestions that the behaviour of some of the senior players left much to be desired by their failure (some say refusal) to implement Clough's tactics.

Brian Clough had no time for dossiers. For example, he had what he believed to be a simple, yet very decisive plan last season to deal with QPR: 'Stop Stan Bowles. That's all you need to know about QPR,' he is reported to have told his players before the game at Elland Road. 'Stop Stan Bowles.' He may have been right, but the result did not support his confidence. Leeds lost 1–0 at home to QPR that day. Shortly afterwards, having alienated most of Leeds' top players and won only one game out of the six matches played, Clough lost both the support and confidence of the directors. He departed after just forty-four days as Manager of Leeds.

Saturday, 17 January 1976: 8.45 a.m.

From a distance, I immediately think 'tennis', but as I draw closer it's obvious that it's the handle of a badminton racquet that's protruding from the top of Marianne's basket.

'What happened to the jogging regime, then?' I enquire.

'Too bloody cold,' she says icily.

'So you're taking up badminton?' I ask, trying not to sound sceptical.

'Have taken it up,' she corrects me. 'This is my second week. I got the complete kit in Shopertunities.'

'In Shepherd's Bush? On the Uxbridge Road?' I ask. I know the place as it's quite near Loftus Road.

'No, the one up in Holborn, opposite Chancery Lane,' she corrects. 'I got it for £2.95 all in, net, shuttlecocks and two racquets — although we've only used one so far.'

And with that she scowls up at the bedroom window. I look up too but the curtains are drawn, although not quite fully drawn and I have the distinct impression that Marjorie is watching.

When I look back, I think I denote the faintest hint of a smile flickering across Marianne's lips. I smile back and then, on the spur of the moment, I decide to risk it:

'I don't suppose you've seen Bernie Trout recently in your travels?'

Wrong move. She is obviously annoyed that I would even ask.

'Why ask me?'

'Dunno. Just asking.'

'I don't frequent his establishment.'

'Okay.'

'Why don't you ask someone that knows him?'

'Good suggestion, Marianne. I'll do that.'

'What about that Italian woman?'

'Italian woman?'

'Yes, the one with the fur coat and cheap perfume who keeps trying to run me down in that noisy car of hers.'

'Svetlana?'

'Yes, if that's her name. Why don't you ask her? I'm sure you'd enjoy that.'

'But why Svetlana?'

'Well, she used to work in the Horsemans, didn't she? I know she doesn't work there any more, but she must be making money somewhere to pay for all those expensive clothes because that husband of hers can't be earning much.'

'Eddie?'

'Whatever he's called. Assuming he is her husband, of course.'

All this delivered with such ill-concealed venom that it is difficult for me to take it all in. What is she trying to tell me? That there was something going on between Bernie Trout and Svetlana? That she actually worked for Trouty at one stage? That she may have a 'sugar daddy' who is keeping her now? And that she may not even be married to Eddie?

The bit about Eddie's lack of money was the only part that was not surprising. But why would Marianne come out with all of this in response to an innocent question? It's not the behaviour I would have expected of her. It's as if she had been storing it all up for a long time, just waiting to let rip.

We stand opposite each other for what seems like an eternity, saying nothing. Then she starts again on her 'I don't know why you are asking me' rant.

'Let's just leave it, Marianne,' I say and start to walk away.

The traffic is bumper-to-bumper and Marianne cannot find a gap into which to hurtle, so I leave her 'harrumphing' loudly on the edge of the pavement and continue on to the corner of Aunt Sally's — or Odd Sally, as I'm tempted to call her. I conclude from the numerous *cheeky double honks, that some of the drivers are exacting their revenge on Marianne by keeping her stranded on the pavement this morning. A brief glance behind me confirms this. She waves her fist at the driver of a new Leyland Mini Clubman who has accelerated suddenly to close the gap between himself (actually, it turns out to be a she) and the white Chrysler Imp in front.*

The railings at Aunt Sally's have all been freshly painted black and Daisuke is now painting the fleur-de-lis finials with gold leaf paint. The railings look good but the overall appearance is let down somewhat by the distressed condition of the walls. There are two builder-types having an argument about something — probably the repairs required to the walls.

Daisuke stands up and remonstrates with them, his voice rising in short, staccato bursts. This isn't a discussion that I can make any meaningful contribution to, so I push on and cross the road at the intersection and on to Beane Row.

I arrive at Eddie's just in time to hear a car door slam and engines revving, and I have to jump out of the way a bit nifty as Svetlana drives out the gate, without as much as a sidelong glance at me. A bit rude, I think, not what I would usually expect from her. But I can tell right away from Eddie's demeanour that they've had a row. Blimey, everybody's at it. What's happening around here this morning? Maybe Marianne has a point about Eddie and Svetlana's relationship.

'Somebody got out of bed on the wrong side this morning, eh Eddie?' I say, trying to keep things light and humourous.

I immediately regret using that saying, because Eddie doesn't really understand our English figures of speech; that they are not meant to be taken literally.

'Last night, last night,' Eddie corrects me humourlessly. 'She got out of wrong bed last night.'

My conversation with Marianne ten minutes ago comes to mind again. At this stage, I don't know if this is typical Eddie, mixing up his language and his tenses, or if he is trying to tell me something. And if it's the latter, then I don't reckon I want to hear the full story. Actually, on reflection, I would love to hear the whole story — but not from Eddie, I don't.

It's obvious too that Eddie doesn't want to engage in conversation today. He continues whatever it is he is doing, ignoring my presence.

'Birmingham today,' I intrude as cheerfully as I can. 'Birmingham City.'

'Bluddy spaghetti junction,' Eddie grumbles, without even looking up.

'Okay, suit yourself,' I mutter under my breath and walk slowly on, thinking he might relent and call me back to discuss his thoughts on Birmingham's football team or at least the city's road infrastructure.

But he doesn't.

Popping into Noah Berrie's provides some very welcome relief after all of the altercations I've witnessed this morning. The shop is an oasis of calm — which suits me this morning but cannot be good for Noah's business.

'Has it been this quiet all week?' I ask.

'The calm before the storm, young man, the calm before the storm.'

As if on cue, Colonel Martin blunders in, all sweating and gasping for breath. He ignores me and rumbles forward, demanding Noah's attention not so much by calling him as by his very arrival in the shop. This is a man with an inbred sense of entitlement. I almost expect him to rap on the counter with his cane, but I notice he is not carrying one today.

Noah does a very good job at fawning over him. It's not a very pleasant thing to witness but probably necessary in his particular business. I don't really want to hang around, but I feel that Noah probably expects me to. For a few minutes, at least. Surprisingly, it only takes a few minutes for them to transact a deal and the Colonel starts to march out again, this time carrying a cane. I turn my back on him and block his path so that he has to ask me to move. What he does is to mutter something completely unintelligible but in a manner that demands that I move. I think about ignoring him so that he will have to ask more politely, but Noah gives one of his apologetic little theatrical coughs and I decide that it might be better for Noah's business if I move.

'So, a new cane for the Major Fatso?' I say, as soon as he is out of earshot. 'Colonel,' Noah corrects me, testily. 'And it's not a cane, it's a swagger stick. It's shorter than a cane and is usually carried by a person as a sign of authority. It can also be used as a riding crop.'

I raise my eyebrows at this: 'Can't imagine old Fatso on horseback, somehow.' Before Noah can respond to this observation, the next stage of the storm blows in. Aunt Sally, carrying two shopping bags – not matching, naturally – arrives and makes a beeline for a corner of the shop containing colourful bric-a-brac. Noah immediately dances towards her and I take this as my cue to leave, although, given the recent revelations about her background, I would have liked to hang on to observe the interaction between the two of them.

Mick is all dressed up this morning, albeit sombrely. Cathal is helping out behind the counter and there's some of his favourite 'wolf' tunes playing in the background. As soon as he sees me, Mick comes out from behind the counter and greets me at the tail end of the small queue.

'I have to go to a funeral this morning,' he explains, 'nobody in the family – just an old drinking buddy. But I knew you wouldn't want to miss me – seeing as I'm an essential part of your ritual – so I decided to hang around til you came in.'

'Thanks, Mick, I really appreciate that.'

'Well, we've come so far in this together, Dawhee me bucko, I would hate to be the one to break the spell and spoil things for you. Not like some I could mention. Although, to be fair, if you had told Mr Trout that he was part of your ritual and how important it was to you, I'm sure he would have changed his plans – or at least told you what he was up to.'

'I suppose you're right. Still no sign of him, I presume?'

'No, and that surprises me. Because, given his fascination for flying, I thought he would have made it his business to be here – and to be flying on the inaugural flight of Concorde.'

'When's that?' I ask. I know nothing about it, but then, why would I? I have no interest in aviation.

'This Wednesday, London to Bahrain — lots of sun there. That would have appealed to your Mr Trout too. Anyway, I have to go now. It's bad luck to be late for a funeral,' he winks, 'except maybe your own.'

Brad is at the head of the queue, with Lisa just behind him. I hear Brad asking for his NME, giving it the full 'New Musical Express' title on this occasion. He obviously wants to avoid leaving himself open to being, pardon the pun, the butt of any jokes from Cathal on enemas and bowel evacuation. But Cathal is being quite pleasant to Brad this morning. 'Enjoy,' he smiles, folding the newspaper and handing it to Brad. But Brad hasn't learnt to quit while he's ahead. He makes a big deal of opening the tabloid at the counter and perusing the listings pages, murmuring the names of the acts he intends seeing and the various venues, punctuated with little exclamations of 'wow', 'far out' and 'fab'.

'Next, please,' Cathal smiles over Brad's shoulder at Lisa. But Brad doesn't move.

'I don't suppose there's anything in here that would interest you, Cattle,' Brad pronounces loudly. 'No Celtic "diddley-aye" stars? No...'

'Page 47,' interjects Cathal, 'Alex Campbell, legendary Scottish folk singer. He's playing at the Albany in Twickenham on Tuesday. You should go.'

'I don't think so,' Brad laughs, nervously.

'Then what about taking in the hardest-working band in the world — "Ceilidh"? Look,' Cathal stubs his finger on a number of spots on the page, 'they're playing at six different venues on the same night.'

'They are, too,' says Brad, sounding impressed, 'look, Lisa.'

Lisa looks bored and impatient. She just stares at Brad, not in a judgemental way but almost pityingly. Brad mutters something about seeing her later and walks off, his head deep in the detail of the listings.

'I don't know how you did that, Cathal,' (she is very careful with the 'Cauhal' pronounciation), 'but it seemed to do the trick.'

The last five minutes — Brad's embarrassment and Lisa's lack of sympathy — have been music to my ears.

'Easy,' Cathal grins, 'a "ceilidh" means a "dance" in Gaelic. All the Irish folk clubs in London have them every weekend. I'm surprised Brad hadn't spotted it before and worked it out, the eejit.'

Lisa smiles, buys her Guardian and indicates that she will wait outside for me. Today has definitely taken a turn for the better.

I pay Cathal for the Mirror.

'Who are you playing today?' he asks.

'Birmingham.'

'Ah. Hit 'em for six,' he says quickly.

I get the impression from his demeanour that there is some little joke or pun hidden in that comment, but I cannot work it out and I don't intend risking the embarrassment of trying to find out. Instead, I hurry outside to meet up with Lisa.

'What was all that stuff regarding your Mr Stanley Bowles in the newspapers yesterday?'

'Whatcha mean?'

'I heard that he had his photograph taken with a topless model. Is it true?'

'Yeah, I reckon it is.'

'Don't you know?' she demands, arms gesticulating wildly.

'Yeah, of course I know. Like you said: it was in the paper yesterday.'

'The photograph was published in the newspaper?'

'Yeah. It was in yesterday's Daily Mirror.'

'But he's married! Isn't he?'

'Yeah.'

'How awful. For his wife.'

'Yeah.'

'You don't seem too concerned?'

'It's not my concern.'

'But why did he do it?'

'Why does Stan do anything?'

'I don't know. You tell me!'

'Money!'

'But he put his marriage at risk.'

'Stan probably wouldn't see it that way. He was offered some money to do it. He needed the money. So...'

'And you believe that's okay?'

'I didn't say that. Why are you so interested in Stan Bowles' private life, or in Stan Bowles at all, for that matter? You said you had no interest in football.'

'I'm not interested in Mr Stan Bowles or his private life. I'm interested in your opinion on what he did. It's a moral issue and I'd like to know what you think – especially since you're asking me to meet you before every home match and you insist on talking about football all the time.'

'Well, for a start, it isn't a moral issue. It's a money issue. Look, all I heard is that the newspaper offered Stan £500 to pose with Jenny Clarke.'

'Oh, so you know her?'

'I don't know her. Jenny Clarke is a topless model who often appears in the Daily Mirror.'

'The Daily Mirror? That's your newspaper, isn't it? One of those red tops as you call them. Is this, eh, model person a redhead?'

'How should I know? Anyway, Stan needed the dosh and accepted. Then it seems that the model was in a motor accident on her way home – crashed her car or something, I don't know – and her boyfriend couldn't get in touch with her and became concerned. Meanwhile, Stan was probably spending the money with his mates at some dog track.'

'Lord, what a bunch. I don't know how you mix with them.'

'Who? Footballers or models? Most footballers I know are okay guys. But I'm not sure I'd trust some of those models. Speaking of which, I hear that you're considering taking up modelling as a career.'

'I most certainly am not. Who did you hear that from?'

'I heard Brad made you a proposition.'

'What a crude way to express it. You're beginning to sound more like the Butlers every day. I bet Jacko or Billy started that rumour, didn't they?'

'Most definitely Not Guilty of that offence,' I say emphatically, before adding under my breath: 'though I wouldn't be so certain of anything else.'

'I beg your pardon, I didn't hear that. What did you say?'

'I said you can ask them yourself. Here they are now.'

But before we can get into any of that, Jacko calls me to one side.

'Can I 'ave a word?' he whispers and I know something dodgy is coming.

'Christ, Jacko, the last bloke who asked me that frightened the shit out of me,' I say, hoping to postpone whatever it is that Jacko is about to ask me.

'Who woz that, then?' Jacko pretends to be interested.

'You remember. A few months back. That bloke in the sharp suit who was hiding under the trees there at Aunt Sally's place. Tough looking bloke. You remember.'

'Oh, yeaaah, I remember 'im,' Jacko lies. 'Wotever 'appened to 'im?'

'He signed for Milwall, I think.'

'Wha?' Jacko looks mystified for a few seconds, then: 'Ah, you's takin' the piss, aintcha?' Jacko starts to roll a cigarette, fumbling with the paper and spilling some tobacco on the ground.

'Never mind. What's up?' I decide I'd better get it over with.

'Well, it's 'bout the Arrow, you see.' He starts kicking away the tobacco while he rolls the cigarette.

'What arrow?

'The dog Arrow. Arrow the dog.' Jacko dangles between his lips the messiest looking rollie that I've ever seen.

'You now have a dog called Arrow?'

'Yeah. Didn't ya know?' He lights up and immediately begins to cough.

'No. I thought your dog was called Roxy Roy or something.'

'Well, 'e woz called Roxborough Roy...' Jacko starts spitting out small pieces of tobacco leaf.

'It's the same dog?' I ask, wiping bits of tobacco off my shirt.

'Same ol' mutt,' Jacko gives a nervous laugh and starts coughing and spitting again.

'Why did you change his name?'

'Well, we wanted a speedier kind of name. And something a bit less posh,' Jacko responds, regaining his composure.

'But you can't change the name of a dog just like that. There must be rules...'

'Why not? Wot rules?'

'Well, there must be a greyhound version of the the Football Association. Isn't there a Useless Greyhound Association or something?'

'F**ked if I know, mate. Anyway, wot's to stop Stan Bowles changing 'is name to Tommy Atkins? All legally like. The FA would just 'ave to accept it, wouldn't they?'

'I suppose they would, but at least everybody would know it was Stan. They know what Stan looks like so there would be no confusion. With a dog, it can be a bit more difficult to...'

And then it hits me.

'You're not going to try to pretend it's a different dog, are you?'

Silence.

'You are! Christ, Jacko, why would you do such a thing?'

'We got our reasons. We got our plans,' he protests and starts to cough again.

'I can't believe you would take such risks over an animal that probably couldn't outrun,' I search for an example, 'that Colonel Martin over there.' I point towards the Colonel huffing his way up Park Road carrying a large bagful of books. Jacko is not amused and looks decidedly offended.

'Now, that's unfair, mate, that is very unfair. Arrow's improved a lot since you last clapped eyes on 'im.'

'I cannot believe that, Jacko.' I'm conscious that I'm beginning to raise my voice. 'That I will have to see for myself.'

'Well, that's wot I wanted to talk to you about,' Jacko shouts. Then he switches to a conspiratorial whisper: 'Tha's the problem, see. You can't. See 'im. You can't see 'im.'

'Why not?' (I find myself whispering too.)

Jacko shrugs: 'Missin'. Again.'

'When?'

'Coupla nights ago.'

I shut my eyes. I give up. 'Jacko, what has any of this got to do with me?'

'Glad you asked, mate. Here's wot I need ya to do.'

'No, Jacko.'

'Hear me out, mate. Hear me out.' He puts his arm around my shoulder, no mean feat, given the difference in our heights. I can smell last night's curry and this morning's tobacco off his breath as he steers me a few yards away from where Billy and Lisa are by now deep in conversation.

'To make a long story short, I fink your friend Echo Eddie 'as nicked 'im − Arrow, that is − and 'as 'im locked up in that garage of 'is. You gets on well wiv 'im so I thought maybe you could 'ave a word and keep an ear out; pay 'im a visit while 'es working like and 'ave a butcher's about the place.'

'That's crazy. Why would Eddie do that?' I ask stupidly, instead of immediately ending the conversation and walking away. But Jacko's arm around my shoulder is vice-like. He's stronger than I thought.

'To get back at me 'cos...' Jacko stops up short.

'Because of what?'

'Well, cos Arrow sometimes gets out at night and prob'ly messes up ol' Echo's garden,' Jacko finally admits, relaxing his grip.

I wrestle myself free: 'And did it never occur to you that once Poxy Roxy or "Arrow" or whatever you call him these days is out, that he might not want to come back again? That he might simply have run away?'

'Nah, mate, 'e'd never do that. Not in 'is nature.'

'Great, so now I'm listening out for a non-existent parrot and greyhound who may already be a hundred miles away.'

'Thanks, mate, I knew I could count on ya.' Jacko pats me on the shoulder before shuffling back to Billy.

'Anything else?' I shout after him sarcastically.

Jacko pauses, then turns.

'Yeah,' he smiles. 'Now I remember 'im. Army man I fink you said he woz. Wearin' a very expensive tin-of-fruit, I seem to remember. And a roller wiv 'is own driver. Asking you about ol' Trouty, he woz. Wotever did 'appen to 'im?'

I say nothing. Suddenly, I'm more concerned about what might have happened to Bernie Trout than continuing a conversation with Jacko.

'Was that all about Mr Trout? Is there any news of him?' Lisa asks, sympathetically, as soon as we've left the brothers. I decide not to go into the shadier details of the ridiculous missing dog story and concentrate instead on the Bernie Trout angle. Lisa can understand my concern but she thinks it's becoming an obsession for me.

'Of course it's an obsession. Football's an obsession,' I retort indignantly. 'I need to have Bernie Trout here in order to stick to the original ritual.'

'But, it doesn't even work.'

'What doesn't work?'

'This ritual of yours.'

'It's working so far.'

'Maybe. But not the way you think it is. You said that if I missed another "date" you would either lose or it would be a scoreless draw. Well, we did bump into each other two weeks ago, but the match against Newcastle still ended scoreless.'

'Yeah, but that was a strange day.'

'It's a strange ritual. Because I read that you lost the replay too.'

I didn't really need to be reminded of that 1–2 defeat, but I make the point to Lisa that it was away at Newcastle. And it was the FA Cup too and not the league.

'You know, I believe you simply adapt this ritual of yours to suit the circumstances. You lost another game last week two to one against Manchester, and I bet you are going to tell me now that it doesn't matter because it was not played at Lotus Park.'

Her knowledge of our recent results cheers me up a bit — even if the results didn't. She must be reading up on it. So I forgive her getting Loftus Road wrong again. I reckon she is genuinely getting it wrong and not being obtuse.

We reach the Glade and she wishes me good luck this afternoon. After we part, my thoughts immediately turn to today's game. Birmingham City are not doing well and, on form to date, we should beat them easily. They've lost 10 of their 12 away games so far and conceded 32 goals — the highest number of Goals Against of any team away from home this season. But with guys like Bob Hatton and Peter Withe up front being prompted by Trevor

Francis and Howard Kendall prowling around the middle of the park, we simply cannot afford to underestimate them.

We'll miss Gerry Francis today but John Beck is a fine stand-in. We drew 1–1 at St Andrews back in September, and although they beat us 0–1 at Loftus Road last season, given their recent record, I expect us to win this one easily – and maybe score a hatful of goals in the process.

Saturday, 17 January 1976: 4.40 p.m.
Queens Park Rangers...2 Birmingham City...1

15. FRANK EXCHANGES

Saturday, 24 April 1976: Half an hour gone in first half

A long raking clearance by Ian Gillard almost lets Don Givens in for a header, but Norman Hunter of Leeds charges across swiftly to avert the danger and head it away to Paul Madeley, the Leeds number 5. Madeley stumbles as he receives the ball on the edge of the penalty area but he recovers his poise, makes a few yards and when confronted by Stan, he slips the ball out to Paul Reaney on the touchline. Reaney passes back to Hunter who hits a long, dangerous raking clearance straight into the heart of our defence. Centre-half Frank McLintock calmly takes it on his upper thigh, lets it drop gently to the ground and then effortlessly lays it off. The ball is moved on to Gerry Francis whose pass goes astray and the move breaks down.

Ten minutes later and Hunter is the instigator of another through ball, this time straight to the feet of Joe Jordon. Almost. In nips Frank McLintock to take it off Jordon's toe. The ball falls into the path of the oncoming Billy Bremner. But Frank's momentum has carried him on after the ball and he stretches out his right leg to flick it away from the feet of the Leeds captain. Full-back Ian Gillard hoofs it forward, but the attack breaks down and the ball is swiftly returned into our half courtesy of Bremner. Jordon nods it down but before he can control it, in steps Frank, and although still retreating from the earlier play and now facing his own goal, he still manages to deftly hook it over his shoulder, where Don Masson is waiting to receive it and start another Rangers attack.

Neat, incisive interceptions are part of Frank McLintock's stock in trade, built up over a stellar career. His reading of the game and his instinctive positional skills are second to none. He is a great role model for the younger players at the club. But he will also let you know if you are not quick or accurate enough – no matter who you are. I've already felt the lash of his tongue on a couple of occasions this afternoon. And we're only twenty minutes into the game!

Frank exchanged his Arsenal shirt for the hoops of QPR about three years ago, having spent nine seasons with the Gunners. During his time with Arsenal he captained the club during their great period of success under Manager Bertie Mee. He led Arsenal to that Inter-Cities Fairs Cup Final win in 1969–70 beating Anderlecht 4–3 in the final. The following year, he lifted the Gunners' first League and FA Cup double. He captained Arsenal again in the FA Cup Final in 1972, but this time they lost – to Leeds United. Which might explain why Frank in particular is really up for it today.

Saturday, 7 February 1976: 8.50 a.m.

It's a mild morning but I quickly encounter a bout of turbulence as soon as I reach Palace Pleass. Marjorie is shouting something while leaning out from her open window of the reception room on the first floor. Marianne is gesticulating frantically, but silently, for her to shut the window — presumably in the hope of not attracting the attention of passers-by. Some hope. Marjorie is bawling. My arrival at Marianne's side appears to do the trick, however, and Marjorie immediately withdraws and slams the window shut. But I can see her standing with her back to the window, obviously still sobbing away. I decide to forget about what happened the last time I met Marianne — at least temporarily — as there is obviously something going on between herself and Marjorie this morning.

'I don't wish to intrude, Marianne, but...'

'Don't!' Marianne is standing rigidly still on the pavement, one hand steadying her bicycle, the other extended in my direction like a policeman's, as if halting traffic.

'I was only...'

'Don't!' She pauses, then: 'Just...just don't.'

People are beginning to stop and look quizically at one another, then at me. I just shrug and walk on. I've had enough of this nonsense. I don't know if Marianne is genuinely very upset or if she is using the altercation with Marjorie as a way of avoiding me asking her about Trouty again.

I reach Aunt Sally's and the same two builders are there again, arguing the toss with Daisuke. There's a sense of déjà vu about this morning. I linger idly, waiting for the traffic to pass before attempting to cross the road. With the prevailing mood of most people this morning, I'm not taking any chances. Suddenly there's the chiming of a bell and I feel the impact of the front wheel of a bicycle running over the toes of my left foot.

'Marianne! For f**k's sake,' I yell as she brings the bicycle to a halt by driving the pedal against my knee.

'There's no need for that language. I'm surprised at you, of all people,' she retorts.

'Well, I reckon you've broken my f**king toe,' I grimace. 'And I've got a match this afternoon.'

'Well, I'm very sorry.'

'What were you thinking of, anyway, barging into me like that?'

'I just wanted to say I'm sorry.'

'You just wanted to say you're sorry before you barged into me?'

'Yes. But not for barging into you, although I'm sorry for that too. I wanted to apologise for what happened. It was wrong of me to react to you in that way.'

'Marianne, I'm not interested in what happened this morning. Or the last time we met. I'm more worried about what's going to happen this afternoon. Or more specifically, what might not happen this afternoon. My involvement in a vital f**king football match, for example.'

'Hmmph. Well, now I have apologised. And I'm not going to stand here listening to industrial language any longer. Goodbye.'

And with that she straddles her bike (I jump back) and she propels herself at a 45-degree angle out into the oncoming traffic. Miraculously, she manages to navigate an almost straight diagonal line across to the far lane, missing oncoming traffic by inches and no doubt becoming familiar with a few new words from the lexicon of industrial language en route.

I hobble across the road and try to walk off the pain. It begins to work so I keep going apace, not hanging around to see if Echo Eddie or the Butler brothers are at home. Hopefully, I can pick them up on the way back and maintain the ritual. I head straight for Noah's place.

'Good mornington. I see you are neither buying nor selling today but limping.'

'Oh, it's nothing much. I'll have walked it off by the time I get home.'

'So is it sympathy or retribution you are looking for, my friend? It seems every sportsman is looking for one or the other, these days.'

'How so?'

'Haven't you seen today's newspaper yet?'

'Haven't got it yet, never mind read it. What's up?'

'Well, you know Frank Bough…'

'The Grandstand presenter?'

'That's him. It seems he's had a major row with the BBC because they haven't asked him to host their coverage of the Winter Olympics. He says he was promised it and even gave up Nationwide in order to do it.'

'Who's doing it then? The Winter Olympics. Who's presenting it?'

'This is where it gets interesting, my friend, because the Beeb has given it to none other than Frank's arch rival, David Coleman.'

'That must have really pissed him off. Coleman used to present Grandstand too, before Frank Bough.'

'He certainly did. So you can sympathise with the man. Now here comes the retribution bit: Frank Bough has only gone and sacked his agent. Who also happens to be the agent of…?'

'Not David Coleman?'

'Yes, David Coleman.'

We agree it would be disappointing if the BBC were to lose either of these heavyweight sports commentators. Both are very knowledgeable about sport, but about football in particular.

'What happens next?' *I ask, as a potential customer in the form of Colonel Martin suddenly fills the doorframe and bumbles in.*

'I've no idea, but I'm sure your newspaper will speculate wildly about it,' *Noah booms, waving his hand in a dismissive gesture. I take this to mean that the audience with Noah has ended and that I should go buy the paper in The Cabin, while Noah deals with the rare challenge of converting the curious into a customer.*

'That was a good win for us last Monday night,' *I suggest.*

'Mick Leach's testimonial? Ah, a great club player. Versatile and very committed. He deserves every penny he got. I'll bet there was a big turnout for that game.'

'Actually, the crowd was a bit of a disappointment. Only about 8,000 people turned up.'

'Was it the weather d'you reckon, Dawhee?'

'Don't think so, Mick. Most people I spoke to blame the bombings in the West End on the Thursday. Twelve IRA bombs in one day: I reckon that's enough to keep most people at home.'

Mick braces himself by putting his two hands on the counter in front of him, leans forward, hangs his head, stares down at the counter and sighs. He says nothing and I feel really sorry for him. I'm even sorrier that I mentioned the bombings.

'Good win, though,' I say to break the silence, '4–0 against a famous European side like Red Star Belgrade can't be bad. That was the team that Manchester United had just played when their plane crashed in Munich back in 1958.'

Mick is still staring at the counter.

'Was it? I don't remember.'

He raises his head: 'I think it was. The Busby Babes. I'm sure it was.'

'Probably was, then.'

'All those wasted lives,' he sighs.

I'm not sure if he is referring to the players who lost their lives in the air crash or to the people who have died in the IRA bombings. Probably both.

There's an awkward silence after this that I take as a hint that I should leave.

I cross over to the Green, hoping I might bump into Lisa there. I see her through the window of the Olde Fayre Green café. She is heavily engrossed in her newspaper. There's also some other stuff on the table — loose sheets of yellow foolscap paper filled with notes and a gum-bound pad of similar paper, plus lots of 'post-it' notes — that she stuffs into the large manila envelope beside her the moment she spies me coming towards her.

'Hello stranger,' she says, without much warmth, as I approach. 'I haven't seen you around for, oh, about three weeks. I thought maybe you had been injured. Or moved.'

If she did think that, she didn't appear too concerned about it.

'No, I'm a Ranger 'til I die,' I reassured her.

'I meant moved house,' she says rather sharply.

'No, not that either. It's just that we had a couple of away games on the trot,' I explain and I pause before adding: 'So you missed me, then?'

She looks up slowly from the table and sighs gently, as if I had asked her a deeply personal question.

'Brad asked me this morning if I had seen you, and when I thought about it I realised I hadn't seen you for a while,' she says matter-of-factly, as if explaining something simple to a child.

I took this to mean no, she hadn't missed me, and that Brad was still on the scene.

'So, why did you think I had been injured these last couple of weeks?' I ask in the jolliest tone I can muster.

'I didn't,' she replies emphatically. 'I only thought that when you walked in just now. Or perhaps "hobbled in" would be a more apt description.'

For a moment I wonder if it would be best to simply make some excuse and walk out, but she suddenly pushes her newspaper to one side and tells me to sit down.

'So what did happen to that foot of yours?' she enquires.

I explain about Marianne and the bike, and Lisa emits lots of 'ouches', 'oohs' and sympathetic grimaces. By the end of the conversation she has cheered up a little and appears to be less preoccupied. But she tells me that she cannot stay too long and is already late (for what, she doesn't say). She half-apologises for not being able to stay and asks if there is another home game next week, as there have been two away games in succession. I tell her that the fixture list doesn't work like that.

'We've got an away game next Saturday, but maybe we could meet up anyway.'

'How so – if you've got an away game?'

'It's a London derby. Just up the road. Against Tottenham.'

'I wouldn't say Tottenham was exactly "just up the road" as you call it. Are you not worried about being late?'

'We could meet early. Eight o'clock?'

'Hmm. That's usually a little early for me on Saturdays, quite frankly, but let's see.' She makes a big deal of taking a slim pocket diary out of her bag and flicking through it. 'Next Saturday? Hmmm. Where are we? February. Ah yes. Saturday February 14th,' she announces.

'That's it,' I say without out further comment.

She consults the diary again.

'Yes, I believe I can do that,' she says matter-of-factly, raising her eyes to look at me over the top of the diary.

I look away and say nothing.

She smiles briefly and then concentrates her attention on flattening out the pocket diary on the table and taking the top off her green ballpoint pen. Writing slowly and deliberately, she makes two short entries that seem to take her an age to complete. The writing appears very legible but at this distance I cannot read it upside down – even if I wanted to.

We leave and stroll up Park Road together.

She takes the Mirror out of my hand without asking and scans the front page.

'Alvin says a gentle goodbye,' she reads the headline aloud. 'Pop. Star. And. Wife. To. Part,' she adds before folding the paper and handing it back to me. 'Do you think that Alvin Stardust's marriage break-up is the most important story in the world this morning?'

'I'm not responsible for what they put in the newspaper,' I retort.

'But you buy it. Every day,' is her instant rejoinder.

'I buy it for the football – as you well know. Look, it's been three weeks since we last met so I'm not getting into a row about this. Some people like to read about famous people's marriage break-ups – even if you Guardian readers don't.'

She says nothing for a minute, then: 'Speaking of marriages, how is Mr Bowles these days?'

I turn to her in surprise but she is smirking: 'Us Guardian readers like to hear about famous people's relationships just as much as anybody else.'

'Stan's doing okay.'

'But what about his wife?'

'Ann is upset, obviously.'

'How insightful of you. What does the poor thing do now?'

'She's already done it. Gone back home to Manchester.'

'Good for Ann. And how's your friend Mister Bowles feeling?'

'Dunno. Most likely depends on whether the two dogs came home at good odds at White City greyhound track the other night. Seriously, though, Stan is obviously upset too. He's handed in a transfer request.'

'So he's leaving QPR?'

'Well, I wouldn't go that far. You see, this wouldn't be the first time that Stan has asked for a transfer to another club. Most likely he'll change his mind after a few days.'

'And what does the club think? What about the Gaffer, as you insist on calling him – that nice Mr Sexton you keep telling me is a decent man – what will he do regarding all of this?'

'Well, the Gaffer only deals with on-field issues. The three Ts as we call them: Training, Team selection and Tactics. Personal issues are dealt with by Mr Gregory, the Chairman.'

'So Mr Sexton did nothing?'

'Well, he dropped Stan for the last two games.'

'What about the next match?'

'Today against Wolves? Stan's back.'

'And what will Mr Gregory do?'

'Well, he tends to indulge Stan a bit. Regards him as a bit of a wayward son.'

'I'll bet he does. So you're telling me that nothing more will happen?'

I look at her sheepishly, holding out my arms in a 'what can I do?' gesture.

She suddenly grabs the newspaper back from me and scans the back page.

'Imagine reading this kind of stuff every day. Imagine mixing with these people. Oh. It makes my blood boil.'

'Boiling blood, heh, heh, just like vampires.' We have arrived almost without noticing at Eddie's gate.

'Oh, nothing as dramatic as that,' Lisa replies, quick as a flash. 'We were just discussing a film I saw recently: *Young Frankenstein.*'

'I see that too, heh, heh,' Eddie exclaims excitedly as if this was some kind of a huge coincidence. 'Where you see it? When you see it?'

I was hoping that this morning's exchanges with Eddie would be of a passing nature, but Lisa stops.

'The Odeon in Richmond. Last Sunday week, I believe.'

'No,' says Eddie, without any hint of his trademark smile. 'No,' he repeats, emphatically. To Eddie, it obviously cannot be the same film if they both saw it in different cinemas or on different dates.

'So ol' Eddie's denying everyfink, is 'e?' comes the unmistakable voice of Jacko, as the brothers-in-arms hove into view. The veneer of cheerfulness about them this morning doesn't quite mask an underlying sardonic air.

'I deny nothink,' says Eddie. 'Polis come to you.'

'Police? What's he on about?' I ask Jacko.

'Ah, he must 'ave seen the Ole Bill call to the 'ouse.' Jacko waves away the issue, then whispers to me confidentially: 'It seems they wozn't exactly totally convinced about ole Finchley's retraction of 'is original statement.'

'You threaten Finch,' interjects Eddie. 'He nice, Finch.'

'Finch? You've got birds on the soddin' brain, mate,' responds Jacko icily, tapping his temple with his forefinger at each word before turning back to face me: 'Anyway, there is sweet bugger-all they can do about it now. The upshot of it is that the Ole Bill said that we is no longer suspects in the case. Still, we did 'ave wot you might call a frank exchange of views.'

'Did you threaten him, Jacko?' I ask him quietly. 'Old Mr Finchley. Did you threaten him?'

'Look, mate, I said it's over. Okay? Case closed. No problem. Why don't you concentrate on solving your own little problems? Bowles is dropped. We've slipped to fifth in the table. And we could be really up against it today.'

'Shouldn't be too much of a problem,' I reply unconvincingly. 'Actually, for your information, we've got Stan back again. Okay, we're fifth in the table. But then, they're nineteenth.'

'Nineteenth or not, I'd be wary of 'em today, if I woz you,' Jacko says dismissively. 'I saw 'em on the telly, a few weeks back,' he adds, 'and they were good, were Wolves.'

'Werewolves?' Eddie's jaw drops. 'Who play like werewolves?'

'Bobby Gould and John Richards,' laughs Jacko, sarcastically. 'They're a couple of werewolves all right. Once the ball is in the Rangers penalty area, those guys will smell blood. You mark my words.'

'But Rangers got the silver bullets,' interjects Billy, giving Jacko a playful nudge in the shoulder with his fist.

'Silver bullets? Wot you on about, Billy, you dozy c**t,' Jacko responds, giving his brother a less than playful punch in the chest.

I notice Lisa wincing out of the corner of my eye.

'S'wot they use to kill werewolves, Jacko; silver bullets,' protests Billy, giving his older sibling a sharp prod in the ribs.

'Yeah. But 'e don't know that does 'e?' gasps Jacko. Then, turning back to Eddie he shouts, 'An' why don't ya learn proper English, ya thick Swede. Not that pigeon-English ya keep spoutin'.'

'Parrot-English, even,' Billy mutters to Jacko.

'Parrot-English? Wot are ya on about this mornin'?' Jacko jabs Billy in the stomach with the point of his elbow. A bit of 'handbags' follows before the brothers suddenly break and slope off in sulky silence, a few yards apart like two stray dogs who have just engaged in an inconclusive test of strength over territory. I deliberately decide not to enquire if there has been any change in the status of the missing dog.

Lisa looks after them, obviously disappointed at their behaviour. I give her a well-I-did-warn-you look. We walk on to the corner making small talk.

'Why do the Butlers refer to QPR as "we"?' *she asks suddenly.*

'Because Rangers is the team they support,' *I shrug.*

'I realise that — but why do they say "we" and not "they"? The Butlers don't actually play for the team, they just support it.'

'All supporters do that. You've heard of "the Royal we", that the Queen uses, so that, instead of saying "I like that", she'll say "We like that".'

'Of course, it's sometimes called "the majestic plural".'

'Yeah, well, anyway, this is "the loyal we". Supporters invest a lot of time, money and emotion — especially emotion — in the club they support. The connection between the team and serious, loyal supporters is like, I dunno...'

'An umbilical cord?'

'Exactly. Both feed off each other. Each needs the other. We're all in it together.'

But that preoccupied look is back again. I think about asking her if something is wrong, but given her reactions earlier I decide not to risk it. It might be something very personal. Hopefully it doesn't involve Brad. I decide that this is not a good time to ask about the meaning of 'trifle' either.

Suddenly, she hails a passing taxi, apologises, says a quick 'cheerio' and jumps in.

I wonder about all of this as I walk the last few hundred yards home. But by the time I reach the gates, my attention has begun to stray to today's match. We drew 2–2 at Molyneaux back in August, and won 2–0 at home last season. We should do it.

Just about.

Saturday, 7 February 1976: 4.41 p.m.
Queens Park Rangers...4 Wolverhampton Wanderers...2

16. YELLOW CARD

Saturday, 24 April 1976: Thirty-five minutes into first half

An opening goal for us is looking less and less likely. We are applying huge pressure on Leeds' defence but not making any headway. They are well drilled and hugely experienced in handling this kind of pressure, and they're more than capable of pinching a goal on the break. We need to commit more players forward and attack them in greater numbers.

I shout to full-back Ian Gillard to push forward. He has the measure of his relatively inexperienced opponent Carl Harris, so he can take that chance. Ian obviously shares my analysis. He almost immediately powers forward, cuts in from the wing and runs straight at the centre of the Leeds defence. He steadies himself to shoot but centre-back Madeley does just enough to put him off his stride and Ian's shot misses the target. But his momentum carries him on and he bounces into Trevor Cherry, who is arriving in support of Madeley. The two become entangled and for a moment, it looks like they are about to exchange blows. The referee has stern words with Gillard.

This time next season that could be a yellow card offence.

It was an English referee – Ken Aston – who first came up with the idea of the yellow and red cards. It was during the 1966 World Cup finals in England in the wake of the confusion surrounding the sending-off of Antonio Rattin in the quarter-final between Argentina and England. The problem was that Rattin did not appear to understand that he was being sent off by the German referee, Rudolf Kreitlein, and he refused to leave the pitch.

This led Ken Aston, who was a referees' supervisor at the World Cup, to conclude that there simply had to be a better way of assisting the referee in making his instructions crystal clear to a player who might not speak the same language as the referee. The story goes that as Aston drove away from the stadium after the game, the solution came to him as he drove down Kensington High Street when the traffic light turned red. He thought: 'Yellow, take it easy; red, stop, you're off.' The benefit of the red card and yellow cards system is that it allows both players and fans to clearly understand when players have been booked (yellow) or sent off (red). Red and yellow cards were first used in the 1970 World Cup finals in Mexico and there are plans to introduce them into English League football next season.

Saturday, 14 February 1976: 8.00 a.m.

'I wasn't expecting to see you this morning, me bucko. And at this ungodly hour too.'

The Cabin is strangely quiet at this time of the morning. (There were only two people in the queue ahead of me when I first came in. Immediately in front of me was 'Aunt' Sally.

Today, despite the mild weather, she was wearing gloves — one dark blue, the other lime green. In front of her was that other oldie — Colonel Martin. For a moment, I wondered if Mick was going to perform another one of his famous introductions. I was thinking it would help if the two of them got together, as then only one of them would need to come to The Cabin — so it would speed up the queue a bit. But Mick dealt with them swiftly and they both left without speaking to one another.)

Expecting me or not, Mick looks extremely pleased to see me this morning, perhaps as a welcome diversion from the depressing news of more bombings. He picks up the Mirror that I've placed on the counter.

'Bomb Hero,' he reads aloud. 'Arthur Sadler, 61, foils IRA vengeance attack.'

I've already scanned the story while queuing. It seems that Sadler, the Station Manager at Oxford Street Tube station, became suspicious of a black executive briefcase lying on the floor of the booking hall during rush hour. He calmly picked it up and carried it to an empty private office, which he locked before calling the police. Scotland Yard defused the bomb, which was made from 20lbs of explosives packed around coach bolts.

'Brave man,' says Mick.

'Or a stupid one,' I say. 'Why didn't he just tell everybody to get the hell out of the place?'

'He probably did after he called in the police.'

'Is this the start of a new wave of IRA terror?' I ask Mick.

'Could be,' Mick says despondently. 'They promised reprisals if that hunger striker, Frank Stagg, died. And not just in London either. There were bombs in Belfast and Dublin last night, too.'

I get the impression that Mick is readying himself for another day of listening to a stream of understandable anger being directed at his countrymen.

'Well, at least inflation is coming down,' I say, in an effort to cheer him up.

'Is it?' he asks, disinterestedly.

'And cheaper mortgages are on the way too.'

'Are they, now?'

'Well, that's what it says there in the paper,' I say, jabbing my index finger at the other story on the front page.

'And who is promising all that good news?'

'The Chancellor himself: Denis Healey,' I say.

'And when did he say that?'

'Yesterday.'

'And what date was yesterday?' Mick asks in the tone of a man who already knows the answer.

'The 13th. Ah, Friday the 13th...'

'Say no more, me bucko, say no more. Sure what would Denis Healey know about figures anyway; a man who has to take his socks off to count to eleven.'

'So, there's no chance of the price of the Mirror coming down, then?' I ask.

'Still six pence — and good value for it, too.' Mick manages a wheezy laugh. 'Be off with you now, Dawhee me bucko.'

I stop by Noah's but there's no sign of him. Probably getting ready to head off to White Hart Lane this afternoon. He doesn't often go these days because of the distance but I reckon he'll be there today, because it's QPR that Spurs are playing and he'll have plenty to talk about when we next meet.

'So how is "The Ritual" going this morning?' she asks. 'Have you met everybody you need to meet?'

'Don't need to meet anybody today,' I reply. 'It's an away game today. No ritual; no pressure. At least none of that pressure. I did pop in to The Cabin for the Mirror and had a quick word with Mick, but other than that...'

I shrug and tail off at that point, thinking that no further explanation is required, but she looks quizzically at me, raising those high arching eyebrows of hers.

'Well, I wasn't hanging around at this hour of the morning hoping that a Butler might suddenly appear at the gate with a cuppa for me,' I stress.

Lisa smiles lightly.

It's 8.15 a.m. and, for the second Saturday running, we're sitting in the Olde Fayre Green café. Lisa has a newspaper spread out on the table and is poring over the sports pages, an unusual occurrence in itself. She's wearing glasses. I didn't know she wore glasses. The frames are black but instead of making her appear uninteresting and serious, they make her look seriously interesting. I'm waiting for my tea to cool and munching on one of the biscuits from the plate in front of us.

Burning a hole in my inside pocket is a Valentine card. I bought it last Monday morning; one of those funny Valentine cards. I signed it immediately and put it away. On Tuesday evening, I looked at it again and decided that the verse was not really appropriate. Too trivial. Bland. On Wednesday, I bought a replacement. This one was a bit more serious. By Thursday evening I had decided that this was not quite right either. Too serious. I spent Friday morning hunting in vain for something more appropriate. Finally, I dug out the first card and decided it would have to do. Blimey, it's just a silly Valentine card anyway; just a bit of innocent fun. Right?

Beside Lisa on the table is a flat paper bag from WHSmith. It obviously contains a greeting card because there's a piece of scrunched-up cellophane beside it. Also, I can see what looks like the edge of the card protruding slightly from the bag. It's yellow coloured. Beside it on the red cracked Formica table is a green ballpoint pen.

'This is interesting,' she announces loudly without looking up. I'm on alert immediately. She doesn't usually raise her voice and I've learned that when she does it in this particular way, something is coming. 'According to this,' she continues, 'there are two teams called Manchester.'

'Yes,' I say helpfully, hoping to head off whatever it is that's coming. 'One is called City, the other United.'

'But isn't that confusing?' she asks in mock innocence, raising her eyes briefly from the open newspaper.

'Not really,' I explain. 'You see, they play in different grounds, Old Trafford and Maine Road. And in different colours. United play in red and City play in pale blue.'

'Hmmm,' is her only reaction. She refocuses her concentration on the newspaper, while continuing to run her finger down what must be the league tables. Then:

'And I've got two Sheffields here, too.' I'm now convinced by the theatrical tone and feigned surprise that there is a reason behind this performance. I play along in the hope that it will be revealed quickly.

'That would be Sheffield United and Sheffield Wednesday,' I explain. 'They also play in two different grounds and in different colours. United play in red and white vertical stripes, and Wednesday play in blue and white vertical stripes.'

'Wednesday,' she ponders. 'It's an unusual name for a football team don't you think? Why Wednesday, I wonder?' She picks up the pen and taps her chin.

'Simple explanation,' I quickly reply. 'The club was originally formed on a Wednesday and so they called it Sheffield Wednesday.'

'What a novel idea,' she exclaims a little too forcibly, 'one doesn't think of football teams as having novel ideas.'

Ah, I reckon. So that's it: the lack of artistic creativity in football. We've been here before, so I let her continue to peruse the league table in silence while I sip my tea and finish my biscuit.

Then, as if on cue, one of those weird moments occurs. You've probably experienced it yourself on occasions, in a crowded tea room or bar; when, by a strange coincidence, all conversation stops at the same time for a few seconds. The tea room din suddenly dies down, at exactly the same moment as Lisa exclaims loudly: 'And look, I've got two Bristols. What do you think of that?'

It can be difficult to manage a slug of tea when it runs against your breath. Throw in a mouthful of crumbly, caramelised biscuit and the results can be devastating when sprayed across a tea room table. Luckily, I have a napkin to hand and quickly mop up most of the damage, while I regain my composure.

'They have different names, of course,' she continues, ignoring my spluttering embarrassment. 'Rovers. And City.' She pronounces the two syllables of 'City' very deliberately as 'Sit-tee'. 'Do they play in different grounds too?'

I can't answer as I still haven't got my breath back, so I nod my assent.

'And in different colours?'

I nod again and manage to mumble an 'Umm'.

'Red and blue?'

Finally I can speak. 'Yes,' I confirm. 'City play in red and Rovers play in blue and white qua...qua...quarters.'

'Quarters?' she stares uncomprehendingly at me. 'Oh, you mean like this.' In one deft movement, she touches her Adam's apple with her forefinger and runs it straight down between her breasts to her navel, pressing down on the cloth of her dress. Then she places *it just under her left breast and runs it horizontally across under her right. 'Four quarters. Like that?' she asks.*

I say nothing. She says nothing. I'm thinking of all the times I've seen players bless themselves quickly before a match starts, but never quite like that. Finally, she leans forward.

'Why didn't you tell me?' she asks.

'Not really relevant,' I reply, trying to pretend I don't get the point she is making. 'Lower division teams.'

'I mean why didn't you tell me that day?'

I don't answer her immediately because I'm gazing straight into her eyes and trying to work out how to move my eyes from her face down to the table without appearing to stare at her body. Eventually, I move my eyes sideways across the room, then down, and then back again so that I'm staring at a teacup that looks as if it's just survived the first stages of being sandblasted with biscuit crumbs.

She bursts out laughing. 'Stop that! You look just like Marty Feldman in Young Frankenstein!'

'Fronk-en-steen,' I correct her, remembering the way Gene Wilder did it in that movie when I first saw it myself a couple of years ago.

'Okay, Mister Eye-gore, so why didn't you tell me all those weeks ago that Bristol was cockney rhyming slang for breast, as in Bristol City/titty.'

'Dunno. Too embarrassed maybe. It's not the kind of language I use myself.'

'Really? Isn't it part of the argot of the dressing room, all this cockney rhyming nonsense?'

'If you mean the jargon of the dressing room, I suppose it is. For some.'

'But not for you.' A statement rather than a question.

'No,' I confirm.

'Strangely enough, I'm inclined to believe you.' Then, smiling, 'But I still believe you should have told me that first day.' Her mood has softened considerably now to the point where I start to wonder if her whole sense of outrage was just affected in order to test me in some oblique way.

She stands up suddenly and taps me playfully on the head with the folded newspaper. 'Come on. You're already running late for the match. If we hang around here any longer we'll have to call you a sherbet.'

'Sherb...?'

'Sherbet dab. Cab,' she explains, smiling. 'And you've got bits of biscuit on your face. Come here,' she takes out her handkerchief and wipes the crumbs of biscuit away from the sides of my mouth. I breathe in the merest hint of her scent. I can't really describe it. I'm not very good when it comes to things like that.

Later, on the approach to White Hart Lane, I make a decision. I decide to put the whole issue of Brad and 'trifle' out of my mind. Forever. It's obviously meaningless. Something Brad said just to put me on the defensive. It actually means nothing, I decide. And, immediately, I feel better. Sometimes it's best to put these things aside. Bin them.

I start to wonder about the card Lisa had in the paper bag. I'm sure it was a Valentine card but it obviously wasn't for me. For Brad, maybe? On balance, I don't think so. Maybe it was for me but she just forgot to give it to me. Unlikely. Anyway, no way was I handing her a card if I wasn't getting one from her.

I remove the Valentine card from my inside pocket. The bland, trivial one. I look at it once more and re-read the message I had written on the inside in red biro on the pale yellow-coloured card. Yellow-coloured. Two yellow cards in one day. In international football, two yellow cards means a red card offence — a sending off. I hope that's not a bad omen for today against Spurs.

I place the card back in the envelope, tear it in two and drop the pieces in the nearest litter bin on arrival inside the ground.

Too late for that kind of stuff now.

Saturday, 14 February 1976: 4.40 p.m.
Tottenham Hotspur…0   Queens Park Rangers…3

17. SALUTING THE CAPTAIN

Saturday, 24 April 1976: Forty minutes gone in the first half

Eddie to Frankie. Brother to brother. Keeping it in the family. Maintaining possession at all costs. The Leeds way. Gray the younger pushes the ball a few yards ahead and accelerates past Gerry Francis. But Gerry doesn't give up. As Gray nears the touchline, Gerry catches up, harries him, wins the ball and with a deft flick of his right boot lays it back to Frank McLintock who sets up another attack. Moments later, Gerry is on the end of another Rangers onslaught and finds a gap in which to fire in a great volley, but Leeds goalkeeper Harvey reacts brilliantly to push the ball away.

Gerry Francis is a local lad, born in nearby Chiswick and a product of the QPR youth scheme. He made his league debut for QPR against Liverpool in 1969, having joined Rangers as an apprentice earlier that year, and he became a regular in the team during the 1970–71 season.

With his distinctive hairstyle and trademark sideburns, you can pick out Gerry instantly on the pitch. He's a technically gifted central midfield dynamo, who passes the ball well and contributes his fair share of goals – he's already scored thirteen goals to date this season. Gerry is most effective when breaking from the halfway line and attacking the opposition with energy and aggression.

He's forged a terrific partnership with Stan Bowles, and they seem to bring the best out of each other. His brilliant goal against Liverpool on the first day of the season is surely a candidate for goal-of-the-season on BBC's *Match of the Day*: Don Masson collected a short pass from just outside our penalty area. He moved forward unchallenged for a few yards before stabbing a short pass to Stan, who had his back to the defender. Stan did an instinctive back-heeled flick to Gerry, who immediately pushed it across to Don Givens on his right. Without hesitating, Don laid an inch-perfect pass forward into the path of Gerry, who had continued his run. Gerry accelerated into the penalty area, leaving the Liverpool defence stranded in his wake, before slotting the ball past Ray Clemence inside the far post. It was precision football; slick passing with a clinical finish. And it set the trend for our season so far.

Gerry has played seven times for England and has captained his country in their last three matches. He was appointed captain by England Manager Don Revie, after a memorable performance for England against Scotland last year when, still only 23, he scored twice in a very impressive 5–1 victory.

I really believe that Gerry is just the leader England need to become worldbeaters again. I say this despite the fact (and most of the squad is aware of this) that Gerry Francis and I have never really hit it off. Relations between us have always been marked by heated altercations, and things have not improved much during the season to date. Gerry does not always welcome my point of view – my 'interventions' as he likes to call them – at training sessions. But I admire Gerry a lot as a player and, deep down, I do believe he is exactly the captain that England needs.

Saturday, 21 February 1976: 8.35 a.m.

The bag is somehow attached along the right-hand side of the bicycle at a 45-degree angle. I can see the heads of the clubs sticking out over the top of the handlebars. I have no idea how Marianne intends mounting the bike, unless she is well used to sitting astride a horse. But she doesn't even attempt to do so. She just wheels it along the footpath.

'Practice run,' she smiles weakly.

'Nice set,' I remark, trying to give the impression that I know what I'm talking about.

'Pro-master,' she says. 'I got them from MFI up on Wembley Way. £24.95. It's a seven-club set and it came with a free golf bag.' She double taps the bag proudly, the way you would pat a well behaved dog.

'Who's going to caddy for you?' I ask, and look up at the bedroom window before I have time to stop myself.

Marianne utters what I can only describe as a silent hiss. She then places her left foot on the left-hand pedal and 'scooters' along the footpath, occasionally threatening to swing her right leg and mount the bike properly.

'Fore!' yells a wag from the passenger side of a passing Austin Morris, followed by a toot-toot on the horn. This causes a tiny wobble on Marianne's part and a loud two-fisted bang on the bedroom window behind me.

I don't bother to look back.

Daisuke is carrying some sacks in through the front gates of 'Aunt' Sally's from the Reliant, which is parked up on the pavement with the engine still running. The Butler brothers are loitering on the other side of the road, taking it all in.

'We woz just comin' to see ya,' Jacko shouts over.

I cross over to their side of the road.

'What's up?' I ask.

'We woz wonderin' if you're interested in trying your luck at the tables tonight.'

'But there's a game today. You know me. I usually need time to recover. Analyse the game while it's still fresh in my mind.'

'S'only Ipswish,' says Billy.

'All these games are important,' I protest. 'It doesn't matter who the opposition is.'

'Dintya enjoy it last time you came, then?' Jacko looks disappointed. 'You won a few quid from wot I remember.'

'Yeah, I did. But there wasn't a game that day. Look, sorry mate, but I just don't reckon I can make it tonight. To be honest, I don't really reckon it's my kind of thing...'

'Why not?' interjects Billy.

'Well, to be honest, I thought it was a bit dingy. And dodgy too, since you ask. The place was full of Chinese blokes wearing grey vests and worried looks.'

'A bit like 'im?' Jacko nods across the road. 'Maybe he's got good reason to be worried.'

'Daisuke is Japanese, not Chinese. And what do you mean he has good reason to be worried?'

'Nothin' at all, me old china. Ooops. Just thought 'e looked as if 'e woz up to something, you know – "fishy".'

'Fishy? What do you mean, fishy?'

'Don't ya take any notice of me, mate. I'm just being inscrutable,' laughs Jacko. Then his mood goes colder: 'So, we're not sophisticated enough for a man of your refined tastes, now. Is that it? Not good enough for a person of your stature?' He turns to his brother: 'Am I right, Billy?'

'Right on, Jacko.'

And they both snigger like schoolboys, turning at the Glade and cavorting skittishly up towards Forest Hill Road.

There's no sign of Echo Eddie out front as I pass his house. This is unusual, but I'm confident that I will pick him up on the way back. I'm almost past the house when I hear the side gate open and the military click-clack of Svetlana's boots along the small path that runs around the side of the house. I glance back and watch as she strides purposefully towards the rubbish bins. She is carrying a bouquet of wilting flowers – probably the remnants of last weekend's Valentine's Day bouquet from Eddie. She lifts the lid of the bin and tosses the flowers contemptuously inside. She does not look in my direction but I know she's aware of my presence. Then she bangs the lid shut and marches back into the house, slamming the side gate shut behind her.

It's then that I notice Eddie. He is sitting silently in the front seat of a very old Daimler he is working on in the garage. He makes no attempt to come out to greet me, so I do something I have never done before: I actually open the front gate and cross his badly kept garden to say hello to him. No big deal, you might think, and also a bit self-serving in terms of keeping to the ritual, but I was concerned about him, ludicrous as this might seem. Things don't look or sound good between himself and Svetlana.

Eddie gets out of the car as he sees me approaching and pretends to be busying himself by tidying up.

'Morning, Eddie,' I say, trying to sound cheerful. 'Having a bit of a spring clean?'

'Not springs,' says Eddie morosely, 'shocks. Shocks,' he repeats. Then, waving his hands in frustration either at his lack of communication and my lack of comprehension – or both – he shouts, 'Suspense,' and appears content that this explains everything.

Suspense? Shocks? Now it's my turn to be confused at what sounds like a description of an Alfred Hitchcock movie. But I twig just in time to save embarrassment all around.

'Ah, yes, the suspension,' I say, pointing to the car. 'Hmm, nice motor.'

'Nice motor, nice motor, yes, heh, heh,' but there is no laughter in his voice this morning. 'Belongs to The Sid,' he says.

'The Sid? Oh. Right. He's the one's been looking after The Horseman's while Trouty's been away.'

'No way,' says Eddie. 'No way.'

'Well, that's what The Sid said,' I retort, 'he told me himself, actually.'

'No away, no away,' says Eddie. 'He's here.'

'Trouty?'

'He's here'

'Who told you that?'

'The Oriental.'

'Daisuke?'

'The Sukey. Yes, the Sukey.'

'Has he seen him? Has Daisuke seen Trouty?'

Eddie shakes his head.

'Well, then, who has seen him?'

Eddie is silent.

'Tell me. Tell me. Who has seen him? I need to know.'

At that moment, the side gate opens and I hear the click-clack on the driveway, followed by a car door shutting softly, engines revving and then a low growl as the Triumph Herald glides swiftly away.

Eddie holds my gaze throughout this interlude. He says nothing. He doesn't need to. I think I can guess what has happened.

'I said good mornington!' Noah's cheery greeting only registers with me at the second attempt. 'Are we buying, selling or just down in the dumps today?'

'Eh? Oh. Sorry, I'm just a bit preoccupied this morning.'

'I can see that. Surely, it's not The Tractor Factor?'

'Pardon?'

'The Tractor Factor. Ipswich. The Tractor Boys. Surely you're not worried about them today?'

I smile weakly. I had forgotten the nickname. I've no idea why they're called the Tractor Boys. To be honest, I've rarely heard anybody use that particular nickname and it means nothing to me. Not this morning. Not ever. But I know that Noah is trying to be upbeat so I make the effort to exchange pleasantries with him. It's not so difficult — until I spy Brad bearing down on us from the general direction of Threads.

'You went to the game last Saturday, then. White Hart Lane?'

Noah just shakes his head and starts to walk away. He's not really a bad loser. I think he is just hugely disappointed at how Spurs performed. He pauses, turns and walks back to me. 'I tell you something. The two goals that your friend Gerry Francis scored were two of the best I've seen in a long time.'

I have to agree with Noah. About the quality of both goals, if not the description of Gerry as 'my friend'.

'Third in the table now. It's all there for you,' he calls after me as I slip away and avoid Brad. I see Lisa through the window as I am queuing in The Cabin. I signal her to wait and she nods, raises one hand to her lips and tilts it to indicate that she will meet me in the café. Thankfully, the queue is short in The Cabin this morning. Otherwise, I reckon I would have made an excuse to jump it. Mick is ready for some small talk but I want to ask him about Trouty. Why he hasn't told me that Trouty is back? Or never left. Or if there is something going on involving Svetlana. Why nobody has told me anything?

Mick pretends to recoil:

'Whoa, Dawhee me bucko. Now hold your horses and say all that again. But slowly, this time.'

I repeat what I've just said as slowly and as steadily as my anger will allow.

'And who told you that Bernard Trout was back. Or never left?'

'Eddie told me,' I say.

'Eddie. Ah yes. Ek-ko Eddie?' Then Mick leans forward and whispers: 'Sure, what would expect from an ass but a kick.'

'Wha...'

Mick doesn't attempt to explain. Instead he places his hand on my shoulder as if to draw me closer:

'Look here, me bucko. Let me give you two pieces of advice. One: Don't take any heed of Eddie. He's a nice man but an ommadawn — as thick as manure but only half as useful. Two: Forget Bernard Trout. He has gone. Wherever to we do not know; melted off the earth like snow off the ditch. Accept it. Get him out of your head.'

'But what about the ritual?' I plead.

'Is it the ritual you're worried about, Dawhee me bucko? Well, answer me this: when did this ritual of yours first begin?'

'Oh, sometime last season,' I reply a little irritably, 'I can't remember the exact date.'

'And was Mr Bernard Trout part of the ritual from the very beginning?'

'You know he was.'

'And how did the ritual work out for you last season?'

'Well, it was mixed; some good, some...ah...not so good.'

'Exactly. Now, how many games have ye played at home so far this season?'

'Twelve, I reckon, maybe thirteen.'

'And how many of those games have ye lost?'

'None, but...'

'No buts now. And on how many of those match days did you meet Mr Bernard Trout, your indispensable rabbit's foot?' Mick asks caustically, dramatically raising his voice so that a hush descends on the shop.

'None,' I whisper, hoping to continue what is left of this conversation in more restrained tones.

'And why is that do you think, me bucko?' (But Mick isn't waiting for me to reply.) 'Well, let me tell you. It's because you have your very own super-sub,' (raised voice again), 'none other than Miss Dell — the David Fairclough of substitutes.'

The bemused customers queuing behind me break into a desultory applause.

'I suppose you have a point there, Mick,' I concede.

'I have a point? No, Dawhee me bucko, I have the point. Now, that'll be 6p for the Mirror and there's no charge for the advice.'

I take this as my cue to make a hasty exit but Brad, who has just come into The Cabin and is standing at the back of the queue, accosts me as I reach the door.

'Who is Danny Fairclough?' he demands.

I just laugh at first. The farcical side of all of this is beginning to appeal to me.

'It's David Fairclough, Brad,' I reply, removing his hand from my arm. 'The guy who keeps coming on as a substitute for Liverpool and scoring vital, winning goals. "Supersub" they call him. I'll bet even Lisa knows that. Don't you know anything?' I give him a gentle double-tap on the shoulder with the newspaper and walk out.

'For a player to be in an offside position, three conditions must be met,' I begin. 'Are you ready for this?'

For the third week in a row, we're in the Olde Fayre Green café. Although this time we're actually sitting outside. Veronica has just brought me a mug of sugary tea; Lisa is having a coffee. So far there has been no mention of unexchanged Valentine cards and I reckon I would prefer that it stayed that way. Anyway, there's no sign of any yellow envelope sticking out of the open satchel style bag that is sitting on the chair beside her. I've told her about what Eddie said regarding Trouty. Lisa reckons there must be some mistake; some breakdown in communication between Eddie and Daisuke. (I'm happy to hear this, so I resist the temptation to say that there cannot be a breakdown in something that does not exist.) Lisa seems certain that if Trouty were around, we would know it by now. This is what Mick reckons too, so I'm inclined to believe it at this stage.

It's chilly. At least I think it's chilly but I'm not really sure if it's really that cold or if I'm just shivering from nerves.

'I'm ready,' she smiles. 'Go on, confuse me.'

'Right. Rule number one: the player must be in the opposing team's half of the field. Two: the player must be in front of the ball. And three: there must be fewer than two opposing players between him and the opposing goal line.'

'Why fewer than two players?' she asks.

'Dunno,' I say. 'That's the rule.'

'Maybe it has something to do with double-checking your sources? You know, the way newspaper reporters need to check their facts against two sources before the newspaper will print the story.'

'What have newspapers got to do with it?'

'Well, they're the ones who are always running stories about whether a goal was off-site or not.'

'Offside; it's offside, not off-site.'

'Oh, yes. Sorry. What about the goalkeeper. Is it two players plus the goalkeeper?' she queries intently.

'No, the goalkeeper counts as one of the two opposing players.'

'Does the goalkeeper have to be one of the two players?'

'No, he doesn't.'

'So any attacking player that is level with or behind the ball is not in an offside position?'

'Correct.'

'What about corner kicks and throw-ins?'

'If a player receives the ball directly from a corner kick, goal kick or throw-in he cannot be offside. Blimey. All these questions. You've been preparing for this.'

Pause.

'Well, I did have a quick chat with my father about it last night,' she confesses.

'Your dad? Does he follow football?'

'He, ah, seems to know quite a bit about it. I know he's been to see Arsenal but I wouldn't say he follows it, exactly. He's more into rugby and cricket.'

For some reason, she looks a little embarrassed and uncomfortable with my question.

'What does he do, your dad?'

'He's an airman.' She appears relieved that I've moved off the subject of football. 'Well, that's what he calls himself because he used to be in the RAF...'

'Who used to be in the RAF?'

We both turn, to be greeted by Mick's son Cathal, who has just stepped out from inside the café with his artistic friend O'Leary, who is obviously back from whatever 'safe-house' he was hiding in. Cathal nods to me but I'm sure he would have continued on his way out if he hadn't spied Lisa. O'Leary looks a bit disheveled. He has a couple of days' growth of stubble, his hair looks greasy and unwashed and he appears to have slept in the clothes he is wearing. He seems uncomfortable that Cathal has stopped to talk to us and keeps his distance, continuously rubbing his thumb along the tips of the fingers of his right hand and examining his fingernails.

'So, who used to be in the RAF?' Cathal asks again, his smile not quite disguising a certain insistence in his voice.

'My dad,' Lisa beams at each of them in turn, obviously pleased that they seem more interested in her dad than I did. 'Actually he's a commercial pilot now. Captain Roger Dell. Sounds very grand, doesn't it?'

'It does indeed,' grins Cathal. 'Grand. Yes. Where was he based when he was in the RAF?'

'Oh, he moved around quite a bit.'

'That must have been difficult,' Cathal says sympathetically. 'For the family. Your dad moving around so much.'

'Well, you know what they say: "Per Ardua ad Astra",' Lisa replies with a flourish. 'Well, that's what my dad says. Sometimes.'

'Meaning?' I interject impatiently. I'm happy to display my ignorance of what I assume is Latin if it insinuates me into the conversation.

'"Through Adversity to the Stars",' intones a well-modulated voice just over my shoulder. It's O'Leary, who has moved a little closer to the conversation.

'Fancy you knowing that,' Lisa exclaims, excitedly. 'I'm impressed.'

'Merci, la belle danseuse.' O'Leary gives a little bow. 'I must have read it somewhere,' he confesses, scratching his stubble and looking just a little embarrassed, as well he might with all these snatches of foreign lingo he keeps spouting. But Lisa obviously is impressed and starts to blush. Thankfully, O'Leary makes a show of tapping his watch, presumably to indicate some urgent appointment. Cathal gets the message; we say our goodbyes and they both drift away together, striking up an animated conversation as we watch them cross towards the Green.

We decide to leave too. I catch Gregory's attention and pay the bill.

'"La belle danseuse" – the beautiful dancer – well, what did you think of that?' Lisa asks, wide-eyed as we stroll up Park Road.

I shrug non-committally. 'I know what it means,' I lie.

'Well, I mean, O'Leary is obviously not one of your IRA Balcombe Street gang, is he? He's hardly out on bail!' she says teasingly. 'And he seems like an educated man.'

'More like an educated tramp, if you ask me.'

We fall silent for a few moments. All is quiet at Eddie's house. I briefly consider raising the subject of offside again just to clarify a few issues that I don't reckon Lisa quite understands, but on balance I decide not to.

'Are you playing at home again next week?' Lisa asks suddenly, as we reach The Glade.

'Why do you ask?' I'm immediately on my guard.

'Well, because I may not be around next Saturday,' she explains. 'We have early rehearsals that day for a performance we're giving the following week.'

I tell her that this is not a problem; that we are away to Sheffield United next Saturday, but at home again the week after against Coventry on 6 March.

'Ah,' she cuts in apologetically. 'I might not make it to The Cabin that morning, either.'

I start to panic and enquire as to why not.

'The dance group is planning to have a little party at the end of that week,' she explains, 'to celebrate what we hope will be a very successful debut for the show.'

I ask her where they are having this party.

'Well, I suppose I shouldn't really call it a party,' she explains. 'It's just a few drinks in the local.'

'The Horseman's?' I ask, hopefully.

'No. I meant our local pub in Covent Garden. It's just round the corner from where we're based.'

'How many of you are going?' I ask, stepping up the inquisition.

'Oh, around ten of us,' she responds cheerfully.

'That's a lot of girlie talk for one night,' I suggest.

'Ha!' she laughs. 'We have a few guys in the group too, you know.'

'Yeah, but they're all gay, right?'

'Don't know. I've never explored it with them. Maybe I'll know more after Thursday night!'

'Who are you going with?'

'I'm going with Lisa. Why?'

'There's another Lisa in your dance group?' I say, incredulously.

'Yes. Lisa Gaughan. She's Scottish.'

'That must get confusing?'

'Not really. We're known as Big Lisa and Little Lisa, for "ease of reference", as they say.'

'Well, Big is obviously you,' I say, then realising that this could sound as if I reckon she is overweight, I half raise my arm as if measuring her height, then raise it higher again in two more, hesitant, movements.

'Actually, I'm the one known as Little Lisa.'

'You mean that there's somebody in the dance group who is actually taller than you?'

'The Big and Little has nothing to do with how tall we are.'

I obviously appear totally nonplussed.

'We're actually known as Big Bubbles and Little Bubbles. I'm Little Bubbles. And don't pretend you don't know what I'm talking about now. I've seen you staring often enough.'

'How can you mix with guys who refer to you in that way?'

'Oh, Lisa Gaughan and I came up with the nicknames ourselves. They're fun, don't you think?'

What I reckon is that I continue to underestimate Lisa – in all sorts of ways. So I quickly return to the important issue.

'So you're going out on Thursday night. So what's stopping you going to The Cabin on the Saturday?'

'Nothing really, except I'm staying over with Lisa on Thursday and Friday night and wasn't planning to be back until later on Saturday morning.'

'How much later?'

'I don't know.' She sounds agitated all of a sudden.

'Well, if it's only going to be a little later, I'm sure I can delay my trek just a bit. Maybe you could ring me.'

I tear off a piece of the Mirror, scribble my number on it and hand it to her.   'A n d maybe you could give me your number,' I blurt out without thinking.

'Aha. So this is what it's all about.' She smiles. 'It's just a ruse to get my telephone number. Sorry, but I don't want you calling me at all hours to discuss your worries regarding the next match. But I promise I will call you if I'm going to be late. Or if I cannot make it to...'

'Look. Please. It's important to me that we meet up. Promise me that you'll be there.' I realise suddenly that we've been walking on through the Glade and up Forest Hill Road without my realising it. I check my watch.

'Okay. I'll do my utmost to be there,' Lisa blurts out quickly. 'But this ritual thing: it's all in your head, you know. You need to get over it. Even though we've met up this morning, there is absolutely no guarantee that you won't lose the match today.'

'We won't lose now,' I say determinedly. 'Just you wait and see.'

I turn and jog back quickly to the corner. I stop to wave back to her. She is standing in exactly the same place, staring after me. She raises her hand and gives a hesitant wave. I don't want to be the first to turn away but I'm worried about the time, so I have to.

I wish I was as confident as I hoped I sounded to Lisa. We're third in the league table, Ipswich are in eighth place and eight points behind us. Still, it's a pretty useful side that Bobby Robson has put together. Any team with Mick Mills, George Burley, Kevin Beattie, John Wark, Trevor Whymark and Clive Woods in it must be respected. And England striker David Johnson is on the bench. We drew 1—1 with them at Portman Road back in November, and we beat them 1—0 here last season.

I keep an eye out for Daisuke on my way home. I want to ask him about Trouty; about where and when he saw him. But there's no sign of Daisuke. Can it be true, I wonder? Is Bernard Trout really back? Did he ever go away in the first place?

Saturday, 21 February 1976: 4.43 p.m.
Queens Park Rangers...3 Ipswich Town...1

18. HOTHEADS
AND REDHEADS

Saturday, 24 April 1976: Almost half-time
The Leeds United supporters are in full voice:

> Little Billy Bremner is the captain of the crew
> For the sake of Leeds United he would break himself in two
> His hair is red and fuzzy and his body's black and blue
> But Leeds go marching on.
> Glory, glory Leeds United
> Glory, glory Leeds United...

Small of stature but big of heart, Billy Bremner, the redheaded Scot with the ferocious tackling technique, embodies all that Don Revie's legendary Leeds United team stood for. Most of those players are still there but time has moved on and, with the departures of Jack Charlton and Johnny Giles in particular, some would argue that Leeds have lost not just talented players but also a large dollop of that cussedness that made them so combative. Bremner is seen as the one player in whom these values are still deeply ingrained.

It's getting close to half-time and Leeds are piling on the pressure. But Phil Parkes is playing a blinder in goal. Time and again he keeps Leeds at bay.

Now they are attacking again. Jordan plays it to McKenzie but Johnny Hollins cuts it out for a throw in.

'QPR ball,' I shout at the linesman – possibly the only time in my life that I've lied to a Parson. But he just glares back at me. 'Let's play it fair, son. And for God's sake, let's keep the game moving.' (Linesmen also have permission to refer to you as 'son', it seems). But I hold on to the ball, pretending not to have heard the linesman. I hold it in the palm of one hand with both hands outstretched in a querying stance.

Billy Bremner comes racing towards me, calling out to me, menacingly. Bremner is probably one of those people who has earned the right to call everybody 'son'. But he doesn't. Instead he spits out a command in that distinctive Scottish burr:

'Gimme the ball quickly, wee man.'

'QPR throw,' I say.

'Gimme the ball. Quickly. Ye wee Cockney prick,' he jabs back.

That does it. Now the fire is really in my head. I take a few steps backwards, holding on to the ball to antagonise him even more, and let fly:

'You're finished, Bremner. You're all washed up. And so are Leeds. Without Revie, you're nothing. The whole lot of you are nothing. You hear, nothing.'

And I toss the ball to him with a final rejoinder, 'And you'll never play for Scotland again either.'

Billy catches the ball, rolls it around in his hands to get the feel of it before taking the throw, then looks up at me and declares quietly, 'And ye know somthan, son? You London pansies will never win the league. This season or ever!'

And with that he takes the throw-in. It leads to nothing and the half-time whistle sounds shortly after, the ref having played two minutes of added time. I ignore Bremner as he trudges off. He doesn't acknowledge me either. But Mr Parsons, the linesman, has a quiet word with me about 'my behaviour'. Sod *him*.

0–0.

We've still got it all to do. And only forty-five minutes left in which to do it. Maybe Bremner is right. Maybe we are destined never to win the league; never to emulate the golden boys who won the League Cup. Maybe this QPR team, the team that the media refer to as 'everybody's favourite second team', the team that has entertained its way through fifty games this season, is destined to come second. To win silver but not gold.

What's the use?
I'll just give in
Try as I may and I do
I'll never win, never win, baby I'll never win.
Here I go again
Watch me now 'cause
Here I go again

Friday, 5 March 1976: 8.31 a.m.

The radio is usually on in the background while I'm having breakfast but, to be honest, I'm what you might call a passive listener. I probably hear what's being said but I'm not really taking it in.

'…Bombs…'

I'm not into politics either, so unless something that's being said on the news headlines catches my attention, subconsciously, it's all likely to go in one ear and out the other. I'm not proud of it, but that's the way it is. I do turn up the sound when the sports report comes on though.

'…pub…'

We've been living with this for quite some time. Terrorist bombs going off with little or no warnings. Bombs in pubs, bombs on the Tube, bombs in Royal Mail postboxes…

'…Covent Garden…'

'Bloody hell! Did he say Covent Garden?' I reach across and turn up the volume:

'...at least two terrorist bombs went off in the heart of London last night. One of them is believed to have been placed beside a pub in Covent Garden. This follows an explosion which ripped open a commuter train yesterday morning only minutes after 1,200 passengers had disembarked at Cannon Street, one of London's busiest stations...'

I'm out the door in seconds, running down the drive and out the gates. I almost collide with Marianne Pleass as she wheels her bicycle across the pavement. I mutter something as I race past her but I don't hear what says in reply, if amything.

It seemed like a bright day from the kitchen window, and it is, but it's also cold and I'm not dressed for that.

No sign of Daisuke this morning as I accelerate across the road at Aunt Sally's. I look up Forest Hill Road but there is no sign of her there. I plough on. Eddie stares after me open-mouthed as I race past him without as much as a good morning. I don't bother to even look in the directions of the Butlers' place as I hare past. A bit of nimble footwork and I swiftly step around Noah Berrie and a selection of artifacts that he is placing delicately on display. The lights are against me at the crossing from The Horseman's so I do a standing jog until a gap appears in the traffic and then I make a dash for it.

I get to the door of The Cabin and I'm now hot and sweaty – and breathing heavily, despite my level of fitness. I grab the Mirror and wave it at Mick to catch his attention. Mick seems surprised to see me but immediately sees that something is amiss. He calls Cathal to attend to the person he was serving and comes out from behind the counter to me. I explain what I've heard regarding the bomb in Covent Garden, near a pub; about Lisa's party and the fact that she hasn't phoned me. I ask him if he has seen Lisa this morning. Mick says no but points out that it's far too early for her – and for me too, for that matter. I glance at my watch and realise that he's right. Mick then reminds me that this is Friday and, whatever about Lisa visiting the shop occasionally on a Friday morning, he never expects to see me in the shop on Fridays – especially in such a disheveled state. Mick makes some reassuring noises and tells me to go home and 'attend to my other commitments' as he puts it. I ask him if he knows Lisa's address but he admits that no, he doesn't. He walks me to the door and stands there staring after me as I head back across the road onto the Green.

The absurdity of my situation suddenly dawns on me. How do I find myself in a position when the moment I have reason to be concerned about Lisa and need to talk to her, the only constructive thing I can think of doing is to run to the local newspaper shop.

I decide not to go home. If she's okay and decides to head for The Cabin today, then I will miss her and spend the rest of the day wondering and worrying. Instead, I decide to wait and kill time by walking around the Green. There's a small war memorial in the centre of the Green. In all the times I have walked past it, I have never given it a second thought. This morning I read the inscription. It's dedicated to the brave souls who died in the two world wars. I shiver and walk on. There are some things I do not wish to be reminded of this morning. I've always thought of the war as being something that old men keep harking back to. Sitting in The Horseman's, slowly sipping their pints of bitter, constantly rabbiting on about 'the way things were'. But this morning? It's like I'm in the middle of something that

I don't fully understand and I'm powerless to do anything about. As if death and destruction are finally beginning to creep up on my generation.

I find a wooden bench with a view of Park Road and scan the front page of the Mirror. It makes for depressing reading:

BOMBS BLITZ

screams the headline:

Pub target in new wave of terror.

I read on. The police are asking for help from the public to act as 'a million extra detectives' in the fight against the terrorists. They have issued an appeal to every member of London's vast commuter army to help them catch 'these maniacs'. There's nothing more specific concerning the Covent Garden bombing than I heard on the radio this morning. It probably happened too late last night. Neither is there any information regarding injuries – or deaths – in relation to Covent Garden, unlike the Cannon Street bomb where eight people are reported to be in hospital. Maybe they got the Covent Garden location wrong. Or maybe there weren't any injuries or fatalities.

I shift around on the bench for around two hours, getting colder by the minute despite the bright sunshine. From across the road I can faintly hear 'Shine on You Crazy Diamond' from Pink Floyd's Wish You Were Here album coming out of Threads. An unsual choice by Brad. I decide to head home, still clutching the Mirror, which I suddenly realise I never paid Mick for.

I spend the rest of the day 'attending to my other commitments' as Mick so quaintly put it, but it's impossible to concentrate.

This evening I walk up Forest Hill Road towards Hazel Wood and spend a depressing hour or so asking after Lisa, but nobody appears to know her or, more importantly, to know where she lives. One person recognises my description of her but, confusingly, is convinced she lives in Aunt Sally's house. Another says he regularly sees somebody answering Lisa's description out walking a small dog. Yet another claims to have seen Lisa taking a young girl to school, from time to time. A fourth can describe Lisa accurately, says she reckons she lives just up the road but is convinced that her name is not Lisa Dell, although she cannot recall what she reckons it is. I realise then just how little I know about Lisa myself.

On a more positive note, the broadcast news later this evening does not mention any fatalities, and specific connections to Covent Garden become fewer as the evening wears on.

Still, it's going to be a long night.

Saturday, 6 March 1976: 7.30 a.m.

I'm back on the Green again, sitting on a bench just inside the railing. It's even colder than yesterday at this hour of the morning. I didn't really sleep last night. Not for long, anyway. It's hardly the best preparation for the game against Coventry today. The Olde Fayre Green café is not open yet so there isn't even the possibility of a cup of tea to keep the cold out. The early morning traffic is beginning to pick up. A guy wearing a dark blue anorak is posting a large package in the mailbox beside the railings. Other than that, there are no other pedestrians on the Green. Now I'm wondering why I decided to start out so early this morning. I know it was to ensure that I don't miss Lisa; to see that she's okay. But I've put the whole ritual in danger. I'm hoping I will catch them all on the way back home but there is no guarantee, is there?

I walk across to The Cabin. I liberate a Daily Mirror and a couple of other newspapers from the bound bundles dumped outside the front door earlier this morning and head back to the wooden bench on the Green. There's nothing about the bombs on the front page of the Mirror. Absolutely nothing. There's a story about that toff politician, Jeremy Thorpe, and some male model that seems to have taken over the front page. One of the other papers talks about an IRA warning that they will embark on a ruthless campaign of bombing in Britain. Top British businessmen will be in the firing line as well as airports, cinemas, theatres, buses, trains and Tube stations. Postboxes will also be used. I move off the bench and walk in the direction of Cheppington Holt railway station, have second thoughts and meander aimlessly through some of the side streets. I've never walked this way before. Acacia Avenue, Sycamore Road, Holly Gardens – these are names I am totally unfamiliar with. There's a little pub – The Cap & Bells – that I never knew existed and, beside it, a trendy-looking tea shop called The Brown Penny, equally unknown to me. I turn a corner and yet another pub - The Three Beggars – is revealed. I'm suddenly conscious of the fact that I don't know the name of the pub in Covent Garden that was bombed last night. It wasn't mentioned in the newspaper or in the report on the radio, as far as I can recall. What if Lisa was in that pub in Covent Garden? What if she was hurt? Where would they have taken the injured survivors? What if something even worse happened to her, like those eight people at Cannon Street? Where would they take the...? It doesn't bear thinking about. I try to focus on what I should do next.I eventually find myself on the high street so I take a sharp left, pass The Cat and The Moon (another pub, but this one I do know), before taking another left at the post office, through Station Road and back onto the Green again.

It's just 8.30. I decide to try the café again.

And there she is. Sitting relaxed with a cup of tea and a warm scone deeply engrossed in her newspaper. As if nothing had happened.

'You never called me,' I say, planting myself down in the chair opposite her, barely able to contain my fury.

'Good morning to you too,' she says calmly. 'I'm here! What's the big problem?' she answers, as if she hasn't a care in the world.

'You said you would call me,' I shout. 'You promised!'

'Calm down,' she says sternly. 'I said I would call you if I couldn't make it or if I was going to be very late. I'm here. Okay, I'm a little late. But what's all the fuss about?'

'Oh, come on. Don't give me that. You knew I would be worried sick about you after hearing about the bomb near that pub in Covent Garden last night.'

She furrows her eyebrows: 'But I wasn't in a pub in Covent Garden last night.'

'You told me you were. That you were going to be in a pub there. Your dance group party...'

'Oh, that. We postponed that,' she says dismissively with a wave of her hand.

'What? You postponed it? Why didn't you tell me?' I ask incredulously.

'Why did I have to tell you?' Now, it's her turn to look incredulous. 'Look, we meet here every other Saturday and have our little stroll and our little chats and it's mostly enjoyable – even if the conversation is almost always about football – but that doesn't mean I have to report in to you about every other facet of my life, does it?'

'No. Of course not,' I stammer, 'but in the circumstances...'

'There are no "circumstances", as you call them, that I am aware of.' She is pointing the rolled up Guardian at me now. I hold up my hands.

'Look, I was worried, that's all.'

'And what were you worried about, I wonder?' she asks in a sarcastic tone that I hadn't heard her use before.

'Isn't that obvious?' I ask.

'No it isn't,' she shouts. 'You were probably more worried about your precious little "ritual" being disturbed than about any real concern for...anybody else.'

I'm dumbstruck. I have never seen her so angry. I have really done it this time.

She must have seen the shocked expression my face – or maybe it's the looks we're getting from other patrons – because she suddenly softens her tone.

'I'm sorry,' she sighs. 'Look, it's easy for you. You're not as exposed to the dangers. You don't have to use public transport to get up to London every day. I've seen those two posh cars in your driveway. And the security on those enormous gates. What do you have to worry about?'

'How do you know where I live?' I ask, surprised.

'Mick told me. He's always going on about where you live; the enormous house in Wellesley Gardens, the cars in the driveway. So I just asked him for the name or number on the house.'

'Why?'

'I was curious, that's all.'

I stare hard at her and she immediately looks down at her cup. It's the first time I have ever seen her look embarrassed. Neither of us says anything for a few moments.

'Look, I'm heading over to The Cabin,' I say finally.

'Okay, I'll just sit here and finish my tea,' she says, without looking up. 'I'll see you later.'

The Cabin is all decked out in green today. There's green bunting strung across the shop; green balloons hanging from the ceiling; green, white and orange rosettes pinned to the walls; a red-bearded, green-suited leprechaun sporting a hideous grin is perched on a shelf behind the counter and there's a general air of, well, Irish-ness about the place. 'Aha,' I think to myself, 'it's the first week of March; must be St Patrick's Day.' But no. According to 'Aunt' Sally, with the two odd earrings, who is standing immediately in front of me, St Patrick's Day is not for another ten days. The decorations are all to do with a rugby match. It seems

England are playing Ireland today at Twickenham. Mick looks all dressed up in a crumpled kind of way. He's wearing a green and white scarf and appears to be full of the joys of life. His mood appears to be contagious, too. There are lots of phoney Irish accents emanating from the queue ahead of me; the conversations are liberally sprinkled with 'to be sure, to be sure' and 'begorrah' and there's lots of smiling and hearty laughter.

The one exception to all of this merriment is 'Aunt' Sally, who is debating the price of Jaffa cakes with Mick.

'Seventeen pence? Seventeen pence? I can get them for fifteen and a half pee in Fine Fare.'

'Well, that's what you should do,' smiles Mick. 'The nearest Fine Fare is only about a heart attack away.'

The old crone cackles loudly, picks up her preordered Daily Telegraph and pads off, leaving the waft of yesterday's garden trailing in her wake. I finally get to face Mick.

'All dressed up, Mick, I see.'

Mick winks and taps his hip pocket: 'Tickets,' he beams.

'Good for you,' I say. 'What's the plan for the day, then? Do you have a kind of ritual for days like this?'

'Ritual?' Mick savours the word. 'Now that's a good word for it, Dawhee. I like that. It has a religious flavour to it. I suppose if you can call something that happens every two years a ritual, then, yes, I have a ritual. I do indeed: a prayer in the church and a pint in the Pope's,' he reveals proudly, tapping his forefinger in the palm of his hand 'that should see us right today. And God knows…' he adds, throwing his eyes in the direction of heaven, 'we'll need all the help we can get today.'

I nod towards the wall behind him where the picture of a pope is sandwiched between pictures of Liam Brady and President Kennedy:

'Is that him?' I ask, with a straight face. 'I didn't know the Pope followed rugby.'

'Pope's Grotto, me bucko. It's a pub in Twickenham; called after Alexander Pope,' says Mick 'The poet,' he adds, noticing the obvious lack of recognition on my part.

'Maybe what you really need is a rugby version of Liam Brady,' I suggest, knowing Mick's admiration for the Arsenal midfielder and attempting to deftly get the conversation back to a topic I know something about.

'Ah, but we already have one, Dawhee me bucko,' says Mick triumphantly. 'Joseph Anthony Brady; plays in the centre with Wanderers. It's his first cap today but I reckon he could turn out to be our lucky thirteen.'

'Well at least it's a pretty easy name to remember,' is all I can think of to say, 'not like some of those double-barrel surnames that are probably on the England team sheet.'

'Well, there's where you're wrong, me bucko,' says Mick, 'the only player on the Twickenham pitch today with a double-barrel surname will be wearing the green of Ireland.'

'You're kidding?'

'Simon Ernest Fitzroy Blake-Knox,' Mick announces in a town-crier voice and stands to attention, while the whole shop falls suddenly silent. Then he leans towards me and whispers: 'He's a schoolmaster in Northern Ireland,' as if this somehow explains everything,

'*and it's his first cap too. He's at number 11, on the wing — same as in soccer.' He turns away, pauses, then turns back to me: 'And while we are on the subject, me bucko, I assume that you, of all people, would have no objection to players with double-barrel surnames lining out for a soccer team?'*

'*Not if they're good enough,' I say, a little embarrassed to have him pick me up on this issue. I decide not to pick him up on his use of the term 'soccer' instead of 'football'.*

The customers soon resume their blarney-banter. I pay for the Mirror and the other papers I took earlier, after eliciting from Mick all I really need to know regarding today's game at Twickenham: Ireland have conceded over one hundred points in their last four matches and don't have a snowball-in-hell's chance of beating England today.

Lisa is waiting for me outside The Cabin.

'*I've finished this. Here, you have it,' she says, pushing The Guardian at me and swapping it for my Mirror. We stroll over towards Berrie's. 'Look at this on page five,' she exclaims suddenly, stretching out her arms shoulder high and opening up the Mirror to its full width. 'It's a photograph of a naked woman. Now there's a surprise. "The Churchill Touch" the headline says. "Pola Churchill, like her namesake Winston, has a high regard for cigars," it reads. That's because a cigar firm has chosen her to appear in an advertisement. Admen seeking the...' (she pauses here for emphasis) '...soft sell; admire the smouldering beauty of this 18-year-old model from Southampton. Indeed, the sight of Paula bare would probably sell snow to Eskimos. Hmmm.' She peers at me over the top of the newspaper. 'She's very pretty, isn't she?'*

'*Dunno. I haven't seen it yet.'*

'*I'm surprised. Why is she naked, I wonder?'*

'*How would I know?'*

'*Is she a redhead, do you think?'*

'*Dunno. Why do you ask?'*

'*Mick told me the other day that you take home a different redhead every week.'*

'*What?'*

'*Redheads. Mick says you have a different one every week.'*

'*Red tops!'*

'*Pardon?'*

'*Red top. He said red top.'*

'*Redhead, red top, what does it matter? Is it true? Do you go home with a different one every week?'*

'*Red top. It's what some newspapers are called. You know, The Mirror and The Sun. They're called red tops because the name is in red at the top.'*

'*Oh. The masthead.'*

'*What?'*

'*The masthead. The section of the newspaper with its name on the top of the front page is called the masthead.'*

'And you thought he meant a redheaded bird. Ha!'

Lisa gives an involuntary shudder at my use of the word 'bird', but recovers her poise to give me a playful punch on the arm.

'Ouch, that hurt.'

'Good mornington to you both. Are we buying, selling – or boxing?'

'Just joking,' Lisa giggles.

'Today, I'm sure I have a book on the Marquess of Queensbury – in near perfect condition – that might interest you, assuming you are both still interested in books, of course.'

I defer to Lisa's intellectual prowess to respond to this but she looks totally nonplussed.

'Come, come,' Noah chides amicably, 'surely you've heard of the Marquess of Queensbury, the Scottish nobleman who gave his name to the rules that govern boxing?'

Lisa and I look at each other with raised eyebrows.

'You probably know him better as John Sholto Douglas,' says Noah, helpfully, 'the man who played a role in the downfall...'

'...of Oscar Wilde,' says Lisa. 'Of course, I remember him now. He was the father of "Bosie" Douglas.'

'Indeed he was,' beams Noah.

I'm beginning to feel distinctly uncomfortable with the direction that the conversation is taking. I always do when it strays onto a subject I know little (and in this case, nothing) about. So I pretend to be amused.

'Boysie?' I laugh 'What kind of a bleedin' name is that?'

'It's a nickname,' scolds Lisa, which brings my fake merriment to an abrupt end. She spells out the name and pronounces it correctly for me before adding: 'His full name was Alfred Douglas and he was a well-known author and poet...'

'...but even better-known as the lover of Oscar Wilde,' interjects Noah, rather theatrically.

'He was a poofter, then?' I grin, as if to justify my earlier laughter. 'I might have guessed, what with him having such a naff nickname.'

They both look at each other in mock exasperation, as if to say 'What can we do in the face of such ignorance?' and then Lisa and I take our leave. I can hear Shawaddywaddy's 'Three Steps to Heaven' blaring out from Threads but, surprisingly, Lisa doesn't suggest that we pop in. Which is just as well, as I've just caught sight of the Butler boys in animated conversation while crossing the road. I hasten to join them and Lisa has no choice but to tag along.

'Brrrr, fackin' 'ell, it's a bit parky today, innit,' shivers Jacko.

'Mmm. It is a bit crisp,' I reply. It's not a term I've ever used myself before, and I don't know where it came from, but it just seemed to serve the immediate purpose.

'Crisp? Crisp? Fackin' 'ell. Listen to 'im, Billy. Crisp? It's crisper than a packet of fackin' Walkers.'

This is followed by much knee-slapping and wheezy coughing.

'Crisp, eh?' they both repeat quietly to themselves every so often as we walk on in a group up Park Road. They pass their own house without stopping, so they are obviously headed elsewhere. They both appear a little preoccupied, as if trying to find a way to restart the conversation.

'Oh, Gordon Bennett, have a butcher's at 'im,' says Jacko loudly. 'Cheer up, mate. It'll never 'appen.'

We have reached Eddie's house and, as usual, he is in the garden working on the area of driveway that he's extending, tipping in some rubble as hardcore from a wheelbarrow. He has dug very deep foundations, I suppose you have to when it's a driveway and not just a pathway. He looks a bit morose – almost guilty-looking - and definitely not his usual cheery self. Of course, the presence of the Butlers might also account for his less than happy demeanour. Neither party has ever really forgiven the other since the incidents with Roxboro Roy.

'It already happen,' is all Eddie says in reply, but he doesn't stop working like he usually does and come over to chat to us. Svetlana then emerges from around the side of the house, looking resplendent in a fur coat, boots and one of those Russian hats with ear-flaps. She gives a flamboyant wave in our general direction, slides into the motor, starts up the engine and glides off. She doesn't say anything specifically to Eddie, a fact that does not go unnoticed by the ever-vigilant Jacko.

'You in the doghouse, mate?' he asks. He sounds genuinely concerned and sympathetic but unfortunately, he has used the wrong figure of speech. Especially as Eddie is holding a sledgehammer that he's been using to drive wooden pegs into the ground. And Billy's spluttering giggles do nothing to calm the situation. Eddie strides menacingly towards Jacko, who suddenly realises the error he has made.

'This is not doghouse. Not doghouse,' Eddie roars at the brothers, who manage to retreat faster than the entire Inter Milan defence.

'Just askin', mate. Just askin'. Didn't mean no offence,' Jacko mumbles as he buttons up his coat. Eddie continues to brandish the sledgehammer.

'I dunno. All these foreigners comin' into the country,' sighs Billy, stepping back and shaking his head as if in disbelief.

'Some of 'em can't even speak the King's English, right Billy?'

'Right on, Jacko.'

And they both slope off with their tails between their legs, back the way they came, towards their own house.

Lisa then has a few words with Eddie in whatever language it is that he speaks and he calms down. Finally, he takes Lisa's hand in both of his and places it against his heart. There is much 'aah-ing' and tilting of heads as if all misunderstandings are being explained. I decide to leave them to it and head on up Park Road towards the intersection.

'Excuse me, mate!' I still cannot bring myself to call him Daisuke. 'Oi! Excuse me!' I run across the road and try to catch him before he shuts the gate. He hears me and stops short of closing it, but leaves only a small gap to peer out from.

'I hear that you know Trouty...Bernard Trout...I'm told that you met him.'

'Yes, I know him.' He closes the gate.

'Met him,' I shout over the top of the gate. 'I hear that you actually met him — recently.' I'm conscious that there is a tone of desperation in my voice, despite the earlier advice from Mick that tracking down Trouty is now unnecessary and a complete waste of my time.

Daisuke locks the gate.

I swear loudly and swing my foot at a pebble on the footpath. It strikes the gate and ricochets with a ping. Then silence. I look around to see if anybody has observed my childish tantrum. Maybe a few passing motorists did, but thankfully there are no pedestrians about. Then I hear the gate creaking open again. But, to my surprise, it's Aunt Sally who marches out:

'Losing one's temper is not going to solve any problem,' she booms. 'Now, what exactly is the problem?'

I explain to her quietly, as best I can, what I was asking of Daisuke, who has now appeared at the gate again, no doubt emboldened by the presence of her ladyship. Aunt Sally displays no interest whatsoever in why I need to establish the whereabouts of 'this Trout person', as she refers to him. Instead, she turns to Daisuke and engages him in a fairly rapid-fire conversation — all in Japanese. Daisuke is nervous but responds with conviction. Aunt Sally then summarises for me:

'Daisuke says that he does indeed know who this Trout person is. He remembers meeting him, but not recently. He also says that a foreign gentleman called Eddie is continually badgering him about the whereabouts of this Trout person and that he has tried his best to be helpful. He says that he sometimes finds it difficult to understand this foreign gentleman.'

'I know Eddie,' I confirm. 'And I can only imagine what those conversations must have been like. Thank you for being so helpful. I've taken up enough of your time.' I nod, give a half-hearted wave and begin to move off.

'You're Lisa's friend, are you not?' she demands. 'I've seen the pair of you together. She talks rather a lot about you.'

'Really?' I immediately stop and take a tentative step back in Aunt Sally's direction. I want to hear more.

'Yes. She thinks you're an interesting...ah, an interesting project, I think she said.'

'That's nice,' I say, not entirely convinced that I like being considered as a project.

'You have some kind of weekly ritual, I believe; some kind of "good luck" routine that you try to adhere to on match days. And it involves people. The same people every time, too. How very, very brave of you.'

Bleedin' hell. Why did Lisa have to go and spill the beans to this old crone, of all people? I explain the thinking behind the ritual as concisely as I can — and as quietly. Because it seems that this lady does not do discreet one-on-one conversations; this lady uses megaphone diplomacy — without the diplomacy bit.

She suddenly turns to Daisuke: 'Aha, I see that you've not finished painting the gates yet,' she says as she begins closing up. It is then that I notice that the colours on the double wooden gates do not quite match. They are both blue but one is dark blue, the other is a very blackish blue. I decide not to point this out as it might delay my escape.

'A very kind and considerate person is your Miss Dell,' she bellows after me.
Your Miss Dell — what did she mean by that? It has a nice ring to it, though.

There's an ambulance pulled in up on the kerb outside number 21 as I skip round the corner from Aunt Sally's. Marianne is speaking to the driver while his colleague is pulling the rear doors shut after him. I stop, walk on a bit, then stop again.

'What's up, Marianne?' I enquire, tentatively, not wishing to appear intrusive.

'Oh, it's Marjorie,' Marianne says, exasperated by whatever it is that's happened. 'She's just done...she's caused herself...oh, I don't want to go into it all right now.'

'But she's okay? Marjorie? She'll be okay? The ambulance — I thought for a minute it might be serious.'

'Not at all. We had a problem opening the gates so the ambulance couldn't reverse in. That's all. They had to take her out on a stretcher. I think she rather enjoyed that, actually. All that fuss, I don't know...' she continues muttering as she walks away.

I don't know whether I'm more pleased that Marjorie is going to be okay, or by the fact that I've managed to complete the ritual in very challenging circumstances but suddenly, things are looking up again. Coventry at home. Who have they got? No one that we need to worry about. Bottom half of the league. No real threat of relegation. What have they got to play for? Nothing. Should be a cinch. We drew 1–1 with them at Highfield Road back in November, and beat them 2–0 here last season. All we need to worry about today is complacency.

Saturday, 6 March 1976: 4.40 p.m.

Queens Park Rangers...4 Coventry City...1

19. GOING OUR OWN WAY

Saturday, 24 April 1976: Half-time

The Gaffer is waiting for us on the touchline as we troop in at half-time. He's obviously disappointed that we've not scored, but he won't let it show. He rarely gets carried away with emotional outbursts. I feel I know exactly what he is going to say in the dressing room: 'Remember what I said, lads, continue to play your own game. Play it your own way. Let's all be patient and the goal will come.'

This has been a recurring theme with the Gaffer recently. He's been constantly talking about the pressures facing the team as it nears the end of the campaign. He insists that QPR must not sacrifice the tactical footballing principles that have taken the club to the top of the First Division, even though the championship struggle is at its final, decisive phase. I concur.

'We have eight games left to play and we must aim to win every one,' he said at the training session in South Ruislip, before the game away to Everton. 'There is no question of us going anywhere and being defensive. That isn't our style.'

We were as good as his word, and beat Everton 2–0 at Goodison Park.

He was back on the same subject at training the following week before the game away to Stoke City. 'We got to the top by attacking teams away from home, as well as at home. If we are going to stay top, it will be by not sacrificing what we believe in.'

We beat Stoke City 1–0 at the Victoria Ground, that Saturday.

He maintains that QPR must not be looking over their shoulders. Permutating the possible results of the other contenders simply does not come into his reckoning.

So what exactly did the Gaffer say in the dressing room at half-time? Well, there's an established custom in football that what's said in the dressing room at half-time stays in the dressing room, and the whole team abides by that – apart from a few clichés to feed to the media after the match, in order to keep them happy.

Another one of my little habits is that I always take a few seconds to flick through the match programme before the second half. Just a quick glance at the photographs, nothing more. I can't say that it helps me to relax but I always feel better having done it.

Saturday, 27 March 1976: 8.50 a.m.

'How's Marjorie?' I call out. 'I don't see her at the window. She's not still in hospital, is she? It must be three weeks since I saw her going off in the ambulance.'

Marianne is wheeling her bicycle down the driveway. I stop at the gate to wait for her. She looks more relaxed than when I last saw her.

'No, not at all,' she laughs off my concern. 'Marj was home within two days. No, it's the changeover to summer time. Most people seem to get used to it quickly, but Marjorie needs a little more time than most,' she sighs, 'at least a week. She's still in bed — with a headache.'

'Anything interesting there?' I ask, nodding at some LPs sticking out of the basket.

'Well I thought so, but I'm afraid Marj didn't agree. They were great value,' she reassures me enthusiastically, opening the bag. 'Look, Elvis, Neil Sedaka, Max Bygraves — all 85p in Boots on Cheppington High Street. The Pickwick label, they call it. You'd pay a quid each anywhere else. But Marj wanted something more musical, you know...more uplifting, she said. No lyrics. So I'm getting her James Last instead. It's more expensive of course — £2.35 — but at least it will...you know...'

'Be more to her taste,' I say (instead of 'shut her up', which is what I feel like saying and is most likely what Marianne means).

'Yes,' she concurs, 'more symphonic.'

The subsequent symphony of car horns that accompanies Marianne's attempts at making a grand entrance onto the far lane on Wellesley Gardens will do little to ease Marjorie's headache, I reckon.

Daisuke continues kneeling as I approach Aunt Sally's. He is putting the finishing touches to the second coat of paint on the right-hand wooden gate. He nods his greeting and I reciprocate, glancing back to confirm my suspicion that each gate is indeed a slightly different shade of blue. Kind of appropriate, I think. I keep up the brisk pace and decide not to re-open the conversation regarding Eddie and Trouty. Having had more time to think it over, I'm convinced now of two things: one, that whatever Daisuke said about Trouty was misunderstood by Eddie (why did I ever think that it could be otherwise); and two, that I don't really need Trouty as part of the ritual at this stage of the season, given our results to date. Unbeaten at home: seventeen games played, thirteen wins, four draws. Mick is right. Ever since I co-opted Lisa to take Trouty's place, our results have been consistent. Consistently good. Why mess with that by trying to track down Trouty?

I cross at the intersection over to Beane Row. There's no sign of Eddie this morning. Or the Butler brothers, for that matter. Perhaps they are all 'lying doggo' and avoiding contact with each other after the rather tetchy conversation they had last time we met. Still, that was three weeks ago. They must have bumped into each other since then and patched things up.

As soon as I round the corner at The Horseman's, I see that Noah is deep in conversation with Brad in the shadow of the little arcade that houses their shops. I couldn't stomach Brad at this hour of the morning so I decide to pop in to say hello to Noah on my way back.

I enter The Cabin and pick up the Mirror from the pile. There's a hilarious story on the front page — and it concerns football. A hypnotist called Romark has put a curse on Crystal Palace — managed by Malcolm Allison. He is angry because — he claims — 'Big Mal' snubbed him. Romark, whose real name is Ronald Markham (!), says that Crystal Palace's success this season was all in the mind — his mind. 'I concentrated on making Crystal Palace win,' he says, according to the report. Now he is promising to 'reverse the team's winning streak in a trance'. In future, he will be concentrating on making the other team win. Romark says he fell out with 'Big Mal' because the manager broke an appointment with him in his office near Harley Street. This has a ring of truth about it as far as I'm concerned. Because I once had a similar experience involving 'Big Mal'.

The approach to me was made by an intermediary: 'Big Mal' was interested in signing me, had an exciting proposal to make and wanted to talk. Where could he meet me and 'my advisors' discreetly? Now, the exuberant 'Big Mal' and discretion do not exactly go hand in hand. He's an individualist and likes to do things his way. Anybody who wears a fedora, smokes large cigars and has a penchant for expensive restaurants and champagne is unlikely to sit unnoticed in the Old Fayre Green café for too long. And Malcolm Allison attracts tabloid media attention like shit draws flies, resulting in his every flamboyant move and outspoken utterance being deemed newsworthy. So a meeting in public was not going to be ideal – especially as the subject matter was best kept temporarily under wraps. Although joining a Third Division outfit like Crystal Palace was not exactly part of my immediate plans, in the end I agreed that we would meet him in my home, where he could arrive unnoticed by parking in the driveway towards the rear of the house.

He didn't show up.

There were lots of explanations proffered by the intermediary as possible reasons for Allison's no-show. All of them sounded quite plausible, but I suspected that the real reason was probably something more exotic. It didn't bother me too much at the time because I assumed that another meeting would be arranged. But that didn't happen. And later, I did start to wonder how my conversation with 'Big Mal' would have worked out. Despite the managerial trough that he currently finds himself in at Palace, 'Big Mal' has always had thought-provoking things to say about the development of the game.

Allison was a player at West Ham until his career ended prematurely because of tuberculosis. As a coach, he was at his most successful while he was Assistant Manager at Manchester City (our opponents this afternoon, coincidentally), working with Manager Joe Mercer. City won seven trophies in seven years while 'Big Mal' was there.

Romark's curse is due to begin today, when Crystal Palace play Bury in a Third Division clash. So I'm really looking forward to hearing the result of that one later on!

The gnarled features of the red-bearded leprechaun are still in situ behind the counter, his mischievous eyes staring out over Mick's shoulder. Come to think of it, all the green bunting is also still in place.

'I thought Paddy's Day had come and gone,' I say to Mick, when I eventually reach the counter.

'Oh it has, Dawhee,' he replies cheerfully, 'but I want the sweet taste of victory to linger on a little longer.'

Seeing the blank look on my face he quickly adds, in an affected 'posh' accent: 'The rugger match, old boy. At Twickers. Ireland won. Thirteen points to twelve. Pip, pip.'

I've never seen Mick look so happy.

'But that was three weeks ago,' I exclaim. 'You're not still celebrating, are you?'

'What's seldom is wonderful, me bucko,' Mick replies, 'especially against the English.' Then the affected accent again: 'And even more so when it's achieved on that part of England's gree-heen and pleasant land they call Twickenham. We celebrated long and hard that night, I can tell you. Pints of the black stuff at the Pope's followed by fillet steaks at the Richmond Rendezvous.'

To be fair to Mick, he is not in any sense gloating over England's defeat. Just happy in a pig-in-shit kind of way that Ireland won against 'the auld enemy', as he puts it.

'So it's been a good three weeks for everyone, then,' I say, hoping we can change the subject to a sport with which I'm more familiar.

'Yes,' he beams, taking the bait. 'A hat-trick of wins for you bhoys. And two of them away from home. That must have pleased you.'

'Yeah,' I reply modestly. 'It's been going well.'

'And speaking of going,' he leans forward conspiratorially, 'what do you think of Wilson resigning?'

Obviously, I was aware that Harold Wilson had shocked the whole country by announcing his resignation as Prime Minister a couple of weeks ago, but, as I said before, politics doesn't really interest me.

'I don't think about it at all,' I admit. 'Why did he resign anyway?'

'Who knows, Dawhee,' shrugs Mick. 'Personally, I think his health is not the best but he claims that he always intended to resign when he got to 60. To do his own thing, he said.'

'Maybe he just got sick and tired of all those Mike Yarwood impersonations of him on the telly,' I offer by way of feeble explanation.

At this, Mick attempts his own impersonation of the Prime Minister, huffing and puffing on his pipe in the way that Wilson does to buy time whenever he is asked an awkward question. But whatever Mick is trying to say is suffocated by his trademark wheezing laugh, which brings the whole performance to an exhausted halt.

'When does he actually go?' is the only pertinent comment I can think of making to ease Mick's cringing embarrassment.

'He leaves on April 5th,' splutters Mick, recovering his composure, 'and personally I won't be sorry to see him go.'

'That's the weekend we're away to Newcastle,' I say enthusiastically, trying to change the subject, but Mick is not for turning away from the newspaper stories of the day just yet.

'It's poor Princess Margaret and Lord Snowdon I feel sorry for, Dawhee,' he sighs. 'Going their separate ways, like that, after sixteen years.'

I have to confess to having a greater interest in celebrities and gossip than I do in politics, so we chat about the unhappy royal couple for a bit. For a man who calls himself a republican, Mick seems to have a great interest in the royal family and even knows the names and ages of the children. Me? I'm more interested in this young guy Roddy Llewellyn that the princess is supposed to be having an affair with, but Mick won't discuss it. You can see the mask of real disapproval and disgust on his face at the very suggestion of an affair. Must be his Catholic upbringing.

When the conversation eventually peters out, I hand over my 6p for the Mirror ('One and tuppence ha'penny in real money,' Mick reminds me) and I'm on my way.

Lisa is at the back of the shop, skimming through the meagre selection of greeting cards on a revolving stand. She seems very engrossed in what she's doing and, initially, I'm not too keen to intrude in case she's buying a card for somebody I'd rather not know about. But then I reckon 'What the hell' and I barge in.

'What's today's big occasion?' I ask breezily.

'Oh, good morning to you too,' she replies, without even looking around. (She must have seen me earlier when I was queuing.) She stoops to peruse the lower sections of the card rack. 'And the big occasion, as you call it, is actually tomorrow. It's Mother's Day, as I'm sure you've forgotten.'

The rack squeals loudly in protest as she rotates it.

'No, I hadn't, actually,' I lie. 'I fact I'm ahead of you there. All done and dusted.'

'Hmmm,' is all she mumbles, before eventually straightening up and striding off to pay for the card she's chosen. I decide to head across to Threads for a quick gander at some new gear that's recently arrived. No sense in hanging around The Cabin listening to Mick fawning over 'Miss Dell'.

I cross over to the Green, wait for the lights, then cross again to the shops. When I get there, I decide that I don't really want to face Brad this morning, so I hang around outside Threads for a few minutes and run my eye swiftly over the clobber in the window. Nothing there that interests me. Brad's got Fleetwood Mac 'Go Your Own Way' playing on the sound system. I take the advice and do so.

Noah pokes his head out the door: 'Good mornington to you. Today, I have something for you.' He grins and ducks back inside. After a few minutes, he emerges from the dust and hands me an old picture frame. 'For Ima. Perfect.' Then seeing that I am totally flummoxed, he explains: 'For your mother. Mother's Day. Perfect. Very old, very valuable. I kept it for you. I'll give you a good price.' He offers me the frame and I pretend to examine it.

'But it's already got a picture in it!' I splutter, aghast.

'But of course it has! It's second-hand. You take that picture out and put in another,' he says in mild exasperation.

'Who is it? In that picture. Who are the two people in it? They look familiar. Do you know them?'

'No, of course I don't know them. It came in a box of stuff that was cleared out from an attic after...' Noah looks suddenly uncomfortable, '...after they had passed away, I imagine. I never really looked at the picture before — it was the frame that interested me — but now you mention it, they do look like older versions of familiar faces.'

'Look, Noah, I appreciate you keeping it for me and all that, but I've already got a gift for my mother.' I hand him back the frame.

He takes it and sighs loudly in disappointment, blowing a load of dust off the ornate silver frame in my general direction. I hold my breath until the moment passes.

'Sorry, mate,' I add, concluding the conversation.

I bump into Lisa again as I leave the arcade, but she seems to be in a bit of a hurry.

'What's the rush today?' I enquire.

'We're off to Brighton,' she says, chirpily.

'What? Brighton are rubbish,' I say, with mock incredulity. 'Why would you want to watch Brighton?'

She smiles weakly at my feeble attempt at humour. 'We're obviously not going to watch a football team. No, a new shop opened in Brighton yesterday — it's called The Body Shop — and it sounds really interesting. A few of us are driving down to see what it's all about.'

'What is it meant to be all about,' I ask, but what I really wanted to ask was, 'Who's we?'

'Well, it will sell naturally-scented soaps and lotions. The whole theme of the shop will be "Inspired by Nature" — products for the face, hair and body.'

'Bit of a strange name, tho,' what? How did you come to hear about it?'

'Well,' she laughs, 'there was an article in one of the newspapers last week about — you'll enjoy this — a local undertaker in Brighton who complained about the use of The Body Shop as a name.'

'Dead right, too,' I say. I give it a moment to sink in, but I don't reckon her humour sensor is switched on today, so I swiftly change tack: 'How many of you are making the trip to Brighton?'

'Oh, just the two of us — myself and Chris. We thought we'd make a day of it. You know, the seaside and all that.'

'A bit cloudy today for that, I would have thought.' I start to wonder who Chris is. She's never mentioned him before. I decide there and then to ask her straight out. But then I change my mind. If she wants to tell me who he is, then she will — in her own good time. If she doesn't, then what's it to me.

'Well, it's mild enough,' she says, not reading my mind. 'Chris and I hope to fit in a stroll on the beach.'

Now I know she is teasing me but I refuse to respond. Instead I start to mooch a bit as we walk up Park Road. I slow my pace to fall behind and search for something in the newspaper that will allow me to change the conversation. I find it on page five.

'Look, Pola's here again,' I shout gleefully, 'top of page five.'

Lisa glares at me with a mixture of irritability and distain: 'Paula?'

'Pola,' I correct. 'Pola Churchill. You remember. She was in the paper a couple of weeks ago. She's in the cigar ad. I push the newspaper towards Lisa, but she's twigged by this stage and turns her head away from the photo of the buxom beauty, sighing exasperatedly.

I'm delivered from this awkward situation by the sound of the Butler boys in full flow singing 'Mammy'...in the style of Al Jolson — accents and all!

They are walking arm-in-arm towards us, each carrying a bunch of cheap flowers wrapped in cellophane. (I know they're cheap flowers because I can see the price stickers still on the cellophane.) But you've got to laugh at their chirpiness. And we both do.

'Wot's so soddin' funny, then?' asks Jacko of us both. 'Betcha you've got nuffink for yer old ladies, 'ave ya?' We both continue laughing.

'Well go on, then — 'ave ya?' This time it's directed at me.

'Yeah, I'm sorted,' I say, clearing my throat, hoping that he doesn't persist in further questioning. But Lisa saves the day by chipping in:

'Me too. I'm taking my mum to Brighton tomorrow,' she says brightly.

'Nice one,' says Jacko, 'I'm sure Cristiana will enjoy that. Right, Billy?'

'Right on, Jacko.' And off they hop, linking arms, singing and looking to all intents and purposes like Fagin and the Artful Dodger in Oliver.

We watch them dance through the open gate and in along the path to their front door.

'I didn't know your mother was called Cristiana.'

'How would you?' she smiles.

'The Butlers knew,' I say, petulantly.

'That's because we talk about things other than football games.'

'*We* talk about things other than football games,' I retort, defensively.

'Yes,' she giggles, 'we also talk about football rules. And player/manager relationships.'

I'm a bit put out by this, but I see a way back:

'Speaking of relationships. . .'

'Oh, yes?'

So I tell her about Eddie and Svetlana. Well, about my suspicions regarding their deteriorating relationship, to be precise. I tell her about what Eddie thought Daisuke had said, although I know that I shouldn't repeat it now that it's been proven to be a misunderstanding. Lisa looks at me pityingly. She says I have an overactive imagination, caused no doubt by my total immersion in all things football to the exclusion of real life.

'And, anyway, I saw them together the other evening and they appeared, how shall I put it, to be totally committed to one another.'

'Svetlana and Trouty?' I ask, sensing that vindication is nigh.

'Svetlana and Eddie, you imbecile.' She slaps my arm with the folded newspaper. 'Now hush. Here's Eddie.'

'What time you play today?' Asks Eddie, as we approach.

'We play at three o clock.' I reply slowly so that he can fully take it in. But I don't intend stopping. I don't really want to hang around with Eddie this morning. I don't reckon I have the patience for it today. But I don't want to offend him either.

'Ah. Three a.m., heh, heh.' He grins as I continue walking past.

'No. No. P.M.' I yell back at him, with a little wave to indicate that the conversation has ended.

And then as if the penny had suddenly dropped. . .'Ah. No P.M. Heh, heh. Yes. P.M resign two weeks ago, heh, heh,' he shouts after me.

I stop dead, turn and walk back the few yards to where Lisa and Eddie are standing. Lisa must have sensed my irritation because she quickly chimes in:

'He was giving you the time of the match today, Eddie. It's on in the afternoon — p.m. He wasn't talking about Harold Wilson resigning.'

'Poof, heh, heh. Poof,' Eddie laughs.

'Well, he's been accused of many things, Eddie, but never that,' Lisa says, trying to resist the urge to laugh.

Eddie then looks at Lisa, raises his fist and makes this sucking sound twice. It sounds crude and vulgar and Lisa looks momentarily alarmed but then she smiles, looks at me and explains:

'Eddie means puff, not poof,' she says. 'Wilson and his trademark pipe.' She raises her fist also, as if holding a pipe, and makes a similar sucking noise as if puffing on it.

'Oh, I give up,' I say. 'I'm totally confused.'

I say goodbye to them both – Lisa has stayed behind to chat to Eddie. Maybe she'll be able to get to the bottom of the Trouty and Svetlana story. She may believe it's a non-story, but I still harbour my suspicions.

I make my way up the hill and cross over by Aunt Sally's. Daisuke has finished painting the gates and is nowhere to be seen. The gates are gleaming. Dark blue and, eh, darker blue.

On the whole, it's been a good morning. Lots of positive vibes – like Cris being Lisa's mother, for example. From the way Jacko pronounced her name – Cris-ti-ah-na – she is obviously foreign, probably Italian. Which would go some way to explaining Lisa's complexion and all that gesticulating she goes on with. Still. Italians are okay. Bloody good footballers. Yeah, a good day, so far.

So why do I have this lurking sense of foreboding?

It's today's game, of course.

Manchester City will not be easy. They've already won the League Cup, beating Newcastle United (who knocked us out 3–1) in the final. Although they trail us by eleven points and are now out of contention for the Division One title, they will have a galaxy of star names playing today: Joe Corrigan in goal; Willie Donachie and Mike Doyle in defence will be difficult to break down; and Joe Royal, Dennis Tueart and Asa Hartford will be dangerous on the break. The hard pitch will suit them today, so we'll need to be on our guard. They'll be without Colin Bell and Dave Watson and, of course, ex-QPR hero Rodney Marsh, who is being transferred from City to Tampa Bay in Florida. Football in America (or 'soccer' as they refer to it) doesn't impress me. A bunch of has-beens from around the world trying to extend their careers.

We've got Don Shanks in at full-back today. Don played about a dozen games last season but this is his very first game this season, so I'm certain that City will put pressure on him right from the start. We drew 0–0 with them in Maine Road back in December, but beat them 2–0 in the corresponding fixture here last season, so we should get a result today.

Saturday, 27 March 1976: 4.41 p.m.
Division 1
Queens Park Rangers...1 Manchester City...0

Division 3
Crystal Palace............1 Bury...0

Interval

20. A BIT OF FLUFF

Saturday, 24 April 1976: After the break

'Any particular advice for me, Boss?' I ask the Gaffer, at the dressing room door just before the team trots out onto the pitch for the second half.

At first he appears a little taken aback that I should ask.

'You've done well in the first half, but we need you to get to the ball faster; step up the pace and keep the game flowing. We're counting on you to help the team maintain pressure on Leeds in the second half.'

It's good to get that kind of motivation. To realise how important my role will be today.

I have a quick word with our substitute, Mick Leach, as we run out onto the pitch for the second half. The Gaffer has made one tactical switch at half-time. He is moving Stan out wide to operate on the right wing. He has also asked John Hollins to fill the gap in our back four whenever one of the others go forward to take a cross from Stan. He will give it roughly twenty minutes to see if it will help to unlock the Leeds defence, which has proved to be impenetrable so far. Otherwise he wants the team to play exactly the same way. I tell Mick that I agree it's worth a try.

'No sense in panicking and making wholesale changes at this stage,' I say. 'Even if that means that you'll have to stay on the bench – at least for a little while longer.'

Mick doesn't offer an opinion. I'm sure he is just raring to go and is disappointed that he's not coming off the bench, but bellyaching is not Mick's way. He's a real pro and a team player in every sense.

'The Gaffer has probably spotted some weakness on the left of Leeds' defence that he hopes Stan will exploit,' I say as I head off to take up my position.

The Gaffer, Dave Sexton is the son of former professional boxer Archie Sexton. He started his playing career with West Ham United in 1948, operating mostly as an inside-forward as part of the old W-formation. He went on to play for Luton Town, Leyton Orient, Brighton & Hove Albion and Crystal Palace. His greatest playing career success came at Brighton, when they won the Third Division (South) in 1957–58. He started his coaching career at Chelsea, before leaving to take up the managerial reins at Leyton Orient. In 1966, he was appointed as Arsenal coach, but a year later he returned to Chelsea to become Manager. Under Dave Sexton, Chelsea won the FA Cup in 1970 and the European Cup Winners' Cup a year later.

However, shortly afterwards he fell out with several key players, notably big-name stars such as Peter Osgood and Alan Hudson, who were very popular with the fans, and both players were eventually transferred to other clubs.

His early successes as Manager of Chelsea proved difficult to repeat and the situation was further complicated by other problems at the club, most notably financial issues arising from the decision to build a new three-tier stand at Stamford Bridge. With the big-name stars leaving, and operating under severe financial constraints, the club terminated his managerial career at Chelsea at the beginning of the 1974–75 season.

A few weeks later, in October 1974, he was appointed manager of Queens Park Rangers.

From Dave Sexton's perspective, coming to QPR from Chelsea made a lot of sense. For a start, expectations at QPR are more realistic. And there is less pressure than there was at Chelsea. But he also had the vision to see the potential in the club – and in the squad of players.

The Gaffer is a true football lover with a strong belief in Continental-style attacking football. He is a devotee of Rinus Michaels and has a particular fascination for the tactics and training methods of the Dutch and German clubs – what they call 'total football'.

I've heard that he goes over to Holland on Sundays off his own bat to watch matches – he pays out of his own pocket. He absorbs the whole experience so that he can put it into practice on the QPR training pitch.

He took the team to a small town near Hamburg for pre-season friendly games as part of his plans to model QPR on the Dutch system, keeping the ball on the ground a lot; playing it out from the back. It's working for QPR because it is not forced on players who are unable to implement it. 'It suits us,' he says, 'because we have the players to do it.'

He's also arranged for Ron Jones, the former Olympic sprinter, to come to the training sessions at South Ruislip and take the squad through its paces. He's got in dieticians – now there are scrambled eggs and fish on the menu before matches, while most other teams are still ordering steaks.

As his experiences at Chelsea indicated, man-management of wayward stars (and they don't come more wayward than Stan Bowles!) may not be the Gaffer's strong point. At QPR, he sensibly leaves all that to Chairman Jim Gregory. So while Jim Gregory attends to Stan's special financial needs off the pitch, it's the Gaffer's responsibility to get the best out of Stan where it matters most to us – on the pitch. The Gaffer respects Stan, knows how he thinks about football and knows how to get the utmost out of him.

What the Gaffer does best is to create an environment where players can realise their potential as part of a team. He's a quiet, thoughtful man, taciturn by nature and not given to the kind of 'we was robbed' post-match outbursts so beloved of the media. I've heard some of them refer to him as a bit of a 'stiff neck'. I can understand how some people might construe this lack of outward emotion as demonstrating an absence of resolve or an inability to take tough decisions. Nothing could be further from the truth.

He substituted Stan Bowles a few weeks ago when Stan was off-form; around the time of his well-publicised domestic and gambling problems. He had just fluffed a gilt-edged chance in front of goal – a rare occurance for Stan, admittedly – but the Gaffer hauled him off anyway. Refusing to overreact to Stan's subsequent angry V-sign and his vow never to speak to Sexton again, he agreed to Stan's request to go on the transfer list 'in the best interests of the club' and dropped him for two games. After a bout of 'will he/won't he leave' ping-pong in the media, Stan was eventually restored to the team. The question now is can Stan, operating on the right wing, find a chink in Leeds' defensive armour – and quickly.

Saturday, 10 April 1976: 8.40 a.m.

It's a rabbit.

Even from this distance I can see that it's a tiny white rabbit. Not a furry toy or a sculpture of a rabbit but a real live, fluffy rabbit, craning its neck to peep over the top of the basket, straining to see where all the noise is coming from.

The noise is coming from an armada of automobiles whizzing around the corner, most intent on just getting to their destinations as swiftly as possible; but one or two on the lookout for the legendary suicidal cyclist. I quicken my step to catch her before she sails off.

'Marianne, is that what...I...think...it is?'

'What do you think it is?' she replies curtly, stopping just short of the edge of the pavement.

'I reckon it's a rabbit, Marianne – a rabbit that is on its way to certain death.' She is obviously shocked at my tone but I don't wait for her to respond. 'Marianne, you cannot cycle on a public road with a rabbit in the bleedin' front basket without any restraint or protection whatsoever. If it jumps out it will be killed.' (She doesn't respond.) 'Squashed!' (She recoils.) 'F**king flattened!' (She steps back.) 'Not to mention the chaos it will cause among the oncoming traffic.'

Bang on cue there's a toot-toot from a familiar bright green Mini as it whizzes by. Marianne turns the bike and walks away. After three or four steps, she turns it again and paces back.

'Marj doesn't want it,' she says. 'She's allergic to it. I am hoping the pet shop will take it back this morning. Otherwise, what am I going to do with it?'

I cast my eyes surreptitiously in the general direction of the first-floor bay window. I can just about see Marjorie standing inside, not unlike the rabbit, craning her neck and straining to catch what we're saying.

'Give it to me,' I say, without thinking.

'What are you going to do with it?' she asks, frowning, but handing me the tiny cardboard box containing the petrified animal, all the same.

'You know the small pond over there on Beane Row...'

'You wouldn't?' she asks, eyes dilating.

'...well, there's somebody living over there who just might take it.'

'Who? Not those awful dog people?'

'No, not the Butlers. Look, leave it to me Marianne, okay? I'll do what I can, but if I cannot find a home for it, I'll have to bring it back to you. Now I reckon you'd better let Marjorie know what's going on before she breaks that window.'

Marianne leans her bike against the wall and retraces her steps up the driveway to the house, the sound of her feet on the gravel in sync with the frantic hammering on the window.

Both of the wooden gates to Aunt Sally's are open, offering rare expanded glimpses of the gardens. Daisuke, who is sweeping out long-dead leaves, does a double-take as I pass. I smile but don't hang around to explain. I'm the object of a few horn-honks and some choice verbals myself as I linger on the corner at the Glade, waiting to cross over to Beane Row. But I've learned to ignore this kind of stuff.

'Nice morning, Eddie!'

'Nice...mornink...heh....heh. Nice...' Eddie has spotted the rabbit immediately and it obviously throws him a bit. Okay, so it's not the kind of thing he would normally expect to see me carrying. He doesn't approach me but stands there as if assuming I'm going to keep on walking by.

'I have something for you,' I say cheerfully, stopping at the low wall.

'For me? You haff somethink for me? Heh...heh,' he laughs, cautiously.

I give him the nod to come closer.

'I thought that this might be a nice present for you to give to Svetlana.'

Eddie is immediately suspicious.

'Why? She is away. She come back at Easter.'

Bingo! Eddie just gave me the hook I wanted. Why hadn't I thought of it myself? 'But that's just it, Eddie. That's the whole point, mate. It's an Easter Bunny! It will make the prefect present for Svetlana when she comes home next weekend.'

I offer the rabbit to Eddie but he makes no move to accept it.

'It's the ideal make-up gift,' I add stupidly, unable to resist testing my they've-had-a-falling-out theory.

'Make up? Make up?' Eddie's face darkens.

'Even better than make-up. Or perfume. Or a chocolate egg. The bunny is a very traditional British gift at Eastertime.'

'British bunny, heh, heh. British bunny.' Eddie gently takes the trembling rodent out of the box and cradles it in his huge arms. Whatever he made of my rambling explanations, he has obviously reached some kind of conclusion that makes sense to him. I don't hang around to give him time for a change of heart.

'Gotta go, Eddie,' I wave. 'Boro today.'

'He burrows today?' Eddie screeches after me, but I pretend not to hear.

The Butlers are lounging by the front gate. Jacko is leaning against a pillar, hands deep in the pockets of his leather jacket, while Billy is kneeling and fiddling with the gate which has come off its hinges. They both look hungover and disheveled. I slow to a walk.

'Woz that a rabbit, then, d'you think?' Jacko asks Billy. He is staring at the pavement as if I wasn't there.

'Or a hare, maybe,' suggests Billy without looking up from his task.

'Nah, it woz a rabbit, alright. A white rabbit, too,' Jacko says, continuing to ignore my presence.

'A white rabbit for White City,' giggles Billy.

'Can't see that lasting too long. Can you?'

'Some hound will surely 'ave 'im,' Billy concludes, while getting to his feet.

'C'mon, you two. What's up? What's the big deal his morning? I've just found a home for a rabbit...'

'...yeah, and we've still lost a dog,' Billy interrupts aggressively.

'That's nothing to do with me,' I protest, conscious that I have done nothing about establishing if Eddie might have dognapped Roxy or Arrow – or whatever name he answers to at this stage – since the Butlers asked me to some weeks ago.

'Well, maybe it's got a lot to do wiv 'im,' Billy jerks his thumb in the direction of Eddie's place.

'Shut it!' Jacko orders Billy. He finally looks at me – a little too menacingly for my liking – then smiles: 'Ya don't want to be taking too much notice of our Billy 'ere. He loved that 'ound, so he did. Can't understand how 'e went missin'. And neither can I, come to fink of it.'

I step up the pace a bit and the two brothers fall in behind me. We exchange some strained chit-chat about today's game until we reach Noah Berrie's, by which time they've cheered up a bit and they wander off in the direction of the Green.

There's no sign of Lisa so I make my way over to the arcade.

The unmistakable sound of Tina Charles is belting out from Threads' p.a. system. Brad has recently taken to playing music programmes he's recorded (probably illegally). This morning it's good old 'Fluff' – Alan Freeman – presenting the UK's top hits of the week.

'And there it is, pop pickers: Tina Charles and "I Love to Love (But my baby just loves to dance)"...'

You can say that again, mate.

'Good mornington! Dry and mild; a good day for football – but not for trading.' Noah's voice rings out over the music and the rest of the early morning clatter emanating from the arcade. 'How is business, Noah?' I enquire, pausing momentarily in the doorway.

'Slow in coming, my friend, like peace in the Middle East. I need ideas to stimulate sales. Brad has a few ideas, but if they're not working for him I cannot see how they will work for me,' he shrugs.

'Mick seems to be doing well over in The Cabin. It always seems to be busy...'

'Busy with people, yes. But sales? I'm not so sure. Why else would he still be keeping all those little trefoils hanging in place long after—'

'All those what?' I interject.

'Trefoils, my friend. Those little shamrock stickers that Mick has hanging up all around the shop, ever since St Patrick's—'

'Why are they called trefoils?' I interject again.

Noah sighs in mild exasperation.

'Because they have three leaves, my friend. You probably stand on them every time you play football.'

'Oh. Right. And does it have any other meaning? Trefoil?'

'Like what?'

'Dunno. Just wondered. It sounds so…so erotic – exotic! Whatever. You know what I mean,' I fluster.

'It has no other meaning – at least not to my knowledge, my good friend,' Noah starts to adjust the positioning of some of the small stuff he has on display; a sure sign that he's beginning to lose interest in this conversation. 'If it's got three leaves, it's a trefoil. Now, are you buying or selling today?'

'I'm goodbying, I'm afraid, Noah. I'm running a bit late as it is. Cheerio.'

'Kol tuv, my friend.'

As soon as I exit the arcade, I see them. All three of them together on the Green. Lisa is chatting to Cathal under the shade of a large tree and, a few feet away, O'Leary is sitting on the bench beside the postbox looking in the other direction. Keeping watch? They obviously cannot see me, perhaps because of the long shadow cast by the arcade entrance. Lisa is handing something to Cathal and receiving something in exchange. I speculate on what this might be. And I'm shocked at the extent of my own suspicions.

O'Leary sees me first as I cross the street and he stands up immediately to greet me. Or maybe to intercept me? His hands are thrust deep into the pockets of the long, crumpled houndstooth overcoat he is wearing (on a dry, mild morning like this?) and he stretches both arms out as he yawns (an attempt to block Lisa and Cathal from my line of vision?). His greeting is loud, perhaps as a signal of my arrival to the other two. In any event, they are totally unfazed by my presence and do not appear in the slightest bit embarrassed. Cathal is in no hurry to go and asks me how I reckon the game will go today. Lisa looks affectedly bored; perhaps feeling trapped by the prospect of yet another dreary football conversation. O'Leary definitely looks as if he wants to go and is constantly looking at his watch. He finally has his way and we part company, although I notice that Cathal and O'Leary go their separate ways shortly afterwards, with O'Leary looking back in our direction a couple of times before he heads on through Station Road and on to the High Street.

'What was all that about?' I ask as casually as I can in the circumstances.

Lisa frowns: 'I was giving him some tickets he asked me to get for him. Why?'

I ignore her question: 'What kind of tickets?'

'Not tickets for a football match, obviously,' she says, dismissively. 'The tickets were for Sadler's Wells, if you must know.' She appears a little rattled by my questions so I keep them coming.

'I didn't know they were into opera,' I observe, sarcastically.

'Hmm. Sadler's Wells does have a historical connection to opera, as you so rightly observe, but these days it is better known as "London's Dance House". I know some people there, which was why I offered to get the tickets for them.'

'I didn't know they were into dance,' I smirk, delighted at how I've boxed her in.

'They're not. There's a folk music concert there tomorrow that they are interested in: June Tabor & Maddy Prior — I don't suppose you've ever heard of them?'

I shrug to buy time. It's obvious I've made a complete fool of myself once again.

'Me neither, to be perfectly frank,' Lisa volunteers, helpfully, thereby presenting me with the opportunity to steer the conversation elsewhere.

'Sadler's Wells is up Islington way, isn't it?' I observe. 'Highbury: Arsenal territory.'

'It is in Islington, but how close it is to any football stadium I couldn't say with any certainty,' she sighs.

'It's a long way from Covent Garden, though. Bit of a cheek asking you to go all the way up to Islington to collect tickets, if you ask me.'

'Well, I wasn't asking you,' she says pleasantly. 'And anyway, Sadler's Wells is on Roseberry Avenue, on the southern end of Islington. It's only a couple of stops on the Tube from Covent Garden. Now, I have to see Brad about something.'

And she begins to move off. I say nothing. I want to raise the subject of trefoils or trefulls. Somehow. But I don't know how to do it comfortably. I certainly cannot do it here in public. But where? When? And now she is heading off to see Brad — who claims to know all about the trefull or trefoil, whatever that means in relation to Lisa. According to Brad, she has already 'shown it to him'. Thankfully, Lisa resolves the first part of the problem for me.

'Wait for me here after you been to The Cabin,' she calls back as she strides towards Threads.

Phew.

I sit on the bench for a moment and try to compose my thoughts. I cannot see how the trefoils described by Noah can have anything to do with what Brad was referring to. So, I have possibly two different meanings from two different people from the same family. I'm no closer to knowing what it is. And I need to know. At least, I need to know more before I can raise it with Lisa.

My reverie is suddenly disrupted by two sweaty hands encircling my eyes from behind and covering them tightly.

'Piss off, Jacko. Not now.'

'Howdya know it woz me, mate?' Both hands immediately relax their hold.

'I could smell you.'

'Charmin', I'm sure.' Jacko comes round to confront me: 'Tha's a nice way to greet one of your mates, innit, Billy.'

Billy is standing downwind so I don't quite catch what he mumbles in reply.

'It's the tobacco. That rollie stuff. I could smell it from your hands.'

'Aah. Tha's all right then, me ol' china.' Jacko's indignation appears suitably mollified by my explanation.

'Have either of you blokes ever heard of trefoil?' I ask in desperation, stammering over the word to allow for the widest possible interpretation.

'Ol' 'Arry? Haven't 'eard from 'im in ages, mate.'

My antennae are immediately on alert. 'What? What did you say?'

'Arry Threlfall. Ain't clapped eyes on 'im in yonks. 'Ave you, Billy?'

'You what it…who it…you know him?' I stand up to face Jacko, but resist the urge to hug him.

'Knew 'im,' Billy's pipes in from downwind.

Jacko and I both turn to face Billy, who is staring at some twigs on the grass he is poking with his foot.

'Arry Threlfall's inside. The Scrubs. GBH. Three years.' With each revelation, Billy stabs his foot at one of the twigs and kicks it away, as if the memory is causing him severe anguish.

'What's Billy jabbering on about? C'mon, Jacko. Tell me. Quick.'

'Iss all comin' back to me now.' Jacko is stroking his chin, savouring the fact that he holds some information that I obviously badly need. 'Ol' 'Arry Threlfall – bit of a villain that he is – woz caught bang to rights after wot ya might call "an incident" involving 'Arry and a couple of 'is mates. In Whitehall…'

'Whitehall? An incident?' I'm immediately alert to the possible political ramifications of what Brad had only hinted at.

'Do let me finish, mate!' Jacko smiles. 'Wot I woz about to say before you so rudely interrupted me woz…Whitehall Park Road. In Chiswick. The incident woz an attempted robbery that included a bit of GBH – that's "grievous bodily harm" to you and me, mate. As a result of which our 'Arry is now doing his porridge in Wormwood Scrubs.'

'What happened to his two mates?'

Jacko gives a polite cough: 'They woz never appre'ended. Just 'Arry. Three years. Seemed a bit 'arsh at the time but then he did have a bit of "previous wiv the grevious" did ol' 'Arry Trelfall. Right, Billy?'

'Right on, Jacko.' Billy gives us the thumbs up, swings his right foot in a final hefty arc but mistakes a protruding root for a twig and does some painful GBH to his big toe as a result. Jacko goes to assist and helps Billy as he limps away.

'Wot's your particular interest in 'Arry Trelfall, anyway?' Jacko calls back. 'Someone bin askin' about 'im, 'ave they?'

I pretend not to hear him and the two brothers eventually shuffle off. I plant myself back down on the bench again. I've learned nothing. I should have known better than to even bother asking the Butlers. Brad said 'her' Trefull or Trefoil or Threlfall or whatever, so it is highly unlikely to be a person. More like something she owns, something she has – part of her. I stand up again. I feel decidedly uncomfortable about the whole thing. I just wish it hadn't raised its head again. I decide to head for The Cabin. Try to get my thoughts back on track. Why does every conversation with Jacko and Billy end up with a discussion about the police, the courts, prison, guilt or innocence? It's impossible to avoid it.

PETER HAIN IS INNOCENT!

The headline on the Daily Mirror front page screams out at me from the shelf. The leader of the Young Liberals walked free from the Old Bailey after the jury found him not guilty of stealing £490 from a bank in Putney. I quickly switch my attention to the sports coverage on the back pages. Milwall Manager Gordon Jago, who managed QPR for four seasons, has some positive things to say about the team and wishes us well today. Jago left QPR in strained circumstances, so it's a very sporting gesture from him to go on the record in this way.

'Well, what do you think, Dawhee?' Mick asks when I arrive at the counter. But it's Peter Hain he's referring to, not Jago.

'It was all a case of mistaken identity, apparently,' I say to Mick.

'Maybe, me bucko, but young Hain says he suspects that South African secret agents used a double in the bank raid in order to discredit him because of his anti-apartheid activities. It seems that only one witness out of six had picked him out of an identity parade.' Mick continues with his forensic analysis of the case but I don't really pay too much attention. It's a complex case and my mind is complicated enough this morning already.

'But you're not really interested in all that, are you me bucko? You've got bigger things on your mind today.'

'You don't know the half of it, Mick,' I feel like saying. But instead, I just shrug and hand Mick a quid.

Then I peel off one of the little trefoils from the display while Mick is digging out the shrapnel for me.

'Do you have any other interests outside of football?'

We are sitting in the café sipping tea, having met up on the Green as agreed.

'There is nothing interesting outside of football,' I reply matter-of-factly.

Her eyes open wide and she half smiles through her exasperation: 'I cannot believe you can say that with a straight face. You're observant, you're knowledgeable, and you're intelligent. How can you not be interested in things outside of football?'

'Such as?'

'Well, music, for example?'

'Hmm. Okay, I admit to having a passing interest in music.'

'Classical music?'

'No. Rock music, pop music, whatever you want to call it. The stuff they play over the public address system...'

'...at football matches! Lord, give me patience. Name some of the stuff you like.'

'Pass.'

'Pardon?'

'Pass. I cannot think of any. But then I did say it was a passing interest,' I explain with a smirk.

'Very droll,' she sighs, unimpressed, 'what about politics?'

'They're all the same,' I shrug. 'All corrupt.'

'Oh my God.' She half extends both arms in exasperation and the fingers of both hands part like talons: 'There must be something,' she looks at me almost pleadingly. 'Poetry?'

'You must be joking!'

'Why? Poetry is beautiful.'

'Football is beautiful. It's been called "The Beautiful Game", or haven't you heard?'

'Football: the beautiful game?' she muses, is silent for a moment, then: 'No, never heard that one. I must have missed college on the day of that lecture. But, to be serious for a moment, don't you know any poetry?'

'I was being serious. And I did know a lot of that stuff a few years ago. When I had to know it. But those old poets are, you know, not really relevant to today's world.'

'So you don't believe that their observations on life are still relevant today?'

'Not really. In fact, definitely not. And the language they used has no relevance to today.'

'Not even to football?' she teases.

'Especially not to football,' I reply emphatically.

She smiles that enigmatic smile again.

'So what's making news this morning?' I ask, nodding at her folded newspaper and trying to change the subject.

'Politics mostly.' She opens The Guardian and scans the news pages: 'There's that story about Peter Hain being cleared of stealing from Barclays Bank. Lots of stuff regarding Jim Callaghan being elected as the new Prime Minister last Monday...'

'Let's hope he turns out to be a lot better than Harold Wilson was in dealing with those IRA terrorists,' I interject.

'Well, there's only so much that any Prime Minister can do...'

'Then they should let Maggie Thatcher have a go. She'd soon sort them out. There'd be no pussy-footing around if Maggie was in power.'

'You don't know that. Politicians promise everything when in opposition but when they get into power it's a different story. They campaign in poetry but govern in prose, as the saying goes.'

'What's poetry got to do with it?' I ask.

'Just on old cliché,' she explains, before returning her attention to the newspaper. 'And, of course, they're still discussing the circumstances of Harold Wilson's resignation as leader.'

'Old Enoch Powell got it right, didn't he, when he said that all political careers ultimately end in failure.'

'Ah, so you do know something about politics.' She smiles, raising her head slowly from the newspaper. 'Well, I hope that you're not an Enoch Powell supporter and I'm certainly not, but in the interests of fairness and historical accuracy, I should point out that Powell said a little more than that. What he actually said was,' and here she puts on an accent that I don't recognise, but I assume is an attempt at mimicking Enoch Powell, 'all political lives, unless they are cut off in midstream at a happy juncture, end in failure, because that is the nature of politics and of human affairs.'

'Same thing, really.'

'Actually, it isn't. What Powell suggested was that successful politicians should get out while they are still on top. If they don't, they will stay in the game just that little bit too long and inevitably their careers will end in failure.'

'Okay, what about it? It's politics. They all deserve their comeuppence in the end.'

'And is it not the same in sport? In football? Don't most footballers' careers end in failure?'

'Maybe too many of them do hang around too long. But not me. I'll know exactly when to call time on my football career.'

'Okay. But have you thought about what you are going to do after your career in football is over?'

'Dunno. Maybe I'll become a pundit. You know, on a TV or radio panel commenting on football games. Or maybe I'll write.'

'In a newspaper? About football?'

'Not necessarily. I meant write. Like a story. Or a book. Whatever.'

'Well, you are full of surprises! I didn't know you could write.' This is said with a heavy hint of sarcasm.

'Well, I don't know that I can. But sometimes I think that I want to.'

'But have you ever actually written anything?'

'Only when I was younger. You know, stuff for the school magazine. That kind of thing.'

'Was it any good? I'd love to read it.'

'Well, my old English teacher, Mr Wattles, used to say that my writing skills were like my football skills.'

'Brilliant?'

'No. Solid. But with very occasional flashes of creativity, punctuated by intemperate outbursts.'

'Oh. Damned with faint praise, then. But did you always want to be a writer?'

'No. As a kid, I always wanted to be a magician or an illusionist.'

'An illusionist? Where did that idea come from?'

'From a book I read. It was all about illusion and the power of suggestion. How you make people think in a certain way simply by allowing them to draw conclusions from facts that you give them selectively.'

'Maybe that could work in football?

'How do you mean?'

'You know, you could use body movements to suggest to an opponent that you are going to do one thing and then you do another.'

'I reckon we do that anyway — but it's instinctive.'

'Maybe it could be developed further.'

'How do you mean, exactly?'

'Well, when your team is setting up a free-kick, you could use choreography to trick the opposition into believing that your players are going to...you know...when you really plan to do something entirely different.'

'But we already do that in football.'

'You don't really. You just believe that you do. You certainly don't do it well. I've seen it on the telly and it's pathetic. The free-kick taker holds his arm upright, shouts something and then everybody runs like headless chickens towards roughly where the ball is going to land. What you need is professional choreography.' She pauses for a bit, then: 'Maybe I could help. Why don't you offer my services to QPR.'

'I'll think about it,' I lie. The thought of going along to a training session at South Ruislip next week and suggesting that a classical dancer is hired to choreograph the set pieces doesn't bear thinking about.

'No you won't,' she smiles, slides her chair back and stands up to go. 'Come along. We should be going.'

I remain seated. There is some unfinished business I am determined to settle. Today.

'You'll be late,' she says, tapping her watch impatiently. 'And stop fidgeting with that piece of paper. What is it, anyway?'

'Just one of those decorations that was hanging from the ceiling in The Cabin. It fell down so I picked it up.' I turn it over and show it to her.

'Oh, it's a shamrock,' she says.

'Mmmm. A trefoil,' I half mutter.

She sits down again.

'What?'

'It's a trefoil.'

'It's funny that you should use that term, "trefoil". Not like you at all.'

'But that's what it is,' I shrug.

Silence. I wish I could say I feel as much in control of this conversation as I would like, but the truth is I feel nervous about where it might be leading to.

'You're the second person in the last twenty-four hours to use that word, "trefoil". I wonder why that is. I believe I shall have to have a word with Bradley.' She doesn't sound upset, just disappointed. I start to wonder who, why and in what circumstances some other person used that word.

Silence.

'I suppose you would like to see it?'

I have my hand covering my mouth, so she won't have noticed how hard I've just swallowed. My stomach has turned to jelly.

'Of course,' I shrug in my best I've-seen-it-all, man-of-the-world manner. 'Where do you suggest we go?'

'I'm not suggesting we go anywhere. Let's do it here.'

'Here?' I feel I'm beginning to lose control of this situation. There is obviously a side to Lisa that I wasn't aware of up to now.

'Yes, here. Because I'm only going to let you see it. I'm not going to let you touch it, okay?'

My throat has gone dry.

'Okay?'

I nod.

Then, very slowly, she unties the knot of the scarf she is wearing over her shoulder and pulls down on the scarf with her right hand so that it slides across the back of her neck and down. Then, she leans forward and turns slightly to the right. On her left shoulder, just where it meets the nape of her neck, are three small, perfectly formed birthmarks. Each appears to be exactly the same size and the three are grouped together in a perfect triangular shape.

I lean forward to get a closer look. I can clearly detect that scent of apple blossom again. Our cheeks are almost touching and I can feel her breath just below my left ear.

'It's just like a tiny tattoo,' I exclaim. 'Nature's tattoo.'

She sits back and smiles, and her eyes are moist as she drapes the scarf over her shoulders again and ties the knot at the front.

'People used to comment on it as soon as they saw it, so now I tend to keep it covered all the time.'

'It's beautiful,' I find myself saying.

She smiles and gives a little shiver with her shoulders.

I feel a great sense of relief that the 'trefoil' wasn't a euphemism for any of things I had speculated to myself about. Also, that Lisa's character is as I always assumed it to be. Why did I even think otherwise? How could I have doubted her?

'Now it really is time to go,' Lisa says quietly, after a moment's awkward silence. We pay the bill, leave the café and set off up Park Road.

'Let's talk about football!' she says suddenly, sensing that I am totally tongue-tied. 'Who have you got today?'

'Middlesboro,' I say, absently-mindedly, still thinking about those three little pearls.

'And what are your chances?' she is trying to jolly me back to normality, but I'm reluctant to go.

'Well, we're still in first place, Boro' are ninth. They've got some really useful players – Graham Souness, Phil Boersma, Terry Cooper. The manager is Jack Charlton, who won a World Cup medal with England. He has them playing a fairly direct style. The pitch will be hard and dry which will suit the kind of football that we play. We drew 0–0 with them back in September up in Ayersome Park, and also at Loftus Road in the corresponding fixture last season, so goals may be difficult to come by for both sides today. But the way I'm feeling right now – I'm confident that we will win.' My last observation owed as much to the events of this morning as to the current form of both teams.

'Good,' she says, chirpily. 'What else?'

'Football-wise?' I ask.

'I'm not so sure that football and sagacity go hand in hand but, yes, what else on the football front?'

I've never heard Lisa sound so genuinely interested in football before, so I decide to take advantage of the situation.

'*Now that you mention it, next weekend is Easter. As it happens, we're away on Saturday to Norwich but we do have a home game on Monday 19th. Easter Monday. It's against the Arsenal. And it's a morning kick-off. Eleven o'clock.*'

'*What are you asking me?*'

'*Well, I'm not really doing the ritual thing, it's a Monday after all and people do different things on Mondays than they do on Saturdays; then it's a Bank Holiday too and...*'

'*What are you asking me?*'

'*I'm asking you if we can meet up on Easter Monday in the café.*'

'*Is it open on Easter Monday?*'

'*Yes. I saw a notice when we were in there earlier. Open Easter Monday.*'

'*So even though you cannot do your "ritual" next Monday, you want me to give up my Easter Monday holiday morning lie-in to meet you...*'

'*At the earlier time of 7.30.*'

'*...at the earlier time of 7.30.' Then she opens her eyes wide in amazement. 'At the earlier time of 7.30? No chance.*'

'*Okay, eight o'clock. Let's say eight o'clock.*'

She pretends to consider it for a moment.

'*Okay. For an Easter egg. A large Easter egg. A very large Easter egg.*'

'*Agreed. What kind?*'

'*Surprise me.*'

*The rest of the journey home is a bit of a blur. I feel so relieved that the trefoil issue has been resolved. It had never really gone away, try as I did to put it out of my mind. Now it's sorted, I can move on – we can move on. Now the problem is to decide what kind of Easter egg I will buy? What brand? Maybe one of those foreign eggs. French. Or Swiss. Dark chocolate. Yes, Swiss! Class. Maybe I should ask Marianne. I still remember our conversation about Toblerone. She seemed to know something about Swiss chocolate. Then again, what's wrong with good old English chocolate? Cadbury's. Or Rowntree's? Do I get a very large egg like she asked for? Or go for quality and maybe smaller?**

By the time I get home, I realise I haven't really thought seriously about this afternoon's game at all.

I need to refocus. It's important that we win today.

Saturday, 10 April 1976: 4.40 p.m.
Queens Park Rangers...4 Middlesboro...2

The
SECOND
HALF

21. EARLY BIRD. SPECIAL!

Saturday, 24 April 1976: 3.55 p.m.: Early in the second half

Early in the game is a good time to score a goal. Late in the first half can be even better. Especially if the goal puts your team into the lead. It deflates the opposition just before the break. They've probably defended heroically for the whole of the first half, then…BANG…they're a goal down. They go into the dressing room at half-time feeling cheated but also beginning to question themselves – and each other. This might not be their day, Lady Luck may have deserted them this afternoon.

But we didn't quite manage that goal.

For all the possession we had, all the pressure we exerted, all the chances we created, we went in at half-time exactly as we had started: level with Leeds. And scoreless.

Early in the second half is not a bad time to score, either. But the tension seems to be getting to us. Despite a bout of sustained pressure, we don't even come close to scoring. Leeds are beginning to believe that maybe, just maybe, this could be their day.

Then suddenly we get a break. We make some laboured progress down the left wing. The ball is fired across the Leeds goal. Don Givens gets his head to it. But he doesn't make proper contact and only succeeds in knocking it further across the goal. And there's Stan, making his run into the box on the right. Not noted for his heading ability, Stan rises to it perfectly. It has 'goal' written all over it. But Frankie Gray rises with him. There's this awful clash of heads and the ball is gathered safely by Harvey in the Leeds goal. Stan and Frankie Gray look at each other ruefully. Stan looks to have come off worst. Christ, that's all we need just now. And just when the Gaffer's half-time tactic of moving Stan onto the right wing appears to be working, too.

I shout across at Stan, ask him if he's okay. Stan looks over but doesn't appear to see me. He looks groggy. Concussion, maybe. He keeps rubbing his head. If we lose Stan at this stage of the game, I don't see how we can win it.

Monday, 19 April 1976: 7.30 a.m.

Easter Monday. I have excused myself the need for the full ritual because it's a Monday, it's a Bank Holiday, it's a morning kick-off – and it's much earlier than usual. I'm dressed in a tracksuit and jogging lightly (a) because I'm carrying a large Easter egg and (b) because I don't really expect to encounter any of the usual crew. But I resolve to treat any elements of the ritual I do manage to encounter as auspicious omens of a successful day ahead.

A promising beginning at this early hour: Marianne Pleass is wheeling her bicycle along the footpath, a particularly large and colourfully-wrapped Easter egg in the front basket.

I can't help but notice that it's a 'Tobler 1'. Embarking on another of her good deed trips, no doubt. But why so early? And a day late? I glance up at Marjorie, who is looking a bit forlorn. She is standing at the first-floor bay window, with one hand raised as if in a permanent gesture of farewell, while the other hand is holding a half-eaten Cadbury's Creme Egg.

I decide that this might not be the best moment to engage Marianne in conversation so I jog slowly on, with the merest nod of acknowledgement in her direction as I pass. She seems disappointed. Perhaps she wanted to compare eggs.

I wonder if Daisuke, as I've learned to call him, is on a day off. Perhaps he doesn't work at Aunt Sally's on Mondays. Anyway, it's highly unlikely he'll be working on an Easter Monday. But then it's an hour before I usually bump into him and I cannot reasonably expect him to start out earlier today just to maintain a ritual he knows nothing about.

But there is someone moving about at the gate, and wearing very strange clothes, at that. Dressed completely in white with something weird covering the head, it looks a bit like an astronaut or a character from one of those films about outbreaks of infectious diseases. It's moving very slowly while carefully opening the gates. Then I spot the dirty brown boots. They look a little incongruous, but it's the different coloured bootlaces – one red, the other blue – that give the game away. Then I hear Aunt Sally's loud, cackling laugh:

'I suppose you are wondering why I am walking around all dressed up like this?' she calls out.

I pause but say nothing.

'You're Lisa's friend,' she states, without expecting to be contradicted. She pushes back the head covering to reveal that jowly, weather-beaten face. 'I'm waiting for Daisuke. I'm all dressed up like this because, today, we need to gauge how much honey is in the hives. To ensure that there's enough in there to keep all the bees fed.'

'How do you do that?'

'By hefting the hive.'

'How do you do that?' I repeat.

'You just lift it,' she laughs, as if the explanation should have been obvious. 'If it feels too light then you have to add something to it.'

'Like what?'

'Like fondant.'

'Fondant? Like on cakes?'

'Yes. Do you have a sweet tooth?' she asks, staring at the Easter egg I'm carrying.

'Not really. This is a present. What do you do with the fondant?'

She smiles: 'You just drip-feed it into the hive to increase the bees' honey diet.'

'Why wouldn't there be enough honey in there already?'

'Well, the weather for a start.' She laughs mockingly at my ignorance. 'If it's too cold, then the worker bees will not collect sufficient fresh pollen from early flowering plants, like those crocuses there.' She points at some blue and yellow plants just inside the gates. 'Then the queen bees will not be stimulated to lay enough eggs to keep the hives going with honey.'

'Why do you keep bees in the first place?' I ask , before immediately realising that the answer to this question may detain me here for far longer than I would wish.

'Your friend Lisa asked me that question too,' she says slowly, as if this was a highly significant coincidence. 'I suppose it's because it teaches me to be quiet and patient. If I rush and make too much noise the bees will try to sting me.'

'Oh,' is all I can say, standing well back as Daisuke's Reliant swings in from the road and goes straight through the gates.

'Aha. There goes my batman. In his Robin,' she cackles again at her own little joke. 'Goodbye. And say hello to Lisa for me. I hope she enjoys the egg.'

And with that she follows the Reliant through the swirling dust into the gardens and starts to shut the gates, giving me a little wave as she does so. I give her a thumbs-up and cross the road, pausing only to allow Marianne to free-wheel past me at speed. There is very little traffic on the road due to the holiday and everything seems strangely quiet.

Echo Eddie is not up and about in the garden yet and, not surprisingly, the silence is uninterrupted by any sound emanating from the alleged squawking parrot. No sign of Svetlana either to brighten up the day as I pad past.

As expected, given the time, it's all quiet at the Butler residence too. Which is just as well, as I don't really want to get into a conversation about Easter eggs with those two headless chickens. I pick up the pace as I head down Park Road.

There's nobody out and about at the shops fronting onto the Green either. All closed. So, no cheery 'Good mornington' from Noah Berrie; no mood music from Threads. I know the café is open and Lisa is probably waiting there. But I decide to pop into The Cabin to pick up the newspaper first, so I have something to read if Lisa is late. Or if she doesn't show up.

'We ARE the greatest' screams the Mirror headline over a story about all the great things that Britain has achieved in business and in sport. There's a picture of boxer John Conteh and another of a woman I don't recognise.

I show the newspaper to Mick as soon as I reach the counter. He doesn't recognise the woman either but starts to read aloud from the report.

'"Nobody makes lighter of British achievements than the British. Knocking ourselves is a national pastime." Hmmm. I wouldn't exactly agree with that now, Dawhee me bucko. "That's why the Mirror is…presenting the best of British…today we kick off…with the money spinning fashion business. Later in the week we will spotlight Entertainment, Sport…"'

He peers at me over the top of the newspaper and looks singularly unimpressed. He sighs and turns immediately to scan the sports pages.

'Who the hell is Hans Croon?' he asks loudly.

'He's the Manager of Anderlecht. He's Dutch,' I reply.

'Croon? Sounds more like a singer. Why would Arsenal want him?' he demands incredulously.

'Because nobody else is interested in the vacant manager's job?' I ask.

Mick smiles lightly at my insolence. 'I don't know about that, me bucko. It says here that Miljan Miljanic of Real Madrid is interested in the Arsenal job. He's good, isn't he? And look at what this man Croon says about Arsenal: "They are famous throughout the world and it would be a lucky man who had the chance to manage them." And sure wouldn't any manager worth his salt give his right arm to take over a team with Liam Brady in it? As you will find out today to your cost.'

We then have a brief debate about how this morning's game will go, but I'm reluctant to get into a long conversation with Mick because of the time. I don't want to keep Lisa waiting.

'Have to go, Mick,' I say finally, folding the newspaper.

'I see you have The Egg with you, me bucko.' Mick nods towards the large box under my arm. He actually helped me choose the egg during the week. And never even asked who it was for. But the way he said 'The Egg' just now — together with that gormless grin on his face — means he knows it's for Lisa.

I nod sheepishly.

'Don't let it get too cosy under that arm, now,' he adds, 'or it'll hatch!'

I bump into Veronica as I cross from the Green to the café. I didn't recognise her at first. She usually wears some kind of plain tea room uniform when she's working. And slipper-like shoes that she slaps around in. This morning she looks...I dunno...different. She looks surprised to see me too.

'I'm early,' I explain.

'And I'm late. Gregory will throw a fit.' She pushes the door in ahead of me and I stumble up the step after her. Lisa is sitting at a table towards the back.

'I cannot believe that I'm doing this,' Lisa grins between sips of tea. We've been sitting together for about ten minutes and the conversation hasn't really got going. Maybe it's because the whole thing has been prearranged and the element of surprise — will I bump into her? where will I bump into her? — is missing.

'Look at the time,' she demands, stirring her tea vigorously. 'I'm usually still fast asleep at this hour.'

I say nothing but smile weakly. She certainly looks wide awake to me. And her eyes are alert and sparkling.

But I think she was a little underwhelmed with the Easter egg when I produced it a few minutes ago. I went for large — very large, as I had promised as my part of the bargain — but I think on reflection she would probably have been happier with something that had a bit more of a quality finish to it. Looking at it now across the table, the packaging looks a bit garish. I should have put more thought into it instead of quickly grabbing the largest one I could find in The Cabin.

Now she is turning over the box, examining each side and making admiring little murmurs. But I know she is just being polite and pretending to be impressed. Suddenly, she pauses to read something, gazes up at me and then returns to finish what she was reading.

'Nice sentiment,' she smiles at last, still reading the box.

Now I know I should have given more thought to the packaging. 'Show me,' I demand and reach across the table for the package, but she folds her arms around it protectively. 'I want to read it...'

She frowns.

'...again. I want to read it again.'

'But I would have thought you knew exactly what it said. Yes. I can just imagine you now; examining all the Easter egg boxes in Harrods until you found just the one that expressed exactly the message you wanted to convey.'

I don't know whether she is pleased and teasing me or if she is being sarcastic and the words on the box are totally inappropriate.

'I just wanted to check that the shop gave me the right one. The one I asked for.' I gesture for her to hand over the box. Instead, she puts the package on her lap. Then she places her elbows on the table, rests her chin on her thumbs and looks me straight in the eye:

So sensitive his nature seemed,
So daring and sweet his thought.

I shut my eyes in embarrassment: 'Is that what it says?'

'No,' she replies. 'That's from a poem called "Easter 1916". By Yeats. But the lines could have been written about you.'

When I open my eyes again, her face is just a few inches from mine. For a moment I think she is going to kiss me. I start to close my eyes again but Lisa suddenly pushes back her chair, stands up, swings her coat on and gathers up the Easter egg, all in one fluid movement.

'I have to be going,' she announces, then, noting my surprise, she adds, 'people to meet, chocolate to eat!' with a theatrical flourish while hugging the box as if it were a cuddly teddy bear. We haven't been in the café for very long and I'm wondering now if Lisa will think that the whole thing was a waste of her time.

I fumble in my pocket for the money to pay for the teas. Veronica, who has deglamourised herself since we met earlier, gives me a knowing wink when I pay at the counter.

'She's very beautiful,' she says, nodding towards the door as Lisa leaves. I smile impatiently, keen to make my own exit.

'Everybody thinks so,' she adds, nodding over my shoulder in the direction of the chattering customers. I glance round and there are, indeed, quite a number of customers staring out the window at Lisa who is waiting for me on the footpath and reading one of the signs in the large window.

Veronica then kind of pats my hand as she gives me my change. But I may have imagined that. Still...

Lisa is still waiting outside and we fall into step as we proceed up Park Road. To break the awkward silence, I thank her profusely for meeting me so early, telling her how much I appreciate it and how I now know we will win today against Arsenal. What I'm really concerned about is whether I missed an opportunity back there in the café. Was she expecting me to kiss her? Should I have kissed her anyway? How would she have reacted? My head's a muddle. We don't say a lot as we walk up Park Road. Just idle chit-chat. We are both preoccupied. Maybe we're both thinking the same things.

There appears to be some kind of stand-off going on as we approach Eddie's place. The Butler brothers are gesticulating wildly but Eddie is not making eye contact, concentrating instead on tidying up and putting stuff away, ignoring their raised voices. It all stops as soon as they see us.

'How I get to Shepherd's Bush?' *Eddie asks me, as if this is what they had been discussing, which I doubt.*

'The best way is to take the Tube,' *I say, looking at Lisa. She nods her assent.*

'Ah, the Tube, heh, heh; the Tube. What colour Tube line I take?'

'You can take the Hammersmith & City line, which is purple. Or the Central line, which is red,' *Lisa explains.*

'There are two line Tubes to Shepherd's Bush?' *Eddie is aghast rather than impressed.*

'There's two different stations called Shepherd's Bush, mate,' *interjects Jacko, seemingly delighted to be adding to Eddie's confusion.*

Eddie is even more aghast. To be fair to him, it does seem ludicrous to have two Tube stations with exactly the same names.

'But which station Kipper?' *At this stage, Eddie pulls a crumpled blue and white scarf from a huge pocket in his overalls.*

'Aah, so ya wanna go to Loftus Road, mate,' *Jacko chips in again.* 'Then take the Central line — the red one — but don't get off at Shepherd's Bush.'

'Don't get off at all, mate,' *mutters Billy under his breath.*

'Why don't get off at Shepherd's Bush?' *Eddie looks around pleadingly. He obviously doesn't trust the instructions he is likely to get from the Butlers. But Jacko persists with being helpful.*

'Cos it's not the nearest Tube station to Loftus Road, mate. For Loftus Road, ya go on to the next station: White City.'

'But White City is dogs!' *exclaims Eddie.*

The very mention of dogs heralds an immediate cooling of the atmosphere between Eddie and the brothers. I decide to intervene.

'White City is a greyhound track, but it's also the Tube station that's closest to Loftus Road. You'll see the BBC offices when you come out of the Tube station.'

'Ah, the BBC, heh, heh. It's on Match of Today,' *Eddie grins.* 'Barry Davees. John Motty.'

Billy closes his eyes and shakes his head in quiet frustration: 'The Big Match,' *he says quietly but emphatically.*

'It's the big match on Match of Today, tonight?'

'No, mate, it's The Big Match on ITV,' *seethes Billy, who is wearing a shirt that looks suspiciously like the top of his pyjamas under his jacket.*

'London Weekend Television. Tomorrow afternoon. Brian Moore and Jimmy Hill,' *Jacko strokes his chin, making a goatee beard shape.* 'Right, Billy?'

'Awe, let's go, Jacko,' *Billy mutters in exasperation.*

On the spur of the moment, I decide to risk the ridiculous and ask Jacko about the dog.

'Any news of Roxy…er, Arrow?'

Jacko looks momentarily embarassed rather than amused, but he recovers what passes for his poise, while Billy looks on stonily.

'Aah, yes, actually. Good news. He's back.'

'Oh, great. Where had he got to? How did you get him back?'

'Actually, there was a bit of a mix-up.' Jacko begins waving his arms about a bit, as he does when he's bullshitting. 'It seems that Benny-the-book called to the 'ouse one evening while Billy an' me woz out and the old man…well…' (Jacko starts to scratch under his chin – another sure sign he's feeling uncomfortable) '…well, the old geezer gave the dog to Benny.' He looks away while telling me this, before adding, 'And then forgot to tell Billy and me.' (The last bit through clenched teeth.)

I make a big play of frowning: 'So the two of you were hunting frantically, high and low, for the missing dog over the past few weeks…'

'Yeah…'

'…and all the time, your dad had given him to your friend Benny…'

'Thass right…'

'…but never mentioned this to either yourself or Billy?'

'Correct,' Jacko says, as if this is his final word on the matter.

'Come on, Jacko.'

'Look, you know my old man. You've bin in the 'ouse. You've met 'im. Can hardly remember his own soddin' name.' Jacko taps his temple rapidly as if to emphasise old man Butler's tenuous grip on reality.

'But why did your dad just hand the dog over to Benny-the-book of all people?'

'Coz Benny actually owns fifty per cent of Arrow,' Jacko retorts emphatically.

'Benny does? Fifty per cent? Why would a bookdealer be involved with greyhounds?'

I hear Billy spluttering behind me. Then Jacko puts an arm around me in a very condescending manner, like I'm a bit thick and pretends to walk me away from Billy.

'Who ever said Benny was a bookdealer?' he asks incredulously. 'I never said he was a bookdealer, did I? He runs a book, he's a bookmaker; a bookie,' he explains. 'He runs a kind of private betting shop off the Portobello Road.'

'Then why did you go to him when I wanted to get a copy of that Timothy Albrecht book a few months ago? On second thoughts, don't tell me. I don't think I want to know.'

'Suit yerself then.' Jacko looks mildly offended and turns to go. 'Early Mondays don't seem to suit our footballing friend 'ere, do they, Billy?'

'Me neither,' Billy replies sullenly, and they both fall into step and head towards the shops without as much as a goodbye.

Lisa and I bid goodbye to Eddie too. We smile weakly to one another as we resume our walk to the junction of the road. But we don't resume anything that I would call proper conversation. In desperation, each of us takes a flier in trying to raise topics that the other is interested in. But now it just doesn't work. Eventually, we run out of road and reach the corner. Lisa seems to snap out of whatever it was she was thinking about when it comes to parting company. She is effusive in her thanks for the Easter egg and we arrange to meet in the caff at 9.30 this coming Saturday morning, the day of the final match of the season, against Leeds. I stress the importance of this to me, its vital part of the ritual. She laughs loudly at what she calls 'the childishness of this whole ritual thing', but she promises that she will be there. And I know she will.

She gives me a little peck on the cheek, as we part, as if this is something that she always does. A small gesture it may be, but it sends me on my way with a little spring in my step as I head for home.

We have now already qualified for Europe. We don't know which competition yet. In 1967, QPR was denied entry into the Inter-Cities Fairs Cup (subsequently renamed the EUEFA Cup) after winning the English League Cup because we were a Third Division team! The rules stated that the team must come from the highest tier of that country's league system.

My confidence was a bit dented after our 2–3 loss away to Norwich last Saturday. Stan Bowles claims he was punched in the face by Norwich defender Tony Powell but the referee didn't see it. I'm not offering that as an excuse. Norwich overran us and took the lead, but we continued to play with composure and patience and eventually drew level. We thought we had achieved at least a share of the points, but Norwich hit us with two shock goals – the second one looking very offside to me. We attacked and pulled one goal back but it wasn't enough.

So, we've got to beat the Arsenal today. And we should. Okay, so they beat us 0–2 when we played them at Highbury just after Christmas. And they drew with us 0–0 in the corresponding fixture at Loftus Road last season. But we're first in the table; they're sixth from bottom and struggling, despite the fact that they've got some good players: Pat Rice, Brian Kidd, Alan Ball, John Radford and, of course, young Liam Brady who made such a big impact last season. There is some doubt about Terry Mancini playing at centre-back for Arsenal today. Terry used to play for QPR until a couple of seasons ago, and was a great favourite with the crowd. Arsenal don't have a Manager of course, due to the retirement of Bertie Mee, so their coach, Bobby Campbell, is in charge today. Bobby is also ex-QPR, having worked as number two to Gordon Jago when we won promotion from Division Two at the end of the 1972–73 season. Small world.

Still, there'll be no love lost between the two sides when we meet later this morning.

Monday, 19 April 1976: 12.40 p.m.
Queens Park Rangers…2 Arsenal…1

22. DIGGING DEEP

Saturday, 24 April 1976: 9.05 a.m.

They are digging up Eddie's new driveway this morning.

I hear the noise of the kango from the top of Wellesley Gardens. When I arrive on Beane Row I can see that the garden is cordoned off by that yellow tape you sometimes see on police dramas on the telly. There is broken concrete strewn around the garden and a lot of dust in the air. Although there's a bit of sunshine this morning, it's also very windy and the dust is blowing everywhere.

Eddie is standing there with a group of men. They are all in plain clothes and looking serious. But Eddie doesn't seem too perturbed by what's going on. Not like a guy who has something to hide. Always assuming, of course, that he knows what is going on. There's a little crowd of curious onlookers gathering, but I hang back a little. And I decide not to embarrass him by offering my services as translator.

Earlier, Marianne Pleass had been out on the footpath, filming me as I approached. Well, not me specifically, as it turned out. She was filming the passing traffic and I happened to walk into picture as she panned across Wellesley Gardens and onto the pavement. In response to my enquiries, she informed me that she was collecting evidence. There had been an incident involving two cars and a cyclist during the week that resulted in the cars coming off second and third best. I'd heard about it yesterday, and it appears that the cyclist escaped with only some minor blushes.

I might have guessed it immediately, but it took a little longer than expected for Marianne to admit to me as she started packing away the camera, that she was the cyclist involved. The general thrust of her defence being that most of the cars drive too fast when coming round the corner from the Glade onto Wellesley Gardens. From what I had heard, the two vehicle owners took an entirely different view, believing, not unreasonably in my opinion, that they should be able to drive freely up a one-way street within the stated speed limit without having to encounter a cyclist coming at them with what looked like the contents from a car boot sale protruding from the front basket.

'It's an automatic Super 8 cartridge-loading movie camera. I bought it in Shopertunities,' Marianne revealed, with pride, pointing to the packaging in the basket. 'Camera, Projector and Screen: £22.95.'

'Wow,' I said.

'Including VAT.'

'Wow,' I said again.

'Plus a free roll of 8mm movie film.'

'It's a steal at that price, Marianne,' I concluded, having exhausted my 'wows'.

'Marj got one, too.'

'Oh, wow,' I heard myself say again, only this time with a little less enthusiasm.

I looked up. Marjorie was at the open window with some kind of makeshift tripod, the lens of her automatic Super 8 cartridge-loading movie camera trained menacingly on the advancing traffic.

'Fire!' I almost shouted, but thought better of it.

As I took my leave of Marianne I heard a rat-tat-tat sound, and I half expected a fusillade of bullets to pepper the pavement around my feet, but it turned out to be the sound of the kango drill up ahead.

Daisuke had his fingers in his ears to muffle the sound of the hammer-drill, so he didn't hear me greet him as I passed.

I waved to Eddie as soon as I arrived and he waved back to me but it would have been impossible to have a conversation with that drilling racket going on. Which was a shame, because I would love to know what exactly is going on there. Why dig up the driveway? What has he got buried there? Who has he got buried there, may be more to the point?

The Butler brothers join the growing group of spectators and are soon larking about. This seems to unsettle Eddie.

'Maybe they'll find your mate Bernie buried under all that concrete,' Jacko shouts to me over the din, 'but crikey, there's enough of the fackin' stuff to dig out. You could land a soddin' airplane on that, it's so thick.'

'We could be 'ere all day,' Billy says to nobody in particular.

There's not a lot else happening other than a cacophony of coughing, but I decide to hang about a little longer anyway. What Jacko said just now starts to bother me. Is it really possible that there's a body buried under all that concrete? But who? And why did Jacko mention Trouty? Maybe there is something to that rumour about Bernie Trout and Svetlana? Maybe Eddie found out. Maybe he was actually referring to an affair between them when he made that comment about the wrong bed. But would Eddie actually go that far? Okay, he's a strong bloke. A very strong bloke. But he always appeared to me as being a bit of a gentle giant. More confused than short-fused, if you know what I mean. But you never know what somebody is really capable of until they are pushed too far. And why is Svetlana not out there with Eddie, offering him support. The more I think about it, the more I think that Jacko might have a point. It would certainly explain a lot. Trouty disappearing. All those rumours about a relationship between them.

The drilling stops and the cluster of the curious cranes its collective neck. But there's nothing to see. I suddenly decide I don't need this, today of all days. Typical. Just when I had come to terms with not having Trouty around. Just when all the pieces were beginning to fall into place in terms of my match day ritual, Trouty, or the ghost of Trouty — maybe even the f**king body of Trouty — comes back to haunt me; puts a poxy grey cloud over my preparations for today's game.

No. I cannot let that happen. I won't let it happen. We are on the point of winning the First Division title. A result today is vital. My focus should be entirely concentrated on that.

I decide to ignore what Jacko just said. Put it out of my mind entirely. Whatever they find, they find. It shouldn't impact on my preparations for a game. For this game above all others. It won't. I won't allow it to do that.

The drilling starts again. I shove my hands deep into my pockets and walk determinedly away against the wind. I hear Jacko call my name but I continue walking, pretending not to hear him over the sound of the drill. I've had enough idle speculation for one day.

I deliberately seek out Noah and test my Trouty theory on him. Not a man to waste his time on fanciful supposition, Noah is pragmatic to a fault.

'I know nothing about it,' he states dismissively. 'When I hear about it, I will know.' He stares at me as if daring me to challenge him.

I don't.

I don't want to.

I want to believe that his position, his attitude to what I told him, is the one I should adopt myself.

He compliments me on QPR beating Spurs' great rivals Arsenal last Monday. The various results that day move Spurs up to seventh place on 43 points, way ahead of Arsenal in seventeenth position on 36 points going into today's games. We chat about this for a few minutes. I'm happy for Noah. And even happier for myself.

'Yihiyeh Tov,' he waves as I'm leaving. 'Things will be okay.' I bump into Brad at the exit, fixing his hair into position. He greets me warmly, stops, shakes my hand and wishes me well this afternoon. He seems a bit preoccupied himself but it was nice of him to make the gesture. Maybe he's not such a bad bloke deep down, after all. He asks me if I've seen Lisa this morning as she had been in earlier looking for him. I tell him no, but that I'm hoping to meet her for a quick cuppa now. On the spur of the moment, I promise him that I will mention to Lisa when I see her that he asked about her. I thought it only fair, seeing as how he was being so pleasant himself this morning.

I have no intention of actually doing this, of course.

I head for the caff, feeling a lot cheerier about things. Smug, even.

Same day. 4.00 p.m.: Five minutes into the second half

It's Frankie Gray that's going off. I was worried that it might be Stan after that clash of heads, but it's Gray who's leaving the pitch. He's being replaced by Peter Lorimer. Bloody hell. What riches. To have a player of the calibre of Peter Lorimer to spring off the bench. Scottish international and one of the big successes at the last World Cup. Almost 400 league appearances and over 140 goals for Leeds. Lorimer will play in midfield with Trevor Cherry, who is moving to left-back in place of Gray. You wouldn't say that Leeds have been exactly weakened by these enforced changes.

From the restart, there is a moment of light relief for the crowd as Lorimer and Johnny Hollins bump into referee Gow. Almost immediately senses are on alert again, as Don Given runs onto a defence-splitting through ball. But Harvey is equal to the challenge and smothers Don's shot.

Lorimer is now beginning to make his presence felt, linking up with McKenzie and Jordon to stretch our defence and create chances. Suddenly, we are really under the cosh again. Leeds have had continuous possession of the ball for the last few minutes. We just cannot win it back.

It's funny, isn't it? The things that can suddenly strike you when you are under sustained pressure and trying to maintain your concentration. There was a newspaper clipping pinned to the wall of the dressing room when I arrived earlier today. It was a piece that was in the paper last Tuesday; a report on our game against the Arsenal. I read it a couple of times. This is the gist of what it said:

> There was a ferocity about Arsenal's tackling and a determination about their play that confirmed their reluctance to let Rangers supersede them as the last London club to win the league. Brian Kidd, whose darting runs always caused Rangers problems, put Arsenal in front in the 52nd minute.
>
> Frank McLintock equalised two minutes later to send the game into a frantic finish with Arsenal goalkeeper, Rimmer making three superb saves.
>
> A draw – and the virtual end of Rangers title dream – looked odds on against an Arsenal side who refused to yield an inch until Bowles weaved his way into the 18 yard box and then fell in the face of a challenge from Ritchie Powling. Referee David Nippard showed no hesitation in pointing to the spot. Francis kept his cool to clinch it with the penalty three minutes from time.

Of course, the clipping was pinned to the wall for a very good reason. To remind each and every member of the team of the importance of resolve; of digging deep. Even – especially – when you fall behind in a match.

We dug deep against the Arsenal last Monday. We were 0–1 down and after losing 2–3 to Norwich away two days earlier, our whole season lay in the balance. Losing that game – even a draw – would have put paid to our title chances. But we clawed our way back, equalised after two minutes and went on to take both points to keep our title hopes on schedule.

Against Leeds today, we cannot afford to find ourselves in that position. To go even one goal down. Leeds know how to defend a 1–0 lead; to close a game down, stifle the opposition and not let them play.

One simple error and our hopes – our whole season – could collapse.

23. SUN, MOON AND STARS

Saturday, 24 April 1976: 9.30 a.m.

'Why is this game today against Leeds so important?' Lisa is already in the Old Fayre Green caff when I arrive, cradling a green mug of steaming hot coffee in both hands. Cathal and O'Leary are heaving themselves up from a nearby table, each having just finished a full breakfast. They nod to me as they leave but, unusually, do not acknowledge Lisa. And she doesn't look up or after them. I order a tea from Veronica, who wishes me well today. Veronica is not known for her interest in football, hence Lisa's query.

'We are on the point of winning the First Division,' I reply, hopefully without any obvious irritation in my voice. I'm sure I've explained all of this to Lisa before. 'QPR has won nothing of any substance since 1967,' I continue, patiently. 'This team is a better team than that 1967 team. They won the League Cup back then, against a First Division side —West Bromwich Albion — when QPR were in the Third Division. And after being two goals down at half-time too.'

Veronica brings the tea. I thank her and she gives me a big smile and a little pat on the back.

'And that team also won the Third Division championship that very same season,' I reveal to no particular reaction. 'So they were heroes, those guys were — the golden boys of their generation. Still are the golden boys, even today.'

'The golden boys,' Lisa repeats, as if mulling it over. 'Golden, hmm.' She pauses and purses her lips as if pretending to think, then: 'The golden apples of the sun,' she announces, waving her arm with a theatrical flourish.

'What?' I ask, between gulps of hot tea.

'The golden apples of the sun. It's a line from a poem.' She looks up. 'By Yeats. You've heard of Yeats?'

'Yeah, Ron Yeats. Legendary Liverpool centre-half,' I say confidently. 'I didn't know he wrote poetry.' I'm getting my own back now.

'Now you're being obtuse,' she scolds. 'I'll bet you know exactly who I'm talking about. And anyway, why all this fascination with being first. About winning gold? What's so bad about coming second?'

'You know what they say,' I shrug, 'nobody ever remembers who came second. Coming first is the only game in town.'

'You mean the only team game. Olympic athletes strive for gold but, equally, they accept coming second and winning a silver medal as an achievement too. Even bronze, for goodness sake, can be a measure of their success.'

'Of their failure, more like,' I interject.

Veronica brings us two sticky buns. She leans over quite close to me as she places the plate on the table and gives me another gentle pat on the back. Only this time gives my shoulder an extended rub as she does so. 'On the house,' she explains and gives me a wink before sashaying off. I tuck into mine immediately but Lisa pushes hers gently away. She pretends to sulk and neither of us says anything for what seems like an age.

'What colours do Leeds play in?' she asks suddenly.

'White,' I reply, a little more curtly than I intended to.

'White and...?'

'Just white. All white. Like Real Madrid.'

'Oh. How unusual. And when did you last play against them?'

I suspect she is just feigning interest in order to instigate a different conversation but, never one to miss an opportunity, I give her the full works.

'We played them earlier in the season, but it was at their ground in Elland Road. We lost 1–2 in front of over 30,000 people. Over the moon, they were, when the final whistle went.'

'That was close,' she observes, matter-of-factly.

'Yeah, but Leeds are very difficult to beat on their own ground in front of their fanatical supporters. They put enormous pressure on opposing teams.'

'Really?' she asks but without any great enthusiasm.

'Yeah. They work tirelessly for each other and they deny you space. I can remember at one stage in that game, Stan had the ball out near the corner flag and there were approximately six Leeds players surrounding him. They were like, I dunno...'

'...like white moths on the wing?' she interjects, waving her arm theatrically again in an exaggerated arc.

'Exactly, that's a perfect description of it,' I say, ignoring the slight smile playing on her lips. 'Maybe you should take up writing about football. Anyway, it wasn't just Stan who got this treatment. The same thing seemed to happen whenever any Rangers players had the ball. The way Leeds players hustled and harried us – their stamina was incredible.'

'But didn't I read in the paper during the week that Leeds are a team in decline?' she asks.

'Don't you believe it,' I say. 'In transition, maybe, but hardly in decline.' (And since when has Lisa started reading about football?) 'They have some good young players coming through and have made a few new signings, but the established players – the stars – still have a few good years in them.'

'So their stars are not...' she pauses here, as if for emphasis, '...flickering out, just yet?' And then there's that enigmatic smile again.

I have to say, she does have a nice way of phrasing things, for somebody who knows next to nothing about football, but before I can begin to compliment her on this, she stands up to go.

'I need to meet someone,' she announces.

I say nothing. Someone?

'It's important I see them this morning,' she adds, as if noting my disappointment. Them? Not her? Or him?

'Okay. Actually, Brad told me he wanted to see you,' I reveal, sheepishly, 'when I bumped into him earlier this morning.' This news seems to cause her some discomfort, which may have been my intention, but now I'm immediately sorry I told her and I don't quite know why. Is she concerned that I didn't mention it earlier? Or is she uneasy about the possible outcome of the conversation she is about to have with that 'someone'.

'Look, I'm sorry to have to dash away. I'll explain later.' She starts to gather up her things distractedly. 'Maybe we can meet up on the green as soon as I've finished, then we can walk up together,' she suggests, perking up a little.

'How long will you be?' I ask, perking up a lot. 'I want to pop into The Cabin to get the paper first.'

'Oh, not long,' she sighs, dolefully.

Then she hurries out, pausing only to pay Gregory on her way.

I call Veronica over, ostensibly to order another tea, but really so that Lisa can see her chatting to me as she walks by the window. But Lisa is far too preoccupied to even glance in as she rushes by.

The games people play.

The old Colonel is ahead of me in the queue this morning. Just my luck. I can see the pink pages of the Financial Times sticking out from under his arm, but he seems to be dithering over whether to pick up the copy of Private Eye magazine that he is peering intently at on the rack. It's got a picture of Prime Minister James Callaghan on the cover and a speech bubble that says: 'Goodbye, Roy'. The PM appears to be giving the fingers à la Harvey Smith's famous V-sign. Colonel Martin picks it up — probably to check the price — just as Mick finishes serving the customer in front of him.

'It's a great read,' beams Mick, nodding at the magazine in the Colonel's trembling hand. 'So long as you're not in it!'

'Roy Jenkins. That's Roy Jenkins he's giving the fingers to!' the Colonel blusters, looking decidedly unimpressed. 'One of his own!'

'Well, not any more, Colonel. He's just wesigned,' Mick makes a big to-do about mispronouncing the R the way Jenkins does.

The Colonel lets out an involuntary laugh. Wheezy and phlegmy, it's a bit like Mick's laugh — except done in an echo chamber and accompanied by some spray. The latter causes a little collateral damage to Mick's shopcoat.

'I don't know, these Labour chappies have no idea how to conduct themselves,' he bellows and throws a few coins on the counter. He then appears to lecture Mick for a couple of minutes. Mick can hardly get a word in edgeways but I cannot make out a word that the Colonel is saying.

'It's a joke, Colonel,' Mick tries to explain. 'Satire…'

But the Colonel turns away brusquely and leaves. And the magazine is back on the rack.

'What was all that about, Mick?'

'You don't want to know, Dawhee me bucko. In truth, I probably brought it on myself.' Mick smiles while dabbing his shopcoat with a handkerchief. 'You know, Oscar Wilde had a point when he said that if one could teach the English to talk and the Irish to listen, society would be quite civilised.'

'Interesting thought.'

'Well, maybe it was the other way around. Anyway, enough of that, me bucko. This afternoon, Rangers will be asking the questions. But will Leeds have the answers?'

I'm not quite certain what Mick means specifically by this. I tell him I feel confident (most of the time) that we will win. But I also worry that if we go all out – as we have to – and commit too many players forward, then Leeds will hit us on the break.

'Hit you on the break, is it?' Mick is aghast at the suggestion. 'To hit you on the break, me bucko, requires speed, acceleration…and the great Leeds United don't have that any more. Hit you on the break? Most of this Leeds team couldn't hit sand if they fell off a camel.'

The blokes immediately behind me in the queue guffaw loudly and Mick joins in. I laugh lightly along with them but deep down, I don't think it's a fair analysis. This Leeds team is entitled to respect and if we underestimate them, well…

'Don't be looking so serious, me bucko.' Mick leans across the counter and places a hand on my shoulder (what is it with pats on the shoulder this morning?) 'Sure I'm only plaw-mawsing you.' (At least, that's what I think he said.)

'Well, okay, but most football pundits…'

'Football pundits, is it?' Mick stands back, hands on hips, almost spitting out the word 'pundits'. 'Now, don't get me started, me bucko. Sure what do they know?' The queue mutters its assent.

'Well, they're like critics, they…'

'Critics, is it? Critics? Listen, me bucko,' Mick knows he has a captive audience now and is obviously playing to it, 'as my countryman Brendan Behan once said: "Critics are like eunuchs in a harem. They know how it's done; they've seen it done but they can't do it themselves." That's critics for ye. That's most football pundits.'

Mick sticks out his chest, or rather he pushes out his stomach and stands there, hands on hips, swaying slightly from side to side, soaking up the laughter from around the shop. I just stand there until it dies down, trying to remain polite. I know Mick is acting this way to give me a boost on the day, but it's over the top and it makes me feel uncomfortable. There's something unprofessional about me being part of it.

'I'd better be off,' I say, looking at my watch. I go to hand Mick the money for the Mirror, but instead of taking it he starts to handclap slowly, staring straight at me, then faster, then faster still until his single ripple of applause is taken up by everybody else in the shop. I'm tempted to run out of the place but I manage to turn and walk slowly out, head bowed, pretending to scan a folded newspaper. I hear Mick above the din shouting after me but I cannot make out what he is saying.

I stand outside on the pavement for a moment feeling a mixture of elation and irritation. Then I hurry across to the Green to meet Lisa as planned.

Same day: Ten minutes gone in the second half

Leeds force a corner on the left. True to form, Lorimer strikes it hard. The ball flies past the near post and everybody misses it. Billy Bremner is in like a flash and almost gets a flick on it. I cannot see what happens next but Bremner immediately appeals for a penalty. And from the look of conviction on his face, I don't think he is doing so lightly. The ball certainly struck something hand-high as it flashed across the goal. Bremner chases after referee Gow but the ref, who has been firm but fair all afternoon, is having none of it and waves away his appeal. Typical Bremner, he will fight for everything. This is one opponent who will keep this tie going until the final whistle.

24. LOVE, BITES AND SCORING

Saturday, 24 April 1976: 9.55 a.m.

She's not there when I return to the Green. I immediately become irritated. The most important game of the season and I'm running behind schedule. I sit on the usual bench and wait. I can hear the mood music from Threads wafting over. It's 10cc:

> *I like to see you, but then again*
> *That doesn't mean you mean that much to me.*
> *So if I call you, don't make a fuss*
> *Don't tell your friends about the two of us.*
> *I'm not in love. No, no...*
> *Oh, you'll wait a long time for me.*
> *Oh, you'll wait a long time.*

Where can she be? Who could she have met that would detain her for so long? Cathal? O'Leary? On the other hand, I've already met Lisa this morning so, technically speaking, the ritual is still intact. It's finished, in fact. I've met everybody so far this morning. Except Trouty — but he doesn't count any longer.

I manage to open the Mirror *without the wind whipping the pages into a flap.*

HAVE-A-GO RANGERS

reads the story on the back page, above Harry Miller's byline. He says that anything less than a Rangers victory will hand the Championship to Bob Paisley's Merseyside men and take the title heat out of Liverpool's last game against Wolves on 4 May.

He then goes on to reveal that Leeds United will be without some key players today — Clarke and Yorath, for certain; while Eddie Gray is doubtful — and he quotes the Gaffer, Dave Sexton, as saying, 'We know what we have to do and that is to put the pressure on Liverpool. Whatever happens I'm proud of what we have achieved at Rangers this season. We've bound together a set of talented players who have got to the top as a team. It's a side that is going to get better and better.' Then Miller finishes by publishing the top-of-the-table placings:

	Played	Won	Drew	Lost	Goals	For	Against	Points
Liverpool	41	22	14	5	63	30		58
QPR	41	23	11	7	65	33		57

So, no pressure then.

I decide to give her five more minutes. After that, I'm out of here. It's the last game of the season so, who knows, I probably won't be making this trip on Saturday mornings any more. No need to. Maybe this whole ritual thing was of no importance after all. Maybe we'd have done it anyway without Marianne and Eddie and the Butlers and Noah and Mick. And, yes, Lisa, too. Come to think of it, I will really welcome the break from all that pressure on Saturday mornings. Not having to worry about whether I will catch up with each of them on my trip to The Cabin. Next season will be different. Hopefully we'll be the reigning Division One champions so we won't need to have superstition on our side. Who needs them?

> *I'm not in love so don't forget it*
> *It's just a silly phase I'm going through*
> *And just because I call you up*
> *Don't get me wrong; don't think you've got it made*
> *I'm not in love. No, no...*
> *Oh, you'll wait a long time for me.*
> *Oh, you'll wait a long time.*

Who could she be meeting, and what does she want to talk to them about that is taking so long?

> *I keep your picture, upon the wall*
> *It hides a nasty stain that's lying there*
> *So don't you ask me to give it back*
> *I know you know it doesn't mean that much to me*
> *I'm not in love. No, no...*
> *Oh, you'll wait a long time for me.*
> *Oh, you'll wait a long time.*

Finally, Lisa hoves into view, stepping out of the shadow of the arcade and into the strong wind and weak sunlight. A few drops of light rain begin to fall as she crosses the street. Brad comes to the front of the arcade and looks after her a little forlornly. I wonder what she wanted to speak to him about. Now she stops to speak to Cathal and O'Leary, who have just driven round the corner in an old banger and stopped at the lights. This is the last straw. I make a big play of sighing loudly in exasperation, patting the Mirror back into some kind of windblown shape as I stand up to go, banging my wrist against the back of the park bench in the process. Luckily my watch takes the impact and there's no damage to my wrist. Glancing over, Lisa suddenly cuts short her conversation with Cathal and O'Leary apologetically and glides across. O'Leary winds down the driver's window and watches her as she crosses.
'Are you leaving already?' she enquires, sensing my frustration as soon as she arrives.
'Well, it is starting to rain,' I say irritably, extending one hand as if to catch the droplets.
'It was, but it's stopped now. Why don't you sit down and tell me what's on your mind.'

I sit down reluctantly and she joins me on the bench. I tell her there is nothing on my mind; nothing, that is, except the game today. But she suspects that I'm being tetchy because she kept me waiting and she reckons that I'm being unreasonable. I don't want to get into a conversation about that, so I go off at a tangent. I ask her if she had seen Eddie's driveway being dug up this morning.

'Yes, I did. It was very noisy – and dusty.' She makes a great play of wiping non-existent dust off her clothes.

'I'm worried about Eddie,' I say. 'I'm worried about what they will find under all that concrete.'

'And what do you believe they will find that is worrying you?' she asks, not entirely sympathetically.

'Trouty?' I sigh, resignedly.

If it wasn't for the fact that it's at my expense, her spontaneous outburst of schoolgirly laughter, which can probably be heard as far away as the high street, would be infectious. But I keep myself in check and give her a stern look of disapproval.

'You may laugh,' I warn, 'but I'm betting that they will find Trouty buried there. I'm afraid that Eddie has done him in. I've suspected this all along and you didn't believe me. Nobody did. But there must be something to it if the police are on the case and all over his garden.'

Lisa fixes me with that condescending stare that I've seen before.

'And you saw the police there, did you? In uniform?' she asks, not unlike, well not unlike somebody cross-examining a witness.

'Not in uniform. Plain clothes cops,' I reply emphatically.

'And you saw the police cars?'

'No. They were unmarked cars.'

She laughs very loudly again. I just stare at her impassively.

'They were not policemen, you silly oaf. Those men are from the council. Eddie does not have planning permission to carry out the work he was doing and the whole thing has to be scrapped. Dug up. Eddie has known this for weeks and is resigned to it. And you would have known it too, if only you talked to Eddie about things other than f…' (for one moment I really did reckon she was going to use the f-word) '…other than football!'

I scratch my right eyebrow.

'It still doesn't mean that Trouty is not buried under there. Just because it's not the police on the case, it doesn't mean that…'

'Mr Trout is in Spain,' she says quietly.

'You don't know that,' I say petulantly.

'No, I don't know that – but I do believe it,' she says with great finality.

We sit there silently for a few minutes. Then I start to laugh skittishly at the stupidity of the whole scenario. At my stupidity. Of course Lisa is right. There is no reason to believe that Bernie Trout is not in Spain. It's something he's done before by all accounts – gone off for a couple of months without making a big fuss about it. Leaving a few of his confidantes in charge of his business interests. This is all the fault of that fool Eddie and his poor understanding of English.

But then again, who was that attorney geezer who stopped me outside Aunt Sally's place all those weeks ago and asked me about Trouty? What was my interest in him? That's what he asked me. What was my interest in Trouty? I could hardly tell him that I needed Trouty for my ritual; that he was essential to it. Well, he was, back then. Or at least I thought he was. Turns out he wasn't so essential to it at all. Weird, that attorney geezer; all flashing eyelids and wincing any time I appeared to be on familiar terms with his 'Mr Bernard Trout'. What explanation does Lisa have for that bloke, I'd like to know. But I don't ask. I decide to say nothing and just play along. Old Trouty may not have been done-in by Echo Eddie, but I'm convinced now more than ever that someone did him in. Otherwise somebody would have heard from him.

Then Lisa laughs. Probably at my stupidity, too. There's a break in the clouds and the sun peeps through again.

'Haaaaaa,' Lisa exhales, like she was soaking up the sun. 'You know, I used to go for regular walks here on the Green with Angus.' Her tone is suddenly upbeat, as if recalling pleasant days.

'Angus?'

'Yes. We used to go for a walk here practically every Monday morning.'

'Why Monday?'

'It's my day off. Don't you remember me telling you that?'

'Oh, yeah,' I lie. 'Did he live nearby? This Angus?'

'Near enough.' She laughs. 'He lives with me, actually.'

I swallow hard. Oh shit. Do I really need to hear all of this? This morning of all days.

'Used to?' I light on her use of the past tense. 'But not any more? Walking here on the Green, I mean?'

'No, it didn't work out,' she says ruefully.

'I'm sorry to hear that.' Actually, I'm delighted to hear that it didn't work out, but I can't admit it just yet. I feign concern: 'What happened?'

'Oh, he had a propensity to wander,' she explains.

'What, right here? On a public green?' I laugh.

'Mmmmm. I'm afraid so. Yes.'

'The bastard!'

'Well, I wouldn't call him that. It's in their nature after all.'

'Not all guys are like that.' I try to appear reassuring.

She gives me a strange look.

'I would certainly hope not, but Angus was.' She smiles.

'What exactly did he do?'

'Well, as I said, he wandered.'

'Yes, but how exactly'? I ask, annoyed that I'm unable to frame the specific question I really want to ask.

She stops, turns and stares straight at me with those big brown eyes and whispers very, very softly. 'He tried to bite people's legs.'

'Angus?'

'Yes. He tried to bite people's legs.'

'The d-d-d-dog?'

'Yes. You didn't think...'

'No. 'Course not!'

She smiles gently. She knows. I know she knows. At this stage she has me well copped. Did she do it deliberately, I wonder. Feeding me just enough information to let me draw my own stupid conclusion. That's what illusionists do, I'm told. Pretend to tell you everything but leave out one key piece of the jigsaw. Enough to let you make a fool of yourself. Well, if she did, I certainly fell for it.

I say nothing while I try to recover my composure.

'Whaat k-k-kind of dog is he?'

'Scottish terrier. Very loving, very loyal but a bit stubborn. Some people believe that Scottish terriers are a rather aloof breed.'

'Really?' I can't resist the next bit. 'I've heard it said that some dogs take on the personality traits of their owners. Is that true, d'you reckon?'

She gives me that look gain. But I don't mind. I've sufficiently recovered my composure to ask: 'Anyway, why did you to call him Angus?'

'Well, he's a Scottish terrier? What else would you suggest?'

'I reckon if I had a dog like that I'd call him Norman.'

'Norman? Why Norman?'

Same day: Fifteen minutes into the second half, thirty minutes left on the clock

I double-check the time with one of the coaching staff: an hour gone. Thirty minutes remain. We're not making much progress in breaking down the Leeds defence. Norman Hunter, the Leeds United number 6, has just slide-tackled Don Masson. It's a fair tackle but Don hits the deck. Hunter's momentum carries him through and I just manage to get out of the way as Hunter and Don slide along the greasy surface and come to a halt on the touchline. Remarkably, given Norman's reputation, there is no damage done.

Hunter joined Leeds United as a 15-year-old, having been spotted playing for a local amateur side. In the beginning he was an inside-forward, before Leeds turned him into a central defender. He formed a highly effective and intimidating partnership at the back with Jack Charlton. His nickname, 'Bites yer legs', was earned from his ferocious strength and commitment in the tackle. Once, when informed that Hunter had broken a leg, Les Cocker, the Leeds trainer, is reputed to have asked: 'Whose is it?'

He made his debut for the England team in 1965. When told that Hunter had been in the England squad which won the 1966 World Cup but never kicked a ball, Stan Bowles is reputed to have quipped: 'I've played against Hunter a few times and he never kicked a ball either – and my shins were black and blue to prove it.'

Having committed himself to the sliding tackle on Don Masson, Hunter is now out of position. Sensing an opportunity, I react swiftly and retrieve the ball once Don is on his feet again. Stan calls for it and moves down the touchline before finding Frank McLintock with a lovely pass.

And then?

Well, this is how Brian Moore, commentating on ITV's *The Big Match* described what happened next.

'McLintock puts it over...a header by Givens...and it's IN! Dave Thomas has scored. As the cross floated over, a flick of the head by Don Givens and Dave Thomas was coming in on the far post to put Queens Park Rangers 1–0 in front. And send Loftus Road wild with blue and white delight.'

The players all pile in to acknowledge the goal. I raise my arm to the crowd in the Ellerslie Road stand. They're going berserk with joy, relief and renewed confidence:

So now you're gonna believe us,
So now you're gonna believe us,
So now you're gonna belee-eve us,
We're going to win the League.

Not to be outdone, the boys in the Loftus Road terrace behind the goal are now in full voice too:

So we're saying goodbye to them all
United, West Ham, Liv-er-pool
We are the Rangers and we are the best.
We are the Loft Boys so f**k all the rest.

Then, in unison, all over the ground, the staccato, rata-tat-tat:

We are Q – P – R; We are Q – P – R!
We are Q – P – R; We are Q – P – R!

We wouldn't expect Leeds to take this lying down. And they don't. Their response is immediate and controlled; Bremner wins the ball just inside his own half, finds McKenzie, and he in turn threads the perfect through ball that splits the defence for Jordon to run onto. Jordon steadies himself, then lets fly...

25. MISSED OPPORTUNITY?

Saturday, 24 April 1976: 10.15 a.m.

I'm still feeling a bit foolish over the Angus incident as we leave the Green. In the shadow of the arcade entrance across the street, I can just about make out the figure of Brad. He's still standing there, not moving, probably watching us as we begin to stroll up Park Road. I think Lisa has seen him too. She looks a little morose and every so often she looks over her shoulder, as if half expecting Brad to approach us. I catch her eye every so often but she says nothing. Then suddenly, just as we've passed the Butlers':

'There's something I want to talk to you about.'

'Okay, shoot,' I say, stopping dead and trying to appear nonchalant about it, 'go ahead.' *But my mouth has gone dry. I fear something's coming that I won't like.*

She turns to face me and I just know from her expression that this is not something trivial. She doesn't make eye contact, which is unusual for her when speaking, but stares into the middle distance over my right shoulder.

'Oh, Lord,' *she sighs,* 'not now. Please not now.'

'Wotcha Lis, wotcha cock.' *I glance behind me to see the Butler brothers coming out onto the garden path.*

'Please turn right,' *I hear Lisa mutter through clenched teeth,* 'please turn...damn it, too late.'

The demon duo are kitted out in blue and white hooped shirts that look like they've not seen the inside of a washing machine since 1967.

As usual, they are full of the joys of life, but Jacko appears to sense immediately that they have intruded into a private conversation. But then it would be almost impossible not to pick up on Lisa's sense of frustration. She is positively bristling with irritation. Such sensitivity, however, is not a social skill that Billy has ever taken the time to hone.

'We woz thinkin of poppin' in to the 'Orseman's for a few quick bevvies before headin' on to the Bush. Why dontcha join us?'

'I thought you blokes were banned from The Horseman's?' *I ask, and I can feel Lisa almost hiss in exasperation that the conversation is continuing.*

'Ah, that woz only ol' Trouty...'

'And 'e ain't around these days, is 'e?' *interjects Jacko, knowingly.*

'So how 'bout it?' *Billy asks Lisa directly, but she has already turned away disinterestedly, something she would never do normally. Thankfully, Jacko comes to the rescue.*

'Don't be stupid, bruv. You can't ask 'im to go to the boozer. How would it look if 'e turned up in the dressing room today wiv the smell of Watney's Red Barrel off 'is breaff?' *Jacko extends his hand to me by way of ending the conversation:* 'Best of luck today, mate. Do your bit. C'mon Billy.' *The younger Butler mumbles some kind of garbled good wish and they drift back down the hill towards the town. Surprisingly, Lisa says nothing.*

'You blokes are going to the game, then?' I call after them, just so we all depart on amicable terms.

Jacko triumphantly brandishes a couple of match tickets.

'See? Ol' Benny-the-book came through just like 'e always does. Right Billy?'

'Right on, Jacko.' And the brothers slither off about their business.

There follows the most awkward silence I have possibly ever experienced in my entire life. We both just stand there saying nothing. Lisa purses her lips and gently punches her open palm with her right fist. I feel like taking her to task about her rudeness in ignoring the Butlers. She certainly wouldn't hesitate to do it to me, if positions were reversed. But I know there is probably a genuine reason for it. And unfortunately, I may be just about to hear it.

'They'll never get in,' I say emphatically, trying to postpone the inevitable. 'Sid Scabbard will never serve them. He knows what Trouty thinks of them.'

'What?' Lisa looks at me as if I have just uttered the most stupidly inane thing she's ever heard. Then she sighs again and walks on. I follow a few steps behind. It seems the right thing to do. She stops and turns again as we reach Echo Eddie's.

'Look, we need to talk. It's important.'

'Okay. Talk.' I'm getting a bit irritated myself. I don't need all this tension – today of all days. Lisa looks around her and notices that Eddie is in the garden tidying up the debris from the drive. Svetlana is in the garden with him. It's unusual for her to be at home at this hour and she is rarely in the garden – usually clack-clacking her heels on the paving and driving off in her red Triumph Herald, with a wave to the world.

She is gazing wistfully at us as we approach, with a warm smile playing over her face and in her eyes. Obviously everything is okay between them.

'Hello,' we say in unison but keep on walking. My reprieve is likely to be a short one. Lisa obviously does not want any further distractions this morning.

'Halo, halo, heh, heh,' says Eddie as usual. Svetlana keeps on smiling and gazing at us as we walk by. Then she walks slowly to Eddie and whispers something in his ear. I cannot see Eddie's reaction as we have now passed them by, but I hear him give a kind of loud chuckly-growl.

'Yes, love birds, heh, heh. Love birds.'

I don't dare glance at Lisa and I know she isn't looking at me. What should I say? If I miss this opportunity I will never get one like it again. But my heart is pounding. Not just in my chest but also in my head. It's like when you have a cold and your ears are blocked. You hear nothing else except your heart. Pounding. And a pounding at the back of your skull. I'm slightly dizzy and disoriented from it all when I suddenly notice that Lisa is not beside me any more. She is standing a few steps behind me with a look of surprise and a slight smile on her face. Her arms are extended and she is asking me something. When my head clears a little I hear her enquire, laughingly: 'Can't you hear it? Can't you hear it?'

And then I do. Clear as a clarion call. A sharp squawking sound coming from the open window of Eddie and Svetlana's kitchen.

'Love birds, love birds, love birds, love birds.'

A sudden downpour saves our blushes and we run for cover under the trees at Aunt Sally's. Crossing the road without even checking for traffic, Lisa grabs hold of my hand and we weave our way over and arrive breathless on the other side. Lisa is either red-faced from running or from sheer embarrassment. She is wet through; her hair is soaked and little rivulets of water are running down her face. She is trembling. There's a strong breeze beginning to build momentum. Lisa takes my hand again and leads me to a secluded spot just inside the open gate. We huddle together under the canopy and wait for the rain to stop.

Now, you're here, so close to me.
I can't resist you.
And I knew when I kissed you
I'm gonna say now.
Here I go again
Watch me now 'cause
Here I go again
Falling in love, in love.
Falling in love, in love.
Falling in love, in love.
Falling in love.

The sun peeps out again. The breeze is still blowing but it feels gentler now, warmer even. And it dries us quickly.

'Look, I have to go now. I'm late. But I'll talk to you after the game. Give me your phone number. I'll call you.' She writes my number in the little leatherbound notebook that I've seen her use before.

'You may not be able to reach me at home after the game,' I say, with one eye on possible after-match celebrations.

'Tomorrow, then,' she says, hurriedly. 'I'll call you tomorrow.' She turns to go but immediately hesitates and rummages in her large satchel of a bag.

'Here. I want you to have this.' She plucks out a little plastic bag and hands it to me.

'What is it?'

'Just a little...gift.'

Her eyes start to well up, but then she turns abruptly and walks away without looking back. This is definitely the most momentous day of my life. In more ways than one.

I stand there for a few minutes watching her as she disappears up Forest Hill Road. I want to open the package now, but I also want the moment to be just right. I consider walking back down to the café but I'm worried about the time. I look at my watch, but it's stopped. Must have been that bang it took against the back of the seat on the Green earlier. I finally decide to open the package at home. I hurry across to the other side of the road, just as Daisuke emerges from the gates of Aunt Sally's...

Same day: Thirty minutes gone in second half, fifteen minutes remaining

...Phil Parkes plucks the shot from Jordon out of the air and punts it long and hard, deep into the Leeds half. Hunter wins it back and Leeds are pressing. Again. Eddie Gray crosses. Frank McLintock manages a firm-headed clearance that goes straight to Gerry Francis. Gerry lays it off to Don Masson and looks for the one-two. Masson pushes it past Reaney's outstretched leg back to Francis. Gerry turns Norman Hunter. Once. Twice. Then he almost fumbles it but regains control before Billy Bremner can reach him, carries it on, straightens and lets fly with his left foot. But the shot goes just a foot or two wide of the post.

Gerry should have scored. He knows he should have scored. We need the cushion of a second goal. I lose it a bit with Gerry and scream at him in frustration. I tell him that he needs to concentrate, to hit the target, at the very least. Gerry ignores me at first but when the ball goes out of play for a throw-in, Gerry takes the opportunity to have a go back and tells me that I need to be quicker.

He probably has a point. Now is not the time to single out individuals for criticism. It's a team game. Everybody has to play his part. There is so much at stake. Not just a first ever Division One league title. There are other records to be achieved too.

Today we are also attempting to extend our unbeaten league run at home to twenty-three matches. If we finish the season unbeaten at home, it will be the first time that QPR have gone through a complete season without losing a home game.

So it's an opportunity not to be missed.

Will the 1–0 lead be enough? Should we drop back and defend this slender lead, let Leeds come at us, then hit them on the break? Easier said than done. Many teams have found that if you allow Leeds to dominate you, it is almost impossible to seize back the initiative. No, the best tactical option is to continue to take the game to them. To force them to play the game in their own half.

If we can...

26. ALL WRAPPED UP

Saturday, 24 April 1976: 11.35 a.m.

On an impulse, I ask Daisuke if I can have a quick a look around Sally's garden. To my surprise, he says yes without giving it a second thought, and he doesn't even go back inside with me.

'Watch out for the bees,' he warns, 'and do not forget to shut the gate when you leave,' he adds, wagging a stubby forefinger at me.

The area by the gates is fairly dark and chilly because of the number of trees, and there's a bit of a breeze blowing too, but once I step beyond the trees, it's like emerging into brilliant sunshine after spending all afternoon at a matinee. Now, I know next to nothing about plants. And the only bush I'm really familiar with is Shepherd's Bush. But the garden is every bit as wild and as colourful as Lisa described it. I stand there for a few minutes, blinking in the morning sunshine while trying to take it all in.

Further along the path, there's this kind of apple-blossomy tree with a wooden seat underneath that I'm immediately drawn to. I plonk myself down on the seat and take in the full panorama.

I take the package out of the plastic bag and place both on the seat beside me. I stare at the package for a long time. It's soft-wrapped with a heavy dark green paper (not tightly wrapped the way I would do it). And it's sealed with a single tab of sticky tape with a tartan design on it (not hermetically insulated at each and every joining with lengths of sellotape the way I normally wrap a present). I'm swallowing hard, my stomach has butterflies and I'm also breathing heavily. I wonder what it is. Actually, I know what it is. It's a book. It has to be a book. It's thick, too; lots of pages. But which book? I know it's not going to be some piece of popular fiction. But what?

I manage to tear the wrapping paper as I remove it with shaking hands, not realising that the tab is resealable and I could have preserved the paper intact. Inside, there's tissue wrapping. It's pressed into place but without any tape. Yet all the folds remain intact. It has obviously been wrapped and kept in this tissue paper for some time. I unfold it carefully so as not to tear the tissue paper. The book reveals itself to be The Collected Poems of W. B. Yeats. Now usually, receiving this as a gift would leave me decidedly underwhelmed. But this is different. The next thing I notice is that the book is not new. It's not tatty or dog-eared; quite the contrary. But I can see immediately from the slightly worn corners of the hardback covers that the book has seen some use. This doesn't disappoint me. Quite the opposite, in fact. What she has given me is obviously something of her own. Something she herself must have treasured. And now it's mine.

I turn the pages haphazardly, reading an odd line or two. Maybe it's the garden setting; Aunt Sally's wild Robinsonian style, as Lisa called it, with all the exotic imported trees and flowering shrubs and the aroma changing slightly with every twist and turn in the direction of the light breeze; but I suddenly start to take an interest in some of the writing. A line here, a word there; some of it conjures up momentary memories or feelings long suppressed. In my mind's eye I see a quiet drawing room, sun filtering in through large windows, a tinkling piano somewhere else in the house. This is an unusual image for me. It's not the kind of thing

I usually imagine. I start to wonder if I'm changing, maybe already have changed. I know that something in our relationship has changed. For the better, too. We have crossed a line and there's no going back. It will have implications for me, of course. For Lisa too, I should imagine. I hold the book close to my nose in the hope I might breathe in some of her scent. But all I sniff is the musty odour of old book. There's a worn-thin bookmark protruding from the middle pages. I wonder if this is what Lisa was reading last time she opened the book...

Dance there upon the shore;
What need have you to care
For wind or water's roar?
And tumble out your hair
That the salt drops have wet;
Being young you have not known
The fool's triumph, nor yet
Lost love as soon as won

I read it over and over again and speculate on what it might mean. Just like we used to do in Mr Wattle's English class.

Same day: Second half, 4.35 p.m., still 1–0 to QPR

Bremner takes a throw-in about fifteen yards from the corner flag. It's a big one, and reaches Lorimer standing to the right of the QPR goal but with his back to it. Lorimer executes a perfect overhead kick that's dropping straight into the path of Trevor Cherry. Cherry lines up the volley. But somehow Gerry Francis throws himself into the tackle and blocks the shot. The ball runs clear. Givens, foraging back in his own half, picks it up and lays it off swiftly to Frank McLintock. Gerry Francis arrives in support. Stan is out on the right wing, where the Gaffer moved him for the second half, in acres of space. It's four-on-three and the break is on. Frank finds Stan with a long, floated pass. Stan, lurking in the lengthening shadow of the Ellerslie stand, takes it in his stride without challenge. He cuts inside a defender. Gerry Francis times his run perfectly into the box. The move has goal written all over it. Inexplicably, Stan elects to go for goal. The ball is on his favourite left foot. But Stan's shot is weak. It bobbles a bit. But then Harvey fumbles the ball as it bounces it front of his diving body and it rolls agonisingly (for Leeds) across the line and into the net.

2–0.

Only seven minutes to go. Seven minutes to defend a two-goal lead. If we cannot do that, we don't deserve to be title contenders.

But here come Leeds again...

27. INJURY TIME

Saturday, 24 April 1976: About 4.40 p.m.

The latest onslaught from Leeds breaks down. Don Masson is moving down the right flank. He hits a long diagonal pass. Don Givens gets a flick on with his head over the nearest defender but Reaney clears, long and high. David Webb waits for the bounce to come up nicely for him but Jordan nips in and heads it forward. McKenzie chases it. As he tries to tackle McKenzie, Frank McLintock stumbles into the path of the recovering David Webb. And McKenzie is away with a clear path to goal. Ian Gillard races across to head him off, but McKenzie has a few yards head start on him and races on to the edge of the penalty area. He hits it low and hard with his left foot towards the right of Phil Parkes' goal, but Phil dives low and stretches far enough to push the ball out for a corner.

Brilliant save. Two goals ahead, about five minutes to go. All we need to do now is to hold our nerve and we'll win it.

Some of the crowd are beginning to climb over the low perimeter wall, and as more and more excited supporters join them they are starting to encroach onto the pitch, particularly behind the Loftus Road end.

Leeds are attacking again but Phil Parkes is playing a blinder, plucking the ball out of the air from another dangerous cross by Lorimer. All we need to do now is to hold our nerve.

I immediately see the possibility of a quick break, and scream at Phil to give the ball to Ian Gillard, who is unmarked. Instead, Phil decides to punt it up-field as far as possible, presumably in an effort to play out the remainder of the game in the Leeds half. But Paul Madeley, the stylish Leeds centre-back, is first to the ball so we've given possession away. I give Phil a bit of a bollocking. Phil isn't having any of it. 'You just concentrate on *your* job,' he says, giving me a withering look. He adds a few choice expletives and leaves me red-faced and determined to show him.

Hunter wins the ball back from Francis in the Leeds half and sends a long, looping ball towards the touchline near the halfway line. David Webb and Eddie Gray, the Leeds number 11, go for it together, oblivious to the fact that the ref has already blown his whistle for a late tackle on Hunter. To be fair, I don't reckon anybody in that part of the ground – player or pilgrim – heard the whistle. I definitely didn't.

There's a bit of 'previous' between Webb and Gray. In the 1970 FA Cup Final between Chelsea and Leeds, when Webby was playing for Chelsea at right-back, Eddie Gray tormented him with his skill on the ball. He went past Webby almost at will and poor Dave had a nightmare. The match ended in a 2–2 draw.

But in the replay at Old Trafford – one of the most physical matches English football has ever witnessed – Webby had his revenge.

With the score standing 1–1 in extra time, Chelsea's Ian Hutchinson took one of his trademark long throw-ins which bypassed every player in the Leeds penalty area, then came off Jack Charlton's head and on towards the far post, before Webby gratefully put it into the unguarded net to give Chelsea the lead and ultimately to secure their first ever FA Cup.

Anyway, with the attention of the crowd and the TV cameras distracted by the foul on Hunter, both Webby and Gray go for it together, roughly ten yards from where I'm standing.

Although I am nowhere near the ball when the tackle is made, I become part of the collateral damage.

The impact of being hit by both of these highly committed players as they slid along the ground at speed in an attempt to reach the ball first is something I will never forget. I went down like a sack of potatoes and their combined momentum carried me off the grass, onto the hard concrete track and smack into (of all things) the *Daily Mirror* advertising hoarding on the perimeter wall, beside the entrance to the dressing rooms.

I don't remember much for a few minutes afterwards, but I gradually come round, thanks to the effective intervention of the medical staff.

'Are you okay, son?' asks one of the medics. (Son? Christ, he wasn't much older than me!) Then he does that thing where they move one of their fingers from side to side and check that you can focus on it. If you see two fingers, I suppose you're in serious shit. Anyway, I don't really recall much of that, as they loaded me onto a stretcher.

'We think your leg may be broken, son,' says a second voice.

I'm more worried about the bang on the head I received as I hit the ground. I'm feeling decidedly dizzy but I can see past the medics now as the stretcher is raised. Some of the crowd are staring at me, others are watching the game. I learn afterwards that play was resumed fairly quickly, as I had ended up off the field of play.

Then, suddenly – oh my God – I hear Lisa's voice.

'Dave, Dave. Are you o-<u>kay</u>*?'*

And there she is, leaning over the perimeter wall. *'Dave. Look at me. Are you all right?'*

I try to raise an arm to signal to her that I hear her. Hear her call my name. Hear her express *concern.* Then, almost screaming...

'David! David! Day-vid!' (She's never called me David before.)

As they begin to move me towards the dressing rooms, I can still see her face staring after me, with anguish etched all over it. Then she swims back into the crowd and is gone from sight.

At that moment, the ref blows the whistle for full-time. And the crowd goes ballistic...

4.43 p.m.
Queens Park Rangers...2 Leeds United...0

The fans stream onto the pitch, cheering and leaping around the place as if we had just won the league title. It's crazy, I know. After all, Liverpool have yet to play their final game and could easily pip us for the title. But the crowd is just living for the moment. This moment. We have played our last game and we're top of the table. And they won't be denied their moment of ecstasy. I try to sit up on the stretcher and raise a clenched fist, but the medics manage to restrain me and the best I can do is shout my support as the chanting fans rush past me towards the players still standing.

> So now you're gonna believe us,
> So now you're gonna believe us,
> So now you're gonna belee-eve us,
> We're going to win the League.
> And then:

> We are Q – P – R,
> We are Q – P – R!

Later that day
So, that's it.
We're unbeaten at home in the league for the whole season. We have qualified for Europe – either the European Cup or the UEFA Cup.
But have we done enough to win the First Division? Well, we could do no more.
I certainly could not do any more – although I'm battered and bruised by the fall and have been told to rest up for a week because of the bang to the head, I'm in seventh heaven.

Sunday, 25 April 1976
Thankfully, the head and leg injuries were not serious enough to warrant hospitalisation, so I was allowed home and told to rest in bed for a few days.
Mick Hanrahan sent a few newspapers round to the house this morning, so that I can fully savour the moment. It's been a roller-coaster of a season – but it's not over yet. Nothing's been won. As the *Sunday Mirror* succinctly puts it:
Queens Park Rangers have played their last card in the most exciting League Championship battle for years. They must now wait until Tuesday week, May

4th, to see whether Liverpool can lay the winning trump and take the pot. Liverpool, one point behind Rangers but with a better goal average, must win at Wolverhampton or draw 0–0, 1–1 or 2–2 to take the title. A 3–3 draw, or higher will leave Rangers champions for the first time.

I read every single match report in all the newspapapers. There's a bit on the telly about the reaction from Liverpool. Some of the squad were not particularly impressed by the sight of QPR players waving to the crowd from the upper stand after the final whistle, as if they had won the championship.

'They seem to think it's all over,' Phil Thompson says with a wry grin, 'but we're really going to show them. It's going to be ours!' he adds emphatically.

Tuesday, 4 May 1976: 10.00 a.m.

Today, like yesterday, is another day of 'agonising inactivity'. The leg injury has healed up pretty quickly and the dizziness persists, but the long ten-day wait to know our fate has been pure agony. And I'm mentally exhausted. Because of their involvement in the UEFA Cup, Liverpool have had to wait until tonight to play their final First Division game of the season – against Wolves at Molyneaux. The game at Wolves is crucial, as Liverpool are now only one point behind QPR.

Same day: 12.00 noon

A number of the QPR team are invited to a private screening of the Wolves versus Liverpool tie at the Television Centre tonight. Players don't usually like watching football live or on the telly when they're not playing themselves. I definitely could not sit through that game as a TV spectator, given what is at stake. I resolve to find some way to distract myself until the match is over. I pick up the book that Lisa gave me: *The Collected Poems of W. B. Yeats*.

But I can't concentrate. My thoughts are torn between QPR winning the First Division and Lisa. I still haven't heard from her. Okay, it's not unusual because we only ever met up on match days a week apart. Sometimes two weeks. But this is different. The season is now over. Doesn't she care about how I'm feeling. About her? About tonight? Then I think back to that look on her face that afternoon at the Leeds match. The tone of anxiety in her voice. Then there was that 'something' she wanted to tell me. What was that all about?

Same afternoon: 3.00 p.m.

Still no word from Lisa. Why, in all of our conversations, did I never manage to get her address or her telephone number? But then, I thought, she knows where I live. And she did take my phone number. So she could contact me anytime she wishes. If she really wants to. This is not like her at all. So why have I not heard from her?

Later that evening: 8.30 p.m.

I manage to pluck up the courage to get an update on the Wolves versus Liverpool game. It's being played at Molyneux, so Wolves have home advantage. Also, they are playing for their very survival in the First Division. Surely that incentive alone will be sufficient for Wolves to put on a powerful performance.

The news is encouraging. Wolves are leading Liverpool 1–0 with less than fifteen minutes to go. Liverpool only need to draw 1–1 to deny QPR the title. Liverpool are on top but Wolves are holding out. This could be it. But I cannot bear to listen, so I shut the radio off.

Still no word from Lisa. On this night, of all nights, I thought I would have heard from her.

I return to the book and idly flick through the pages, not really taking anything in, until one catches my eye:

> Now all the truth is out,
> Be secret and take defeat
> From any brazen throat,
> For how can you compete,
> Being honour bred, with one
> Who, were it proved he lies,
> Were neither shamed in his own
> Nor in his neighbour's eyes?
> Bred to a harder thing
> Than Triumph turned away
> And like a laughing string
> Whereon mad fingers play
> Amid a place of stone,
> Be secret and exult,
> Because of all things known
> This is most difficult.

The poem is called 'To a Friend whose Work has come to Nothing'.

I start to worry once more.

Later still: 8.50 p.m.

I turn on the radio again. And I cannot believe what I'm hearing! The game is over. Liverpool scored three times in the last fifteen minutes, through Keegan, Toshack and Kennedy. Wolves are relegated and Liverpool have won the First Division Championship – by a single point. By a point. One miserable, f**king point. We should never have allowed it to come to this. The whole season, gone. All that graft; all that expectation.

I try calling some of the team. Nobody answers. I can't watch the telly or listen to the radio. Cannot bear to hear any more about Liverpool as champions. They should be calling us champions. We deserve to be called champions. To be – what was Lisa's phrase? – The Golden Apples. That was it. The Golden Apples of the Sun. And what are we left with? Nothing. Second place. Silver medals.

Wednesday, 5 May 1976: 9.00 a.m.

I wake with a start from a deep slumber as if by the metallic bang of a loud explosion followed by an echo. This is strange, as I hadn't been dreaming about bombs going off or anything like that. At least as far as I can recall. I'm breathing heavily and sweating profusely. I'm also on edge. Whatever I'd been dreaming about has unsettled me. But try as I may, I cannot pin down any of those elusive remnants of the dream. I drift back into slumber again. Vague, incomprehensible snatches of the earlier dream return but when I awake again, I still cannot fit them together. I'm left with a feeling of what I can only describe as aftermath. It's as if I'm experiencing the end of something but don't know what that something is. I read somewhere once that in the aftermath of a bomb explosion, there is an eerie silence for about ten seconds. And then the screaming starts.

I listen intently, pulling the covers around me as if I might need to suddenly duck deep for safety. Being half awake does that to me sometimes. Through the vented window I think hear a commotion in the distance, but it turns out to be nothing much above the ordinary.

I pick up the book Lisa gave me and open a page at random.

The girl goes dancing there
On the leaf-sown, new-mown, smooth
Grass plot of the garden;
Escaped from her bitter youth,
escaped out of her crowd,
Or out of her black cloud.
Ah dancer, ah sweet dancer!

Feeling decidedly heavy-lidded, I slip back into drowsiness again. I dream. That dream again? I'm being followed. Whoever – or whatever – is in pursuit is gaining on me. Try as I may, I cannot put distance between me and him or her. Or it. My knees weaken but I keep running. A siren in the background signals my attempted escape from...

I sit up. Sweating again. The sound of the siren restarts in my head. I feel a sudden sense of panic. Then I realise the sound is coming from outside on the street. It's close but less persistent now, slowing until, eventually, it just seems to shut off in mid-bleep.

I'm wide awake now. I try once again to trap and retain more details of the dream, but the harder I try, the more frustrating it becomes to piece together all the seemingly unrelated elements into any coherent meaning. I'm running away. From what? There was a room somewhere. A man sitting behind a desk. Lisa was there. But the person didn't look like Lisa, although she acted just like her. She was annoyed with me. Something I said. Or did. The urge to run, to get away, appears to be my overriding objective. But away from what? Maybe I'm actually running <u>towards</u> something. Striving to get there in time before my knees give up. But why the urgency?

I collapse back in the bed, totally exhausted. The book slips off the edge and onto the floor with a thump. I lean out and retrieve it. A small piece of onion-skin paper is protruding from between the leaves. I gently prise open the pages and remove the delicate swatch of paper. Some words have been carefully transcribed, probably from the pages of this book in very fine, ornate, handwriting:

I had this thought a while ago,
'My darling would not understand
What I have done, or what would do
In this blind, bitter land.'

And I grew weary of the sun
Until my thoughts cleared up again,
Remembering that the best I had done
Was done to make it plain.

And every year I have cried 'At length
My darling understands it all,
Because

And there it ends. In mid-sentence.

Nobody ends a verse of poetry like that, do they? A line with one word on it? Well, maybe Timothy Albrecht does. I scan both pages of the open book but the extract is not from a poem on these pages. I check the pages immediately before and after, but it's not there either. She (and it *is* Lisa's handwriting; I recognise it from the Christmas card she gave me) has not written down the title of the poem either. So it could be on any of the 800 or so pages. Why did she not complete transcribing the words? Did something or someone interrupt her? Or was it the words that followed that caused her to stop in mid-sentence? I resolve to investigate as soon as I am up and about again.

Thursday, 6 May 1976

I cannot bring myself to get up and face the world today. My anger has subsided but the disappointment remains. Not just with the Liverpool result, but because

I still haven't heard from Lisa. Somethings's up, I *know* it is. But I'm afraid to confront it.

I start to wonder again about that unfinished poem she transcribed onto that flimsy swatch of paper.

I retrieve the book and start to flick through the pages in some trepidation, looking for any other 'bookmarks'. There's a football ticket. Arsenal v QPR, last December. Is it possible she went to that match? And didn't tell me? That would be a strange thing to do. Why would she hide the fact that she had gone to the game? I remember how embarrassed she seemed when she told me that her dad sometimes went to Highbury. Maybe that was the reason she felt uncomfortable. She went to the game herself. But why didn't she tell me? It would have been nice to know. Why hide the fact? Then again, maybe she just picked up the ticket to use as a bookmark after her dad left it lying about the house.

But there's more. There's also a ticket to an Ike & Tina Turner concert. That's the one that Brad went to last year. Did Lisa go with Brad? And stood there in The Cabin that day while Brad discussed it – and said nothing? Why? How else would she have come by it? I suppose it's possible she might have picked up the ticket after Brad discarded it. But that could mean she was in his house. After a tennis lesson, maybe? Were she and Brad closer than I had imagined?

It gets worse. A torn piece of ticket to Sadler's Wells for the Maddy Prior & June Tabor concert a couple of weeks ago. Why would Lisa keep that? Why would she even have it? She told me she was getting the tickets for Mick's son, Cathal, and O'Leary. Is it possible that Lisa went too? With O'Leary?

I can't think of any other plausible explanation, other than that Lisa attended these events. And deliberately decided not to tell me. Okay, the Arsenal ticket might be easily explained away as something she picked up at home. But the others? Well, Brad hardly matters now, judging from his expression on the morning of the Leeds game. That was definitely an 'end-of-any-relationship' look.

But O'Leary? The self-styled 'artist' with his gleaming white teeth. Looking back on things now, there is a real possibility that there could have been (could still be) something between them. I remember how Lisa commented on how tall he was and as having a nice voice and a 'noble bearing'. Then there was the time she staunchly defended him against my suspicions (which I still harbour) that he was actually an IRA operative.

I think I need to have a serious conversation with Lisa. And I need to have it tomorrow.

Friday, 7 May 1976: 10.00 a.m.

It's a strange feeling when you go out again for the first time, after being indoors for a couple of weeks and spending most of that time in bed. For a start, you feel a bit light-headed. You take a second or two longer to take in and process very familiar surroundings and activities. Things appear strangely surreal. You tend to look at familiar everyday things almost as if you were seeing them for the first time. What should be comfortably familiar suddenly appears slightly detached. It's almost as if you were observing them, but not really part of the scene. And the slightest change to what you expect to see is also disturbing, and slightly disorientating.

This morning, I notice that there's a FOR SALE sign outside number 21 – Marianne Pleass's house. I'm surprised at this, as Marianne never gave me any inkling that they were considering moving house. I look upwards in the hope of attracting Majorie's attention, but she's not in her usual place by the window. The bright morning sunlight dazzles my house-bound eyes.

At Aunt Sally's corner, the old wall has been broken and there are a few temporary breeze blocks, some cones and a length of drooping orange tape signalling to pedestrians to take a wider berth. I had already heard about the accident. But I wasn't quite expecting the outcome to be so horrific.

The bus stop was sheared off about a foot above the ground, its jagged-topped stump still protruding grotesquely at an angle. The wall of Aunt Sally's must have crumbled easily and there is quite an amount of debris. A single bunch of faded flowers in crinkled, wet cellophane has tipped over from where it had been propped against one of the breezeblocks. It now lies there forlornly, the inked message on the card run and rendered illegible by the tip-tap of raindrops falling from the trees overhead. There are two large indentations on the lower wall where both cars struck it with such force before bouncing off in opposite directions; the smudges of white and bright green metallic paint still visible in places. I wonder why two cars would swerve off the road while travelling in the same direction. Thankfully, both drivers survived. The young woman at the bus stop was not so fortunate, however. She is not being named 'until her relatives have been informed'.

The gates to Aunt Sally's are shut. Daisuke's little Reliant Robin is nowhere to be seen. And not a sound – or an echo – emanates from Eddie's place across the street.

Shivering slightly, I pull my flimsy tracksuit top tightly around me to ward off the early morning chill. Then I turn right and walk quickly up Forest Park Road in search of Lisa Dell.

ADDED
TIME

28. WHATEVER HAPPENED TO...

Marianne Pleass

When the FOR SALE sign went up beside the front pillar of the gate to number 21 shortly after these events, I assumed initially that Marianne had changed her job and was moving house to be closer to her new place of work, because the sound of screeching brakes and loud tooting of horns in the early morning became a thing of the past. However, the sign came down again after a couple of weeks without the house being sold and the sisters stayed put. But I never saw Marianne ride her bicycle again.

Marjorie continued to keep her vigil at the upstairs window.

Aunt Sally

As 'Aunt' Sally got older, her treks to The Cabin became more infrequent, until eventually she stopped going altogether. Daisuke took on that role for her. He eventually moved into her house as a kind of live-in caretaker. After Sally passed away, Daisuke continued to live there. The story was that she had included a clause in her will to the effect that the house could not be sold while Daisuke lived there. I missed her funeral ceremony, but made it to the house some months later when her ashes were scattered around the grounds, as Cosimo's had been years earlier. It was a bit like a happy gathering of ageing hippies.

Echo Eddie & Svetlana

Eddie and Svet got married, had a kid and moved to a flat on the other side of Cheppington. By then, Eddie had found full-time work with a haulage company and didn't have the time to mess with cars any more. The job took Eddie abroad quite a lot on long-haul trips and I eventually lost contact with him. Doubtless he used the opportunity to inflict his language skills on unsuspecting locals as he traversed the continent.

Svetty opened her own gym. Members reported that there was nothing more invigorating than having Svetty put you through your paces. However, rumours that she dressed as a leather-clad dominatrix and lashed lazy members across the buttocks with a riding crop were probably as exaggerated as they were tantalising.

The Butler Brothers

The boys finally got to experience the joy of being detained at Her Majesty's pleasure – in the slammer at Wormwood Scrubs. (Something to do with a robbery and involving 'menaces'.) They were put in separate cells initially, but Billy became so disconsolate at their being apart that the authorities relented and put them together in one cell. I went to visit them a few times but the 'screws' wouldn't allow me to see both of them together, and it wasn't quite the same meeting them individually. A bit like having a conversation with Eric Morecambe without Ernie Wise being there. They needed to be together to act as a comforting foil to one another. For some reason, they were subsequently moved apart again, and after that Billy went rapidly downhill. Meeting them became more and more painful, with excruciatingly long silences. I could sense Jacko straining for the day he would be released, but Billy just seemed to go into himself and give up. After a while I just stopped visiting.

Billy passed away shortly after he was released. There were rumours that it was suicide but I didn't look for confirmation. I only became aware of his death because he included me in his will. A parcel arrived one day out of the blue from a legal firm dealing with what they referred to as 'William Butler's estate'. Inside were some books, part of a TIME-LIFE series on The Old West, the kind you send away for on thirty-day approval and only pay for if you commit to purchasing the set. It was all about the founding of the American Old West, with each book focused on a different topic, such as cowboys, American Indians, gamblers, gunfighters and thieves. It was obvious from some of the letters on TIME-LIFE headed paper being used as bookmarks that 'William' had fallen into the latter category and had 'overlooked' paying for any of these books. There were also a few Jimmy Rodgers albums, mostly ballads about cowboys, also acquired from some direct mail outfit. I never played the albums or read the books but I still have them. Somewhere.

Among the books was some football memorabilia, including a ticket for *that* game against Leeds and a match programme. Billy was obviously a stickler for detail (not a character trait I had noticed in my dealings with him back then) and had faithfully recorded the team changes, goalscorers, half-time score and attendance on the back of the programme.

Prison changed Jacko. And not for the better, from what I heard. After his release following Billy's death, he became more hardened, lost the 'lovable rogue' persona and fell in with a fairly tough 'firm'.

I've only seen him once in recent years. Very briefly, in the distance, near Hay's Mews in Mayfair. He looked different. He'd lost that pasty pallor and looked tanned and toned. But it was Jacko all right. I'd know that profile anywhere. He was getting out of a smart-looking chauffeur-driven motor up the West End with a very tasty bit of fluff on his arm. Very tall and tanned, she looked. At least she did from the rear. I strolled along in their direction on the opposite side of the street – okay, I followed them – for a couple of minutes. Then they turned into Curzon Street. At one point the woman bent down to pick something off the pavement. As she stood up, she made to swing round as if she sensed I was following, but I quickly turned away and pretended to stare into a nearby window. When I eventually looked after her she was loping along after Jacko. They looked to be heading into the Clermont Club.

I'm sure I heard her call him John.

'Arrow' (aka 'Roxboro Roy')

I never found out the truth about what happened to the dog with two names. To my knowledge, he never returned to Cheppington. At least, nobody I spoke to ever laid eyes on him again. But then, nobody seemed terribly interested. A year later, when a grey-coloured dog named Roxboro Roy won a race at some nondescript venue, I guessed that the Butlers had – somehow – finally made a killing with the bookies. I reckoned that there couldn't be two dogs with that unique name. But then, the Roxboro Roy I knew was black!

Go figure.

Berrie & Threads

Noah continued to run the little antique shop for a few years until his health failed. Fashion is a transient business, which probably goes some way to explaining how the skills that Noah Berrie had developed in himself and attempted to inculcate in his scion Bradley – an eye for second-hand/used products of enduring value – did not transfer quite so seamlessly to the fashion business, where built-in obsolesence is de rigueur. Never one to be heard dropping an 'aithch' himself, Bradley nevertheless dropped it from Threads as part of what he called 'upsizing and rebranding', while also replacing the 's' with a 'z' (or a 'zee' as he called it) to become 'Treadz'. In any event, the bottom line of 'Treadz', with or without an aithch or a zee, continued to have a threadbare look to it and eventually unravelled a couple of years later.

Undaunted, Bradley dedicated himself to his nascent career in local politics, and appeared to be on the cusp of great things nationally a few years later when that infamous 'BRAD AND THE LAD' story broke in the tabloids. Readers of a certain vintage will doubtless recall the sordid details that, despite his initial vehement denials, eventually brought Bradley's burgeoning political career to an inglorious end. Headlines such as 'BERRIE BRAD BOY' and 'BRAD'S CAREER DEAD AND BERRIED' caused much public merriment at the time.

In a futile attempt to convince the world of his heterosexuality, Brad employed the services of a PR agent who came up with this wheeze of having Brad seen constantly in public with a young woman on his arm. The woman obviously did not wish to be recognised, because she always wore a scarf on her head that she wrapped over the lower part of her face. This gave her a slightly mysterious appearance as she trailed after him, and the media soon switched their attentions to establishing her identity.

Having singularly failed to do this, they then refocused their attentions on Bradley. He recovered somewhat from the ordeal, of course (his sort inevitably do), and made a name – and, I understand, some considerable wealth – for himself subsequently. Which is more than can be said for the young lad involved in the scandal. I will refrain from elaborating upon the details of the story for the benefit of younger readers, lest I be accused of wallowing in the discomfort of a man whose doubtless talents I was never quite able to recognise or appreciate. I believe that great Irish philosopher, Mick Hanrahan, got it just about right when he once said of Bradley: 'If he was even half the man he thought he was, he'd be double the man he is today.'

Mick Hanrahan

Life went on more or less exactly as before for Mick until he passed away in 1982, shortly after his wife died. There was a huge turnout at his cremation, with much swapping of stories by people who had met and become friends as a result of Mick's 'introductions'. Many of Mick's infamous insults were also rehashed and re-traded on the day. His ashes were later buried in Ireland.

The Cabin

It's not there any more. After Mick passed away in 1982, his son Cathal took it on for a time but the place was never quite the same. Many of the original clientele were no longer around for various reasons (Cathal's politics was probably also a factor) and the place was simply left behind by more modern developments. It transpired that there were also issues regarding planning permission for the building, which his son Cathal discovered when he looked at developing it into a retail outlet more in keeping with today's needs. When I visited Cathal about a year ago he showed me some old photographs of The Cabin and, in truth, it is difficult from today's perspective to see what the attraction was about the place. It had to be Mick. And when he was gone, The Cabin died too

Bernie Trout

Pardon the pun, but old Trouty surfaced again approximately twelve months later. I unexpectedly bumped into the silver-haired hobbit, looking fresh and effulgent, on one of my rare excursions down to The Cabin. It seems he had spent those 'missing months' that season in Spain 'until the heat died down'. Despite my natural curiosity, I decided not to ask him whether this was a reference to a change in the weather on the Costa Brava or an issue pertaining to the forces of law and order here in Blighty. I still felt that he had let me down by absconding at such a crucial stage in the football season, and this probably influenced my lack of warmth towards him. Unaware that he had been part of my 'ritual', Bernie probably took my recitance towards him as being indicative that I 'knew something' about him that disappointed me.

After that encounter, Bernie seemed to avoid me. At least, he never seemed to be around when I visited The Cabin or on those rare occasions when I popped into The Horseman's. I asked Mick about it. At first Mick was non-committal and gave the impression that he would be betraying a confidence if he discussed Bernie with me. Eventually, he told me that Bernie had bought a second pub over in Weybridge. Big deal, I thought. Finally, Mick revealed that he'd heard on good authority that Bernie had returned from Spain with a new woman. About half his age. Mick hadn't actually seen her, but from the reported sighting she certainly looked Spanish – and was definitely much younger than Trouty. Mick didn't seem to approve but I couldn't see what all the fuss was about, when he first told me. 'Maybe she dances the flamenco for him,' was all I could think of to say. Mick looked at me wistfully: 'I think she could probably do that alright, me bucko,' he said, rather sadly. Mick obviously disapproved of the relationship. I never raised the issue with Mick after that. And I never crossed paths with Bernie Trout again.

The Horseman's

It's still standing. Bernie Trout sold out his interest in the place shortly after his return from Spain. You might find me in there some weekends, sipping a mineral water and watching football on Sky Television. But there are too many games machines in there for my liking.

QPR in Europe

Drawn against Norweigian side Brann Bergen in the first round of the UEFA Cup in September 1976, QPR won 4–0 at home, thanks to a Stan Bowles hat-trick. In the return game, the score was 7–0, including another hat-trick from Stan.

The second round saw QPR pitted against Slovan Bratislava. The first game was a 3–3 draw in Czechoslovakia with QPR being behind twice, and Stan Bowles notching another brace of goals. In the home game at Loftus Road, QPR won 5–2 with another hat-trick, this time from Don Givens, with Stan also getting on the scoresheet – his ninth goal in the competition.

In round three, QPR played FC Cologne, winning 3–0 at home. Stan scored his 10th goal, which meant he had now scored more goals in Europe in a single season than any other English player. Cologne won the return leg in Germany 4–1, but QPR made it through to the quarter-finals on the away goals rule.

In the quarter-final against AEK – conquerers of Derby County in an earlier round, – QPR won the first leg 3–0 at Loftus Road, with Stan scoring his 11th European goal of the season. But in the return leg in Athens the scoreline was reversed. And so it went to penalties. At six penalties each, Dave Webb missed the vital kick that sent QPR tumbling dramatically out of the UEFA Cup. This was in March 1977, by which time, of course, my association with QPR had already ended.

The First Division
On 20 February 1992, all the First Division clubs, including QPR, resigned from the Football League. Three months later the Premier League was established. Television rights were assigned to Sky Television. Things were about to change utterly. A new chapter in the history of the beautiful game was about to be written.

The famous QPR blue-and-white hooped shirt
It's still there, although it too has changed slightly in the intervening years, due no doubt to the overriding commercial imperative to accommodate the demands of sponsors and kit suppliers. We seem to have arrived at a point where, because of the amount of away strips, third strips and training strips each club produces each season (usually in colours chosen for their leisurewear fashionability rather than any real connection to the club), the sponsor's logo is now the most immediately recognisable aspect of most club replica shirts. But it's quietly reassuring that in today's melange of colour strips, the familiar blue-and-white hoops continue to proclaim an enduring and endearing association with QPR.

The Birmingham Six
An appeal against their convictions was dismissed in 1976. In the mid-1980s, several *World in Action* TV programmes were broadcast raising doubt regarding the men's convictions. In 1986, a new book, *Error of Judgment – The Truth About the Birmingham Pub Bombings*, written by Chris Mullin, detailed a case supporting the men's innocence. The case was then referred back to the Court of Appeal by Home Secretary Douglas Hurd. After a six-week hearing, the men's convictions were upheld.

New evidence of fabrication and suppression of evidence, the discrediting of the men's confessions and of the 1975 forensic evidence resulted in a successful third appeal in 1991, which led to the men's release. Ten years after their release, the six men were awarded compensation ranging from £840,000 to £1.2 million.

The Balcombe Street Gang
The four gang members were found guilty at their Old Bailey trial in 1977 of seven murders, conspiring to cause explosions, and falsely imprisoning John and Sheila Matthews during the siege. Three of them each received twelve life sentences, the fourth member received eleven. During their trial the men instructed their lawyers to 'draw attention to the fact that four totally innocent people were serving long sentences for three bombings in Woolwich and Guildford'. Despite claiming to the police that they were responsible, the Balcombe Street gang were never charged with these offences.

The Guildford Four

The Guildford Four appealed their convictions almost immediately. The appeal was unsuccessful. They then tried to make an appeal under Section 17 of the Criminal Appeal Act 1968, but were unsuccessful.

In 1987, the Home Office issued a memorandum recognising that it was unlikely the Four were terrorists, but that this would not be sufficient evidence for appeal. It later transpired that two of the Four – Gerry Conlon and Paul Hill – had an alibi for the very moment the Guildford pubs were blasted by IRA bombs. The prosecution hid that key alibi from the defence.

In 1989, a detective reviewing the case found material that implied that the police had manipulated notes to fit with the case they wanted to present. An appeal was granted on the basis of this new evidence. The convictions were reversed and the Guildford Four were released in 1989.

Noah Berrie

I had occasion to visit Noah Berrie's antique shop shortly after the release of the Guildford Four. I hadn't been there for a few years and I was surprised at how he had aged. But he recognised me immediately. Always had a sharp eye for a face, did Noah. Good for business. As ever, he tried to be his usual ebullient self, but I think the circumstances surrounding Brad's brief notoriety had taken some of the edge off his zest for life. We chatted a bit about football.

As I was leaving, Noah suddenly thrust an open newspaper across the counter at me. 'I suppose you know who that is in this photograph?' he asked, jabbing his forefinger at a photograph beside the story of the Guildford Four's release. 'It's that Irish bomber bloke, Conlon,' I replied immediately without even picking up the paper. (Versions of the photograph had been all over the newspapers and on the telly of this guy in his shirtsleeves charging around outside the court.)

'Not him, my friend. Look at the people in the background,' Noah demanded impatiently. I bent down and started scanning the photograph. 'There, there,' Noah prodded a particular section of the picture, his impatience growing. I picked up the newspaper and peered at the sea of faces among the jubilant family and supporters. Suddenly I saw a face that had once been familiar to me. I'm pretty certain that I recognised 'Lofty' O'Leary among the crowd, smiling in the background. It was difficult to make out any of the faces clearly. It was a very grainy photo and O'Leary was almost obscured by a tall woman wearing sunglasses and a beret standing just in front of him with her arms folded. But it was him alright. 'O'Leary,' I shouted, feigning excitement. 'What's he doing there?' Noah sighed irritably, almost whipped the newspaper out of my hand, looked at the picture again and was about to say something when he suddenly thought better of it.

'Do you think those guys are really innocent?' I asked, just to make conversation. Noah paused and stared at me as if searching for an appropriate response. 'Some people just cannot see the wood for the trees,' he said finally in exasperation, and wandered back into the interior of the shop, smacking his thigh gently with the folded newspaper as he went.

I couldn't fathom what he was on about. He seemed confused and irritable. Not like the Noah I knew. It came as no great surprise to me when I learnt a few months later that he was suffering from Alzheimer's disease.

Flick Colby and Pan's People

Pan's People made their final appearance on *Top of the Pops* in April 1976, dancing to 'Silver Screen' by The Four Seasons. When the dance group disbanded, Flick set up and choreographed a mixed-gender troupe called Ruby Flipper which appeared on *TOTP* to a mixed response from audiences. An all-girl group – Legs & Co – replaced them until Flick finally persuaded *TOTP* that the inclusion of some men would be beneficial. The result was ZOO, comprising some twenty dancers which made intermittent appearances on the show until sometime in the early eighties. But with record companies now supplying free promotional videos with high production values to the TV stations, the era of the dance troupe drew to a close. Flick Colby returned to the United States and bought a farm.

The number 10 shirt

At Queens Park Rangers, *the* shirt has always been the number 10 shirt, occupied for so long by the flamboyant skills of Rodney Marsh and then Stan Bowles. The number ten shirt at QPR was subsequently worn with distinction by a host of great footballers, including Paul Goddard, Tony Currie, Simon Stainrod, Mike Flanagan, Leroy Rosenoir, John Byrne, Wayne Fereday, Les Ferdinand, Trevor Francis, Roy Wegerle and Peter Reid.

The advent of the Premiership, with its huge squads of players and designated numbering, means that, today, the shirt worn by a club's most iconic player is as likely to be number 69 as it is number 10.

Gerry Francis

Gerry went on to win twelve caps for England between 1974 and 1976, and was captain for eight of those matches. In 1976, he suffered an injury that was to end his international career. He left QPR for Crystal Palace in 1979, although he subsequently returned to QPR for a second spell, but by this time I was no longer involved with the club – a fact that will not have displeased him.

He spent some time at Coventry City and then Exeter City, where he finished his playing career.

In 1990, he managed Bristol Rovers to the Third Division title, but a year later he returned to QPR as Chief Coach.

In 1992–93, QPR finished fifth in the inaugural Premier League – highest placed of all the London teams – but in November 1994 Gerry left Loftus Road for Tottenham Hotspur. Mid-table finishes in the next two seasons led to Gerry resigning in November 1997, with Spurs battling against relegation from the Premier League.

In September 1998, he was named as QPR Manager for the second time, but they were now Premiership strugglers. He later resigned as Manager and briefly became Director of Football. Gerry regularly appears as a football pundit on TV.

Stan Bowles

Stan spent seven years at QPR, playing a pivotal role in what was probably the club's greatest ever team, under Manager Dave Sexton. A 2004 fans poll saw 'Stan-the Man' voted QPR's all-time greatest player. In 1979, he left to join Nottingham Forest, where he played for a short spell under Brian Clough and was sold in 1981 to Leyton Orient for £100,000.

He joined Brentford the following year and remained at the club until his retirement from league football in 1984.

In his autobiography, Stan talked about the extent of his drinking, womanising and gambling during his playing days. He was something of a cult icon because of his chaotic personal life and is amongst the few footballers to have a single released bearing his name, in this case the 2004 release by the The Others. Stan is also the only footballer I know of to have a piece of serious music composed around his talents. In 1992, Michael Nyman composed a concerto entitled 'The Final Score' with footage featuring Stan from the QPR v Leeds match on 24 April 1976 (yes, that match).

Jim Gregory

After Manager Dave Sexton and Stan Bowles left QPR, Club Chairman Gregory appointed former player Terry Venables as Manager in the early 1980s. Venables and Gregory were instrumental in having an Omniturf pitch installed, to become the first English team ever to play on what became known as a 'plastic pitch'. At the time, it was heralded as a great innovation in English football. A few other clubs followed this QPR 'innovation', each believing that the synthetic surface represented the future of football. However, they quickly fell out of favour and were banned in 1988.

Under Venables, Gregory saw his beloved QPR reach Wembley in the 1982 FA Cup Final. Rangers lost after a replay but promotion to the top flight followed a year later. After promotion, Gregory announced that he was leaving QPR after twenty years at the club.

Jim returned to football as Portsmouth Chairmen a few years later, but ill health forced him to step down and hand over the reins to his son, Martin. Sadly, he passed away three years later.

Dave Thomas

Dave's most successful season was undoubtedly 1975–76. He was a pivotal figure in the team, providing outstanding service from the wing. Dave continued to enjoy success in the 1977–78 season following his transfer to Everton.

He won eight England caps overall whilst at Queens Park Rangers. His first England cap was given to him by Manager Don Revie on 30 October 1974, in a 3–0 win against Czechoslovakia. He set up the first goal in that game. In 1981, he played a single summer season with the Vancouver Whitecaps in the North American Soccer League.

Afterwards, he worked as a PE teacher at the Bishop Luffa School in Chichester.

Dave Clement

It was during that 1975–76 season that Dave deservedly received his first senior international cap against Wales in 1976, coming on as a substitute at half-time in a game England won 2–1. He made four more appearances over the next year, his last cap coming in February 1977, against Holland.

Then, after fourteen years at the club, 472 appearances and 28 goals in all competitions, and with QPR by that stage relegated to the Second Division, Dave was sold to Bolton Wanderers for £170,000 in 1979. He subsequently went on to play with distinction for Wimbledon and Fulham before his sad death in 1982, aged 34.

I was a great admirer of Dave, a very talented full-back and a great pro.

Frank McLintock

Frank made a total of 127 League appearances for QPR before he finally retired from the game in 1977. After retiring, he became Manager of one of his old clubs – Leicester City – but they finished bottom of the First Division and were relegated in his first season in charge. Between 1984 and 1987 he was manager at Brentford, before joining Millwall as a coach, and he assisted the club in winning promotion to the old First Division. Frank later became a successful after-dinner speaker and a pundit for BBC Radio and Sky Sports.

The two Dons

After three seasons at QPR, and seventeen caps for Scotland, **Don Masson** moved to Derby County in 1977 in exchange for Leighton James (yes, that Leighton James). After a second spell at Notts County, he played in the United States. On returning home, he was appointed Player-Manager of Kettering Town, before eventually retiring from football.

Don Givens left QPR in 1978 after six successful seasons, making almost 300 appearances and scoring over 100 goals. He joined Birmingham before moving to Sheffield United, and ended his playing career in Switzerland with Neuchâtel Xamax, where he made 144 appearances and scored 34 goals. He retired from club football in 1987. Don Givens was Rangers' most capped player, making 56 appearances for the Republic of Ireland and scoring 19 goals, including a record four goals against Turkey, and became his country's leading goalscorer at that time.

Mick Leach
Mick continued to play for QPR until 1978, in many instances coming off the bench to score vital goals. In total, Mick scored 61 goals in 313 league games for QPR. He then moved to the US to play for Detroit Express in the North American Soccer League, before returning home to play for Cambridge United, where he ended his career. After retiring as a player, he had a short spell as a coach at Chelsea. Sadly, he died in January 1992, aged just 44.

Dave Sexton
Twelve months after he almost guided QPR to the First Division title, the Gaffer was enticed away to take over as Manager at Manchester United, replacing Tommy Docherty, who had just been sacked. However, his time at Old Trafford failed to deliver any trophies, the highlights being an FA Cup Final appearance in 1979, losing 3–2 to Arsenal in a dramatic match, and finishing in second place behind Liverpool in the 1979–80 First Division championship. His thoughtful, contemplative approach was probably not best suited to the demands of such a high-profile club and he was dismissed by Manchester United in April 1981. He then managed Coventry City for two years before leaving in 1983.

Dave also had a very successful period as coach of England's Under-21 side, and won the UEFA Under-21s Championship twice, in 1982 and 1984. After that he went on to become the FA's first Technical Director at the FA's National School at Lilleshall in 1984. He also wrote a book on coaching a football team for coaches of all levels called *Tackle Soccer*. He died in 2012.

Billy Bremner
Six short months after our sharp exchange of words on the touchline at Loftus Road, after I told him 'you're finished...washed up' (though I'm sure entirely unrelated to that comment), Billy Bremner left Leeds United to join Hull City, having played 772 games for Leeds.

Though winding down his career, Billy Bremner was anything but washed up and emerged as a major success at Hull over two years, retiring at the age of 39.

In 1978, he took over as Manager of Doncaster Rovers, guiding them to promotion to the Third Division in 1981 where they remained for two seasons, and again in 1984.

Billy's life after playing was mainly notable for his topsy-turvy spell as Manager of Leeds, following in the footsteps of old teammates Allan Clarke and Eddie Gray to try to restore happier days to the club after their relegation in 1982. They never regained promotion under Bremner but came close, losing a play-off final to Charlton Athletic in 1987 and reaching the FA Cup semi-finals in the same season, losing to eventual winners Coventry City.

Billy was sacked by Leeds in September 1988. In July 1989, he went back to Doncaster as Manager, but left in November 1991. This was the last position that Billy held in football.

He suffered a suspected heart attack at his Doncaster home in Clifton, South Yorkshire and died two days before his 55th birthday.

A statue of Billy Bremner in celebratory pose was erected outside Elland Road as a tribute to the club's greatest captain and, according to an official poll of supporters via the club website, the club's greatest ever player. In 1998, the Football League, as part of its centenary season celebrations, included Bremner on its list of 100 League Legends. Bremner was later inducted into the English Football Hall of Fame in recognition of his impact on the game.

So, belated apologies, Billy – game, set and match to you.

Leeds United

Leeds continued to compete, albeit less successfully, in the First Division until 1982 when they were relegated to Division Two. They did not return to the top flight again until 1990.

They were league champions again two seasons later.

Despite competing for places in Europe and reaching the semi-finals of the UEFA Cup and the UEFA Champions League in consecutive seasons, Leeds ran into severe financial difficulties and, following a mass sale of players, they were relegated from the Premier League.

Despite their travails, Leeds United continue to enjoy the support of a large and committed fan base and I believe that top flight football is the poorer for their continued absence.

The Men in Black

They don't really exist any more. Not in black anyway. Black was the traditional colour worn by officials, and 'the man in black' was widely used as an informal term for a referee.

However, at the 1994 World Cup finals, new rules were introduced that allowed match officials to wear a choice of burgundy, yellow or white. At the same time, the creation of the Premier League in England resulted in referees being allowed to wear green jerseys. These changes were driven primarily by the needs of television.

The Red Tops

The daily circulation battle between the *Daily Mirror* and *The Sun* continued throughout the late 1970s. In November 1978, a new newspaper, *The Star*, joined the battle of the Red Tops. At the time of its launch, Derek James, its Editorial Director, when asked to describe what qualities *The Star* would embody, was quoted thus: 'All tits, bums, QPR and roll-your-own fags.' With a mix like that it was bound to be a favourite on the terraces. I continue to buy the Red Tops to this day, particularly the *Daily Mirror* and, with the advent of more full-colour pages, it is now possible to establish that many of the beauties that appear on page 3 are in fact redheads.

'Big Mal'

Malcolm Allison was definitely one of the most charismatic characters in the annals of Crystal Palace and 1975–76 was the most successful season for 'Big Mal' at Selhurst Park. Having suffered relegation in two consecutive seasons, Allison led Palace to the club's first FA Cup semi-final appearance after a succession of victories against higher league opposition such as Chelsea, Leeds United and Sunderland. But having failed to reach the final in Wembley, Palace subsequently also lost out on a promotion place and Allison resigned in May 1976, moving on to manage Galatarasay in Turkey.

He returned to Crystal Palace in 1980–81 for a two-month period in a doomed attempt to avoid relegation from the top flight. He then went to Portugal to manage Sporting Lisbon, where he won the league championship and the Portuguese Cup in 1981–82.

Allison's outspoken nature and behaviour were constantly reported in the tabloid press. One of the more notable incidents occurred in 1976, when a *News of the World* photograph showed him in the Crystal Palace players' bath with film star Fiona Richmond, whom he had invited to a training session.

Veronica

Ah. Now that's a story for another day...

Dave Lee-Royd

Modesty dictates that I relegate myself to the penultimate paragraphs. Sadly, the 1975–76 season was the last time I was involved with the club as a sort of unofficial ballboy. Shortly after that final game against Leeds, the club issued a letter saying that my special sideline pass would not be renewed for the 1976–77 season. I had become too involved with the action on the pitch, it said and, whilst they valued and appreciated my enthusiasm for the club, they felt that persons in my position needed to demonstrate a greater degree of detachment from the play. Also, my consistent uninvited appearances at the training ground in South Ruislip had become a distraction to the players and my advice from the sideline was sometimes in direct contradiction to the tactics being worked on by the coaching staff. That I had refused to desist from this practice despite the very reasonable overtures that team captain Gerry Francis had made to me on a number of occasions, only served to confirm to them that it would not be in the best interests of the club that my special sideline pass be renewed.

It didn't help that this epistle was addressed to my parents, since it was through their efforts that I was given that special sideline pass at Loftus Road in the first instance. Both of my parents were casually acquainted with Chairman Jim Gregory and it was through this connection that I secured the pass.

Matters were made worse by that letter from QPR coinciding with a missive from John Brightening, the headmaster at St Iago's, to my parents, expressing concern at the number of mornings I had been absent from college mid-week and bemoaning the recent dip in attention to my studies.

My parents were Alice Lee and Robert Royd. Ring any bells? *Doctor* Alice Lee and *Doctor* Robert (Bob) Royd? If you are of a certain vintage or interested in medicine, you'll probably remember that research breakthrough back in the late sixties? If not, don't worry about it (I'm not that interested in medical research myself). Anyway, that was them. So you can imagine I wasn't short of pocket money. Trips to away games were not a problem for me, money-wise. And, with the amount of time my parents were working late or away from home, skipping my studies and covering my tracks presented no great problem.

I don't reckon that my parents were unduly concerned about – or fully understood – the reasons why my sideline pass was not being reissued. And I was able to muddy the waters a bit by explaining that at 17 years of age, I was probably getting a little old for that unofficial ball-boy role anyway, and that the observations made by the club were attributable to my natural overenthusiasm and commitment.

The education issue was a bit trickier to resolve. But ultimately, I managed to get through it. However, I was the subject of pretty intensive supervision for the rest of my time at St Iago's and severe restrictions were placed on my after-school and weekend activities. Unfortunately, the Saturday morning ritual walk to The Cabin and all that went with it became a thing of the past.

My football career at school suffered too. This was primarily my own doing. I stopped playing as a kind of protest and refused to take it up again, despite the best efforts of the school sports master, Mr Clay, to persuade me to change my mind.

Sometimes, when I look back, I think I should have pursued that enquiry from Big Mal at Crystal Palace. Maybe I would have made it. Playing in the Third Division would not have been my ambition but at least it would have been a start. It could have launched my career. In the event, no clubs of any note came looking for me after that; my form dipped and eventually I had to accept that I would not make a career in the top flight of professional football, never mind captaining England one day.

After I finished school, I did a writing course at a local college and held various jobs as a reporter with local newspapers. But the big news-reporting role has so far eluded me. I tried sports reporting too, but I have never been able to muster up sufficient enthusiasm to write well about games that did not involve my beloved QPR.

The notes that form the basis of this book represent a period in my life when everything seemed possible. A future waiting to be tasted and relished. The very uncertainty of this future held its own irresistible appeal. The course of every year was charted by the vagaries of the First Division fixture list. Home and away. Top-of-the-table clashes; mid-week match-ups with mid-table mediocrities; stirring battles with relegation-threatened strugglers; the elation of victory; the anguish of defeat, the unsatisfactory, sour aftermath of a drawn game. An emotional roller-coaster, week-in, week-out.

And the Saturday ritual. That ridiculous construct of random, oscillating, childish superstition. An unnecessary layer of nervous pseudoscience applied to an already over-burdened, nerve-wracked activity.

And throughout it all, there was Lisa Dell. Enigmatic, beautiful, elusive. Easing her way in and then, just as quietly, drifting out of my life. Always questioning, making me believe that alternative attainments were not only possible but infinitely more desirable.

But in that particular season of my life – those nine long months, suspended over two calendar years – the ultimate prize, that torment of Tantalus, the one I really yearned for, lusted after, coveted with a passion, ultimately proved heartbreakingly elusive.

Lisa Dell

I didn't see Lisa that day. And I've not seen her since.

What she probably wanted to tell me was that she and her family were leaving Cheppington. That must have been the reason why Brad looked so forlorn that morning. I didn't ask him. In the end, whatever the reason for her leaving at short notice, I didn't want to hear it from Brad. Or from anybody else, for that matter. Nobody who did know the reasons volunteered the information to me. They probably assumed I knew. And, of course I *would* have known if I hadn't been in such a hurry on that morning of the Leeds match. And if I hadn't been injured at the end of the game.

I never knew her address, so I couldn't trace her. I didn't even have a photograph of her. Not many of the contacts that knew Lisa were much help or seemed that interested. Mick looked as if he was carrying a dark secret. I asked Noah, being artistic, if he would draw a little sketch of her from memory. It was incredibly accurate and captured her mien just perfectly. I tried to persuade Mick to put it in the small ads window but, surprisingly, he resisted. 'She's gone, Dawhee,' he said, sadly. 'Just…just let her go.'

But I couldn't.

I withdrew into myself. Became a bit of a recluse. My parents became concerned about my health; about my inability to face facts and live with the truth of what I knew. They arranged professional help for me on numerous occasions but I never 'stuck with the programme'.

Over the ensuing years, I put huge efforts – too numereous to recount here – into trying to trace Lisa. Sometimes I would think I had a lead, but, like all the others, it would eventually peter out.

'*She's gone, Dawhee.*'

The advent of social media offered new possibilities in terms of finding Lisa, but ultimately yielded nothing to date except a dispiriting sense of failure and frustration.

'*Just let her go.*'

But I still can't.

I never will.

I will find out where she has gone,
And kiss her lips and take her hands;
And walk among long dappled grass,
And pluck till time and times are done
The silver apples of the moon,
The golden apples of the sun.

QPR RESULTS: 1975–76

Saturday 16th August 1975.
Queens Park Rangers........2
Francis, Leach.
Liverpool........0
Attendance: 27,113

Tuesday 19th August 1975.
Queens Park Rangers........1
Francis.
Aston Villa........1
Attendance: 21,986

Saturday 23rd August 1975.
Derby County...1
Queens Park Rangers........5
Thomas, Bowles 3 (1 pen), Clement.
Attendance: 27,950

Tuesday 26th August 1975.
Wolves...2
Queens Park Rangers........2
Givens 2.
Attendance: 19,380

Saturday 30th August 1975.
Queens Park Rangers........1
Givens.
West Ham United........1
Attendance: 27,113

Saturday 6th September 1975.
Birmingham City ...1
Queens Park Rangers........1
Thomas.
Attendance: 27,305

Tuesday 9th September 1975
(Football League Cup Round 2)
Queens Park Rangers........4
Webb, Masson, Thomas, Leach.
Shrewsbury Town........1
Attendance: 11,250

Saturday 13th September 1975.
Queens Park Rangers.....1
Webb.
Manchester United.....0
Attendance: 29,237

Saturday 20th September 1975.
Middlesboro.....0
Queens Park Rangers.....0
Attendance: 24,876

Tuesday 23rd September 1975.
Queens Park Rangers.....1
Leach.
Leicester City.....0
Attendance: 19,292

Saturday 27th September 1975.
Queens Park Rangers.....1
Leach.
Newcastle United.....0
Attendance: 22,981

Saturday 4th October 1975.
Leeds United.....2
Queens Park Rangers.....1

Bowles (pen)
Attendance: 30,943

<u>Tuesday 7th October 1975</u>.
(Football League Cup Round 3)
Queens Park Rangers.....1
Bowles.
Charlton Athletic.....1
Attendance: 20,434

<u>Saturday 11th October 1975</u>.
Queens Park Rangers.....5
Givens, Thomas, Masson, Francis 2.
Everton.....0
Attendance: 23,435

<u>Wednesday 7th January 1976</u>.
(FA Cup Round 3 - Replay)
Newcastle United.....2
Queens Park Rangers.....1
Masson
Attendance: 37,225

<u>Saturday 10th January 1976</u>.
Manchester United.....2
Queens Park Rangers.....1
Givens
Attendance: 58,638

<u>Saturday 17th January 1976</u>.
Queens Park Rangers.....2
Masson 2
Birmingham City.....1
Attendance: 16,759

<u>Saturday 24th January 1976</u>.
West Ham United.....1
Queens Park Rangers.....0
Attendance: 26,437

<u>Saturday 31st January 1976</u>.
Aston Villa.....0
Queens Park Rangers.....2
Hollins, Francis
Attendance: 32,223

<u>Monday 2nd February 1976</u>.
(Mick Leach Testimonial)
Queens Park Rangers.....4
Francis 2 (1 pen) Masson , Thomas
Red Star Belgrade.....0
Attendance: 8,506

<u>Saturday 7th February 1976</u>
Queens Park Rangers.....4
Thomas, Givens 2, Francis
Wolves.....2
Attendance: 17,173

<u>Saturday 14th February 1976</u>
Tottenham Hotspur.....0
Queens Park Rangers.....3

Givens, Francis 2.
Attendance: 28,200

<u>Saturday 21st February 1976</u>
Queens Park Rangers.....3
Wark og, Webb, Thomas
Ipswich Town.....1
Attendance: 22,593

<u>Wednesday 25th February 1976</u>
Leicester City.....0
Queens Park Rangers.....1
Thomas.
Attendance: 24,340

Saturday 28th February 1976
Sheffield Utd.....0
Queens Park Rangers.....0
Attendance: 22,949

Tuesday 2nd March 1976
(Friendly)
Queens Park Rangers.....1
McLintock
Moscow Dynamo....0
Attendance: 8,710

Saturday 6th March 1976
Queens Park Rangers.....4
Givens, Thomas, Masson, Francis
Coventry City....1
Attendance: 19,731

Saturday 13th March 1976
Everton.....0
Queens Park Rangers.....2
Bowles, Leach.
Attendance: 25,186

Saturday 20th March 1976
Stoke City.....0
Queens Park Rangers.....1
Webb.
Attendance: 22,847

Saturday 27th March 1976
Queens Park Rangers.....1
Webb
Manchester City....0
Attendance: 29,833

Saturday 3rd April 1976
Newcastle United.....1
Queens Park Rangers.....2
McLintock, Bowles.
Attendance: 30,134

Saturday 10th April 1976
Queens Park Rangers.....4
Francis 2 (1 pen) Givens, Bowles.
Middlesboro....2
Attendance: 24,342

Saturday 17th April 1976
Norwich.....3
Queens Park Rangers.....2

Thomas, Powell og.
Attendance: 31,231

Monday 19th April 1976
Queens Park Rangers.....2
McLintock, Francis (pen)
Arsenal....1
Attendance: 24,342

Saturday 24th April 1976
Queens Park Rangers.....2
Thomas, Bowles
Leeds United....0
Attendance: 31,002

Final League table positions after all games were completed:

	P	W	D	L	F	A	Pts
1. Liverpool	42	23	14	5	66	31	60
2. QPR	42	24	11	7	67	33	59
3. Man Utd	42	23	10	9	68	42	56
4. Derby County	42	21	11	10	75	58	53
5. Leeds Utd	42	21	9	12	65	46	51
6. Ipswich Town	42	16	14	12	54	48	46
7. Leicester City	42	13	19	10	48	51	45
8. Man City	42	16	11	15	64	46	43
9. Tottenham H	42	14	15	13	63	63	43
10. Norwich City	42	16	10	16	58	58	42
11. Everton	42	15	12	15	60	66	42
12. Stoke City	42	15	11	16	48	50	41
13. Middlesboro	42	15	10	17	46	45	40
14. Coventry C	42	13	14	15	47	57	40
15. Newcastle U	42	15	9	18	71	62	39
16. Aston Villa	42	11	17	14	51	59	39
17. Arsenal	42	13	10	19	47	53	36
18. West Ham Utd.	42	13	10	19	48	71	36
19. Birmingham City	42	13	7	22	57	75	33
20. Wolves	42	10	10	22	51	68	30
21. Burnely	42	9	10	23	43	66	28
22. Sheffield U	42	6	10	26	33	82	22

The Silver Apples of the Moon is a work of fiction, loosely based around the actual events described within. The footballers, certain members of the management teams and other prominent people in public life at the time are recognisable. All other characters in the novel are products of the author's imagination, as are the incidents concerning them.

The author has endeavoured to ensure that all facts relating to real people were correct at time of going to print and would encourage readers to contact him with any relevant updated information that can be included in future editions.

CREDITS

ACKNOWLEDGEMENTS

'EASTER 1916'. W. B. Yeats, 1917. *(Chapter 21)*
'TO A CHILD DANCING IN THE WIND'. W. B. Yeats, 1912. *(Chapter 26)*
'TO A FRIEND WHOSE WORK HAS COME TO NOTHING'. W. B. Yeats, 1913. *(Chapter 27)*
'SWEET DANCER'. W. B. Yeats, 1938. *(Chapter 27)*
'WORDS'. W. B. Yeats, 1910. *(Chapter 27)*
'THE SONG OF WANDERING AENGUS'. W. B. Yeats, 1897. *(Chapter 28)*

BIBLIOGRAPHY

QUEEN'S PARK RANGERS – A COMPLETE RECORD, *Gordon Macey. The Breedon Books Company, 1993.*
BOWLES, *Steve Bidmead. Virgin Books, 2002.*
THE MAVERICKS, *Rob Steen. Mainstream Publishing Company, 1994.*
JOHN GILES – A FOOTBALL MAN, *John Giles with Declan Lynch. Hachette Books, 2010.*
KICKING & SCREAMING – AN ORAL HISTORY OF FOOTBALL IN ENGLAND, *Rogan Taylor & Andrew Ward. Robson Books, 1995.*
OUT OF TIME – WHY FOOTBALL ISN'T WORKING!, *Alex Flynn & Lynton Guest. Simon & Schuster, 1994.*
ONLY A GAME?, *Eamon Dunphy Viking/Penguin 1986*
THE GREAT & THE GOOD, *John Giles with Declan Lynch. Hachette Books 2012*

PLUS: DAILY MIRROR, *assorted print and broadcast media and QPR match programmes.*

ND - #0152 - 270225 - C0 - 234/156/16 - PB - 9781780915562 - Gloss Lamination